CONTEMPORARY AMERICAN MARKETING

Contemporary American Marketing

Readings on the Changing Market Structure

Edited by HARPER W. BOYD, Jr., Ph.D.

Professor of Marketing

RICHARD M. CLEWETT, Ph.D.

Professor of Marketing and Chairman of the Department

and

RALPH WESTFALL, Ph.D.

Associate Professor of Marketing

All of School of Business, Northwestern University

1957

RICHARD D. IRWIN, INC.   HOMEWOOD, ILLINOIS

First Printing, August, 1957

Library of Congress Catalogue Card No. 57–12624

PRINTED IN THE UNITED STATES OF AMERICA

Preface

Since this is but one of a number of books of readings in marketing to appear in recent years, we feel some responsibility to explain its mission as well as how it evolved. Its primary purpose is to bring some of the dynamics—the verve—of the market place into the classroom. It is hoped that this will stimulate the beginning student and enable him to grasp more readily the nature and scope of the marketing segment of the economy. It is designed for use with a basic textbook. The editors believe that this book can increase student involvement in the study of marketing, thereby making the learning process not only more palatable but more enduring.

This book is the result of considerable classroom experimentation over the past several years at the School of Business at Northwestern University. It reflects our current thinking that the beginning course in marketing should more and more contain materials which will help the student understand the marketing problems faced by businessmen and also the interrelationships between marketing and other functional areas such as production and finance.

The case-articles selected for inclusion in this book are, for the most part, descriptions and explanations of the marketing operations of particular companies. Our desire was *not* to provide the student with the scholarly writings contained in the various journals. We felt that such material—where pertinent—would be covered in the basic text. To be sure, some of the articles included in this book contain too many superlatives, but this, in part, represents the language and color of the market place.

Our first selection criterion was that each article should focus upon a business illustration or "case." Further, these illustrations should be highly readable and involve firms and types of goods with which the students could "identify" readily. Practically all of the readings focus upon the marketing activities and problems of an actual business enterprise. In only a few instances was it found necessary to deviate in this respect. Also, it was felt that the readings should represent the typical and not the unique. The authors hope that in their selection they have sublimated the natural desire for the unusual.

A second criterion was that the articles should fit into the framework of basic texts. Thus, subject matter was of considerable importance. The organization of the readings centers around seven major sections as follows: (1) Nature and Scope of Marketing, (2) The Market, (3) Product and Product Line, (4) Channels of Distribution, (5) Advertising and

Personal Selling, (6) Price Strategy, and (7) Legislation. Several of these major sections are, in turn, further subdivided. For example, the section on channels of distribution is broken into retailing and wholesaling. In all sections an attempt was made to gain a balance between consumer and industrial fields. This minimum of scaffolding is deliberate since many of the articles cover more than one subject and may be used to illustrate the material in more than one section of a basic text.

The editors did not include articles on all phases of marketing. Such subjects as transportation, warehousing, and marketing efficiency were not covered. This was done deliberately in an attempt to prepare a book of readings of reasonable length. It was reasoned that the seven major sections indicated above comprise the heart of marketing.

It was felt that emphasis should be placed on the recency of the article. This became the third criterion. It is unfortunately true that students are singularly unimpressed with materials which are not of recent origin. Over half of the articles included first appeared in 1956 and 1957 and few of them appeared earlier than 1955.

In our search for materials we covered a great variety of publications. It is surprising how many magazines attempt, in one way or another, to cover some aspect of marketing! There are, however, in the final analysis only a limited number of publications which provide the kind of material desired and, thus, only ten sources were used. Initially, the editors had planned to use several additional articles from *Fortune* Magazine. Unfortunately, this was not possible. The editors of *Fortune* did, however, release two articles for which we are most grateful.

The editors of this volume would like to take this opportunity to express their gratitude to the editors of *Advertising Age, Business Week, Electrical Wholesaling, Fortune, Industrial Marketing, Journal of Business, Printer's Ink, Progressive Grocer, Sales Management,* and *Tide* who made this book possible.

HARPER W. BOYD, JR.
RICHARD M. CLEWETT
RALPH WESTFALL

EVANSTON, ILLINOIS
May, 1957

Table of Contents

VI. PRICE STRATEGY

VII. LEGISLATION

Part One . . .

NATURE AND SCOPE OF MARKETING

·{ 1 }·

*People, Tomatoes and Advertising: The Story of Campbell's Soup**

Campbell Soup Company is catching its second wind. Still inspired by the memory and example of its brilliant merchant-mentor, Dr. John T. Dorrance, it is gaining vigor and vitality from its hard-hitting 47-year-old President William Beverly Murphy.

Probably the two men would have got along together fine. Dorrance, father of the Campbell condensed soup, was by training a chemist and by instinct a hard-bargaining successful salesman. He created a new product in America, learned to make it sell at a popular price and had the good sense to preempt the market with continuous advertising that gave the company an immediate and lasting franchise with the consumer. He was cautious but forward-looking; exacting but fair.

W. B. Murphy is a chemical engineer by education, a sales and marketing specialist by training and inclination. He's sticking with the old Dorrance formula of a good can of soup at a competitive price backed by strong advertising. He's adding a few innovations of his own. Scientific marketing, continually improved standards of quality control and greater delegation of authority are a few of his interests. He feels there is still a lot of money to be made in soups. Like Dorrance, he is ambitious but cautious.

Forecast for 1960

Last year Campbell net sales were $338,667,888. In 1939 they were $65,470,696, less than one-fifth the 1954 total. Unit sales in cases were nearly three times as much in 1954 as in 1939. President Murphy is shooting for $500,000,000 in sales by 1960.

Between the regime of Dr. Dorrance and Mr. Murphy were those of Dr. John's younger brother, Arthur C. Dorrance, deceased, and then James McGowan, Jr., now chairman of the board and a director. Their management served the vital purposes of sustaining growth and expansion in the years following Dr. Dorrance's death.

* Reprinted by special permission from *Printers' Ink*, February 18, 1955. Copyright, 1955, *Printers' Ink*.

But the story of Campbell Soup Company today centers around the spirit of Dr. John and the reality of W. B. Murphy.

It's almost impossible to observe the Campbell operation without being conscious of the long-time influence of Dr. John. He was a dedicated man—dedicated to the job of making and selling soup at a profit. That he did. When he joined the old Joseph Campbell Preserve Company in 1897, he did so with the idea of developing a condensed soup, an idea he conceived in Europe. His starting salary was $7.50 a week. When he died in 1929, his estate owned the Campbell Soup Company lock, stock and soup kitchen. His personal fortune was more than 115 million dollars.

How did he do it? There were no tricks—no interlocking directorates, no lavish executive salaries and no ornate executive suites. The success of Dorrance and his company was largely a result of his all-consuming notion that a good can of soup, competitively priced and consistently advertised would sell. He was right.

Advertising, a Cornerstone

Dorrance believed wholeheartedly in the power of advertising. A year after he joined the company, he fathered its first advertising campaign —a $4,600 car card program. It was the beginning of a continuous advertising program that has few equals in American business. Dr. Dorrance believed that advertising and marketing are as much the responsibility of top management as production and sales. This same basic philosophy persists in the expanded Campbell operation today. He knew the value of a dollar and never forgot it or allowed anyone else in his organization to forget it either.

Dollars aren't spent freely these days. There is a Spartan appearance to the Company's headquarters in Camden that startles the visitor—and would no doubt please Dr. John.

*   *   *   *   *

Constant Quality Control

On the floor of the soup-making plant, where inspectors inspect the operations and other inspectors inspect the inspectors, there is a laboratory for company technologists. A huge sign over the door reads: *Quality is our business.* Into this laboratory samples of the day's production are brought every hour. Cases are taken from the assembly line, cans are opened and contents put under the microscope.

Every day, an executive team of 7, often including Mr. Murphy, meets to taste a sample of the production from each of the company's four major plants. Careful reports are filed, and nobody's feelings are spared.

The company is deliberately rough on itself when it comes to checking the quality of its product. The taste-testing teams literally look for trouble. They single out minor flaws that would seldom be obvious to the consumer. But these men take these extra pains because it's good business.

Take a recent report on a day's output from the Chicago plant. Comments were made on fatty tissues and inadequate amounts of spice and a 16-ounce sample of pork and beans that contained no pork. If the comments warrant it, production is stopped and the difficulty quickly corrected.

A plant rule, explained by Donald M. Mounce, vice-president in charge of production, is that if a question arises concerning the quality of an ingredient, anybody can stop production. The operation can be resumed only on the approval of the plant manager, technologist or chief inspector.

"To Pack Good Foods and Let It Be Known"

Campbell is probably a classic example of advertising successfully used over the years. But advertising is a tool which the Campbell executives don't extol blindly. William B. Murphy says "advertising has many effective media. Of them all, word-of-mouth advertising is the best. Advertising helps a business attain success, but some companies seem to be quite successful without advertising. If we stopped, I think the first year it probably would make little difference in our sales, but then sales would dip seriously."

Oliver G. Willits: "Old John Wanamaker used to say he only got half value for each dollar spent on advertising, but he couldn't tell which fifty cents it was so he kept right on spending dollars."

James McGowan, Jr.: "I like the old slogan of the National Canners Association, 'pack good foods and let it be known.' That is where advertising comes in."

*   *   *   *   *

Decentralization

A big change in the company's operation is its decentralization. But even this has been going on for a number of years. Prior to 1930, the company had only one plant at Camden, New Jersey. It now has other major plants at Chicago, Ill.; Sacramento, Calif.; and New Toronto, Ontario, Canada. These plants operate throughout the year. Smaller seasonal plants are located at Salisbury, Md., and Chatham, Ontario, Canada.

In addition, Campbell picked up plants in Napoleon, Ohio, and Terre Haute and Saratoga, Ind., when it purchased the V-8 business from Standard Brands in 1947. By the end of 1956, it will complete the most modern food processing plant in the world at Napoleon, Ohio. It has leased the DiGiorgio Fruit plant at Lucerne Park, Florida, for its new juice product, FR-8. New plants are now being completed at Camden, Chicago and Sacramento for frozen soups to assure national distribution which will commence on March 1, 1955.

A big reason for decentralization is to cut distribution costs by getting as close to the markets as possible. But no matter how much the company decentralizes and no matter how much its management continues to delegate authority, some things will continue unchanged. Don't look for Campbell to stray from the food processing business. Future expansion may include more frozen soups and perhaps more products under the Franco-American label. There is nothing in the cards that suggests further diversification at this time. Campbell grew healthy because it insisted on becoming a specialist. It's going to stay that way.

From Private to Public Ownership

For over 85 years Campbell Soup Company was privately owned. The trustees recently put up for sale 15% of its stock (13% to the public, 2% for salaried employees).

Two reasons are given for that decision: (1) to set a market value on the shares; (2) to take advantage of the public relations benefits inherent in a publicly owned corporation. As a privately owned company, Campbell apparently found itself during the war and after in a lonely situation when negotiating for tin plate allocations. Legislators and government people seem much more impressed with the power of stockholders, who are also voters, than the authority of a highly paid executive in a private company.

Pricing Is for the Trade

Years ago Campbell used to advertise price. There was a period when wholesaler and dealer resentment crowded in on the company. Some smaller retailers complained that the product was being used by the big chains as a loss leader. Campbell has now divorced itself as much as possible from this whole area of complaint. In its advertising it sticks to the quality story. "We don't want to tell the trade what to sell our products for. Our problem is not establishing prices for retailers. We have one price for all," Mr. Murphy says emphatically.

This desire to stay out of price hassles is a decision firmly ingrained at all levels of management. Board chairman McGowan says simply, "Campbell Soup Company didn't bring on the Robinson-Patman Act." You talk to Mr. McGowan about the problem of loss leaders, and this elder statesman tells you a little story.

"Years ago," he says, "I remember talking to a very prominent agency man. I asked him what he did when he found that grocers were using his clients' products as loss leaders."

"Said he, 'We talk to them, we wire them, but we never let them run out of goods.'"

Mr. McGowan says this philosophy was successful. Campbell will do its best to keep prices in line, but it won't interfere with a retailer's selling job. That's the gospel at Camden.

Campbell's job always began and ended with making a product, getting it into the hands of the wholesalers as rapidly as possible and advertising it to the consumers for all it was worth. That course hasn't changed one iota. It won't in the future.

One of the outstanding impressions gained from spending a week of exploring the Camden plant and talking with executives and plant personnel is that the company is humming along at a quicker pace than ever before. And this is the most obvious in its marketing operations.

Only as recently as 1952 did Campbell go off tin allocation. For years before that, its selling problems were not pressing. Since then, however, it has found itself with a big job. Not only must it continue to stay ahead of the competition in condensed soups, but it must try to overtake Van Camp in the pork and beans business and surpass Libby in tomato juice sales.

For this job, Mr. Murphy has surrounded himself with a first-class marketing team. It is headed by Clarence Eldridge, who retired from General Foods in 1953 at age 65 and who is one of the country's ablest marketing heads. Murphy hired Eldridge on the advice of an old hand at advertising, Ray Rubicam. Murphy, Eldridge and Rubicam form a special strategy team on marketing. This team also includes such men as R. M. Budd, who was made advertising director in 1950 after more than thirty years with Campbell. Backing Eldridge and his team is a group of product managers and specialists who came from such aggressive advertisers as General Foods, Lever Bros., Scott Paper. Mr. Eldridge is responsible directly to Mr. Murphy. The association is intimate and direct. Himself an expert at marketing and sales analysis, Mr. Murphy expects top performance from every man.

One of president Murphy's big jobs is making sure the best people are available for the right jobs. When the right man is found, Campbell keeps him; more than 700 employees are on the 25-year honor roll. In holding his organization, Murphy is thinking 10 years ahead. As he sees it, he must determine what his company's personnel needs are going to be and assume responsibility for filling those needs.

Campbell Soup Company has a background rich in tradition, but it is not complacent. Its past success does not blind it to future opportunities. Campbell Soup Co. looks to 1955 for the biggest and best year in its history. It does so while continuing to operate on the old-fashioned theory of being exacting but fair.

MARKETING—THE KEY TO CAMPBELL'S EXPANSION DRIVE

"Our whole business is making public good-will," says big, precision-minded president W. B. Murphy, "That is, the degree of pleasure that consumers get out of our products. Advertising is a medium for getting people to try our soup so that they may realize pleasure from it, buy it again and spread word-of-mouth advertising about it.

"Our publication and broadcast advertising is a nucleus for the creation of public good-will. The great importance that we place on uniform and high quality products is directed toward it. Everything we do is directed at the consumer. To achieve our objective of pleasing the consumer most efficiently, we delegate responsibility and authority —within specific confines—wherever we can."

In the marketing end of the business this delegation of responsibility and authority is perhaps achieving its most striking results. A plan for reorganization of all marketing activities was developed while Campbell was strait-jacketed by the wartime and postwar shortage of tinplate for cans.

Then—later than in almost every other industry—in November 1952, the lid was permanently off on tinplate, and Campbell had a chance to fight for business for the first time since before the war. That's only two and a quarter years ago. Since then a team of Campbell old-timers and newcomers have brought its assured share of the soup business to the point where the only competition they talk about is the competition from housewives.

President Murphy, with expansion on his mind, will tell you: "Of soup in homes, 40% is still homemade." And James McGowan, Jr., chairman of the board, seems indignant when he admits: "Soup is consumed only 1 to 2 times a week on the average."

"We've only plowed up part of this field," he'll tell you; "and there's an opportunity for 21 meals plus snacks in between."

Eat More Soup

So Campbell marketing strategy is aimed squarely at increasing soup consumption. And it's expanding into other food specialty lines where it figures there's a need for more help for the housewife.

That's the background against which you can pose two fascinating graybeards.

One of these is Clarence Eldridge, who retired from General Foods at the compulsory age of 65. At Campbell a man can retire if he wants to at age 65—but if he wants to and if the company wants him, he can work until he's 67. Vigorous, alert and with a mind that matches that of his new boss for clear thinking on marketing—Eldridge didn't stay retired. We asked him whom he expects to work for next time he retires. We got a quick, laughing reply: "Anybody who'll have me. If you know of anybody, you let me know!" He picks up as executive vice-president in charge of sales, advertising and marketing research. Harry F. Jones (who helped plan the changes that are going on now) was in charge of marketing when he retired in 1953 as vice-president, distribution. Mr. Jones is still a director.

The other new figure is Ray Rubicam, formerly of Young & Rubicam. He came out of retirement about three years ago to work for Campbell as a consultant. He had a lot to do with selection of new advertising agencies recently; and he helped get Eldridge to come down from his New York State farm to the soup factory in Camden. He has contributed a lot to the development of new advertising copy themes—and is influential in copy appraisal. Murphy, Eldridge and Rubicam have been working with each other in one way or another for many years—since Murphy came east from Chicago to head up the eastern end of A. C. Nielsen and before Eldridge moved from Y&R to General Foods.

The Marketing Team

They have a team of experts to work with. Eldridge is in charge of policies and activities in sales, advertising, marketing research and general promotion. He directs this work through a vice-president of sales, a general advertising manager, a director of marketing research and a general promotion manager. And reporting directly to him are three product marketing managers (each of whom is blessed with a product advertising manager—plus staffs and ad agencies).

The sales division is set up as a separate Campbell Sales Company, but it is wedded to advertising as one part of the marketing operation.

Coordination of advertising and sales is accomplished through the product marketing managers.

Product advertising is just one part of complete marketing plans. There are, in addition, over-all advertising activities that cut across product lines. These are the responsibility of director of advertising R. M. Budd, who is handling two big and important new advertising programs: advertising to children and advertising of over-all product quality (as close as Campbell comes to institutional advertising). Mr. Budd also controls such pooled advertising properties as TV shows.

Marketing research is a service operation that guides every member of the marketing team all along the line. As president Murphy (who came to Campbell as a sales analyst) puts it: "We get all the facts we can. We determine the margin of unknown factors. Then base decision on judgment." Campbell researches everything with great intensity before it makes a move: products, markets, advertising themes, its people, the people it wants to sell to. And then it goes back and researches them all over again. The intensity with which the company strives for quality in product laps over into an obsession with accuracy in marketing. Research is used creatively every step of the way.

In this reorganized marketing setup, functions are spread out—with specific authority delegated to a fairly large group of key men. This represents an evolution at Campbell from a general-manager type of operation. The business is expanding so greatly that one man can no longer keep close track of everything that affects the marketing of each product.

"We have done some changing of functions," says Mr. Eldridge, "but except for some necessary additions to our staff, there has been very little change in personnel."

Where Budgets Begin

Every move that Campbell makes is carefully planned. In marketing, complete budgets are developed way in advance. Says Mr. Eldridge:

"We take into account sales objectives, based on sales trends, the information furnished by marketing research, and our knowledge of planned advertising and promotional activities. It is right there that budgeting begins.

"We try to arrive at a general figure of how much of an expenditure is justified and needed. To do this you have to put yourself in a managerial relationship, and make sure that in allowing for expansion you are on sure ground."

The size of advertising budgets bears no fixed relation to expected sales volume—such and such a per cent of sales for advertising as with most companies. Campbell's ad budget on new products is apt to be larger than on old-established lines. A Campbell executive says, "With the introduction of a new line of products it is reasonable to assume that you aren't going to break even within one year." The general attitude of businessmen is that three years is the usual break-even period for a new, major line.

At Campbell the allocation for advertising by product groups depends on the weighting of four factors: (1) opportunities for expansion, (2) size of the holding job, (3) severity of the competitive situation, (4) special considerations for a product with great undeveloped potentials.

The product advertising manager goes to work on specific advertising plans. He gets a general figure to work with, plus an idea of objectives; and starts his planning January 1. He gets the agency to work out a very specific recommendation, including costs, copy themes, etc., which is to be back in the hands of the product marketing manager by April 1. The plan is then worked over for about a month under the direction of the product marketing manager; and passed to Mr. Eldridge on about May 1.

For another month Mr. Eldridge with the executives in each product group can go over and further perfect the plan. In June there is a finished plan for marketing each product. At that time the plan goes to president Murphy for final approval.

Organized Planning

One important aspect of planning is an organized method of plan writing that Mr. Eldridge has worked out. He gives each product group an outline to follow as a guide. This consists of:

1. Statement of facts—
   a. The competitive situation.
   b. The trend of sales.
   c. A sufficiently complete history of the product, its possibilities and its problems, so that if you were to read it you could draw definite conclusions what to do about it.
2. Enumeration of problems that product faces.
3. Objectives—actually setting up what the company wants to accomplish.
4. The plan—how the company wants to do it.

Much of the detail work of writing each plan is done by the advertising agency—always under the close supervision of company marketing executives. It includes specific media recommendations, schedules and costs. It includes copy platforms—primary and secondary advertising appeals. It includes pattern ads in near-finished form. It includes at least a half-dozen finished copy blocks in pattern ads. By the time of approval, much of the work of preparing advertising has been done. The finished ads in the campaigns that started in plan form on January 1 are ready for publication in August issues of national magazines.

The organized method of plan writing results in reasonable uniformity in planning (even under a multiple agency setup), control of the entire operation all along the way, advertising that is based on concrete knowledge of marketing problems and opportunities. It brings everybody into the act of planning—and secures the greatest amount of creative thinking from all quarters. "Ideas," says Mr. Eldridge, "are the responsibility of everyone."

A Franchise on Consumers

New ideas are fed into the mill in Campbell's marketing department all the time—from all sides. But the biggest idea of all is the same one that made a merchant out of chemist John Dorrance some 50 years ago. It is simply to make the best possible soup at a price that almost anybody can afford—and once having done that, to tell the world about it.

Translated into the language of modern advertising that means building an unbeatable consumer franchise. In relation to soups, there's no doubt that such a franchise is what Campbell's has always had. It has never lost leadership in the soup business. And it is continuing the policy of dominant and continuous advertising to maintain that franchise.

But there seems to be a feeling at this old company (it shows through the new policies and new decisions) that you can't be sure of staying on top in an expanding market by simply holding your own. Campbell is not only out to hold its share of the soup business, but to increase the total consumption of soup. And it has every intention of moving into big volume in other lines of specialty foods. The old bromide, "The best defense is a good offense," is being applied here with a vengeance.

So Campbell's is extending its consumer franchise by sharpening up the impact power of its already powerful advertising. And also by slow expansion of the amount invested in advertising—mostly in a tightly budgeted relation to new products in new markets.

To Expand in Its Own Backyard

"Advertising," says Clarence Eldridge, "is a means to our ultimate objective of expanded business. We are not expanding just to keep pace with population increases but to secure a larger share of consumer dollars.

"We have a reputation largely built on our soup business. This is a very high quality product and is recognized by consumers as such. But we feel that still more can be done to make better known the *reasons* behind that quality and the almost fantastic preoccupation with quality that dominates this company. I personally have never seen anything like it.

"Our new line campaign in which advertising of over-all quality of our products is being demonstrated is a means toward this end. And it is our belief that the reputation our soups enjoy can be extended to other products—like those in our Franco-American line.

"Our basic marketing philosophy or desire is to build our business on the basis of a sound consumer franchise, based on high quality products—efficiently made—at minimum cost. To build that consumer franchise, we stress in our advertising: (1) quality, (2) convenience and (3) economy.

New Themes in an Old Market

"Our greatest opportunity for growth is still in soup. This is where we have our greatest volume; and a small percentage increase in soup consumption means a big increase in volume. We can increase this volume, we believe, by presenting new ideas about our soups to housewives, to children and to institutional users. To direct our appeals to children is a leaf out of the cereal advertisers' book. And we are selling directly now to children via the Howdy-Doody, Abbott and Costello, and Lassie television shows.

"But no one medium does all the jobs that we want to do equally well. Some ideas are appropriate to women's service magazines. In our ads in that medium we stress convenience, time saving, economy. Here is where Anne Marshall appears with advice on food preparation. Here is where we lay the greatest stress on serving soup in new ways—such as sauces in casseroles, combinations of two or more soups: 'soup-mates,' we call it.

"Then there is the broad general audience of eaters of all kinds that is important to us. In general magazines and on evening TV we stress appetite appeal. In *Parents' Magazine* we are doing a specialized job on the mothers of young children. Through institutional magazines, where we have about doubled our schedule, we are seeking more business from lunch counters. There is no likelihood that in the near future we will give up any of the media that we use.

"We use local media when we are introducing new products, but for the most part our business is all national—and we use national franchise-building advertising to support and augment it. Color TV, on a national basis, will doubtless some day become a factor for us.

For Greater Impact

"We are trying to get greater impact from all of our advertising dollars. Toward this end we pay attention to: (1) the quality of advertisement content, (2) the consistency of advertising schedules and the consistency of appearance of the ads and (3) the concentration of ad dollars. We use full schedules in whatever magazines we are in."

That is what the famous Campbell consumer franchise means to Mr. Eldridge, who says in summation: "Nobody has a greater admiration for the men who have preceded me than I have. Those of us who are here now are simply trying to carry on the spirit that made this a great company: ingenuity, courage, a willingness to break new ground."

* * * * *

Enter: Marketing Research

To see marketing research at grips with practical problems, we suggest a visit to an intense, hard-working ex-salesman. He's J. F. Merriman, director of marketing research.

If Campbell executives had known what research Mr. Merriman did before coming to work for them in 1950, they'd have been sure they were picking the right man. Merriman searched out every scrap of information he could find about Campbell's (including articles in several dusty volumes of PRINTERS' INK); then decided on the basis of research that he wanted to make the move.

Merriman's job is to service the requirements of the product marketing managers, Eldridge, Nixon and vice-president Philip W. Souder in charge of product research and development. The work gets intense but interesting whichever way it turns. Merriman calls it "a balanced research function serving the over-all marketing needs."

Marketing research became important to Campbell in 1939–40–41 when Mr. Murphy first came to the company. During the war years, marketing research came to an unavoidable standstill. It got going again with one man and a girl in 1948, when William Kingston (now manager of sales research) became Campbell's first manager of marketing research. In 1950 Gordon Scowcroft became marketing research head. And then in March of last year (when Scowcroft moved into the interesting spot of product marketing manager on the new frozen soup line) Merriman was taken out of his sales department spot and given the assignment.

This department now numbers nine people, is growing, reaches out through the research departments of its ad agencies and through outside research services to tap vast and varied sources of fact. But since a large part of the work is on confidential new products, Campbell's own researchers are kept normally busy. They have the main office statistical staff to draw on for tabulations; and have their own consumer panel set-up.

A Service for Sales and Advertising

Merriman says that the work of his department breaks down into *sales* research and *consumer* research. A very direct example of what he means by sales research is a study that is being made now to see what happens when sales manpower in the field is doubled. In a test market, Campbell is now using twice as many salesmen as it normally does. The men in this market are split (for test purpose) into two groups: one carrying soups only, the other carrying the other Campbell products. Marketing research sets up the test situation in a case like this, develops the report of results—in behalf of sales vice-president Nixon.

Under sales research comes also interpretation of such data as that supplied in great quantities by the Nielsen service. "No research," says Merriman, "is worth a dime unless it's used." One reason for the entrance of president Murphy into the Campbell Company in 1938 was to help get more mileage out of the Nielson data. That aspect of his early work for the company is still taken seriously.

In consumer research there is a constant demand for blind product testing. This involves the masking of cans in which old soup formulae and experimental batches are compared. Or it may be the masking of cans containing a Campbell formula and a competitive formula. Many of these are executed through National Family Opinion and Home Testing Institute, and a report of consumer taste preferences comes back. Work of this kind originates in the test kitchens; it comes to marketing research through Mr. Souder, vice-president in charge of product research and development, and it's a constant operation.

As much of the field work as possible—even with product preference research—is farmed out, drawing extensively on the research departments of the advertising agencies.

On Mr. Merriman's status report there are 14 other major projects current, 5 others in the planning stage, 3 just completed. That's the normal load for his department, where it takes from one to six months to complete a survey.

Copy Research

Advertising research also clears through this department. And at the present time the Gallup-Robinson service plays an important role in ad strategy. Gallup clinics (impact scores, playbacks of consumer comments, presentation of over-all findings) are continuous. At these sessions, agency people are welcome—and usually attend.

"We are now trying," says Mr. Merriman, "to convert all our marketing work toward making the greatest impact on consumers. We are trying to fit our products to the needs of the consumer. It's gone from what you can make to what you can sell—and when we find that out, we'll make it if it's up our alley."

Frozen Soups—a New Success

First national advertising on Campbell frozen soups will break late this month. On its network TV shows (Dear Phoebe and Lassie) and in two-color spreads in national magazines this new line of products is set for its first big advertising ride. From now on, Campbell will follow its old stand-by rule of constant advertising. It will be plugging frozen soups for all they are worth.

No dollar figures are available, but it's no secret that this first splurge of national advertising will take a much higher percentage for advertising than is likely to be justified by sales. This may be the case for the next year or so, but it's not unusual. The intent now is to promote hard and long to build consumer recognition and acceptance.

The frozen soup story is perhaps a standout example of the renewed vigor and aggressive marketing approach that stamps the company's operations today. Campbell is moving fast.

In less than a year since Campbell first test-marketed the product in the Philadelphia area, market-by-market distribution has been built up across the country. National advertising is breaking at the same time that national distribution is completed on the West Coast. Behind this big decision is the Campbell attitude that something that is worth doing is worth doing on a big scale.

This attitude comes through in another test-market operation for the new blended fruit juice product, FR-8. The company wasted no time here either. When it ran into snags, the product was withdrawn from the market and sent back to the product development laboratories for more study. When the kinks are ironed out there, you can look for the same aggressive all-out marketing and advertising push that is now behind the frozen soup line.

On the frozen soup line, enthusiasm runs high. Initial market tests set the wheels in motion. Within a two-month period after the product was first introduced in Philadelphia, the market was checked. A survey revealed that 80% of those interviewed knew Campbell had frozen soups; and 50% said they had bought them. Repeat sales and interest by the trade gave Campbell the necessary clues to its marketing course.

Markets were explored and opened across the country. In primary markets (those with population of 500,000 or more), TV and newspapers were used. Secondary markets (200,000 population and under) got heavy newspaper support. The smaller markets are being opened so close to the breaking of national advertising that the decision was made to let the national advertising carry the introductory message in those areas.

National magazine advertising closely resembles the advertising used in the market-by-market build-up. There is plenty of white space with major dominance given to the Campbell name and identification of the soups as frozen. (Leo Burnett handles the advertising for this line.)

Campbell has no intention of letting frozen soups dangle in the consumer marketplace now that the initial testing stage is over. The company is too painstaking and careful to do anything like that. The frozen soup line will be watched like a hawk. Markets will continue to be checked and surveyed; decisions will be altered as marketing conditions change.

Less than a month ago testing was still going on. Over the week end of January 21 a phone survey was conducted among 1,500 consumers. Market research people used a comprehensive 10-page questionnaire to learn consumer preferences and tastes in frozen soups. This information —and other studies from now on—will continue to supply marketing and selling fodder to move Campbell frozen soups off the retailers' shelves.

There'll be other areas of checking. Recently the company started its first product demonstration in a food store. A Food Fair store in the Philadelphia area was used. If successful, tactics like this will probably become a part of marketing the Campbell frozen soups.

One big question still unanswered is just how the frozen soup line will affect the sale of Campbell's bread-and-butter line, the heat-processed soups. This won't be known for some time. The regular soup line isn't expected to suffer greatly.

For Canned Soup—a Big Push

But Campbell doesn't intend to take any chances here. It is mapping out continually aggressive and consistent advertising programs to capture an even larger share of the market for heat-processed soups.

From W. B. Murphy right down to the production line, the good old can of high quality soup is recognized as the mainstay of the company's business. When executives like Mr. Murphy and Mr. McGovern and Mr. Willits say they've only convinced the housewife to serve Campbell soup 1 to 2 times a week, it means these men think Campbell has only just begun to sell soup. They insist that the housewife is still the company's biggest competitor.

A tip-off on the company's marketing thinking regarding soup comes from marketing bossman, Clarence Eldridge. He says the big job for the company is to increase the frequency of soup consumption. Like other top brass, he doesn't appear to be at all worried about Heinz or Lipton or any of the other competitors. He points out that Campbell has a good percentage of the soup market now. He has no intention of letting any competitor squeeze in and take even the sale of a single can of soup away. The real source for new soup business, he says, is in increased frequency of use.

Steps are now being taken in national advertising to accomplish this. As a part of its regular magazine campaign, Campbell features using soups in casseroles and mixing of soups for different taste sensations.

Campaign on the mixing of soups (*the soup-mates* promotion) got under way in January. The promotion is backed by full-page, four-color ads in *Ladies' Home Journal, Better Homes & Gardens, Good Housekeeping, American Home, Woman's Home Companion* and *McCall's*. And main commercials are used on all four of the company's television programs.

There is even a subtle campaign brewing that will attempt to sell soup for breakfast. Perhaps the first break in this unusual approach was an article on soup for breakfast that appeared recently in one of the home service magazines. Did Campbell have anything to do with this?

"Well, we didn't discourage it," Mr. Eldridge says.

*   *   *   *   *

More Impact for Franco-American

This line (now handled by Ogilvy, Benson & Mather) offers a real challenge to the company. These are the low-volume products in the company and are the ones getting plenty of attention from Mr. Murphy, Mr. Eldridge, advertising consultant Ray Rubicam and Gordon Scowcroft, product marketing manager in charge.

Although the Franco-American products are made with the same skill and careful attention as the soups, company executives feel that consumers are not as familiar with the quality of Franco-American products as they are with the quality of Campbell's soups. Strategy now is to bring this line under the quality umbrella of the soups. This is being done gradually. First step is listing of Franco-American products in all advertising of other products. And in the Franco-American ads, the Campbell products are listed. In many of the soups ads, the Franco-American name is printed in red for extra emphasis.

Because Franco-American sales are low by comparison with soup volume, individual appropriations are considerably less than for the soups. The problem here, according to Mr. Eldridge, is that of trying to build impact. Campbell is trying something here.

Instead of dispersing Franco-American space, Campbell is concentrating a total of 33 pages in Life for the various products in the line (spaghetti, macaroni, beef gravy, spaghetti sauce with meat). A family resemblance to all the ads will attempt to reap full identification for the entire line. As much as money will permit, Franco-American will be promoted on the company's TV programs.

Competition for Van Camp and Libby

Like the Franco-American line, Campbell's pork and beans and tomato juice represent the company's real competitive lines. With these last two products, Campbell is driving hard to overtake two very active competitors. Van Camp is now No. 1 in pork and beans sales; and Libby's is ahead of Campbell in tomato juice.

For the job, Campbell is driving hard at the consumer. Former General Foods man J. P. Shenfield, now product manager for pork and beans, V-8, FR-8, tomato juice and ketchup, says that today advertising and promotion for these products is better geared to the marketing problems.

The marketing problems in this case are related principally to the competitive situation.

Mr. Shenfield says that pork and beans sales are showing a very substantial increase for the past year and a half. One important factor in this showing has been the addition of a 28-ounce "family size." This has enabled Campbell to sell a large-size can of beans at a lower price than Van Camp's large size, which is 34 oz.

Pork and beans are being promoted more often during the year. The company is using more trade offers. It is getting its feet wet in a few premium deals. The latest premium offer is a pair of white or blue nylon gloves—promoted, as a self-liquidating consumer-deal, on pork and beans labels.

New Interest in Premiums

Deals and premiums are used cautiously. But the company is exploring the field. One of the current offers is a set of self-liquidating premiums, eating utensils for babies—obtained for cash plus 2 Campbell soup labels. The premiums, specially designed, silver-plated cups, fork and spoon set and knife, are promoted in the special campaign in *Parents' Magazine*.

Other special deals have included a Lassie puppy contest promoted over the Lassie TV show. This one brought over 500,000 entries, about twice as many replies as were expected.

Not a Big Dealer

But from all that we can gather premiums and deals aren't going to be permitted to become a top-heavy part of Campbell's marketing strategy. They never have been in the past. And even now they are being used gingerly. Mr. Eldridge (for a long time involved with various kinds of offers in the General Foods marketing operation) says premiums are being used now in a limited way where the basic situation seems to justify their use—especially on Franco-American products, pork and beans and ketchup. But—Mr. Eldridge hurriedly points out—Campbell's fundamental marketing objectives cannot be met by a succession of deals, premiums, and give-aways.

"As a general rule, they are not for us," he says. "We have a basic philosophy. Our aim is to build our business on a sound consumer franchise, based on a high quality of product, produced at a reasonable cost and sold at a fair price. Deals can't be expected to do that. Deals are expensive. They take money away from reason-why franchise-building advertising.

"Deals are a substitute, an expedient of temporary and usually illusory benefit. We don't want to be battling over premiums and deals. We're doing it on a very limited basis for very specific purposes, and we intend to control it vigilantly.

"When a deal is used for sampling it seems to me a legitimate thing," Mr. Eldridge says. "Then it's a fundamental form of promotion. We'd like to find ways to sample. But since house-to-house is so expensive, we have to try to find some substitute form of sampling that we can afford. That's where consumer-deals sometimes have a legitimate use."

No Co-op Ads

Another marketing practice that Campbell is even more inflexible about is cooperative advertising. And here there seems hardly a ghost of a chance that there will be any deviation at all. Mr. Eldridge outlines the Campbell policy on this.

"We have a policy that's firmly against co-op advertising," he says, "Every dollar you spend for co-op advertising is taking away a dollar necessary to establish and maintain your consumer-franchise. Building sales for a particular retail grocery store is the responsibility of that store. We would be diluting our real job of building consumer-franchise if we embarked on a cooperative ad program.

"We have a continuous job of building and maintaining our consumer-franchises. That is a job we must keep at everlastingly. A consumer-franchise once bought isn't yours forever. It has to be nurtured and kept alive and vital by constant attention."

*   *   *   *   *

SOUP, SALESMEN AND SALES PROMOTION— THEY RUN TOGETHER IN THE CAMPBELL SALES CO.

The men who run the Campbell Soup Company are hipped on quality. They have two women out in the plant who do nothing but throw out the broken letters in the alphabets for the alphabet soup!

When you visit Campbell's you hear about quality from everybody you talk to. There are signs on the walls about quality. You can get the idea that this fantastic concentration on the quality of the product is carried to extremes. That is, until you come to—of all people—the man whose concern is sales and salesmen, chain and wholesale buyers, shelf-space in stores, the skeptical retailer in Kokomo, promoters and promotion, competitive prices, quotas, sales meetings.

He's William B. Nixon, vice-president in charge of sales of Campbell Soup Company and president of Campbell Sales Company. "Our most valuable sales asset," he'll tell you, "is product quality. That's what our salesmen have to sell above all. It takes real sales ability to persuade a balky retailer to increase the size of his Campbell shelf space. And I don't want to minimize the importance of personal selling in any way. But without product quality—and the consumers who associate that quality with Campbell's—we wouldn't have much to sell."

Nixon came up through the ranks in the sales end of the business, where he started as a sales correspondent in 1928. Now he is either in the field or in a rather barren metal-and-glass cubicle next to the vice-president in charge of sales, advertising, and marketing research (to whom he is responsible). A hurried man, Nixon seems to have accepted the life of jangling telephones and train-or-plane-hopping.

Sales Are in the Field

The bulk of his sales organization is in the field, working out of four divisional sales offices and 66 district sales offices. The divisions are East, West, North and South and follow state lines. Generally speaking sales districts embrace whole counties. Nielsen figures can be applied directly to them.

The district managers hire and train their own men. Authority and responsibility are delegated to them—but within specific limitations set down in a sales manual. The salesmen, all on salary, sell to jobbers, wholesalers and chains. But they spend much of their time calling on retailers, merchandising the products, the advertising and special promotions, selling vertical soup sections (planned display shelves) and working in behalf of the wholesaler or chain headquarters to keep stocks balanced and complete. "As near as possible the amount of time salesmen spend on each product," says Nixon, "is related to the importance of the item in the business. Sales quotas are set up on a district basis. Each district's quota is the total of the wholesaler, jobber and direct customer quotas in his territory. In setting quotas last year's sales, present conditions and the amount of increase we want are taken into account."

Campbell salesmen ration their time, calling most often on big volume retailers.

Keeping close track of local problems at all times are the divisional manager and divisional supervisors who work for them. Contact with the main office is direct through sales correspondents assigned to each district. Every now and then the fieldmen come to Camden to get a chance to know the men they write to and telephone to in emergencies. Sales conventions bring groups of districts together at least once a year.

"During the year we spend about a month," says Nixon, "in the field at sales conventions. They last for two days—the first day concerned with advertising and promotion, the second day with personnel relations and straight selling. We think of them as sales-training seminars. And we get a chance to outline in advance the full year's plans for advertising, selling and sales promotion."

Soup Displayed Is Soup Sold

The salesmen are really doing a job for wholesalers and work hand-in-glove with them. They install displays and push regular promotions. They sell hardest on the vertical soup section.

"Our salesmen," says president Murphy, "perform (in addition to their other duties) the function of missionary men. We never get earned shelf space for our line in stores. We should get more space on the basis of volume. But fast turnover items are always behind on shelf space. Our line is typical in this respect."

Campbell does not reveal its sales figures by brands, so it is not possible to specify exactly what Mr. Murphy means by "earned shelf space." However, a look at the soup section in any well-stocked grocery will give you a pretty good idea.

Campbell soups are usually displayed in the vertical section that is so dear to the hearts of the salesmen. And that section often spreads out into about 60% of the total display shelving for soups. If Campbell had its way, its vertical soup section would hold about 80% of all soups in the store. And the Campbell brands would be divided roughly into four equal display sections for chicken soups, vegetable and beef soups, tomato soup (the biggest single seller) and all other varieties.

The Campbell executive mask appears at any question of relative share of market for Campbell products. So this probably corresponds to about as good a guess as an outsider can make of relative sales power of its heat processed canned soup line.

Sales Promotion—a New Package Every Other Week

Salesmen in the field are backed up with a quality product, a strong and strengthening consumer franchise. And they have some new piece of sales promotion material to take with them on almost every call.

Practically all of the material is in the form of sales promotion packages: posters, shelf talkers, case cards, newspaper mats. There's no co-op ad allowance. However, a mat service is provided. Related ads in grocery merchandising papers at the same time are developed as part of the package. Salesmen get brochures to work with in explaining to the retailer what's going on. And (as the brochures inevitably point out) the whole point-of-sale package repeats the themes current in national ads.

There's a new promotion on soup every four weeks. On other products, promotion packages come through about every three weeks. They reach the field through district managers, who are fully instructed how to promote the promotion to their men. District managers get the material about six weeks ahead of time and are able to time meetings strategically.

Preparing sales promotion is the responsibility of the product marketing managers, working through their ad agencies. "We make our promotion events so obvious," says soup marketing manager Stevens, "that nobody can miss the relation to time of year, related item promotion, national copy themes . . . Good headings for these events are: *Children's Favorites, Soup and Crackers, Soup's Ideal for Summer Meals.* We have used all of these with good results. We won't use a theme unless we can make it obvious. Then we let the same idea run through the trade ad, brochure and display.

"We are plugging the relation of soups to sandwich meals in national copy in summer and soup and crackers in the fall. Naturally sales promotion follows this timing."

* * * * *

One Price for All

The Campbell price policy is as simple as it could be: one price for all. Campbell sells to jobbers and wholesalers and direct to chain buyers or to anybody else who is a complete source of supply for a number of retail stores. It believes that warehousing is a job for the middlemen. The intent is to sell the soup to middlemen, let them allow for warehousing costs and set their own prices. Retail prices were once advertised—but now no longer.

"We don't want to influence the trade on how they price our merchandise," says president Murphy. "That's their business. The wholesaler can charge the amount he wants to charge in order to stay in business, to meet his competition and make a profit."

To give the middleman a fair deal, the company makes no exceptions to its one-price-for-all rule. "We have," says chairman of the board McGowan, "one grade—and it's a good grade—in each type of product. There are no competitive price lines. We shoot at the consumers all the time to build their acceptance of this value. Because it is the consumer's dollars that make the middlemen's dollars.

"Our profit per unit gets less every year, but our volume is growing—and over-all profits get bigger. That's the sole reason for being big." As Campbell's volume and over-all profit get bigger, so should that of the middlemen who perform the warehousing and re-selling function efficiently.

Published figures are a quick index of just what has happened. Campbell Soup Company in 1954 made twice as much net income as it did in 1939. But its net income per dollar of net sales dropped from 17.7 cents in 1939 to 7.0 cents in 1954. The consumer is getting a better shake for her dollar.

From 1925 to 1955—Same Price for Tomato Soup

In 1925 your mother could buy a can of tomato soup for 12 cents. Today you can buy it for about 12 cents (less when it's on sale)—and the soup today is a much better product. How come?

"How did we do this," asks Oliver G. Willits, vice-chairman of the board, "in spite of rising costs of ingredients, labor, shipping? By extending automation in our plants, by increasing productivity, by increasing crops and yields, by increasing marketing efficiency.

"In 1914 a good tomato [pronounced *tow-may-tow* by the men who know more about them than anybody else in the world] farmer would grow 4½ to 5 tons an acre. In California in 1955 they are getting an average of 17 tons an acre. They are doing it by feeding and watering their land, growing more plants per acre. Here in the East some youngsters in the Future Farmers of America got 24 tons to the acre last summer.

"We secure savings through decentralization. Shipping costs (we pay all shipping costs so as to deliver the goods at the same price to all) are considerable in our business. Through decentralization of our processing plants, we have vastly reduced these costs.

"In advertising we try to increase our effectiveness. We try new media, new themes. We seek new markets through advertising. And we are constantly seeking to make our advertising more pleasing. We are constantly experimenting for selfish reasons with the betterment of all marketing methods."

Special Discount in the Tomato Season

In keeping with the intention of giving wholesalers a fair deal on the warehousing costs, Campbell makes a price adjustment every fall. In August and September the entire Eastern tomato crop is harvested and canned. The result would be a sudden stockpile of canned tomato soup if special incentives were not given to the trade to draw the big supply into their warehouses. So last year the opening price (now $5.05 net per case) on Campbell's tomato soup, for shipment as packed was cut 20 cents a case. In addition a marketing incentive was offered of 10 cents a case for all tomato soup moved by the wholesale industry into retail stores during a ten weeks period in the early autumn.

There are 48 cans in a case; so the regular wholesale price is about 10½ cents a can on tomato soup. Chains that take both discounts can move the tomato soup directly into retail stores at 10 cents a can. The markup that grocers choose to put on the product is not large. Campbell keeps hands off on retail prices, assumes that the middlemen and retailers know how to take care of themselves on pricing.

In a grocery chain like First National you can buy the tomato soup for 11¾ cents a can (four for 47 cents). The mark up (wholesale plus retail) on cans purchased at the regular wholesale price runs around 12½%. In First National stores Campbell's cream of mushroom soup (one of the more expensive in the line) may sell at two cans for 35 cents (one for 18 cents). Wholesale price is $7.15 net per case of 48 cans—less than 15 cents a can. That leaves a markup (wholesale plus retail) of around 17% on the wholesale price.

*   *   *   *   *

·{ 2 }··

New Products, New Ads, New Brand Loyalties *

BY KENNETH LAIRD †

Two massive dangers threaten top-selling consumer products today. Significantly enough, they are not the well-advertised buyers' market or the tooth-and-claw tactics that get talked about when business drops off. Instead they are:

1. A new and very fickle type of consumer brand loyalty psychology. Proceeding at top speed, it is stimulating the fast consumer acceptance of new products and abandonment of old ones.

2. A new type of effective media strategy. Now an advertiser can cover almost the entire buying population of the country within a few months and build overnight acceptance of the new item.

Closely allied, you find these two elements working together against the *status quo* in an upsetting, fiendish partnership.

Revolution in Buying

There was a time when the American housewife hoarded her favorite product or brand like an heirloom. It was tried and true. It had served her for years and perhaps her mother before her. So she cherished it and clung to it loyally.

* Reprinted by special permission from *Printers' Ink*, July 2, 1954. Copyright, 1954, *Printers' Ink*.
† Vice-president and treasurer, Tatham-Laird, Inc., Chicago.

In contrast, any new item was something of an interloper. She tended to regard it suspiciously. Even if a convincing story of product improvement could be told, she was not swayed easily.

Newness was a distinct handicap.

If you were Colgate sitting on top with Ribbon Dental Cream, you felt sure that to dislodge you would take a newcomer many years—and at a cost of many millions of dollars in advertising and promotion.

But look at today!

Pay-As-You-Go Is Possible

A manufacturer with a genuinely dramatic, improved dentifrice—and a beginning advertising appropriation of $2,500,000—could put a dent in the dental cream leaders as big as the Grand Canyon.

And it could be done with little or no out-of-pocket cost by the end of a year!

Colgate's Ribbon Dental Cream has been one of the great all-time money makers in the drug trade. But all of us know how ammonium and chlorophyll have affected the standings of dentifrices. Now Colgate has closed out Ribbon Dental Cream nationally, launching an anti-enzyme formula as its successor.

The management evidently decided that the product might as well be licked by something with a Colgate label on it.

Just consider the recent breath-taking product successes in the past few years, including:

1. A new lipstick with a no-smear feature.
2. A shampoo with only a minor improvement in form and a girl with a white umbrella.
3. Frozen prepared specialties—pre-fried fish, chicken pie and complete dinners.

Fast Brand Establishment

Obviously, quick product establishment means quick new brand establishment.

One reason is the vulnerability of most brand leaders. Too often they sit back until a fledgling with a new or improved product has taken over.

Stopette is a good example. Essentially it was a packaging improvement that offered a new convenience to the consumer at what was then a high price.

There was very little money back of the product, almost no manpower. It was just a new idea—plus determination.

What did most of the established brands do? They watched Stopette grow! Finally, when Stopette became too big and too powerful to be squelched, most of the competitors swept valiantly into the fray—with imitations!

Today smart competitors aren't waiting. If you bring out an outstanding new product in Minneapolis, and it sells well, and you expand to Milwaukee and Des Moines, the chances are that a shrewd competitor will beat you to Chicago, St. Louis and Detroit!

You will end up in these cities as the second comer, apparently imitating the first-in product.

Brand Mortality High Today

Recently A. C. Nielsen, president of A. C. Nielsen Co., pointed out the high mortality of grocery brands today:

1. Out of 100 leading grocery brands in 1942, heading their respective categories, 30 had lost their leadership by 1948—only 6 years later.

2. In 1953, after another five years, 30% of the *new* 30 leaders had lost their thrones.

This was despite the fact that the new 30 were, in most cases, the product of young and vigorous managements!

Look at the cigarette field, whose leading brands rest on massive advertising foundations. The king-size and filter-tips are causing customers to switch brands as never before. The five leaders had seven-eighths of the market five years ago, now they've dropped to two-thirds or less.

Maybe we can summarize all this change as follows:

Formerly the consumer resisted and mistrusted new products. Today she'll try anything once and expects to like it better!

Post-War Promises

Let's look at a possible reason for all this upheaval.

The development of consumer products was halted during World War II, and we lived in a sort of austerity. Toward the end of the war the air was full of promises about the bright new world ahead because of war-matured science and industry.

Not all the promises were kept. But many were, and some of them have been mighty in their impact upon us.

Consider television. On VE Day it was a laboratory curiosity. Today it's a captured and domesticated miracle, casually operating in 6 out of every 10 homes in the nation!

Let's look at a few more:

1. A washing machine that goes through all the stages of doing laundry upon the setting of a single dial.
2. Plastics that outwear leather.
3. A refrigerator that defrosts itself.
4. Foam rubber pillows that outperform down.
5. Winter underwear made of nylon and Fiberglas that is warmer and lighter than long-accepted pre-war items of different materials.
6. Synthetic yarn that is warm like wool but doesn't shrink.
7. New miracle drugs that easily overcome infections formerly considered lethal.

Why shouldn't the public believe that the genius which created all these will go on pulling fatter and fancier rabbits out of the hat?

Why shouldn't the public assume that the new item is better and put the burden of proof on the old favorite to justify its continued existence?

Media's Increased Tempo

Today, with the addition of television, we have a new knowledge of how to use advertising media with confidence.

It is possible now to cover almost the entire buying population of America within a few months. In fact, *months* should probably be amended to *weeks*. Many millions of consumers can be induced to try a new item of mass appeal, enabling the advertiser to build a solid and broad-based profitable business at a reasonable or even negligible net cost.

The secret is simple: the application of more advertising power than we dared to use in the past.

We have learned that big advertisements on the air or in print, plus frequency, will pay out if the product and the copy are right. The maneuver will work for print as well as for television, but we must give TV some credit for teaching us the lesson.

TV taught us that sums of money (staggering by any ordinary yardstick) pay off on TV. That has given us the courage to try the same strategy in print, and it pays off there, too.

We see many a campaign today with a string of magazine color spreads or a dozen newspaper pages in as many weeks, or we see $200,000 worth of television and radio a month on a single product. And rightly used, we see these large expenditures supported by the business they produce. (This assumes that proper research precautions have been taken to insure that both the product and the campaign are worth spending big money on.)

Trade Wants Sales Quickly

Today the trade does not have the patience necessary for any creeping technique of new product introduction. Unless retailers are convinced that a product has what it takes to get quickly into major volume, they won't give it shelfroom. And they are pretty sophisticated in knowing just what it does take—at least in the food and drug trades.

Quite obviously they are more sophisticated than in the old days when we could wave one single *Saturday Evening Post* color proof and get an order for a carload.

Opportunity

If we combine the consumers' eager and receptive attitude toward new products with the powerful new techniques for presenting the story of new products, it adds up to a broad vista for the new and a danger for the old.

How can you—assuming you are a manufacturer—avoid that danger and convert it into an opportunity?

Here is a program presented with no modest blushes because it isn't original. It was obtained from watching the operations of smart clients.

1. Recognize that the red corpuscles of your business in the next few years will depend on a flow of good new products and worthwhile improvements in old ones.

2. Give this new marketing function the management stature it needs.

Set up a small but high-powered department or committee. Put an able, aggressive, imaginative executive in charge—probably an advertising man. Pay him one of the top salaries in the company. Have him report to top management. Give him able staff assistances in technical research, consumer research and production.

3. Set up a schedule for bringing out new products (or old ones with important improvements) at the rate of one or two a year for the next five years . . . and drive that schedule through at least to the test market stage.

4. Develop a technique of introductory marketing that is in line with today's tempo and that uses the full power of media to spread the news of the improvement to a public that waits expectantly.

With consumers so eager for better mousetraps and the technique of spreading mousetrap news so powerful, there are going to be some casualties in the mousetrap business.

But if companies aggressively develop and launch new brands with added consumer benefits, they will be playing the percentages. Because today the percentages favor the aggressive innovator.

·{ 3 }··

U.S. Steel's New Marketing Plan *

In Pittsburgh's gleaming U.S. Steel building, the managers of the world's largest marketing task force are perfecting and expanding one of the most significant concepts in business today.

U.S. Steel can be truthfully described as the basic company in the most basic U.S. industry. Its preoccupation with market development

---

* Reprinted by special permission from *Tide*, November 5, 1955. Copyright, 1955, *Tide*.

demonstrates that today nobody, not even U.S. Steel, can afford to ignore "the age of marketing."

To trace the growing awareness of market development in the sprawling steel company which sells some $3 billion worth of steel each year would take volumes. But the result of that awareness can be almost simply explained. Today, the nation's biggest industrial marketer spends at least $4,000,000 of its annual advertising budget into carefully wrought promotions telling everyone from manufacturer to retailer to consumer why steel makes better mattress springs, refrigerators, cutlery, swimming pools or just plain chicken wire.

At first glance, this technique seems merely a matter of diversifying distribution, an effort to expand markets for consumer durables or stainless steel cutlery. But the strategy runs much deeper. U.S. Steel's growing commitment to "the age of marketing" is basic recognition that today's order no longer goes to the spellbinding salesman, but flows almost automatically to the individual and the company who can best serve the customer. "Service," a Steel spokesman has said, "is our most important product."

Steel has polished its service theory until indeed it radiates from supplier through manufacturer and retailer to the consumer. Steel's service concept can be described this way: help your customer sell; then help your customer's customer sell. The reason behind Steel's service strategy is obvious enough: by expanding your customer's market, and his customer's market, the total market grows. As it does, so should Steel's share of it.

Steel's relatively simple marketing concept goes one key step further. Help General Electric expand the appliance market and your chances are better for other GE steel orders, such as those for factories and heavy equipment. Or help an electric utility boost appliance sales so that its power sales presumably zoom. That means the utility needs more equipment to generate kilowattage. That, in turn, means steel for transmission towers, generators, wire fence enclosures, etc. And that's when U.S. Steel salesmen start mailing orders to Pittsburgh. Clearly, Steel's service concept is geared primarily to support the line force of salesmen.

If Steel's promotions—and they push both consumer products and steel for farming, building & construction, transportation, etc.—are a kind of insurance for Steel, they surely are a kind of insurance for the economy, too. They help protect existing markets (for example, from competition from aluminum, plastics or rubber); they help build markets and they help develop new markets (Steel is currently heavily pushing the use of cans for soft drinks and milk).

Today, half of the whole industry's 83,000,000 finished tons goes into three industries: automobiles, construction, heavy machinery. Another one-third goes into consumer goods (including automobiles). By keeping ingots flowing into many baskets, not just the big three, U.S. Steel has a better chance of adjusting to market shifts.

Hanging on wall after wall of the gleaming U.S. Steel building is a motto that perhaps best sums up what the world's largest marketing task force is in business for: *Sales objective: to obtain as a minimum that share of all markets for the products sold, product by product, territory by territory, in which The Corporation's capacity in relation to the industry entitles it, and to accomplish this participation ratio through the exercise of judgment so as to insure the maximum continuing return on investment to The Corporation."*

U.S. Steel's share of steel produced last year: 32%. Nearest competitor: Bethlehem Steel with 16%.

The spark behind U.S. Steel's marketing strategy is resolute David F. Austin, who joined the company as an office boy after World War I, and who today is executive vice-president in charge of Steel's now famous Commercial Dept.

The Commercial Dept. rides herd on all marketing activities of U.S. Steel, the giant company which employs 270,000 people in 13 divisions, 13 subsidiaries, including five railroads and two steamship companies and which is owned by some 275,000 stockholders.

This centralized marketing command in a basically decentralized corporation is a trend growing in big business. Each division under the Commercial Dept. operates autonomously, meaning that each has considerable freedom to design, develop, make and market its products. But each must work within a framework of over-all policy constantly guided and watched over by the Commercial Dept.

Basic philosophy behind Austin's job: unifying all Steel's marketing—that is, bringing each division forward so that each division's sales as well as total sales grow along with the economy.

Austin's operating philosophy, of course, is service—beat out competitors with service, the "extra" served up to steel customers beyond price, quality and availability of product.

Explains Austin: "It is in the area of service that the ingenuity of any merchandising organization finds full play. For this reason, there is a marked difference in the services rendered; and it is in this field that a sales department has the widest opportunity to out-distance competition and cement customer relationships. When this is done, obviously it results in improved participation and increased profits."

Austin, who reports directly to U.S. Steel president Clifford F. Hood and who is a member both of the Executive Policy Committee and the General Administrative Committee, has three assistant executive vice-presidents to help him. They are J. D. Darby, in charge of sales coordination; R. F. Sentner, in charge of distribution and pricing, and Bennett S. Chapple Jr., in charge of administration and management, and in direct charge of the four divisions that plan and run Steel's marketing strategy: commercial research; product development; market development; advertising. Here's how each of those four divisions works:

Commercial Research. Under director Bay C. Estes, its two basic jobs are to analyze markets and forecast how markets should grow. Estes' men analyze markets to a fare-thee-well, continually obtain from salesmen reports of how much of every steel product each consumer buys in each salesman's area including what U.S. Steel sells him and what he probably buys from other steel producers. Sametime, Estes' researchers estimate Steel's fair share of the market for each particular type of steel and how much steel-making capacity is needed to produce that fair share.

Product Development. Under director Loring S. Brock, its basic jobs are to improve old products, develop new ones, always with an eye toward attracting new business. Brock's men also field test the products they develop. An example of their work is T-1 alloy steel, which took 10 years to develop, is now being promoted for use in heavy industry.

Market Development. Under director Robert C. Myers, it is staffed by a group of hand-picked project managers who work to build old markets, develop new ones for virtually every type of steel—for the home, farm, transportation, building & construction and heavy industry markets. Each project manager, hired because of his familiarity with the market he covers, directs a staff of market developers who fan out and work in all Steel's sales districts. These men promote the use of steel at every conceivable distribution level—whether fabricator, retailer, trade show, or arranging tours of Steel's mills.

Advertising. Under director G. Reed Schreiner and his new administrative assistant, John Veckly (former Satevepost ad & sales promotion manager), advertising, like Gaul, is divided into three parts.

General advertising, under assistant director Harold W. Hoffman, handles all the Commercial Department's advertising to consumers.[1] That includes all print advertising, Commercial Dept. commercials on television's U.S. Steel Hour, exhibits, visual presentations and motion pictures explaining or promoting the corporation or steel. Last year, 11,-205,935 people saw Steel movies at 18,890 showings throughout the U.S.

Industrial advertising, under assistant director Robert J. Wilcox, is now run under a new plan that may set an example for other industrial marketers. Steel's industrial admen are now trained to be well-rounded industrial admen, not as specialists for a specific type of promotion, such as trade booklets, working virtually as account executives do. Thus, the well-

---

[1] Each U.S. Steel division or subsidiary has its own ad staff, handles its own advertising (including the 43 people in Commercial's ad division, 115 people work on advertising in the corporation). Commercial's ad division, however, coordinates advertising when more than one operating division is involved in a program.

rounded industrial adman can swing from one problem to another—just as market development's project managers help each other on different markets.

The third section of the Commercial Department's ad division is also a new idea. A staff of 15 work with W. H. Crawford, who holds the newly created post of business manager, to take the work-a-day business details (accounting, billing, etc.) from the ad division's creative people.

Ad division men work with BBDO, Steel's agency for the last 20 years, as do admen from each Steel division—bringing the count of BBDO, Pittsburgh, account men on the job to some 13 or 14. Sametime, BBDO, San Francisco, services the Columbia-Geneva division, while BBDO, Los Angeles, services the Consolidated Western division. BBDO, New York, concentrates on television's U.S. Steel Hour, works also with Universal Atlas Cement.

The Commercial Department's big problem, of course, is getting Commercial's divisions both to work together and to work with the market researchers, the product developers and the marketing and advertising men of each Steel division.

The key to that problem is an intriguing one. At Steel, the salesman comes first—that is, the commercial research, product development, market development and advertising divisions basically aim to help the salesmen sell. This is done, on one front, by working with the Commercial Department's sales division, which has on its staff 13 product managers, one for high-strength steel, one for stainless steel, etc. (the sales division also has 90 salesmen who back up the salesmen from other divisions as well as cover territory of their own).

Each product manager is responsible for moving his steel type, seeing its share of market grow. Obviously, each needs all the marketing help he can get, and each literally fights to get his product promoted hardest. The Commercial Dept., for example, is currently pushing stainless steel —ads in women's and home magazines promote cutlery, ads in farm magazines push milk tanks.

How does Commercial decide which steel types to push? The answer is largely "selective selling," or "the exercise of judgment so as to insure the maximum continuing return on investment to The Corporation." For example, T-1 steel, certainly a profitable item, is getting a heavy push on the industrial front these days.

The Commercial Department's liaison with each Steel division's research, product development and marketing & advertising people is through committees. For example, the market development men from the Commercial Dept. and from each division meet twice a year, in concurrent session with the advertising committee.[2] Market development

---

[2] The market development committee, for example, includes Commercial's market developers and those from these divisions: American Bridge (Pittsburgh), American

director Robert C. Myers heads his committee, while advertising director G. Reed Schreiner heads the ad committee.

At this point, Commercial Dept. has had enough experience to settle on a basic pattern for its marketing programs. The sales division's product manager huddles with a project manager from market development and an ad division man. Based on findings from the research division (which are exhaustive enough even to weigh the degree of agressiveness of the competition), the group works out a program to solve the product manager's problem. When all parties are in agreement, the program is detailed down to the last ad dollar and media specification, bound into a single "book," with a total price tag on it.

Steel makes it plain—and this vital concept is growing in business today—that the marketing program is budgeted according to the job needed to be done, not according to what the product has had in the past in the way of advertising and promotion.

The classic procedure for most promotions, whether for garden tools or railroad freight cars, goes like this: Steel market developers and admen bombard the key target, the "opinion leaders" who make the decision to buy the special type of steel product being promoted. If the program is to push the appliance market, the housewife, the opinion leader in that field, is hit with promotion. If the program is to push steel products for the farm, Steel's promoters go after the farmer.

Meantime, Steel informs its primary customer, the steel fabricator, what it is doing to build his market and his customer's market. Project managers, under market developer Myers, constantly criss-cross the country with slides, movies and large visual presentations explaining what Steel is doing to help Steel's customers.

As Commercial's assistant executive vice-president Bennett Chapple sums it up: "We approach the manufacturer by personal calls, direct mail, trade paper advertising, through his trade associations. We approach the distributor through the manufacturer, the retailer through the distributor. And, of course, the ultimate consumer is reached through network television . . . and through advertising in consumer magazines and newspapers."

Currently, the Commercial Dept. has some 50 market development programs in the works—with the principal targets these markets: consumer, farm, building & construction, transportation and heavy machinery.

Steel's consumer market promotions, probably the best known, all aim

---

Steel & Wire (Cleveland), Columbia-Geneva Steel (San Franciso), Consolidated Western (Los Angeles), Gerrard Steel Strapping (Chicago), U.S. Steel Homes (New Albany, Ind.), National Tube (Pittsburgh), Oil Well Supply (Dallas), U.S. Steel Export Co. (New York City), U.S. Steel Products (New York City), U.S. Steel Supply (Chicago), Universal Atlas (New York City), Tennessee Coal & Iron (Fairfield, Ala.), Union Supply (Pittsburgh).

at solving a specific problem for steel end-product manufacturers and distributors:

Operation Snowflake, promoting white goods as Christmas gifts, aims at helping appliance makers and sellers build their market for appliances during a traditionally low point in appliance selling (*Tide*—February 12).

Operation Wife-Saver, plugging all-steel kitchens, aims to pre-sell the housewife on steel kitchen cabinets, gets her to pressure kitchen cabinet makers to improve their currently poor distribution. Youngstown Kitchens, for example, is one of the few manufacturers with national distribution. Since only 25% of the cabinets installed in new homes are made of steel, Steel sees this as a high potential market, perhaps one day totaling 600,000 tons annually.

Quicknic, pushing quick-to-fix family picnics using canned foods and beverages grew from Steel's promotion three years ago to help canners get surplus stocks off grocery shelves. The idea, of course, is to push the use of cans in an age of throw-away bottles, aluminum foil cartons, etc.

Shower the Bride With Gifts of Steel aims at getting young married couples to think steel from the wedding day on. One promotion angle: steel products "packaged" for bridal showers for sale in department stores.

Operation Snowflake is typical of Steel's technique. Indeed, claims Steel, it parlayed its first $100,000 Snowflake campaign (run last Christmas) into a $5–6,000,000 job, counting tie-in advertising from appliance manufacturers, distributors, dealers, utilities and banks (Steel produces 20% of the country's sheets, principal component of appliances).

To launch Snowflake, Steel contacted directly or by mail 100 appliance makers; 550 electric utilities, REA co-operatives, gas companies; all TV stations carrying the U.S. Steel Hour; 1,800 daily newspapers; some 2,500 appliance distributors, their 80,000 retail outlets, plus 15 interested electric, gas and appliance trade associations. In all, 76 manufacturers tied-in—Norge redirected $100,000 of its ad & promotion money to push Snowflake. Sears, Roebuck included major appliances in its Christmas catalog for the first time.

Plainly, Steel has something to learn about promotion, but harkening to criticism (e.g., "the promotion should start earlier") Steel in June launched Operation Snowflake—1955, again themed: "Make it a White Christmas—Give Her a Major Appliance." Last month, Steel sent to more than 11,000 daily and weekly newspapers a 12-page Snowflake supplement with room for tie-in ads from local dealers. This month, among other things, Steel will begin an ad series in 250 dailies, magazine ads, plugs for Snowflake on the U.S. Steel Hour (on which it periodically plugs other promotions—e.g., air conditioners, steel garden furniture).

Just as interesting as Steel's consumer market development programs are similar ones in the agricultural market. Here the problem is often building a market for steel from the ground up, keeping in mind that the nation's 5,000,000 farmers are their own purchasing agents. Steel's first market development program, incidentally, was to the farm market for grain bins. So far, nearly 1,000,000 tons of galvanized steel have gone into grain bins, with Steel providing probably half the tonnage.

Typical of the Commercial Department's farm market development projects is the bulk milk handling promotion—that is, promoting stainless steel piping and tankage from the milking machine to the tank truck to the dairy plant. To sell the idea to farmers, milk haulers and milk processors, Steel barraged them with trade magazine ads. Sametime, it showered direct mail on agricultural leaders such as county agents, agriculture teachers, farm managers, agricultural engineers and dairy plant operators.

As it does with every market development promotion, Steel included coupons in its ads. "Leads" from inquiries mailed to the market development division go every two weeks to steel fabricators interested in bulk milk handling.

Between 1950 and last year, that one program resulted in 10,276 inquiries passed on to steel fabricators and Steel estimates that 25,000 dairy farmers now have a stainless steel bulk milk handling system on their farms.

Steel's promotion (it still runs the magazine ads) helped build what is today one of the top markets for stainless steel (autos is largest single consumer market). The market is especially important since stainless steel costs four times as much per ton as carbon steel and has a considerable markup.

Another farm program: promoting steel farm buildings, a project on which Steel and the University of Wisconsin work together. The university tests the usefulness of steel farm buildings, experiments that attract some 8,000 influential agricultural leaders each year. Steel even studies sweet potato growing. Why? Sweet potatoes are good livestock feed. More livestock means more steel fences.

If the latter idea seems somewhat far-fetched, consider an idea Steel once had for promoting automobiles (which account for 20% of its output): plugging for three cars for every family—a Sunday car, a station wagon and a sports car run-about.

On the industrial front, Steel's marketing development programs are equally comprehensive. It spent nine years talking up curtain wall construction for buildings to architects, builders, contractors, code-writing bodies, municipal designers and engineers. One result: the new stainless steel Socony-Mobil building now rising in New York City.

Steel promotes hard to highway engineers who have a hand in choosing steel-made objects ranging from wire fabrics for roads to bulldozers, graders, cranes, steam shovels, even road signs.

Steel built a 50-ton railroad hopper car to prove the merit of its durable Cor-Ten steel, hustled it around the country for engineers to see.

One of its priority programs is for T-1 steel, a high-strength alloy that Steel promotes for mammoth power shovels, pressure vessels and the like. Promotion is generally confined to engineers and metallurgists who influence the fabricator's decision to buy T-1 steel.

Not all Steel's market development programs promote steel—the huge corporation is also the world's largest cement maker and a vast marketer of coal chemical ingredients for everything from fertilizer to aviation gasoline to anti-histamine drugs. The Commercial Dept. pushes all these products, too.

Like other marketers, Steel has passed through two periods; an emphasis during the 1920's and 1930's on acquisition and consolidation, much of that accomplished by financial deals; an emphasis during the 1940's on production. The steel industry emerged from World War II with its capacity up 17% (1940–1945), vs. aluminum's rocket rise of 600% from virtually nothing, magnesium's 90-fold increase. Thus for Steel, as for other businesses, today's emphasis must be on marketing.

The power of Steel's marketing concept is not lost on its competitors. To spur demand for steel products at the consumer level, Republic Steel Corp. has under way its first concerted effort to promote stainless steel in the home.

Nor are Steel's efforts lost on its Pittsburgh neighbor, Aluminum Co. of America. To counter Steel (as well as Reynolds Metals), Alcoa hopes to boost its aluminum by pouring $3,000,000 into the hour-long television show, Alcoa Theater, hard-selling successor to Ed Murrow's soft-selling See It Now. Key to Alcoa's new ad effort: giving end-product manufacturers ad support on aluminum goods in return for using labels on those products that read: "We chose Alcoa Aluminum."

Neither Steel nor Alcoa can overlook the fact that of total aluminum output this year's first half, building took a huge 19%, transportation 16%, consumer durables 13%, the electric industry 7%. *Fortune* has reported that there is a good chance of doubling in the near future the current average use of 30 lbs. of aluminum per car.

That kind of competition puts more heat than ever on Steel's Commercial Dept. It gives even greater import to David Austin's key job: managing a marketing task force that must keep all Steel's divisions growing, and thus all Steel, itself.

"I suspect," commented a veteran of the world's most basic industry, "that if a man who had been familiar with all aspects of steel marketing in 1939 or 1940 could somehow have slept, Rip Van Winkle fashion, for the intervening years and could now return to become once again an active member of a steel selling organization, he would find that he had much to learn, many attitudes to change, many old ideas to erase from his mind, and many new and challenging problems to attack."

WHAT RETAILERS THINK OF U.S. STEEL'S EFFORTS TO HELP THEM SELL

Tide's cross-country check of appliance retailers indicated mixed reactions to U.S. Steel's efforts to help dealers sell consumer durables. Steel runs national magazine and television ads pushing durables and other products made of steel, also has promotion kits and other aids for dealers to use at the local level. Its biggest, coordinated promotion so far was last year's Operation Snowflake, an attempt to push white goods as Christmas presents (as described above). *Tide* asked retailers for their reactions to Operation Snowflake specifically and to Steel's over-all program in general, got this response:

In New Orleans only seven of 12 appliance dealers contacted had heard either of Operation Snowflake or Steel's dealer aid program. However, the seven who had, all large stores, believe Steel's program helps their business, though they can't estimate how much. Said Charles A. Gay, sales manager of the Radio Center: "U.S. Steel's advertising has been pretty swell. For instance, we have 150 models of TV [sets] on the floor, so we probably get more benefit . . . than does the dealer handling only specific brands."

"I sent out bulletins on the . . . program to all our 260 dealers," reported L. George Maness, sales promotion manager of Frigidaire Sales Corp. "But I cannot tell how much it is helping business. If they tie in with reliable brand names in the appliance field, it might be more effective. Certainly we want it. It means less service work for us."

Los Angeles dealers, few of whom knew of Steel's promotions, believe their own intensive local campaigns are responsible for good business. One dealer complained that the prospect of a rise in steel prices would certainly offset Steel's promotions. Steel companies, said another dealer, should crack down on white appliance makers who use plastic trim on appliances. That dealer said consumers don't want plastic trim.

In St. Louis, ad manager Tom Cowdery, of Franklin Furniture Co., said he hadn't heard of the promotions but that he wouldn't be interested even if he had. "Every inch of space has to pay for us. We wouldn't give a column inch to this kind of promotion. From our standpoint these things are complete flops." "We customarily do not tie-in with things as broad as that since it gets too complicated," added Rosemary O'Brien, ad manager of Carson-Union-May-Stern, St. Louis' No. 2 department store.

In Minneapolis, Don Gabbert, president of an appliance outlet bearing his name, found Steel's efforts "too diluted to be effective." He feels there's too great a gap between the promotion and the retailer's efforts to sell. "You can't just tell people they need clothes. You've got to sell them on new fashion or style." A high merchandising official of Dayton's, the city's biggest department store, commented: "This is just one promotion effort. It's being done in plastics, glass, aluminum and others."

In Chicago, approval is high at Montgomery Ward—but just for the basic idea. Ad manager Raymond Yahnig believes "it is actually set up to help independent dealers. Montgomery Ward cannot use a manufacturer's promotional material as there is so much, and so many would be fighting for space that our displays would look like junk shops. We are planning to pick up U.S. Steel's slogans, however—slug them in our advertisements and display materials."

Yahnig cited Steel's use of ribbons around refrigerators, complained that while colorful, the idea isn't practical because the refrigerators cannot be opened, thus blocking the main selling point—the inside. "U.S. Steel's idea is fine," he concluded, "at the consumer level, which we like."

In Philadelphia, most appliance dealers indicated they're pleased with Steel's efforts. Several critics said Steel started too late last year with Operation Snowflake (which the corporation admits). Air conditioning dealers pointed out that since last summer was extremely hot all the advertising they needed was placement in papers of their names and telephone numbers. "No results can be traced to Steel's air conditioning campaign," said Jack Rosen, vice-president of Raymond Rosen & Co., air conditioning distributor. The Steel effort is "nice but unwieldy . . . an effort too large in scope." Another air conditioning spokesman, B. R. Gates, sales manager of S. S. Fretz, Jr., & Co., suggested that Steel canvass retail outlets "to find out how effective the program really is."

Said retail division manager Donald J. MacLoud, of one of the largest retail outlets for appliances in Philadelphia, the Philadelphia Gas Works: "It would be much better if U.S. Steel had put the money, time and effort into local ad programs instead." MacLoud's nearest competitor, the Philadelphia Electric Co., was even more critical. Frank E. Taylor, manager of residential planning, pointed out that for his company "results were indefinite. We sent out 1,500 display pieces free of charge, got them into windows all over the city and talked the campaign up . . . but we were too late because U.S. Steel was too late."

Maxwell Littman, appliance buyer for Gimbels thought Steel should "see the boss man and sell him. He is the guy who okays the spending of ad dollars." Otherwise, the program is a "terrific idea."

In Washington (D.C.) the local Sears, Roebuck outlet reported "Promotion campaigns by the steel companies are not very helpful to us. For instance, Sears 'White Christmas' participation last year was not successful in Washington." The head buyer of appliances for Montgomery Ward suggested that Steel sponsor a television show similar to the Home show to demonstrate steel products for the home.

In New York, Carl Sonnett, ad manager of Bruno-New York, Inc., largest appliance distributor in the city, stated that he looks forward to such promotions. Bruno distributes to dealers and salesmen promotion kits from U.S. Steel, Youngstown Kitchens and Whirlpool-Seeger. The promotions "could be better."

Part Two . . .

THE MARKET
FOR CONSUMER GOODS
FOR INDUSTRIAL GOODS

··{ 4 }··

How and What the U. S. Pays to Play*

Today's brightest new market lies without a doubt in the growing amount of free time for people of all income levels. And with income continuing to rise and working hours continuing to dip, the potential for 1960 or 1975 is all but phenomenal. Choice surely is the big key to the leisure market, since leisure implies the amount of time one is master of. Yet if the awareness of spare time as a bright new market is scant so far, so—and even more acutely—is knowledge of what people choose to do during their increasing leisure hours.

It's true that national leisure time trends are cataloged to an extent, and that they suggest a movement away from spectator sports toward participation activities ranging from bridge to skin diving. But they do not indicate leisure tastes in the various areas of the country, particularly important to know in view of the way population figures in some U.S. areas are sky-rocketing today. Even more important, they do not chart the leisure time tastes of various groups of people—for example, the hourly-wage earner, some of whom now boast a family income of around $12,000; the growing number of retired people, many with pensions; the farmer who has more leisure than ever before, and other such groups.

Leisure's phenomenal ability to cut across lines of income, age, education and occupation is at its clearest in the changing leisure time habits of the nation's 24,000,000 hourly-paid wage earners (as distinguished from the white collar worker, the proprietor, or the executive). Marketing hay is plainly ready for harvest in the fact that today's hourly-paid worker has more leisure time than the proprietor, white collar worker or executive.

Macfadden Publications' Wage-Earner Forum, a panel of some 1,500 wage-earner families, show, for example, that while do-it-yourself is a "once-in-awhile" affair for the white collar worker, it's "a way of life" for the wage earner. Other taste trends among wage earners: fishing is the most popular pastime (55.7% of panel members fish), followed by hunting (38%), bowling (24.3%) and boating (16.1%).

The emphasis the wage earner places on do-it-yourself only highlights

---

* Reprinted by special permission from *Tide*, March 24, 1956. Copyright, 1956, *Tide*.

the basic clue to his whole leisure philosophy: the home is the wage earner's leisure center. For example, Macfadden's panel shows that partaking of a snack while "just sitting around and talking" with friends and relatives is still, by & large, how the wage earner spends much of his spare time. A wage earner, apparently, has little interest in "going out," yet Macfadden's panelists now entertain friends and relatives at home at least once a month. Why? "More time now;" "more money;" "have nicer things;" "have more interest now in the social side of life."

In short, it appears that today's wage earner shies from ostentatious leisure habits—but mainly by choice, not because of income. For example, the lodge gets preference over the fancy club; the family auto is primarily for getting to & from work, not for pleasure spins or "for getting away from home." It appears, too, though, that the wage earner is growing more conscious of his growing amount of spare time—over half Macfadden's panelists realize they now have more time away from the job than ever before.

This leisure-consciousness among wage earners is creating another special leisure market: some 30,000 firms spend $800 million a year on athletic, cultural and social recreation for their employes—double the amount spent seven or eight years ago. The National Industrial Recreation Assn. finds the top company-sponsored leisure activity is athletics. The importance of this market is obvious from one informed guess that industry buys more sports than schools and colleges combined.

If the active worker is growing more leisure-conscious, what about his older counterpart, the retired worker who has enforced time on his hands? Like the wage earner group, the burgeoning population of 14,-000,000 people 65 & over (who have $20 billion a year to spend) is a ripe plum, ready for plucking by many leisure goods marketers. Today, as a Twentieth Century Fund study of older people remarked, the troubles of the retired (low income, poor health) "do not justify the popular and exaggerated notion that retirement is 'living death'."

The real trouble for many retired people, and what makes the market really unique, was recently put this way by author E. B. White, writing in *Holiday* magazine: "To anyone who has always gone some place in the morning, even a place he hasn't particularly liked, retirement seems like the removal of the most steadying thing of all, his destination."

There's little doubt, as L. C. Michelon, writing in *The Journal of Business*, adds, that "the fundamental problem of retired people is essentially the substitution of a new set of personal values and new kinds of activity for the life-long job of earning a living, raising a family, and overcoming the day-to-day obstacles that affect one's income, status and career."

Some clues for selling the retired person are implicit in Michelon's list of the retired person's reversal in values: the individual often lives alone; he must make new friends after losing work and home relationships; hobbies, once only peripheral when he was active, are the center of his life.[1]

A University of Chicago study does a rather precise job on do's and don'ts when it comes to marketing leisure products to the retired. For instance, while retired men like hobby crafts, such older men are less inclined to use power-driven machinery. This suggests that power tool marketers may need to play up safety factors and speed control if they wish to sell to the retired.

Similarly, the study indicates that retired professional and businessmen go for fly and plug fishing (that is, artificial bait fishing), while their workingman counterpart prefers live-bait fishing. Another clue to marketing to the retired: women and professional and businessmen lean to exotic, decorative types of gardening, while former workers stick to regular gardens, more prosaic floral arrangements. Similarly, professional and businessmen prefer photography more than retired workers.

What tends to be the pattern of a retired person's life? St. Petersburg's publicity man, Gay White, suggests that the retired follow a regular pattern once they settle down. First, they come (8,000 a year) to rest and relax in St. Petersburg. Then they travel, acquire a few hobbies. Gradually, however, after a year or two they settle into a single hobby or part-time occupation. White also sees a vast market for leisure clothing for the retired. As for the hobbies, the *Journal of Lifetime Living*, a magazine edited for people over 40, finds that traveling, reading, gardening, sewing and bridge are the most important interests among 1,000 of its readers (74% of those polled were women). Other interests: hunting, fishing, boating, music, photography, home workshops and movies.

While the retired worker, professional or businessman may have large amounts of leisure time on his hands, *Minneapolis Star & Tribune* poll shows that 89% of farmers surveyed work six or seven days a week. Such findings suggest that the seller of leisure goods must both sell the farmer on leisure and the fact that the leisure product will help him get the maximum out of his limited leisure hours. Further, as Capper Publications' research director Victor Hawkins points out, electrification and mechanization are putting "leisure time" back into the farmer's vocabulary. "Today the farmer has both the time and the money to give to a wide range of leisure activities." One *Capper's Farmer* subscriber survey shows that nearly two-thirds of the households have one member off on vacation a year.

To sell leisure goods and services, Hawkins implies, you must sell the farm family as a unit. "In farm homes, (leisure) life centers around the family. Leisure time and home entertainment are synonymous."

---

[1] *The Journal of Business* finds that most retired persons live in the New England states and the midwest. Few live in the southeast, with Florida as a notable exception. St. Petersburg is the city with the most retired people. Its nearest rival: Pasadena.

Other groups important to leisure time product marketers: teenagers and the 2,700,000-member undergraduate market who have, for example, long summer holidays and other vacation time at their disposal. (*Time* magazine recently counted some 8,000,000 pieces of luggage possessed by college students).

Behind selling the teenager and the undergraduate, of course, is introducing them to today's new "life of leisure"—showing them early that leisure time should be enjoyed (a belief not yet universal, thanks to a Puritan past).

If the teenager may need special treatment by leisure time marketers, however, today's 15,000,000 Negroes may not. Leo Shapiro, director of the survey division of Chicago's Science Research Associates, points out that Marketers need not treat the Negro as a special market group. He thinks you can sell the Negro on leisure the way you sell it to the majority of consumers—simply because the Negro is eager to join the majority and will listen to and watch it. The Negro, Shapiro adds, wants what the majority wants—comfort and convenience, and he has more time and money for it. For example, more than $10,000,000 in new hotels and motels have gone up in the south to cater to Negro travelers.

Possibly, the most fascinating question for today's leisure product marketer is who sets leisure time tastes. Sociologist David Riesman makes a strong case for the "peer groups"—a man's age-mates, job-mates and playmates. Author A. C. Spectorsky has a different idea at least for upper-income groups: "What they do will be done, a few weeks or months later, by their counterparts in Lake Forest and Santa Barbara and on the Main Line." Who is "they?" The "exurbanites," who live just beyond the suburbs surrounding New York City. Adds Spectorsky: what these exurbanites talk about "will all too often be picked up and actually talked about in Beverly Hills, Grosse Pointe, and Sewickly. What they tell us to buy, by god, we buy. . . . When a foreign manufacturer has a luxury item—like the Jaguar—that he wants the American people to accept, he is fully aware that his purposes will be served and his job three-quarters accomplished as soon as he can contrive to cajole the exurbanite into buying it. (The job of selling, of course, is entrusted to other exurbanites). The man from Schweppes whispered first into an exurbanite ear. The man in a Hathaway shirt is an exurbanite."

While Spectorsky finds the exurbanite a taste-molder, he also finds him a specific kind of leisure product consumer. For example, the Fairfield County, Conn. exurbanite (average buying income: $7,431) "does not strive for conspicuous display, or conspicuous consumption. . . . He buys old farm houses and remodels them. He effects the open-collared plaid shirt and the rough boots." Every fourth Fairfield resident quietly takes a holiday winter and summer; Fairfield residents "lead the nation as buyers of foreign cars." Leisure time tastes and who influences them indeed is important enough for *Holiday* magazine to have a study of the subject under way.

While tastes may tend to be similar within various groups, such as wage earners, retired persons or exurbanites regardless of geographical location, there are certainly vast taste differences when it comes to leisure time pursuits among the nation's various regions. A recent *Sports Illustrated* survey reveals, for example, that while women of the northwest and midwest rank bowling as their favorite sport, the southwest woman sails first and golfs second, while her southeast counterpart gives basketball top billing. The northeast woman goes most for swimming.

As for the east's leisure man, four regional taste trends are immediately apparent:

1. *Groups Quickly Grow Around Leisure Pastimes.* In Boston, observers find the stay-at-home group (who go for backyard barbecues), winter vacationists (swelling guest lists of Florida and Bermuda hotels), boating cliques (with motor boat sales near lakes leading those on the ocean shore), "hi-fi couples" and ski crowds. In New York, Abercrombie & Fitch points out the "groupness" of Long Island boatsmen. Thus, if you can catch a few fanatics, you'll soon have a flock of enthusiasts.

2. *Leisure Pastimes Are a Family Affair.* In Philadelphia, where 115,-000 suburban homes have gone up in the last five years vs. 38,776 homes in the city proper, families are herding into travel tours as fast as agents make accommodations. Says Paul P. Shepherd, assistant manager of Thomas Cook & Sons' Philadelphia office: there is no longer an off season for family travel since middle income groups vacation at all times of the year today. A recent study of boat buyers by researcher Ernest Dichter showed, among other things, that people buy boats because the entire family can use them.

3. *Leisure Habits in the East Are Often Shaped by the Business Environment of the Leisure Man.* In Boston, for example, one observer reports that lawyers almost require a Florida vacation to keep their standing in their profession.

4. *If Any One Leisure Activity Is Booming, It's Boating.* "We're exploding in this aspect of the leisure market," says Robert Farren, the *Boston Herald's* travel & boating advertising director. Nonetheless, he thinks "we're in the Model T era of boating." In Philadelphia, retailers report that fishing is booming. R. D. Hall and Morton R. Moskowitz, vice-president and secretary, respectively, of the five-store M & H chain, see lower and middle income customers filling the gap left by a decline in wealthy sports enthusiasts. "Few people today come in to buy $100 rods. Today we're selling more customers but unit sales average $3 and $4."

While leisure activities in the east seem to be generally on the rise, leisure pursuits in the south are growing sporadically.

Says the Reverend Joseph H. Fichter, chairman of Loyola's (New Orleans) sociology department: "The trend to fewer working hours and more leisure time is spreading all over the nation but more slowly in the south. However, the trend is definite in the south and the two-day weekend is more & more prevalent." Fichter finds that, aside from the obvious sports of fishing and boating in New Orleans waters, cultural pursuits are leaping ahead (music, night school, reading).

As in the east, leisure in New Orleans is mainly a family affair. Newcomb College sociology instructor Warren Breed, currently studying family relationships, finds that visiting relatives over the weekend is a favorite pastime. "This leads me to believe that in New Orleans at least habit and tradition are great influences on the use of leisure time."

Dr. Robert Stone and Dr. Leonard Reissman of Tulane's Urban Life Research Institute believe leisure choices in New Orleans are influenced by 1) personal idiosyncrasies, 2) friends, 3) advertising and 4) television. Stone, for one, feels the biggest influence is television—watching what other people do. Reissman, who remarks that leisure time today is growing by leaps & bounds, worries about the standardization of leisure: "Even in the do-it-yourself movement, a person is conscious that thousands of others are doing it by themselves, too, with them."

Florida, a totally different leisure dish, may well be one of the best test markets for leisure time goods & services. For Florida appears to reach the apotheosis of leisure—integration of life and play. As *Sunrise* editor Warren H. Pierce puts it: "The integration factor is more tangible, but nonetheless important. It means, for instance, that a family builds a home on the waterfront with the deliberate intent of going fishing immediately after dinner instead of washing the dishes. Or that they go swimming before breakfast in the morning as an eye-opener before spending a day at work. It means that boats are a normal, accepted possession just like an automobile. It means that recreation is an ordinary part of daily living, rather than being a separate project."

Pierce points out that thanks to the climate of Florida and other southeastern states, outdoor activities the year-round are of far greater importance than in most parts of the country. "In specific leisure activities, fishing appears to be the majority favorite across a wide range of age and income levels. The only exception to this popularity is among young marrieds with very small children. Other young couples with older children call it the ideal, all-family activity. Middle-aged couples and older people who are retired also put it at the head of their leisure time list." Some families (and this includes younger families where the husband goes to business) report that fishing brought them to Florida.

Very significant, according to *Sunrise* editor Pierce, "is the fact that boat ownership in Florida is not limited to higher income families. To see five or six boats in a block where houses cost an average of $10,000 is not unusual." Unlike fishing, boating is not too popular among older people.

Other favorite leisure activities among Floridians are swimming, motoring, travel, golf, tennis, workshops, hunting, photography and, among older people, shuffleboard. "People who call swimming a favorite leisure activity often spend most of their Sundays through the warm weather months (April through September) at the beach."

Evening leisure hours during the week follow the national pattern more closely—watching television, reading and entertaining friends or being entertained by them.

Pierce reiterates that "leisure time activities are usually enjoyed by the Florida family as a unit." Only among older retired people are divergent activities seen to some extent. With young and middle-age couples it is a matter of having fun together. Where there are children, recreation is often chosen to suit their tastes. Few wives whose husbands go to business report any daytime activity that can genuinely be called recreation —mostly this involves civic duties.

Despite Florida's reputation as a vacation paradise, Florida residents occasionally take vacations from it. For long trips, planned by upper income families or those who are retired on a "comfortable income," Europe, Mexico, California and Canada are the popular places. Cuba, only an hour distant, is "enormously popular," for short trips, says Pierce, and the adjacent Caribbean Islands are receiving more play every year. "An increasing number of young people are moving here today and this ability to pull up roots and take chances in an entirely different environment often indicates a craving for new experience which travel also fulfils."

The amount of money Floridians spend on leisure pursuits varies enormously—from a small percentage of their incomes up to one-third of their income. Specific figures for leisure pursuits, according to *Sunrise* research, $35 a month for husband and wife with an estimated income of $5,000; $50 to $70 a month for a family of $7,500; and one-third of their total income for a $15,000-a-year couple with a son in college.

Today's Texan can be approached by the leisure marketer in any one of three different ways:

1. *As a Sportsman.* Hardware and sporting goods firms report the "sky is the limit" on good guns and ammunition. The Texas leisure man mounts his boat on a special trailer to weekend at one of the state's numerous man-made lakes (where he often has a cottage) or to vacation in Colorado to beat the famed Texas heat.

2. *As a Traveler.* One trailer firm "has had its hands full" for five years building all-aluminum trailers (equipped with butane gas, ice compartments and screens for windows). The "native" Texan travels—but not too far. He may go to Mexico City or Acapulco (for fishing). New York City is thought of as a jumping off point for Europe.

3. *As a Family Man.* The station wagon carries the Texan's family on weekend camping trips with the ever-present western barbecue kit (often $50 to $100 apiece). Even at home, the native Texan almost invariably barbecues some food for family or friends.

"The westerner thinks he's different because he got a lucky break: he is living in the west." Because the westerner feels he has a good life, he won't be rushed into new ideas and this is more conservative than his reputation would indicate. That's the way psychologist Ernest Dichter of the Institute for Motivational Research, looks at today's western man. The "oldtimer's" resentment of newcomers and a resistance to change, however, is only a slight block, feels Dichter, to the launching of new, untried products in the west. But the accent, suggests Dichter, should be on friendly, personal advertising that avoids the cold, impersonal approach. For example, the westerner's strong personality means he may resent advertising using testimonials of famed personalities.

Sunset traces the rise of today's western way of living this way: climate and geography bred the outdoor barbecue, which, in turn, changed conventional landscaping and house design. "Patio living" is the result. With all that, westerners have "nature's recreation within their reach— the mountains, skiing, the ocean, all within a short day's drive." *Sunset* describes the western atmosphere as "youthful, vigorous." "This is an active place."

Comments Pierre Martineau, research director of the *Chicago Tribune:* "the midwesterner's leisure philosophy is just getting to that of the easterner." For example, Martineau cites skiing, long a big sport in the east, and now catching on in the midwest.

Martineau points to the change coming over midwesterners in their use of Sunday time. Until recently, midwesterners and their children wore their best attire on Sunday. Now they are beginning to change: after Sunday dinner they slip into casual clothing and seek companions for golfing, or perhaps boating.

Aside from the east (suggested by Martineau), the far west influences midwest leisure time pursuits—at least, according to Leo Shapiro, director of the survey division of Chicago's Science Research Associates. Shapiro points to the west's outdoor living, now rising in the midwest.

Leisure pursuits in Cincinnati, Minneapolis and Detroit indicate the complexity of the leisure market. One Cincinnati observer doesn't think leisure pursuits amount to much in that city—which suggests that marketers may have a missionary job to do in that area. What leisure pursuits there are, such as trips to Europe, seem to be confined to upper income groups: single men ($6,000 or more); widows ($12,000 or more); married couples ($18,000 and up).

By contrast, leisure pursuits in Minneapolis and Detroit appear to be growing faster than leisure salesmen can follow them.

For example, 33% of the state's population weekend during summers at lake cottages. While winter vacations are off (according to the *Minneapolis Star & Tribune* some 50% planned a winter vacation in 1950, 10% have the same idea today), summer resorts are booming. "The resorters," comments Harvey Hammergren of Grand Rapids' Chamber of Commerce, "are selling vacations for the whole family rather than the fishing trip for dad." Further, foreign vacationing is up. Passport applications of state residents in the first half of 1955 virtually equaled the total for any previous year. "Norway a Minnesota Suburb?" headlined the *Minneapolis Star* last year. Even the local CIO plugs three-week package tours to Europe for its members. Do-it-yourself for expansion attics and play rooms makes a Minnesotan's trip to the hardward store "a regular Saturday morning occurrence."

Perhaps Detroit—the fastest growing U.S. market—best spotlights how more time and money for leisure has affected leisure product buying patterns in the last five years. Detroit, of course, is the automobile capital—which means that union hours and wages predominate. In recent years, it's been a boom area. Also important is Detroit's geography —it's near mountains, lakes and rivers, all powerful influences on Detroit's leisure. Here's what's happening to Detroit's leisure market:

The biggest sports boom is in skiing and skating (even though the more sedate sports of croquet and badminton continue to rise). Says a buyer of Detroit's giant J. L. Hudson department store: "Skis and ski equipment is the best seller unitwise. Our high price skis at $85 are the best sellers. Even office girls who make less than $85 a week demand the best aluminum and plastic skis. In other articles, the middle price is most in demand. But not in skis." The pattern for ice skates is similar. Says Henry Fishman, ad manager of Lippman's, a Detroit sporting goods and tools store: The big trend is toward winter sports equipment, while hunting and fishing don't get as many followers because they're handed down from father to son. "Tools for the basement handyman have fallen off in the last two years, though they boomed before that." Outboard motor sales are 34%–50% ahead of a couple of years ago.

Further, fishing, once strictly a spring & summer sport, now is big in winter, thanks to ice fishing. Archery is up "by leaps & bounds," with the major reason revived interest in deer hunting by bow & arrow. Another interesting trend: farming as a hobby is growing. Members of Detroit's Agricultural Club meet once a week to talk about the farming they do on weekends.

APPENDIX: HOW THE U.S. SPENDS ITS SPARE TIME
Spectator Sports about Hold Their Own

	Attendance Figures*			Attendance Figures	
	1953	1954		1953	1954
HORSE RAC-ING	49,748,000	50,473,000	TRACK & FIELD	2,500,000	2,500,000
BASEBALL	37,681,000	35,660,000	HOCKEY	2,426,000	1,949,000
FOOTBALL	15,281,000	15,833,000	SOCCER	1,500,000	1,500,000
WRESTLING	4,000,000	3,600,000	TENNIS	915,000	915,000
BASKETBALL	2,683,000	3,139,000	DOG SHOWS	255,000	225,000
BOXING	857,000	1,590,000			

* Source: *Morning Telegraph*

Participant Recreation Is on the Rise

Boating: In 1952, 3,700,000 racing craft were registered in the U.S., compared with 2,500,000 in 1948. In 1953, boat sales totaled $122.7 million, up from 1947's $118 million. In 1954, an estimated 20,000,000 people in the U.S. sailed, triple the 1945 count. In 1954, people spent $1 billion on boats & equipment, nearly double 1953.

Books: In 1954, people spent $518 million on books & maps, compared with $504 million in 1952 and $476 million in 1950.

Bowling: Some 17,000,000 people bowl today—about the same as in 1953.

Bridge: Between 25–30,000,000 people play bridge today. Roughly 60,000 play tournament bridge, double the figure of five years ago.

Clubs: In 1954, people spent $557 million on clubs and fraternal organizations, compared with $551 million in 1952 and $470 million in 1950.

Fishing: In 1955, people spent $18,854,809 for fishing licenses, up from $17,127,896 in 1952. An estimated 25,000,000 people fish, with lake & stream fishing most popular. Of the 25,000,000 who fish, 47% say they fish frequently. Last year, sales & expenditures for fishing equipment totaled $125 million, double 1945.

Gardening: In 1954, people spent $697 million for flowers, seeds, potted plants, etc., compared with $641 million in 1952 and $527 million in 1950.

Golf: Today, probably 6,400,000 people play golf (74% men), with roughly one-third under 30, one-third between 30–40, one-third over 40. There are 5,000 golf courses in the U.S. In 1954, people spent $40,000,000 on golf equipment. Casual wear sold in golf pro shops jumped 25% in sales over 1953.

Hunting: In 1955, people paid $14,191,552 for hunting licenses, up from $13,902,428 in 1952. Sales of hunting equipment totaled $40,000,000 in 1955, compared with about $37,000,000 in 1952.

Magazines, Newspapers: In 1954 people spent $1.69 billion on magazines, newspapers, sheet music, compared with $1.62 billion in 1952 and $1.47 billion in 1950.

Movies: In 1954, people spent $1.28 billion going to the movies, compared with $1.28 in 1952 and $1.39 billion in 1950.

Pianos: In 1952, piano sales (manufacturers') totaled $63,630,000, compared with $55,086,000 in 1947.

Radio-TV Sets: In 1954, people spent $2.2 billion on radio-TV sets, compared with $2.1 billion in 1952 and $2.38 billion in 1950.

Records: In 1953, record sales (manufacturers') totaled $92,000,000 compared with $110 million in 1947.

Skiing: Probably 2,000,000 people ski, compared with 1,500,000 in 1953.

Tennis: In 1955, 8,500,000 people played tennis, on some 15,000 tennis courts, compared with 5,750,000 in 1945. In 1954, tennis equipment sales totaled $6,919,553, compared with $5,119,397 in 1952.

Theater: In 1954, people spent $211 million on the theater, compared with $185 million in 1952 and $177 million in 1950.

Travel: In 1955, 85,000,000 Americans traveled away from home—6% of them traveling outside the U.S. In 1955, money spent on U.S. vacations totaled $10 billion—up from $8.5 billion in 1954 and $5.4 billion in 1947.

Sources: Dept. of Commerce (Census of Manufacturers, Annual Survey of Manufacturers, Office of Business Economics); American Contract Bridge League; Outdoor Life: Sports Illustrated.

But Consumer Expenditures for Recreation Are Barely at the Rate of 30 Years Ago When There Was Much Less Leisure Time

CONSUMER EXPENDITURES FOR RECREATIONS

Year	Amount (000,000)	% of National Income	Year	Amount (000,000)	% of National Income
1925	$ 2.84	3.9%	1945	5.42	3.0
1929	3.84	4.4	1950	9.15	4.2
1935	2.25	4.0	1952	11.37	3.9
1940	3.27	4.0	1954	12.22	4.1

·{ 5 }·

What Are the Real Reasons People Buy Today?*

BY DR. ERNEST A. DICHTER†

As Told to Ray Josephs

What man who sells—or manages the activities of salesmen—hasn't said, "If I could only get inside my customer's brain and find out what *really* makes him buy, my troubles would be over."

Sometimes, listening to the talk that spins round about the new science of motivation research, you get the feeling that the answer to this seemingly impossible miracle has been discovered.

For the last two decades, motivational research has been my day, night, week-end and even holiday activity. Today, when The Insitute has opened a new research center on a 10-acre estate overlooking the Hudson, and when we have begun to see the international implications of our work with the undertaking of a study for the Japan Air Lines Co., Ltd., I still cannot say that we've gotten anywhere near the goal of final solution to the No. 1 problem of everyone who sells. Still, there has been progress in the search to learn why buyers tick. It is appropriate that, at this confluence of circumstances, we take stock. We can at least say this: If you and your firm are not taking advantage of the new psychological insight into consumer behavior now available, you may be missing one of the most important selling tools.

Many people in selling still regard motivational studies as pure bunk or just interesting experiments, O.K. for someone else but far removed from their businesses. On the other hand, an increasing number of successful firms, large and small, are using the findings of social scientists.

As Robert Whitney, president, National Sales Executives, Inc., explains, there are two major reasons: "First, the probers often come up with answers which, when tried, have worked. Second, even if recommendations haven't panned out exactly as hoped, they have lifted

---

* *Sales Management*, February 1, 1955. Copyright, February, 1955 by Ray Josephs, author of *How to Make Money From Your Ideas* (Garden City, N. Y.: Doubleday & Company, Inc.).

† President, Institute for Research in Mass Motivations, Inc.

managements out of mental ruts. And re-examining worn-out approaches has caused many concerns to come up with fresh ideas."

Last year, it is estimated, U.S. businesses spent approximately $9 million for such studies. Expenditures for 1955 should be at least a third higher. Most believe they're getting their money's worth.

Some businessmen insist that seeking out customers' motivations and giving them new names and rationals is simply Freudian mumbo-jumbo. "Human nature," they insist, "remains pretty much the same over the years. The only way to sell is by appealing to four fundamentals: the desire for sustenance, recognition, sex and security."

There's no doubt that whatever terms you use, these are the four horsemen of buying motivation and behavior patterns. But you can't ignore the fact that the relative importance of each in the lives of most of your customers has changed since World War II. And the speed of events is altering attitudes accordingly.

Just think what has happened in three months, any three months, of the post-war years. Recollect the headlines and ask yourself: "Can all this occur without an impact on my customers? Will they remain the same?"

The answer, we believe, is no. What moves people today is not necessarily what made them reach for checkbooks last year. Customer attitudes and states of mind influence your sales, as much as need or logic. More Americans today buy discretionary items not when required, but when they're in the mood. That mood can be natural or created through stimulation. Psychological factors, rather than need, are the motivations of almost 60% of our yearly purchases.

Since successful use of the right appeals at the right time and place so often determine your sale, it is wise to ask: What is the psychological climate influencing American customers today? What are the top-ranking appeals and the best ways to use them?

We have conducted some 500 major research studies, and compiled over 100,000 individual consumer case histories, for such blue-chip firms as the American Broadcasting Co., Ralston Purina Co., Brown & Williamson Tobacco Corp., Equitable Life Assurance Society of the U.S., General Electric Co., General Foods Corp., Jewel Tea Co., Inc., Endicott-Johnson Corp., Goodyear Tire & Rubber Co., Inc., General Mills, Inc., Lever Brothers Co., The Andrew Jergens Co., Miles Laboratories, Inc., and Associated Merchandising Corp. Over 300 psychologically trained interviewers in 55 major markets funnel information to our analytical staff.

These studies show the four principal factors affecting today's sales climate, why they have become important and are likely to become more so in the immediate future. They also demonstrate how some firms and associations—our own and others—have taken the vital step in using this research, switching old appeals to new ones geared to the thinking of today's customer.

Our method is to study the firm and product personality. Then, rather than check questionnaires along, we have trained researchers make hundreds of interviews in depth so that hidden motives may be dredged out and analyzed according to psychological knowledge. From this procedure come facts that you, the businessman client, can use to reorient or improve your sales appeals.

But down to cases. These are typical. You may not agree with all of them or even with the terminology, for motivational research is still far from an exact science. But they will certainly give you challenging ideas to mull over—and to act on in your own business.

Major Shifts in Our Thinking

Since World War II there have been four major shifts in our thinking, strongly affecting buying attitudes:

1. Puritanism Is on Its Way Out.   More and more Americans have adopted the attitude that it's not wrong or sinful to get as much pleasure out of life as possible; that it's not necessary to pay in pain for each pleasure. And they're purchasing accordingly.

2. Why-Shouldn't-I? We are increasingly willing to give vent to our whims and desires, to say: "Why shouldn't I have this or that?" We also realize that often an emotional, irrational basis lies behind many of our actions. But we are more willing to let out instincts and emotions determine "I'll take it," particularly if the seller knows how to follow up emotional appeals with convincing evidences of benefits that make us believe our purchase wise and indicative of our good judgment.

3. We Are More Mature.   Since we are increasingly giving in to our whims, this may sound like a paradox. Yet the constant series of crises and fears under which we live have forced us to think ahead in long-range terms—and buy that way.

4. We Would Be More Individual.   We admire America's mass-production, assembly-line products. But there's a reaction, a desire for expression of individuality and for recognition, manifesting itself in countless activities—and purchases.

Perhaps you are already aware of these fundamental changes and are using some of the new appeals developed from them. But unless you are employing all to the fullest, you may be missing your best untapped sales opportunities. As many astute businessmen have discovered, one added appeal for your product or service, properly employed, can mean the difference between success and failure, profit and loss.

The real selling secret, we have found, is not concentrating on one appeal in your product or service as applicable to everyone. It's discovering how many different, directly personal appeals, based on major consumer thinking changes, you can send out, like a series of radar beams, seeking potential customers. Some must be used head-on, others obliquely. For while all basic human motivation boils down to the desire to stay alive

WHO'S DICHTER? Dr. Ernest A. Dichter is president and founder of the Institute for Research in Mass Motivation, Inc. He began pioneering in the use of psychological research for marketing studies in the U.S. some two decades ago, and since that time the Institute, under his guidance, has completed 500 major studies and over 100,000 consumer case histories.

WHAT DOES HE SAY? Since World War II, Dr. Dichter declares, there have been four major shifts in consumer thinking, strongly affecting buying attitudes: (1) Americans are throwing off the Puritanical cloak and purchasing for pleasure, without twinge of conscience; (2) they are saying, "Why shouldn't I have this or that?" allowing emotional appeals to influence their purchasing; (3) they are more mature in their buying attitudes, thinking ahead in long-range terms; (4) there is a desire for individuality, self-expression and recognition.

HOW CAN YOU BENEFIT? As an astute sales executive, you can perhaps find among the new motivations one added sales appeal for your product or service which will tap new sales potential. Ignoring these motivations for buying could be costly, if not disastrous.

WHAT'S COVERED HERE? In Part I of a two-part series to appear in Sales Management, Dr. Dichter discusses several motivations to buy, which are a positive expression of the American trend away from Puritanical concepts. Labeling them Comfort, Luxury, Prestige and Quality, he cites case histories of companies and agencies that have employed these new sales appeals profitably. He suggests various applications of them which may be adopted for a variety of products and services—both consumer and industrial.

WHAT'S COMING? In Part II, which will appear in the February 15 issue of Sales Management, Dr. Dichter expands on the other three new motivations: The why-shouldn't-I philosophy, the new maturity, and the desire for recognition. The author points up still other sales appeals which have been and can be used successfully.

as happily as possible, there are infinite ways to appeal to this desire—and to make your sale.

Factor One: Puritanism Is on Its Way Out

What psychologists call the "Puritan complex" in our national mentality is a result of our total history and culture. For generations most Americans believed that it was somehow sinful to get too much pleasure out of life. Self-denial and thrift were key virtues. Worldly goods, beyond certain requirements, were considered the prerogative of spendthrifts and millionaires. Since the Puritans and those who followed them had to conquer virgin territory and lead lives of hardship, they made a virtue of their frugality. But as we became more secure, settled and prosperous, modern technology provided more products for more people at lower prices. With income rising—and in part, because of it—advertising to encourage consumption of more products and distribution to make them more available, helped to dissipate the Puritan heritage. Both these factors also broadened every kind of communication: greater interchange, national and international, have brought people new, direct personalized impressions, made the forbidden familiar and not only desirable but available. World War II made moral standards more lax, self-denial less restrictive on our purchasing moods.

What New Appeals Has This Put Forward? Sales-wise, the lessening of Puritanism has pushed forward three major sales appeals: (1) the desire for *comfort*. This doesn't mean Americans are getting lazy, but rather that they realize that unnecessary work is something to be legitimately avoided, and the time thus gained spent for other things; (2) the desire for *luxury*, to enjoy sensual pleasures that go beyond mere comfort, to enjoy new sensations, to permit secret dreams to find realization; (3) the desire for *prestige* and improved social status reflected primarily in the desire for products and services which not only connote *quality* and improved, upgraded social position to the individual, but which the customer can use to show others where he now stands.

Firms That Have Switched to the Comfort Appeal. The appeal for comfort works everywhere, not only with products obviously sold for that purpose. Today even a tractor can be sold more readily when comfort is stressed. Not long ago a major producer, finding sales of heavy equipment below quota, called us; asked what motivations we could research out that might be helpful. Customarily the firm sold on the basis of engineered performance, adaptability for many jobs and related factors—all important. Studies revealed one overlooked aspect, fully as vital: what the man who ran the machine, and who had a major voice in its selection, had in the back of his mind—even if unwilling to express it openly before the boss—was comfort on the job. Motivation studies showed he wanted such passenger car comforts as automatic gear shifts, upholstered seats, heaters, arm rests and glove compartments. All were installed. And to win the boss, stress was put on the fact that the comfortable man does a better, safer job. The comfort approach, based on sound psychological proof, has not only raised sales for this major tractor manufacturing company, but other leading equipment makers have also successfully employed it.

No Need to Sweat

Power tools long sold primarily on the basis of increased efficiency. Now, as the result of seeking out real purchaser motivations, more and more manufacturers appeal to the growing belief that there's no need to sweat. An example of smart exploitation of this appeal is Hiller Engineering's Yard Hand. A brightly colored little power vehicle, its psychologically perfect extra is a seat enabling you to ride astride while doing lawn chores or even snow plowing. That rider seat offering comfort, pleasure and family sport not only sells Pop and the kids on Yard Hand, it has made more sales to envious neighbors than any similar product in years.

Dayton Rubber Co. not long ago developed a new type of foam with infinite use possibilities. The big question: What to make of it? Psychological studies were run to discover the product with likeliest consumer appeals. "Offer comfort," Dayton officials were told, "and you'll get more people to pay more for your product than for one with only utilitarian use." Dayton decided on pillows, called them Koolfoam to stress comfort and get over the hurdle of the popular conception of rubber as hot; developed a slogan: "Gives you the rest of your lifetime." In three years Dayton has become a leader in its field.

Simmons Co., long an industry leader, puzzled by dragging sales, learned through studies that at least one-third of the bedding market currently buys a mattress worth only $60. Today's approach to selling higher-price Beautyrest mattresses is "new comfort hitherto unavailable," rather than stress on spring coils and permanency.

W. A. Sheaffer Pen Co., spent a vast sum to develop its Snorkel when motivation probers came across the fact that a prime objection was the uncomfortable business of dunking and wiping after refill.

The Florsheim Shoe Co., Inc., headed in new directions when it put its finger on proof that more and more men wearing loafers at home wanted shoes providing the same comfort, yet dressy enough for town wear. Result: a new type of lighter "Lo-Top" slip-on shoe, combining ease and appearance.

Manufacturers of every kind of home furnishings have found informality, based on the desire for comfort, so strong it has created a whole new "casual period." The National Association of Summer Furniture Manufacturers, for example, eager to increase business beyond seasonal sales, mapped an extensive campaign to sell the idea that summer comfort is available for finished basement playrooms and enclosed porches —and is rolling up year-round sales heretofore believed impossible.

Comfort on the Farm

Not long ago the farmer was the counterpart of the Puritan. Examine his publications today, however, and you'll note that more and more alert manufacturers are, as a result of motivation studies, stressing the comfort their products offer. Farmers are buying everything from mechanical milkers to tape-recorded music for the henhouse. It has been proved that chickens actually lay more eggs when they are made comfortable. And cows, treated like luxury animals rather than duty beasts, increase milk output.

Appliance makers have been most vigorous in developing comfort appeals even over efficiency. When, not long ago, Lewyt Corp. decided to enter the vacuum cleaner field, motivational studies of 5,000 housewives showed that, more than anything else, women often enjoyed a sense of accomplishment in cleaning—but hated the aftermath. So Lewyt created its no-dust-bag-to-empty cleaner and subsequently a low-slung dolly on which cleaner and attachments glide easily from room to room. This, more than anything else, has put Lewyt in top rank.

General Electric Co. stresses the comfort appeal for everything from ironers ("no need to sprinkle") to washer-dryer combinations ("do your laundry in less than two hours; start at nine and your washday is over before 11").

A classic purveyor of the comfort appeal is Carrier Corp., a leading home air conditioner manufacturer. While always stressing the comfort of the cool house in blazing summer months, with the added motivational appeal of heat for winter, Carrier won over many customers reluctant to spend for a device they believed to be useful only certain months of the year.

How to Use the Comfort Appeal Yourself. Study thoroughly your service or product to determine how it can offer new and different ways to meet consumer desires for comfort—and play up these advantages as fully as possible. Can you show ease of maintenance? Launderability at home? No need to carry, lift, walk? Can you make your product more comfortable by reducing bulk or weight, as have some of the hat, suit, overcoat, shoe and related apparel manufacturers? Or by new design, usage?

Philip Morris, a major cigarette maker, recently spent hundreds of thousands of dollars on its new "Snap-Open Pack" permitting neater, faster opening and refolding, after sutdies showed that comfort and convenience were a prime consideration in smokers' minds.

The multibillion-dollar frozen food industry, and notably orange juice, was built not so much on promises of freshness as of comfort—less work for you, the user. There is little doubt that more industries will, in the next decade, build with the same approach.

Can you find new ways to improve comfort by simple self-demonstrations? General Electric and Maison Blanche Co., New Orleans department store, promoted the idea and topped a $100,000 four-day goal in three by allowing all household appliances to be taken home for 10 days on a no-risk, money-back guarantee. The high percentage of keep-it sales overcame minimum spoilage.

Have you made it as comfortable as possible for your customers to shop—given them places to sit, provided undistracting areas to close important sales? Checking 150,000 food transactions, The Coca-Cola Co., not a firm to let grass grow under its feet, found proof that customers who stopped for a soft drink while shopping spent an average of $9.39 compared to $5.20 spent by non-stop shoppers. Then the company put the facts to work—showed super marketers that 80% of the customers accepted offers of free Cokes and increased average purchases to $7.64.

Firms That Have Switched to the Luxury Appeal. Recently the Kudner Agency, Inc., asked us to study the "typical high-price car buyer"—and specifically the Buick buyer—his habits, earnings, job, thinking patterns, so the agency could sharpen appeals. Researchers quickly recognized one contradiction to previous statistical research: There just weren't any "typicals." Butchers, grocers, farmers, all kinds of people who traditionally "weren't supposed" to be high-price owners, were. In line with findings of our motivational studies, we advised Buick: "Go beyond customer groups you're appealing to now and into more mass-circulation media. Broaden direct mailings to include all income groups. Don't show cars in unattainable estate settings but adventuring on the open road. And tell dealers not to form snap judgments from shoppers' clothes. The guy in the beat-up pants might buy a Roadmaster convertible, too." Already the advice is paying off, for mass markets not only accept but actively want luxury at every price range.

Heads of Chevrolet's Car Clubs, making their own motivation exploration of sales appeals that closed the deal, found luxury and appearance most important; economy way below; reliability third. Another national study revealed that while customers are still choosy when they buy cars, they want luxury: power brakes and steering, white walls, the extras. Almost the only purchasers of "plain vanilla"—without additionals—are fleet buyers. Cadillac is still a waiting-list product primarily because, with keen insight into buying motivation, it has emphasized the luxury appeal consistently, even when unable to fill orders. And Chrysler, checking to discover why it slipped on sales when other firms moved ahead, found that the answer lay mainly in styling. Engineering-wise, Chrysler is the equal of GM and Ford cars. For most drivers, psychologists learned, getting behind the wheel of an important-looking car lifts morale, increases the feeling of self-importance, enhances gratification. And since they have come to think "long slinky" cars are automatically "better," they have bought the luxury look.

Even in the maintenance end of motoring, our study for Socony-Vacuum Oil Co., Inc., showed that price wasn't the primary objective—rather it was the desire for the luxury of *special* service and "being cared for." Proof of findings influenced Socony to shift from strident claims as to what gasoline would do (which, it was found, motorists usually ignore anyway) to better and amplified station facilities.

The Frank H. Lee Co., a leading hatter, has altered its approach from needling men into hat-wearing to avoid that "harried look" to offering luxury—"Nothing makes you look and feel so important as a Lee." Lee has even put rich brocade linings in its hats, adpated from increasingly popular male vests. Though seen only by the wearer when he doffs his sombrero, these linings give him the feeling of the ultimate in the individual luxury—"what a woman gets from a coat lined in mink."

How to Use the Luxury Appeal Yourself. Demonstrate in every possible way how your product or service provides luxury at least cost. The package alone might make the difference: Extensive studies have shown that most women can't tell perfumes by odor—packaging makes more sales than contents. And it works just as well for ice cream. A leading maker had us seek out buyers' reaction to a series of proposed new containers. We found that one in Wedgewood blue, simple in design and pictureless, caused eight out of ten customers to consider its contents more expensive, better tasting, with more flavor than previous packages depicting the ice cream itself. Placed in production, the motivationally chosen design proved to be the best seller.

Similar results came from a study for the Jewel Tea chain. Our probers found that customers did not consider expensive steaks wrapped in plain paper as good as those in special wraps. Some with sliced meat spread out to look richer, others beautifully wrapped ready for the freezer, jumped sales so sharply that Jewel used its research studies to sell butcher groups on prepackaging. The firm has since adapted the system for most of its super markets, gaining far higher volume and markup in less space. One California super market went even further— found that by creating the idea of luxury through putting a pat of butter atop each of its better steaks, sales increased 15%.

A study for Schenley Distillers, Inc., showed the Luxury appeal so strong that it lead to introduction of new decanters. Results: The whiskey looks costlier and better in buyers' eyes; new decanters are a powerful merchandising attraction.

Whenever your product is made to look less utilitarian, we have found, the more luxury it usually connotes to the customer.

L. Bamberger & Co., Newark department store, learned that wrapping all possible items in cellophane not only enhanced luxury appeal, but saved on returns, inventory and soiling particularly with multiplied units. One line of slow-moving linen ensembles, for example, sold out the day after being cellophane-packaged in groups.

Grouping items in kits, or selling associated products together, is another way of appealing to the luxury yen and increasing sales tickets. McGregor Sportswear, for instance, began boxing slacks with shirts, stockings with walking shorts, under the name International Sets. When President Harry Doniger noted that a $5.95 shopper frequently signed a $12 to $15 check, McGregor redesigned its $50 million yearly output. Today almost every item "goes with" other things in color, design, wearability. Sales of wardrobes, instead of individual items, have paid off handsomely.

Variety packs of good cheeses, fine crackers, special occasion components, all express the luxury notion to many customers. Numbers of complete kitchens and bathrooms are sold this way. Often an inquiry for a single item can be built into a complete sale if adequately followed through. Psychologically, buying grouped products provides satisfaction, a sense of completeness and accomplishment, makes most customers feel a little closer to the ultimate perfection we all seek. It also arouses a feeling of "getting a better buy." The carnival pitchman, you'll recall, showed you a kitchen paring utensil, then told you he'd toss in a pear slicer, a carrot grater, a celery shredder, all wrapped up in one package. It was a hard lure to resist; it is as effective today when coupled with a luxury appeal.

Firms That Switched to Prestige and Quality Appeal. The desire for prestige, quality, improved social status, as much as for comfort, is the real reason behind purchase of many better homes, apparel, automotive and other products. It's an appeal to the American sense of pride, a desire for recognition; not social climbing in the old sense, but a desire for self status. Prestige is more social than actual in present-day psychological terms—what people think about a product or service is paramount to what it really is. And your appeals must reflect this to succeed.

For example, seeking clues for Lord Calvert (Calvert Distillers Corp.) we learned that today Americans are less concerned with looking up to outstanding personalities in unquestioning admiration than they were a decade ago. Rather, since most people believe that they can reach the top, they are primarily interested in how Mr. Big did it. Adding "how to" details in the advertising copy gave the Man of Distinction appeal an extra push.

General Mills, Inc., had us check its advertisements for Wheaties to see if they could be made more effective. As a result of psychometric tests for degree of consumer involvement in the appeal, for positive emotional reaction developed, and for degree of mental rehearsal of purchase and use of the product, we advised: "Have a youngster appear in the advertisement with the champion. The kids will identify themselves more readily with your message." Knox Reeves Advertising, Inc., Minneapolis, interpreted these findings ingeniously. It has worked out exactly as forecast.

Adding prestige luster to a product or store can be done in many ways. Ohrbach's New York department store, to get away from its one-note price consciousness, not only ran an extensive institutional advertising campaign to stress high fashion, but put on the town's biggest show of Paris originals to drive it home.

Foley's Federated Department Stores' big Houston store, with a primarily middle-class clientele, advertises $15,000 minks. Doesn't expect to sell many, but tests have proved that such conversation-makers give prestige to labels on lesser items. The same store group spent thousands of additional dollars adding impressive decor to its Fedway Stores to create what President Fred Lazarus, Jr., calls a "$5 blouse atmosphere," though many blouses go at $2.95, because "you can sell a $5 customer a lesser item in better settings, but it's hard to up-trade the other way round."

Prestige in Dime Stores

More and more variety and F. W. Woolworth Co. stores have up-graded presentation, store design and appearance, aware that they're not only selling more expensive items than in the past, but that customers choose the store that gives them the satisfaction of prestige.

Radio Corporation of America is stressing the appeal with Limited Edition collections. Assembling sets of Beethoven, Toscanini, and even Glenn Miller, RCA bound them handsomely, had a good explanatory book written and, though most of the recordings had been in the catalog for years and could be bought individually for far less, the prestige albums sold out. Henry Holt & Co., Inc., publishers, did the same with several of Robert Frost's poems. A $12.50 fine-binding, numbered collection edition of 80th birthday favorites, twice as expensive as his complete works, was gone a week after publication.

C. F. Hathaway Company's eye-patch man gave the shirtmaker national fame in short order because of prestige stress. Snob-appeal advertisements, franchising only top name stores, added an extra prestige value that gradually trickled down. A similar appeal is now being used to sell beverages for "The Man from Schweppes"—red beard and all.

Prestige often stems from what others think of your product. From this premise Caterpillar Tractor Co., Peoria, has developed a unique device: Yearly it invites 200 barbers for a look-see. Since barbers reputedly love to talk, Caterpillar, in giving them something to enthuse about, gets its prestige message across in the most effective manner via word-of-mouth.

The quality appeal is part of this same picture. Williamson-Dickie Mfg. Co., that sells $18 million of work clothes yearly, found that its desirable is the look of quality plus comfort. Studies showed that since factory workers have up-graded their living scale and women come into many plants, the boys are far fussier about the cut of their jib—and willing to pay, if you can show them how to achieve the quality look on the job.

Cluett Peabody & Co., Inc. recently checked suburbanites in 10 cities; found 94% Mr. Fixits, 80% of whom were dissatisfied with clothes they wore for do-it-yourself tasks. Result: a newly styled working line, with the quality appeals of the fashion show. McGregor discovered that many men weren't using sportswear for leisure at all, but for work; somehow they felt that sport clothes gave them a quality feeling impossible to get in overalls. As a result, McGregor has upgraded appearance, smartness and color of its sportswear, extended sales to many stores that formerly carried no such items.

The same quality appeal is fully as effective in the mechanical field. R. M. Oakley, sales manager for John Deere Plow Co., Des Moines, formerly showed two evenly matched used products when offering equipment to younger or less prosperous farmers. What we call the "misery of choice" often made the customer hesitate to such an extent that he bought neither. When Oakley concentrated better tires and best paint job on one tractor, the visible quality difference was immediately apparent. In practically every case, the quality product sold first—even though priced higher.

How to Use the Prestige and Quality Appeal Yourself. Anything you can do to dramatize and enhance appearance and focus attention on highlights of your line or service can add prestige. Do it with packages, lights, display, special effects. A Detroit car dealer employed a psychological approach in his showroom by guarding his prestige car with a red plush rope. His trick: telling favorite customers it was O.K. for *them* to duck under and inspect the car closely.

Koch of California thought it had a good approach in stressing how its fiberglas luggage could take a beating—even if dropped from a plane. Consumer reaction was negative—and our motivation study showed why: It conjured up thoughts of crashing. Another previous appeal, "so strong you can clean it with steel wool," didn't win customers either. Instead of ease, it made them think of the work they might have to do. When studies showed that most people want the admiration of other travelers and of the redcaps handling their bags, a new prestige appeal was put forth and translated by J. J. Weiner Co., San Francisco, advertising agency. It has made sales where other appeals failed to attract. Admiration from others, another way of expressing prestige, has also become the Pacific Mills theme. All its men's clothing advertisements, are now additionally directed at women, emphasizing, "Does your husband carry the world on his shoulders? Tell him about the suit with the weightless feel." Enhancing *his* status in *her* eyes has helped to sell both.

Tools of Prestige

If you seek to build prestige by testimonials, endorsements, awards, make sure they are believable and real. Effective publicity in prestige media is another good way of achieving prestige for services or products. Tie-in promotions of nationally advertised brand name merchandise can bring prestige. The manufacturer who omits window and store displays, point-of-purchase and cooperative advertising, and the retailer or service firm that doesn't employ such aids in full, are missing some of selling's best prestige-making tools.

As to use of the quality appeal, remember that, except where real savings are offered on standard price-fixed items, price is the one factor most customers dislike about shopping. Yet so many salespeople repeatedly open with "how much," rather than "here's what this item or service will do for you." To sell quality, you must be able to demonstrate it in terms the customer seeks, expressed or unexpressed. Often, however, explanations are so technical that the customer can't sense the advantage. In fact, our studies proved that in case after case customers, seeing a specific technological claim made for one brand, attributed it to another within 15 minutes. Looking for the little things which denote quality isn't easy. One investigation for the Kwick-Set Lock Co. of California showed that home buyers are apt to judge quality less by important basic construction than by hardware and locks. Publicizing its motivational findings, Kwick-Set increased sales to builders. A study for General Motors proved that, realistic or not, it was the "feel" prospects got from slamming doors that made them believe one car to be a quality product, another "tinny" or cheap.

Astute garment manufacturers have learned that women often judge quality by buttonholes or hem depth. And in the men's field, hand-picked stitching on the collar, pearl buttons, non-stick zippers often create the belief that the rest of the item must be of similar quality.

Sometimes quality can be demonstrated by telling how your product is produced. Univis Lens Co., Dayton, for example, skipped nuts-and-bolts details, of interest only to technicians, concentrated on convincing ultimate wearers how each production step meant additional quality for their own benefit. And Luchow's, famed New York restaurant, discovered how one little difference can put across a quality idea: When it began serving a few diners beer in old-world pewter steins instead of glasses, people at other tables immediately asked for the same. Luchow's was happy to oblige—and beer sales have foamed up 40%.

·{ 6 }··

Selling to an Age of Plenty*

It was in May, just 29 years ago, that Henry Ford gave his famous order to the factories to shut down production on the Model T—the most successful car in the history of the automobile industry—and told his engineers to start tooling up for what became the Model A. In so doing, Ford put a full stop to one era in economic and social history and, however reluctantly, committed himself to a new one.

If a date can be put on it, May, 1927, marks a great divide in modern times. It can be used handily to date the transition from the Age of Production to the Age of Distribution.

Although few realized it at the time, the car industry in 1927 was leading the way into an era of enormous production and of high-level consumption in which industry must perforce listen closely to what the consumer wants. This era has now reached full bloom—as most people realize more or less clearly.

Marks of the Era

It is an era that has disturbed many people. They are upset by what they see as an enormous emphasis on materialism and triviality and as a saturation of American life with the false standards of the market place.

1. It is an age in which "style" and other basically nonessential factors are more important to consumers than price.

2. It is an age in which continual change—innovation—is a major spur to buying.

3. It is an age in which consumer credit permits people to borrow from future income in order to buy goods—particularly expensive ones— that they couldn't otherwise afford.

4. It is an age in which advertising has assumed a major role as the stimulator of people's appetites for goods that they may not have known about or felt a need for.

New Maxims

Finally, it is an age in which all the old admonitions appear to have been outdated: Make do. Neither a borrower nor a lender be. Penny-wise, pound-foolish. Waste not, want not. A penny saved is a penny earned. A fool and his money are soon parted.

Just past the midmark of the 20th Century, it looks as though all of our business forces are bent on getting everyone to do just the reverse: Borrow. Spend. Buy. Waste. Want.

REFORMING AN INDUSTRY

Even by 1927, the change that had overtaken the auto industry had been clear for some time to everyone who cared to see. That didn't include Ford himself. He stubbornly clung, up to the last minute, to the wonderful and beloved "universal" car that had revolutionized American life and touched off the era of the mass-production of major consumer durable goods around the world.

Forcing Ford's Hand

Ford sales of passenger cars had hit their peak of 1.7-million in 1923, had been slipping steadily since. In 1926, General Motors Corp. and Ford Motor Co. were running neck-and-neck, each with about 1.2-million units that year. GM's low-priced Chevrolet, which had puny sales in 1920, alone accounted for more than 600,000 of GM's output.

Ford had turned a deaf ear as early as 1923 to pleas from his dealers to redesign and upgrade the Model T, but finally even he couldn't ignore the sales figures. As the genius of production, he had put the masses on wheels with a cheap mass-produced car, a stripped down, tough, inexpensive utility car that admirably suited the needs of a raw nation that traveled to town on rutted dirt roads. In all, he sold 15-million Model T's for the staggering sum of $7-billion. But eventually he had to give way to a complete change in the nature of the country, the market, and the competition—a change that, ironically, he had done an enormous amount to bring about.

Only the Beginning

What Ford failed to see was that he had run headlong into an era of high-level consumption in which the first major industry to be affected was the auto industry.

Before this extraordinary new development could sweep through the entire U.S. economy, the nation first had to go through a major depression and a war. But the auto industry 30 years ago contained most of the main elements—with some important exceptions—that have since produced what is now widely called the Consumption Economy.

The significance of the changeover from the Model T to the Model A was summed up cogently a few years ago by Keith Sward in his book, The Legend of Henry Ford:

"What gave the coup de grace to the world's best-known car, and what its producer was reluctant to face, was permanent shift in consumer demand from price to style. By the middle of the 1920s, the American car buyer was asking for 'class' as well as economy in his mode of transportation. Price alone had lost its charm. By the new standards, the bony T had finally become 'too cheap.' Its severe and simple form was not up to the cult of color-styling, four-wheel brakes, shock absorbers, balloon tires, gearshift transmission, roominess, or smooth engine performance and streamlining. Nor did its rigid makeup allow for survival once General Motors had made a national habit of the desire for an annual change of model."

Left at the Post

Price alone—the rock on which the Model T had been built—no longer served Ford. Model T's had pushed the prices of autos down so that by 1923 no less than 70% of all cars sold were in the under-$875 class. Ford's own cuts, which brought his price down from $780 in 1910 to $290 in 1925, had been achieved through the production economy implicit in sticking to one car that, except for minor changes, stayed the same for 18 years.

Meanwhile, the rest of the industry was moving ahead. There was the closed car, which accounted for 30% of Detroit's output in 1923,

70% in 1926. People were willing to pay $150 or so extra, over the price of the open car, for the comfort. The price of a Model T, even when you added in such extras as demountable rims and self-starters—things that came as standard equipment on other cars—was still about 25% under Chevvy. But people were willing to pay the difference.

Color Blindness

Henry Ford's attitude toward these extras and accessories is the key to his business philosophy. He regarded them, and said so publicly, as "knick-knacks." He maintained that he was selling transportation—and only in black.

From this it is clear that Ford never understood the implications of the revolution he himself had created. He could not grasp the fact that the day was ending when there was one car for the masses and a very different car for the classes. He couldn't see that the day was coming when everyone would drive around in a car just about as big, shiny, and begadgeted as everyone else's.

New Principles

Beneath the surface of the enormous and growing American market were still other developments that doomed the Model T—factors that were novel in those days but have since helped to transform many U.S. industries, markets, and consumption patterns.

By the mid-20s, with some 20-million cars rolling and bumping along U.S. roads, the used-car business and the trade-in pattern had been established firmly. A man in the market could pick up a usable car for less than a Model T—and his used car would have a gear shift, shock absorbers, and other refinements he liked.

This was the beginning of what might be called the trickle-down principle of car distribution. It worked then and since to doom a mass-produced American stripped-down or economy car. It was also the beginning of what might be called the disposable society—one in which people willingly get rid of a perfectly good item in favor of something newer and better.

Advertising

The market was also transformed by mass-advertising, which the automotive industry helped to create. By 1915, the industry had become the nation's No. 1 national advertiser. Ford, however, who had early shown brilliance in promotion—"Watch the Fords Go By" dates to 1908—was notoriously an in-and-outer where advertising was concerned. (He once called it "an economic waste.") In 1926, Ford, still a shade the largest producer of cars, was outspent in magazine advertising by seven other makes of cars.

Easy Payments

Another development that doomed the Model T was auto installment credit. As early as 1919, credit had become a potent force in the auto market; by that year, 75% of low-priced cars were sold on installment. But during the 1920s—and this was the significant point—more and more expensive cars came to be sold on credit. From 1919 to 1926, the percentage of all GM cars sold on credit rose from 32% to 56%. It was clear that installment buying was enabling the mass of consumers to upgrade their car-buying habits, to indulge their taste for more expensive cars than they could afford for cash on the barrelhead.

GM recognized this early by founding the General Motors Acceptance Corp. in 1919, to expand its financing both for dealers and for customers. Ford did not set up his credit corporation until 1928.

THE ROCK OF DEARBORN

Henry Ford was not by nature the man to sense or comprehend these trends. Obsessed by the hard facts of wheels, gears, and production lines, he was an authoritarian in social and economic affairs, a man whose instincts in these matters were shaped by an older, rural society.

Ford fits rather neatly into sociologist David Riesman's definition of the "inner-directed" man, who follows the dictates of a conscience formed through rigid discipline in early years. As Riesman points out, this type was well suited to—and was also the product of—an era whose main concern was to wrest a living from a tough physical environment.

Holdout

Ford was the archetype of the production man. His drive took the form of giving people what he thought they ought to want rather than what they really wanted. And it was Ford who could say, "I don't know how many cars Chevrolet made last year—and I don't care."

It was that GM who cared about these things, particularly about what the customers wanted. Secy. of Defense Charles E. Wilson, when president of GM some years ago, quipped that, in buying a car, the U.S. consumer "wants a blonde who can cook."

General Motors' success was largely due to the fact that it pioneered in the new area that Henry Ford ignored. As early as 1921 it started developing a psychological research section, which acted as a listening post to find out what consumers wanted.

In the '20s it also built up the concept of Fisher Body as the style leader. It adopted the annual model change, helping to establish the auto industry's renowned principle of "planned obsolescence." It poured money into advertising in steady and ever-larger streams. It offered the public a range of cars in several price classes.

The Model A

When Ford finally capitulated, he went a long way toward meeting the competition. The new Model A came in four colors and 17 body styles, had a gear shift, hydraulic shock absorbers, four-wheeled brakes, battery ignition, and a lot of other refinements, including a new one—safety glass. And Ford spent $2-million in advertising to introduce the car.

But still Ford hadn't grasped the whole lesson. He froze the Model A for five years, while GM made annual changes, including Chevvy's switchover to the six-cylinder engine. This change helped Chevvy to regain its sales lead over Ford. It also touched off the power race that has possessed Detroit ever since.

In 1932, Ford scrapped the Model A and began retooling again, this time for the Model B—which shortly became the V-8. This time the shutdown lasted only two or three months; the switchover to the Model A, and to a new assembly plant, had shut Ford down for fully five months.

Near Disaster

The two Ford shutdowns were vaster and more complete than anything the industry had known, and they lasted weeks for each day it now takes Detroit to change models. To Ford Motor Co., they were nearly disastrous. The company directly lost millions of dollars in sales; GM with its briefer annual changes grabbed more of the market; Walter P. Chrysler was able to gain a position in the low-priced field.

Moreover, the Ford dealer system was nearly wrecked, and tens of thousands of Ford employees were thrown out of work—the second time coming at the trough of the country's worst depression. The social and business consequences of Ford's 1927 and 1932 shutdowns left their mark on a whole generation.

New Emphasis

The first upheaval at Ford acknowledged the fact that it was no longer enough to roll cars off the production line at more than one a minute.

The second upheaval was an admission that the industry had passed the point of no return in its shift of emphasis to marketing and distribution rather than sheer ability to make cars cheaply.

The age of distribution, of the consumer and his foibles, of General Motors had begun. And autos became the first of all major industries to tie production and distribution together in one tight package.

CONSUMER IS KING

There is no turning back from the era that was born with the automotive industry back in the 1920s.

Today in the United States, as in no other country in the world, considerations of marketing and distribution saturate the thinking of businessmen. At a recent conference of the American Management Assn., to pick an example at random, one speaker said the consumer is "the king" who determines "what and how much will be made, when it will be made, and how much he will pay for it." Another speaker called mass-distribution and mass-production the "Siamese twins" on which depend "this country's welfare, standard of living, ability to defend the free world."

These remarks, which can be matched by similar remarks from dozens of talks by businessmen, give full recognition to the nature of an era that Henry Ford tried stubbornly to deny. It is a recognition, however, that had to wait through 15 years of depression and war for its full flowering.

Setback

The buoyant hopes of the 1920s fell clattering after 1929, when in a few short years individual annual savings plummeted from $3.7-billion to minus $1.4-billion in 1932, and personal disposable income from $82.5-billion to $45.2-billion in 1933. Faced with a catastrophe of such proportions, there was little that businessmen could do but retreat.

Their new-found faith in the potency of marketing and selling wilted before such an enormous loss in purchasing power. This was something you couldn't advertise your way out of, a fact that business tacitly recognized in cutting its advertising expenditures from 4.1% of the nation's disposable personal income in 1929 to 2.8% in 1933.

Price Conscious

The market that remained was dominated by price. It was an age of spectacular price-cutting, in which the chain store made huge strides and the supermarket was born. One of the New Deal's first problems, in fact, was how to push the general price level up again.

In this predicament, the thinking of marketing people by and large turned negative; they were interested mainly in protecting what they had. They fought off newer and cheaper forms of distribution through restrictive devices ranging from resale price maintenance and loss leader-laws to the Robinson-Patman Act.

The Big Change

Some of this negative thinking still persists in business, but the Depression itself, with its social and economic legislation, and the war, with its mass-employment, redistribution of income, and creation of a vast reservoir of purchasing power, have radically changed the climate.

In short, the conditions that now underlie the U.S. economy are very different from those of before the Depression. These are the conditions that have brought about our present high-level consumption:

1. Through improved technology and productivity, the U.S. standard of living has gained enormously.
2. Income has been redistributed so as to spread the fruits of productivity among the masses of Americans.
3. Our accelerated gain in population has expanded the physical market.
4. An increase in leisure time has whetted people's appetite for goods and services of all kinds.

Living Standard

It's hard to be specific about how much the standard of living has improved, since it is affected by a number of factors that are very difficult to measure. The sheer increase in cash income doesn't accurately reflect the improvement in the way people live, because you have to contend with such things as the size of families, the disappearance of household help, the shift from rural to city life (when fewer people raise their own food, there's less bartering "in kind").

Various estimates exist. One, by an economist named William Fielding Ogburn, pins down the increase this way: "The standard of living as measured by money has doubled within the the first half of the 20th Century, and the standard of living as measured in quantity of goods and services has probably doubled in slightly over 50 years."

The basic cause, of course, has been the remarkable strides in technology and, in turn, productivity.

Income Shifts

Of equal importance in the shaping of a new society has been the redistribution of income. Arthur F. Burns, chairman of the President's Council of Economic Advisers, once called this shift "one of the great social revolutions in history."

This revolution produced the great American middle-income market, the growth of which can be illustrated best by these figures:

1. In 1935–36, nearly half of all U.S. spending units (wage-earners singly or in household groups) had annual incomes—measured in 1950 dollars—of $2,000 or less. Only 14% received incomes in what is now the big, broad middle band of incomes, the $4,000-$7,500 bracket.

2. By 1950, only 23% were in the under-$2,000 class, and 31% were in the $4,000-$7,500 group.

The shift since 1950, as over-all national income expands, has been in the same direction.

In 1950, the 31% of units in the middle bracket received about 39% of all personal income after taxes; in 1953, 39% of spending units were in the $4,000-$7,500 band, and they pulled down about 44% of income after taxes. Meanwhile, the next higher bracket—$7,500-$10,000—increased from 2.6% of spending units to 7.6%, and its share of income after taxes increased from 3.8% to 9.5%.

Profile of a Market

This broadening of the middle-income class, the backbone of the new American market, has had far-reaching effects on markets and the economy generally. Perhaps the outstanding characteristic of the new market is its homogeneity.

The old distinctions that used to divide peoples sharply—by race and national origin, by urban and rural living, by educational background, by section of the country, and so forth—have largely disappeared. No matter where they live or what their backgrounds, people in the same income groups today tend to resemble each other in the way they live, the things they buy, and their aims in life. This is true more than at any other time in the history of any western nation.

Plural Pay Envelopes

This leveling within middle-income groups has proceeded farther and faster than is generally supposed, partly because most people have overlooked one new factor: The differences in family income within the middle-income groups, up to about $8,000 a year, are due mainly to the number of breadwinners in each family.

In other words, as you move up the family income scale, there is little difference in the annual income earned per worker. It is the number of earners that determines the family's financial status. So earners in the middle-income groups all earn about the same pay, do the same work as everyone else.

Easy Go

A second major characteristic of the modern middle-income market is that the consumers that make it up voluntarily save very little money. This applies, in fact, to Americans as a whole, except those in the topmost income brackets and those who might be called entrepreneurs—roughly, the self-employed, including farmers. What savings they have (using the word in its technical sense) are mainly in the form of big, long-range commitments—insurance and mortgages.

Undoubtedly this is the product of the enormous social changes that helped to create this new society. Social security, pensions, health and medical plans, the prospect of guaranteed annual wages, and a general sense of security and prosperity have eliminated the driving need that people once felt to save for a rainy day. Easy-to-get consumer credit of all kinds has helped generally to change spending and saving habits.

Baby Boom

Our increasing population is another product of and stimulus to our basic prosperity. It gives an enormous impetus to industrial expansion as companies push to keep up with the physical increase in the market.

It is clear now that projections of population growth have fallen sensationally short of reality. Having learned the hard way, the Census Bureau took no chances when it made its 1952 estimates. Its predictions of population growth for 1960 contain a spread of 15-million between "high" and "low" estimates—165-million to 180-million. We passed the 165-million mark this year, so it looks as though 180-million should be a safe bet for 1960—and 190-million for 1965.

Households now number about 48.5-million. They have grown about 5-million since 1950.

There is an interesting interrelation between unexpectedly large population increases and economic conditions in general. In attempting to explain the increasing birthrate, Census Bureau officials concede that prosperity, plus a sense of well-being and security, must have had a hand in boosting the number of babies per family.

Leisure

A second potent fact in booming the American market has been the increase in leisure time.

This has already had a major impact on people's buying habits, but it still has a further impact to make. One thing seems clear: The more time people have outside their working day, the more marked is their propensity to consume goods and services of all kinds.

This brings us back once again to the essential factor behind the upthrust in our economy—the same factor that has doubled our living standard in 50 years. It is the startling productivity of our industrial machine. Our steadily improving productivity, with all that it has meant in the way of an outpouring of goods, has given us our leisure, our high incomes, and our prosperity.

It has made us a wealthy people living in a high-consumption era which had its false dawn in the 1920s but which has become a solid reality, thanks in part to the removal of the inequalities in income distribution that existed 30 years ago.

BURDEN OF RICHES

We are a wealthy people. This itself has created new problems barely dreamed of in less affluent eras.

Putting the matter in its simplest terms, it is clear that as soon as a man is raised economically above the subsistence level—once his basic need for food, clothing, shelter, and other necessities has been satisfied—a totally new situation arises. He has some room to move around in. He can make a choice of various goods and services offered him and can decide on which he will spend his excess income.

Jumping the Fences

In the view of an older generation of economists, consumer spending was pretty much a function of income, tied to it by an iron law. They could, with confidence, predict how people would spend their money.

This theory undoubtedly had greater validity when the masses of people lived on a lower, more necessitous economic level. They got so much, they had to spend so much. This, of course, put a major emphasis on the function of price, which was regarded as determining the demand for a commodity. The lower the price, up to a point, the greater the demand would be.

Today, almost nobody believes in these mechanical, rigid relationships between income and demand. It is widely recognized that though consumers as a whole tend to spend almost all their income, a very small change in the spending-savings ratio can seriously affect the over-all economy. This was the lesson of 1951, a now-classic instance where the individual savings rate hit its highest level since World War II—and a sales lull set in.

Matter of Choice

This kind of situation has led to a profound preoccupation with the nature of the consumer—with people, that is, in their role as purchasers of goods and services—and with the consumer's habits, needs, and desires.

We now have a society in which many nonessential goods, from TV sets to power tools, are available, and in which the purchase of many large and expensive durables, such as cars, bulks large. These are largely postponable purchases.

As a result, businessmen and economists are much concerned with what is now frequently called "discretionary" spending, or the outlay of money on things which there is no pressing need to buy.

Overdoing It

This preoccupation has led to considerable exaggeration. An economist for an advertising agency, for example, recently figured out that an average family with an income of $4,500 has $4,165 disposable income after taxes. Of this, he said, $1,840 goes for "basic" living costs—food, clothing, housing, household operation—to maintain a 1941 standard of living. Left over, he figured is $2,325 in "discretionary" spending power. Study of this example can only lead to the conclusion that the average family—in 1941—was living on a remarkably primitive level.

"There is some danger," says government economist Arthur Burns, "that the whimsical nature of consumer spending will now be as roundly exaggerated as was its mathematical determinacy only a short time back."

Questions Raised

Even though exaggerated, the concern over how the consumer will spend his money is entirely legitimate in an era of plenty. If nothing else, the consumer has the power to shift his purchasing from one kind of goods to another, or to change the mix of his purchases within reasonable time limits.

For instance, it has been clear for years that as consumer income rises, consumers do not spend their new money according to their old pattern of spending. Out of each new dollar, the consumer tends to spend relatively much less on clothing than he does on housing.

Therefore, an array of new questions has become vital to businessmen and economists.

Among these questions are:

1. How do spending patterns change as consumers climb up the income ladder? How long does it take them to take on the characteristics of the new income group?
2. What effect have innovations and new products on demand?
3. Does advertising change demand and how?
4. To what extent does welfare legislation—public money spent on roads, schools, social security—change consumption patterns?
5. Will people prefer to take the fruits of increased productivity in more leisure time or in the form of higher pay?
6. How does the "confidence" of consumers regarding general economic conditions affect intentions to buy?
7. How does size of family affect buying habits—and what size families will people choose to have?

Inquiring Minds

The emergence of such questions is keeping economists, psychologists, historians, anthropologists, sociologists, and others busy re-examining human actions, behavior, and motives in the light of new conditions.

Work in these diverse fields is linked together by the realization of a fundamental difference between the economic behavior of the American people today and those of yesterday. Researchers along a broad front realize that they are dealing with the consequences of prosperity, with the consequent effects of abundance on the nation's character and habits.

Taken together, these efforts add up to an over-all evaluation of the individual in relation to the economic world in which he lives. From it we are getting a new view of such factors as the role of innovations, of advertising, of price competition, of distribution costs, and a host of other vital considerations—including what makes people tick.

WORLD OF ABUNDANCE

In his book The Lonely Crowd, David Riesman deals with the problems presented by abundance. He develops his thesis around the change of people's character that has accompanied the transition from an era primarily concerned with production to one concerned with consumption.

The "inner-directed" man of the Henry Ford type who dominated an earlier age, he says, was shaped in a world that didn't yet have enough of worldly goods to go around. Consequently, the older virtues of hard work, thrift, prudence, and abstinence set the tone.

The New Man

Today the dominant type of American, Riesman says, is the "other-directed" man, who has developed out of society's shift of emphasis to nonessential functions—or what used to be regarded as nonessential. These include distribution, service trades, the professions. People are generally less concerned with conquering their physical environment than with pleasing other people. They are less likely to be entrepreneurs than employees.

This has produced a different type, one whom Riesman describes as having a radar set always tuned in for guidance from the outside, rather than the inner gyroscope that gave direction to his ancestors. Gone are the old guideposts that had served past generations that geared their consumption patterns to fit a given station or role in life.

Of the other-directed man, Riesman says:

"He bespeaks a western urban world in which, with growing economic abundance, work loses its former importance and one's peers educate one in the proper attitudes towards leisure and consumption."

He also remarks on the other-directed's "tremendous outpouring of energy . . . channeled into the ever-expanding frontiers of consumption."

Less Conformity?

The chief value of Riesman's book is not its logical development of an organized view, but rather the insights it contains.

One of Riesman's ideas is that we may be passing out of the age of conformity and anxiety that afflicts people today in their role of consumer. Riesman suggests that our Puritan heritage has been "responsible for much of the rigidity and unimaginative use of our leisure." He also speaks of the enormous acceleration of style change and of the flood of goods differentiated from each other only by small gradations.

"The consumer trainee," says the author, "has a lot more to learn than in the early days of industrialization."

Riesman thinks that we are entering a more sophisticated era in which the "art of consumership" will be developed. He thinks that this will come about through more creative use of leisure, through a revival of craftsmanship in leisure pursuits, through increasingly high standards of taste, and even through the gradual replacement of salesmen in some fields by what he calls "avocational advisers."

Role of Sales

Meanwhile, abundance in the U.S. is altering the attitude of thinkers toward those twin American phenomena: salesmanship and advertising.

Traditionally economists as a group have been distrustful about advertising, questioning whether it has a true economic function. At worst, they felt, it created a demand for trivial goods, urged false standards on people, tended toward monopoly, and fostered a situation in which sellers could dodge price competition. At most, they said, advertising merely tended to shift demand from one brand or product to another.

"There are a great many things about the U.S. that can only be explained by its wealth," says J. K. Galbraith in American Capitalism: The Concept of Countervailing Power. His chapter on "The Unseemly Economics of Opulence" is devoted to explaining how this shapes the present role of advertising.

Cope of Waste

Much of advertising, says Galbraith, is economic waste, stimulating only a desire for frills. But he shrugs his shoulders: We are a rich society that takes care of its basic wants and can afford some frills and inefficiencies.

Furthermore, something else happens in a wealthy society. "The need and opportunity to persuade people," Galbraith says, "arise only as people have the income to satisfy relatively unimportant wants, of the urgency of which they are not automatically aware." The fact there are more goods to be sold in a society of abundance "means that psychological, not physical considerations, should control desire."

Supporting View

David M. Potter, chairman of American Studies at Yale University, in People of Plenty, carries the Galbraith argument a step farther. He finds that advertising is indispensable in our kind of economy. It is the force that creates demand for the flood of new products that keeps the economic wheels turning.

"Advertising is not badly needed in an economy of scarcity," he says, "because total demand is usually equal to or in excess of total supply. . . . It is when potential outstrips demand—that is, when abundance prevails—that advertising begins to fulfill a really essential economic function."

As a historian, Potter is concerned primarily with describing and defining American national character. Abundance, he thinks, is the key. Borrowing the insights of Riesman and the social scientists, he traces the impact of plenty on American democracy, social structure, and economy. About advertising, which he calls "the institution of abundance," he says:

"The productive capacity can supply new kinds of goods faster than society in the mass learns to crave these goods or to regard them as necessities. If this new capacity is to be used, the imperative must fall upon consumption, and the society must be adjusted to a new set of drives and values in which consumption is paramount."

Psychology

Time and time again in economic writings, the psychological factor underlying demand and consumption becomes the prime factor.

Economists no longer regard price-output relationships in themselves as sufficient explanation of the interplay of competitive forces. Increasingly they call on psychology to round out theories.

Here, for example, is what Lawrence Abbott, an economist at Union College, says in his book Quality and Competition:

"In a primitive society, the niceties of discrimination have not yet been developed. . . . But as a society matures and education improves, people learn to develop more acute powers of discrimination. Their wants become more detailed. They begin to pride themselves on being connoisseurs in certain fields—to develop a preference, say, not simply for white wine, but for 1948 Chablis."

Abbott makes this point in attempting to fill in the "serious gap" in the structure of economic theory. He wants to construct a theory of competition that takes into account the "product or quality" variable as well as price behavior.

A corollary of this interest has been the development of a field that now touches the daily life of almost all businessmen—motivations research. The business of examining consumer behavior has now become a major force in modern economic life.

Where Now?

What will be the upshot of this intensive effort to find out what the consumer thinks, feels, wants? Will it be the conformity in American life that so bothers Riesman and others? Will this sensitivity to people's wants and needs end with a greater catering to individuality by businessmen? Or will it lead to a greater emphasis on finding out what mass-man wants.

It is still difficult to foretell the outcome.

In our wealthy society, there are powerful drives in both directions. On one hand, there is a drive toward conformity, as witnessed by the fact that American cars today are very nearly as much alike as they can be made. On the other hand, there is the example of the frozen food industry, which every day adds to the array of prepared foods that cater to the increasingly catholic American palate.

But one thing can be said with certainty: No major company will ever again turn such a deaf ear to the consumer as did Henry Ford back in the 1920s.

In a series of articles following this introduction, BUSINESS WEEK will explore some of the consequences of this basic fact. It will take a closer look at the new role played by consumers and the impact that this is having on advertising, pricing, new products, the cost of distribution, and related areas of business.

·{ 7 }··

Buyer Wants Not Facts Alone, but "Reassurance of Adequacy,"*

BY STUART SIEBERT †

I am not a psychologist. I am an advertising man.

And as an advertising man I am more concerned with the *application* of motivation research findings than with the techniques of the research.

What is the purpose and value of motivation research in connection with every type of product, industrial as well as consumer? Not to provide a dramatic, magic formula for guaranteeing sales. Not to replace the creative talents of writers, art directors and planners. But simply to help us understand our customer a little better and so to reach him with the words, illustrations and ideas that will hit that "pocket-book nerve." It is now seven years since our agency began to use motivation research in this manner to stimulate the creation of new sales and advertising approaches. Today, it is not only a practical, but an indispensable tool in every phase of our agency service.

Only for Chewing Gum?

And that brings us to another question. Does motivation research help us create better advertising for the Inland Steel Co., General American Transportation Corp. or the Visking Corp. as affectively as it helps us to sell Toni home permanents, Mogen David Wine or Spearmint chewing gum?

Our experience is that motivation research does help . . . and for a

---

* Reprinted by special permission from *Industrial Marketing*, June, 1955. Copyright, 1955 by Advertising Publications, Inc., 200 East Illinois Street, Chicago 11.

† Vice-president, Weiss & Geller, Chicago.

very good reason: industrial customers are people, too. People who are subject to the same kind of hidden emotional judgments, beliefs, prejudices, desires and fears when they buy for business as when they buy for their personal consumption.

In both industrial and consumer purchase, our studies have shown, the combinations of motivations that lead to the buying decision may be compared with an iceberg . . . one-tenth visible and nine-tenths submerged. The visible tenth is the conscious, rational evaluation of need, price and quality upon which every industrial purchase is theoretically based. But the submerged nine-tenths, we have found, the unconscious, emotional motivations, play just as great a part in the purchase of a carload of widgets as they do in milady's selection of her Easter bonnet.

For one of our industrial clients, this conflict between conscious and hidden attitudes was interestingly revealed by an opinion survey which was conducted simultaneously with a series of projective tests.

Our client was a large corporation supplying a basic material to manufacturing customers of every size. These clients, in turn, manufactured many different types of finished products.

Uneasy Feeling

The problem was not to solve any particular or immediate sales crisis, but simply to learn if a more effective advertising and selling approach could be discovered. Sales executives of the company had long had an uneasy feeling that the company's relationship with many of its customers was not all it should be, and we were interested in looking at the image of our client as it was reflected in both the conscious and emotional opinions of its customers.

The opinion research survey, conducted in the most impartial and objective manner by a well-qualified independent research organization, painted a glowing picture. Customers felt that prices and policies were fair, equitable and keenly competitive. The company's contribution to civic affairs, to the economy of the community and to the technical advancement of industry in general, was known and praised. Labor policies were considered good, and the customers felt our client was dedicated to a high standard of quality and craftsmanship. The company's attitude toward technical advice and other services seemed to be all that the customer could wish.

In each of these respects, our client was usually ranked second, often first, and never less than third in an industry known for its comprehensive public relations efforts. This was a highly creditable showing since our client was neither first, second or third in size in the industry.

Tests Trip Up a Test

On the surface, therefore . . . the visible tenth of the iceberg . . . no problems existed. The company was doing fine.

But our projective tests . . . uncovering the submerged nine-tenths of the iceberg . . . told a far more complete story. True, they confirmed that our client was held in high regard in all of the important fields touched upon by the opinion study. The difference, however, was in the deeper emotional reactions of a very important segment of the market . . . the small customer.

Through our tests (role playing, sentence completion and a modified Thematic Apperception Test) these customers told us the attitudes they thought *other* buyers might have toward our client. And in so doing, they clearly revealed their own attitudes . . . an underlying feeling of hostility.

This hostility, we found, was caused not by any deliberate action or policy of the company but by an imagined attitude which the customer read into the company's advertising and the manner of its salesmen.

Hostilities Uncovered

This attitude, customers imagined, was one of condescension toward the little fellow, an indication that the little customer was tolerated rather than appreciated . . . and that his problems were neither interesting nor important to the large supplier.

From the tests, the causes of this hostility could be easily understood. The client's industry is one of giants . . . organizations of basic importance to the economy. In their laboratories, these great corporations were constantly solving important technical problems of other industrial giants. And it was natural that these dramatic accomplishments should be the basis of the company's advertising. It was also natural that the company's salesman would feed his own ego by a little industrial "name dropping" when calling on a small customer.

Once exposed and understood, this hostility was easy to combat. Our client's advertising began to speak with pride of contributions toward solving the problems of small customers as well as large. And it was indirectly emphasized that these problems taxed the ingenuity, skill and research facilities of our client fully as much as did the problems of larger customers.

In addition, the new advertising touched with friendly humor upon the complexities and importance of the purchasing agent's job . . . it was no cinch discharging such responsibilities, the ads implied, and the supplier realized it.

Coupled with a new, similar approach in sales training and sales meetings, the effectiveness of the advertising increased and the client benefited measureably in both increased sales and improved customer relations.

Test by Mail

Incidentally, the projective tests used in this particular research were circulated by mail. As far as I know this was the first time projective tests were ever given in this manner. The practical results of this experiment were highly satisfactory in stimulating more effective advertising and we plan to develop the technique for clients where cost, the wide scattering of customers, or other factors may prohibit personal interviews.

One of the most useful findings to come out of our industrial motivation research has been the recognition of three emotional elements present to some degree in almost every purchase: the reassurance of competence, the search for an authority figure, and a post-purchase anxiety.

Inside the Buyer

These findings were confirmed by a motivation study in consumer buying patterns. I will tell you about these emotional factors in the consumer study, for this reason: The elements are the same as in industrial buying, we have found, but the explanation is necessarily more directly and less technically described in the consumer study.

For the consumer study, one of our psychologists spent five weeks as a retail salesman on the floor of one of the country's largest appliance dealers. His mission was to observe and analyze customer reactions as the purchase decision was made.

His report stressed the three emotional elements: the reassurance of competence, the search for an authority figure and a post-purchase anxiety.

Needs Reassurance

Stripped to their essentials, these expressions simply mean; first, that the customer needs to find in every sale some reassurance that his role in life is important . . . and that he is filling that role with competence.

To a woman buying a washing machine, for example, the transaction is an important way of reassuring herself and demonstrating to her husband that her responsibilities in the home *are* important and necessary to the family's well being. And by being a shrewd and knowledgeable buyer of the washing machine she demonstrates to both her husband and herself that she knows how to handle this important job of homemaking.

But the fact of the matter is that she is not always completely sure she *will* make the *right* decision in selecting a washer. So the need for reassurance of her competence is matched by an anxiety lest she prove to her husband, and herself, that she really is incompetent after all.

And that's where the authority-figure comes in . . . someone or something who can be trusted to make the decision for her without appearing to do so. In a good many cases, of course, this authority-figure turns out to be the salesman. Or it may be a friend or relative whose advice is sought, or *Consumer Reports,* or the reputation of the manufacturer or some symbol contained in the manufacturer's advertising.

Post-Purchase Anxiety

Once the purchase has been made, with the help of the authority-figure, the third element . . . post-purchase anxiety . . . usually appears. This anxiety, familiar to all of us, is the conviction that we have done the wrong thing. We should either have bought the other brand or else not made the purchase at all.

A common antidote for this anxiety is to return to the manufacturer's advertising for reassurance of our good judgment.

Now this may be very interesting, you are probably saying, but how can this woman's emotional attitudes toward buying a washing machine be likened to those of an industrial buyer? After all, the purchase of a washing machine is an infrequent and important event in this woman's life. No wonder she is anxious about her decision. But an experienced, practical buyer of industrial products is a different breed of cat. These decisions are daily occurrences with him, and he ought to be pretty calloused against such anxieties.

More So

Well, there *is* a difference, true enough. But the difference, according to our findings, is not that the industrial buyer has *less* anxiety . . . he is apt to have *more.* For in making his decisions, frequent as they are, he is under the pressure of many different people at various levels of importance and he must reassure himself of his competence in the eyes of each of them.

It is somewhat as if our washing machine buyer not only had to be concerned with her husband's reaction, but also that of her father, her children, her mother-in-law and the cleaning woman. (And, incidentally, that is not altogether an unknown situation either, according to our psychologists.)

The recognition of these three emotional elements now plays its important part in the creation of all advertising for our industrial clients. How can we acknowledge the importance of the buyer's work and his skill in discharging it, we ask ourselves. What authority-figure will the customer find in the ad? And what reassurance will he find if he returns to the advertising during his period of post-purchase anxiety?

As a final example, you may be interested in the findings of a motivation study where industrial buyers revealed some of their attitudes toward advertising itself.

Diversification Problems

The client was a large corporation serving many different types of industrial customers in many different ways. For example, it manufactured products for some customers, while for others it performed industrial services.

The problems for which we sought answers arose out of this combination of activities:

1. How did the customers of the manufacturing division feel about the company's service activities? And how did the service customers feel about the manufacturing?

2. Was a horizontal campaign stressing the company's diversification needed . . . or should the client's advertising be broken down into separate campaigns, each aimed at separate industries?

The answers to these questions were obtained through a series of depth interviews held with industrial executives and with executives of financial and banking firms. Through these interviews we learned that *in this particular case* the size and diversification of our client apparently influenced the customer toward acceptance rather than rejection of the company. Indeed, in this case, the manifest knowledge gained by such diversification made the corporation a very acceptable "authority figure" to most of its customers.

The result of these findings was a highly successful horizontal campaign stressing the advantage to *each* customer in the experience gained by our client through serving *many* clients.

Buried Reactions

But possibly the most interesting results of this study were the by-products . . . the buried reactions of these executives toward industrial advertising in general.

On the surface . . . that exposed tenth of the iceberg . . . our respondents indicated a low opinion of the value of industrial advertising. Personally, they said, we don't have time to read trade advertising, unless it is genuinely newsworthy, announcing a brand new product or process. Oh, occasionally we may have time to leaf hurriedly through business papers, but we almost never read the ads.

But, indirectly, the executives interviewed told us something very different . . . that they *do* follow and *are* influenced by industrial advertising far more, in fact, than they, themselves, realize. In such advertising they seek more than practical information. They seek the reassurance of their own adequacy, and an acknowledgement that the supplier appreciates their skill.

We learned that industrial advertising can offend a customer's pride by not talking as one professional to another . . . by saying, in effect, your job requires no real specialized knowledge, therefore we can capture and hold your interest merely by flippant headlines, clever illustrations or analogies to commonplace things outside the realm of your business life.

For example, we learned to beware of humor unless it leads immediately into man-to-man professional talk based on a sound, not a superficial, knowledge of the technicalities involved.

People in Ads? Maybe

We learned that to feature personalities in industrial advertising can be dangerous. Buyers interviewed showed a buried resentment against what they called "publicity" for those of inferior business "rank" to themselves. On the other hand, they equally resented being confronted with company executives of "superior rank" whom they have never met. Thus a purchasing agent may be equally unimpressed and resentful of advertising presenting a mill worker or a chairman of the board.

But if to present individual personalities in industrial advertising is often dangerous, to picture the scenes and situations in the client's plant can be quite desirable. To take the buyer "behind the scenes" may provide him with that very important reassurance of his competence, at the same time proving the company a very acceptable "authority-figure."

To sum up, it is possible that historian Henry Adams may have stated the real importance of motivation research to industrial advertising when he said, nearly 75 years ago: ". . . above all, we must recover that which we have lost through the very techniques of scientific knowledge and invention; the power to *feel,* which is at the basis of all truly human relationships . . ."

·{ 8 }··

The P.A.'s Dilemma*

Have you ever sat behind a desk and had five different soap salesmen try to sell you the greatest product in the world—all different and all in the same day? It is one of the greatest frustrations in the life of a purchasing agent and not for the reason you might think.

It does get tiresome listening to individual pitches which, matched against each other, can only be ridiculous. But the source of my frustration comes from the fact that I cannot tell which pitch is correct. And I cannot, really, test these various products to find out.

This is my basic problem and I think it would help salesmen and marketing men if they understood it better.

---

* Reprinted by special permission from *Industrial Marketing,* February, 1956. Copyright, 1956, by Advertising Publications, Inc., 200 East Illinois Street, Chicago 11.

Quality? Who Knows?

I am director of purchases for a metal-working and manufacturing company with five major divisions. I also act as purchasing agent for one of these divisions. The five divisional purchasing agents are largely responsible for purchases in their own divisions. Each has a staff of assistant purchasing agents, buyers and expediters and we are all confronted with the same problem: How are we going to tell which product is best?

And if we can't, how are we going to make a decision?

Last year we bought $33,000,000 worth of materials. It has been fairly universal experience that 45% to 51% of the gross business of a company is in material cost, and this applies to nearly all companies. So while we are far short of being the largest company in the United States we do buy a substantial amount.

A surprising volume of these purchases have to be made with insufficient information.

We buy everything to engineering specifications. But that doesn't simplify our problem, believe me, when we are dealing with standardized products, perishable tooling, and so on.

For instance, time after time we have salesmen come to us with materials of the same specifications as other suppliers.

Let's take a screw. It is a standard item and is bought strictly on price within certain limitations. Thirty different fastening houses call on us and every one can supply us with the same screw. Their prices are very close. How are we going to decide?

First, we limit the number of inquiries we send out. We probably ask for a quotation from six or seven. They are houses which meet the following requirements:

1. The salesman has made a good impression on us.
2. The company has a good background and history.
3. It has given us good service. By this I mean it has provided extraordinary service at times. It hasn't held us up in the past. It has given us straight answers and not a runaround if it got into trouble with our order.

Can't Afford to Test

This is a straightforward case. We evaluate all the factors, including price, and write our order accordingly . . . not really too much of a problem but I think we have to admit that we give the order rather arbitrarily.

Now let's look at something a bit more difficult: cutting oil, for instance. Many people make cutting oil. All of them are in here trying to sell us. But the only way we can find out whether it's any good is to use it. Now are we to risk interrupting our production to test 30 different brands of cutting oil, every one of which is claimed to be the best in the country?

Suppose we did test them all? Maybe one of them would ruin a machine. Another might not show up best because it was used wrong. So, frankly, we don't test them all. We can't allow all these people into our plant for test purposes. We don't know what is best. So again we take an arbitrary stand. We test until we find an oil that will work with a whole group of machines. Then we close the door. Are we right or wrong?

The only thing that will open that door again is for some individual company to arouse our interest with some unusual product that will promise substantial savings in the cost of the oil or increase in tool life. It will have to be backed by concrete facts.

P.A.'s Won't Admit It

This is not unique. It is the general situation with all kinds of perishable tooling such as drills, grinding wheels and so on; with housekeeping supplies such as floor compounds and waxes, and with all those usable supplies on which we spend millions of dollars each year.

I suppose that few purchasing agents would admit all this, and even I am hiding under a cloak of anonymity. But it's time we did admit it, I believe, and it's time that sellers understood it.

Yet at the same time I insist that my approach is rational. I take it because I seriously question the costs of tests in these areas to determine the best product.

Steel warehousing is another source of supply that falls into the same category. Why do we buy from one and exclude the other? It's a good question.

We can't research the product, therefore we depend upon the selling abilities of the company and of the salesmen. A steel warehouse salesman has absolutely nothing to sell but service. He has everything we need and so have his competitors. So it's his own personal selling ability plus the service his company is able to give that tips the scales.

It seems to me this opens up a wide approach to selling—but it must be selling of the highest type. It must be selling based on helpful ideas, on service, on integrity, on straight-shooting.

We're Wide Open

When we buy heavy equipment and capital goods the situation is entirely different, but here we are talking about expendable supplies and standard items. We don't always buy strictly on quality because we don't have any way of determining it. We are wide open to the right kind of selling.

Putting it bluntly, we can't measure the quality absolutely. Who can measure it for us? The plant clean-up force? The machine operator? The foreman? Who knows the answer? I don't.

Part Three . . .

PRODUCT AND PRODUCT LINE

·{9}·

To Make Them Buy—Try Science*

These last three years have been bitter ones for the cigarette business. It's been a time when just about all the troubles that could affect the industry came to a head simultaneously. There were the long-foreseen effects of the Depression-time birth rate—a factor that necessarily meant that each year for several years there would be fewer new smokers. There were climbing taxes. There was the sudden surge of public demand for filter-tip and king-size cigarettes. And then came the cigarette-lung cancer scare.

After the first buffeting from all these troubles, the industry quickly began trying to regain its losses. Now it's working feverishly at that task. By and large, the companies' research on their product, its development, and its market is strictly a serious matter.

You can see just how serious it is when you consider the case of Philip Morris, Inc.'s new red, white, and gold cigarette pack, which hits the market this week. The new pack replaces the 22-year-old cedar-colored package around the company's major product—Philip Morris cigarettes.

The Idea's Cost

Philip Morris labored two years to bring forth this pack. On the job it spent at least $250,000 of accountable expenses. And you can add to that figure the cost of intangibles, like salaries paid to Philip Morris' Pres. O. Parker McComas and to other company top brass in proportion to the time they spent sweating the new design through its creation.

At first glance it seems unbelievable that all this money and time was expended on just a new pack. After all, the cigarettes inside the pack are exactly the same. When you look into the history of the change you see how all this time and money accumulated.

THE CUSTOMERS' DEMAND

In early 1953 pollster Elmo Roper's continuous survey of cigarette consumers' habits and brand preferences showed that significant numbers of customers were getting pretty tired of Philip Morris' conservative brown pack. They thought it was old fashioned.

They were right, too. The original Philip Morris cigarette, sold in England to Oxford students in 1848 by the antecedent of the present company, was marketed in a flat cedar box, and from this evolved PM's familiar brown pack.

But consumer survey or no, Philip Morris obviously wasn't going to toss its traditions away without first making quite sure that it got to the source of the trouble.

Group for the Job

PM decided to get a task force together to handle the job. It was made up of the company's top management and it gathered quickly under George Weissman, in charge of market research, new products, and public relations.

First step was for the management men to make sure that it was the package and not the cigarette that was at the root of the consumers' attitude. They sent out researchers who selected smokers at random, offered them PM cigarettes and other brands, all packaged in plain white packs. The affirmative responses on flavor and mildness tallied with results previously gathered by market research. This, Weissman felt, confirmed the Roper survey's indications.

"So we knew then we had a major packaging change on our hands and that we had to start from scratch," he says. The task force saw a long job ahead, decided to christen the program, and named it "Project Mayfair." The name helped mask the task force's intentions from the competition. Many outsiders who heard that work was moving at PM on "Project Mayfair" assumed a new Philip Morris brand was being prepared, and the company did nothing to disabuse them of that idea.

Eye to Future

Mayfair's charter was to produce a modern colorful package with maximum brand identification and visual registration. Moreover, with Philip Morris' heavy commitment to TV ("I Love Lucy," for example), the new package would have to fit the demands of color television advertising.

Project Mayfair collected under its banner a wide range of color researchers, market researchers, and package designers:

1. A team from the Color Research Institute in Chicago, under Dr. Louis Cheskin, studied the psychological and physiological effects of bright colors suitable for cigarette packs.

2. A package design competition was set going and three package design consultants entered it.

3. Container Corp. of America's design laboratory began testing various package colors, shapes, and designs.

Information from these sources poured back into Weissman's office. Some 4,000 pack designs were submitted by the packaging consultants alone. By June 1, this year, the task force had rejected all but 50. A few days later the number was cut to 10, and on June 17, the team selected the winning package, prepared by New York designer Egmont Arens.

PROVING THE PRODUCT

The new pack was about as unlike Philip Morris' old brown pack as it could be. Most of it is colored a warm red—because red gets attention. It also had a white band around it—this, researchers said, connoted purity of ingredients. Then there was the light gold striping with which, the color scientists claimed, the customers would associate quality.

Next step for Project Mayfair was pre-testing the pack. It sent the pack back to the color laboratories, where it was subjected to rigorous tests for:

1. Visual acuity. (Does it stand out among competitors' packs?)
2. Color vision. (Does the color outshine other brands?)
3. Peripheral vision. (Does it catch your eye even if it's not right in front of you?)
4. Light and shadow. (Can it be seen even way back on tobacco stores' shelves?)
5. Legibility tests. (At what distance can you first read the brand name?)

Field tests were also run off by Philip Morris' own people, the company's ad agency for Philip Morris, by Elmo Roper's researchers, and other market testing groups.

Color's Appeal

In other tests, shoppers were picked at random as they entered grocery stores, given a shopping list (soap, starch, cereal, cigarettes, mayonnaise). The list allowed them a free brand choice and the researcher told them "It's all on us." When the shoppers finished, the researcher met them at the checkout stand and questioned them on the reasons for their choices. The main point of interest: How much of a part did color play in impulse buying? Of this, Weissman says: "We have a lot to learn from the cereal and soap manufacturers."

In tobacco stores, Philip Morris men and researchers worked for days behind the counters. When a man asked for Philip Morris, they handed him one of the new packs and sought his reaction.

The new pack tested well in almost every case. Some slight typography changes were made, and then the design was put into production.

Philip Morris, fifth in the tobacco industry (last year's sales, $283-million; net income, $11.4-million), has moved more slowly than the rest of the top manufacturers in reacting to recent changes in smoking habits, most observers feel.

Punch at Volume

But with its new Philip Morris pack, made in two sizes for king-size and regular, PM wants a 25% sales increase in a year's time. It will hit hard, with heavy promotion, at the big volume outlets, like supermarkets. As Philip Morris' Pres. McComas points put, that's where the swing is under way from purchase by the pack to by the carton. McComas also guesses that cigarette makers should take a marketing lesson from Detroit. He asks: "Why not change the styling of your pack once in a while, if it gets attention?" PM's newly jazzed-up Marlboro is part of the campaign, too.

All the emphasis that Philip Morris and other tobacco companies are paying these days to new and scientific marketing management may already be paying off. According to Walter E. Knight, who is a director of the Louisville Chamber of Commerce's Research Div., cigarette sales are up in the first six months of this year for the first time since the bleak days of 1953.

··{ 10 }··

The Dentifrice Market: Battle of the Additives*

Right now there are two ingredients in the hectic tooth paste market: fluoride and money. Dentifrice marketing strategists, and that's what they are or they wouldn't survive a minute, have great respect for both.

They respect fluoride because they have seen what other additives have done. With ammoniation, and the publicity to back it, Block Drug rammed Amm-I-Dent into second place in the market in 1949–1950, faltered with the brand when bad publicity took some of ammoniation's magic away, and competitors—adding it to their own products—took much of the rest.

Then, in 1951, chlorophyll jammed in with about the same tactics and took a third of the market before chlorophyll foot pads and dog food got the ingredient laughed out as a major factor. Less spectacular, but not to be ignored, Lambert (whose Listerine tooth paste was all but a dead duck) got back in with an anti-enzyme additive. Now, with three big dentifrice makers test marketing fluoridated tooth pastes and others readying their own compounds in the laboratory, fluoride is one of the market's promising new ingredients.

The other ingredient, however, is also new to the market—money, spent in the profligate quantities that only steel-nerved soap makers are

* Reprinted by special permission from *Tide*, August 13, 1955. Copyright, 1955, *Tide*.

conditioned to spend. Using the soap maker's philosophy of investment spending with a three to five-year return (and at a cost estimated at $20,000,000), Procter & Gamble blasted its way into second place, now has 23% of the market. Competitors thinks P&G is a long way from black ink with Gleem, but find the theory only mildly consoling in view of their own increased advertising costs and diminished share of market.

Currently the market is catching its breath before the storm everyone knows is coming. P&G, apparently satisfied with Gleem's share of market, is expected to cut back advertising. Colgate, which fell to 37% last year is back almost to 40%. Pepsodent and Ipana, both hypoed by trade and consumer deals, are down only a little—Pepsodent from 1954's 11.6% of the market to 10.1% this year, Bristol-Myers' Ipana from 9.0% to 8.1%.

Also holding on while the giants pause are Lambert's entries: Listerine and Antizyme. Right now they share 3.8% of the market, down from 4.4% last year. Ironically, the two brands which find sledding toughest both got into the market on the strength of additives: Block Drug's Amm-I-Dent and Lever Brothers' Chlorodent. Amm-I-Dent, which had 6.2% of the tooth paste market last year is down to 3.7% and Chlorodent, whose highwater mark may have been 30%, fell from 4.6% last year to 2% this year.

Despite the problems of the older additive-based brands, no one is dismissing fluoride tooth pastes lightly. Currently in test markets are P&G with Crest, Block Drug with Super Amm-I-Dent and Lambert with a "fluoride-like" ingredient. The other majors are still in the laboratory watching their rival's test cities with hawk-like vigilance and pitching an occasional test market curve to try out their own counter fluoride strategy.

Typical curve, pitched in test city Portland (Ore.) is Colgate's solicitous message to the town's parents: "MOTHER! A word of assurance . . . Colgate's is Absolutely Safe . . . even for Toddlers." The ad is a counter to P&G's Crest, which, like other fluoriated tooth pastes, is required to carry on its package a warning against use by children under six. Colgate, however, will not be caught short with only negative strategy, is considering marketing a fluoride itself, or adding the ingredient to its present formula.

A new ingredient and accompanying whoopla are proven bellringers in the dentifrice market place, and there is every indication the public is ready to bite again. But there are a couple of tantalizing questions still unanswered. Unlike the days when Tom Ryan of Pedlar & Ryan could invent a new disease (pink tooth brush) and the cure for it (Ipana) in an afternoon, clinical evidence in growing file cabinets indicates there really is something to Colgate's Gardol and a similar anti-enzyme ingredient in Lambert's Antizyme. The same thing is true of the fluorides, and even though the American Dental Assn. and American Medical Assn. have not approved fluoride tooth paste, they are backing fluoridization of community water supplies. If fluoride tooth paste got their approval it could change all bets in the industry. Even without medical endorsement, fluoride has its charms for the manufacturers.

For one thing, the fluorides have already had scads of publicity. All of the brands now test marketing have picked cities where fluoride is in the water, or is being considered along with a few markets where it is not yet an issue. More national publicity is certainly on the way.

Miracle ingredient money has also won grudging respect from the dentifrice makers. After a bad finger-burning with Teel, P&G's liquid dentifrice, the big soap maker repaired to Cincinnati to lick its wounds, reappeared in test markets with Gleem in 1954. Gleem's success, if it turns out that it is, [is] a tribute to free spending and a catchy slogan: "For people who can't brush after every meal." With a whopping budget, P&G started a rolling barrage of advertising and consumer sampling market by market the likes of which dentifrice makers had not seen before.

Following up the ads, P&G sales squads swarmed into grocery stores with more money to buy display space. Since the brand's ingredient, GL-70, is dismissed by competitors as "another detergent" and apparently will not support very strong copy claims, it is clear that the market can be bought. P&G competitors, however, are not so sure it will stay bought.

In terms of strategy, two divergent trends are now in motion. With limited funds, Lambert, for example, is pumping big money into a few markets and maintaining national distribution for its Antizyme with thinner national effort. Their hope is to pick up a profitable share of market in one city, then use the profits to fight for another. This is a tricky thing to accomplish in the face of heavy advertising pressure from Colgate and Gleem. Then, too, there's always pressure, in the form of deals, from Ipana, Pepsodent and others. Lambert's advertising vice-president, Ernest P. Zobian, thinks it can succeed and believes time will favor the therapeutic tooth pastes: "There will be a ground swell of realization among the public that a dentifrice can stop tooth decay . . . we're sure the therapeutic dentifrices will be accepted eventually." Warner Lambert, with heavy ethical experience, believes Zobian is in a better position to develop and test the increasingly complex additives than the soap companies.

On the other hand, marketing factors seem to favor P&G, Lever and Colgate. Toothpaste, traditionally a drugstore item, now gets an estimated 58% of its volume through grocery outlets and their share continues to grow. It is here that the big sales forces of the soap makers can be brought to bear to get vital shelf space. Bristol-Myers, Block, Lambert and the other drug & cosmetic houses cannot hope to match the retail selling job of the soap world's big three. Block Drug's George Abrams, advertising vice-president, expects the market to become more like the soap business, less like the drug business: "I think it's going to be a dealing sort of business with coupons and deal merchandise, one promotion after another. I see it as a business where P&G and Colgate will bring out new products regularly and the one solution for smaller brands will be their hard core of users."

However the battle ends, if it ever does, one thing is appallingly clear about the immediate future. For the next couple of years, nobody is going to make much money out of the $100 million dentifrice market. Money that isn't spent on advertising and promotions will go back to the laboratories to search for a fluoride topper. The trouble is, tooth paste miracles never end.

IT'S IN THE MIND, NOT THE MOUTH

Quipped a motivational researcher recently: "The difference between a fad and a permanent change in the market is that the fad fades." It is a phenomenon dentifrice marketers have viewed frequently in the past five years, sometimes with fascination, sometimes with trepidation—but always with curiosity. What, they ask, happens in the market when an unknown substance, sometimes of questionable value, captures consumers' imaginations and drives well-established products and appeals into adopting the ingredient or fading in the marketplace?

For an answer, during the rapid upsurge of chlorophyll, one dentifrice maker, Bristol-Myers, turned to Alfred Politz Research and got some interesting answers. One answer (that they will now talk about) shows how chlorophyll was accepted by upper educational groups, which means upper income groups, too, but failed to make a hit with the lower educational groups. When interviewed by Politz researchers in the winter of 1950, 32% of the college educated group said that they thought chlorophyll was helpful. As the figures below show, their numbers grew until the following winter, 1951, when almost half of the college group believed chlorophyll helpful. Surprisingly, the lower education groups either didn't hear, or didn't accept the green miracle's claims as swiftly. By winter, 1951, when upper education group faith in chlorophyll was peaking at 48% the lower educational group stubbornly resisted, only 15% agreeing that chlorophyll was helpful. Result: Politz believes the failure of chlorophyll to win acceptance at the broad base of the market spelled the ingredient's downfall.

PERCENT OF CONSUMERS WHO REGARD CHLOROPHYLL AS HELPFUL

	College Educated	Grade School Educated
Winter, 1950	32%	11%
Summer, 1950	45%	9%
Winter, 1951	48%	15%
Summer, 1952	39%	19%
Winter, 1952	38%	25%
Summer, 1953	38%	22%

·{ 11 }··

Users Help Design The Product*

[Housewives were asked to help] design a new kitchen range for Borg-Warner Corp.'s Norge appliance division. It's an example of how more and more manufacturers are turning to the motivational type of market research (*BW* Aug.14'54,p50) to find out what the customers want and need, and why they will or won't buy.

When a manufacturer decides to market a new product—or redesign an old one—he can't just go out and ask the consumer what he would like in the way of design. Or anything else, for that matter—advertising, pricing, distribution. By and large, people either don't know what they want or why they want it.

The problem gets even tougher where product design is involved. Questions alone may not be enough, because it's hard to envision what the researcher has in mind. People may talk about design in terms of a Cadillac when all they can afford is a Chevvy. In other words, you often may have to show the potential customer the real thing.

Show the Product

That's what Borg-Warner did in setting up its cross-country clinics. By this method, the company got women to see, feel, and examine mockups of stoves so that B-W could intelligently design the kind of stove the women wanted at the price they would pay.

General Electric used somewhat the same strategy to line up opinion on designs of washing machines, driers, refrigerators, and other appliances—except that it put the machines in a trailer and took them to the housewife. And Philco and other manufacturers have used similar techniques.

Norge hired Nowland & Co., Inc., market researchers, back in 1950, to make the most comprehensive study to date on how customers wanted their kitchen ranges designed, and why. There was good reason for the study: Norge, at one time considered a leader in sales of both gas and electric ranges, had watched its competitive position melt to the danger point.

The results of the study are just beginning to show. And Norge is pretty happy with them. Sales of its redesigned 1955 models are climbing. Last November and December, volume was up more than 2½ times over the final two months of 1953.

Pilot Study

To probe the psyches of potential range buyers, Nowland's first step was to set up what it calls a pilot study—standard practice in most of the company's research programs. These pilot surveys are qualitative rather than quantitative—in other words, they are more concerned with finding out what people like or don't like, and why, than in how many will buy what item.

In the Norge case, Nowland discovered that housewives prefer electric to gas ranges by about 3 to 1. It also found that about 85% of the people it interviewed were dissatisfied with existing ranges for two reasons:

1. The traditional cluster arrangement of the surface unit burners was too crowded.

2. Ovens were too narrow and too deep. Where a range had two ovens, both were designed for baking with dry heat, and weren't adaptable to broiling and roasting.

Forums

Armed with this basic information, Nowland set up what is called "forums" in appliance and department stores in nine cities. There were special rooms where store customers were invited to come in and help design a new range. Over the eight-month survey period, more than 3,000 accepted.

Starting from the premise that you can't just ask people what they want and need, Nowland set out to show them. The forums used actual mockup models of ranges. The customer—in most cases a housewife—passed through five different rooms.

In the first, researchers asked her general questions about her income group, what type and size range she was accustomed to. Then she looked at models of five different gas and electric types—large and small, four-burner and two-burner, double-oven and single-oven; even one old-fashioned model with a high oven above the cooking surface on the right.

After the customer had picked the type that appealed to her most, she went into the second room, where she was confronted with mockup models of range tops only, with the burner units arranged in different combinations in various positions.

After she had indicated her preference here, she went into the third room, where she selected an oven arrangement in much the same way. The choices were between a high oven or a low one, or a single or a double.

In the fourth room, she made up her mind between any conflicting choices she had made, or took a compromise model. If, for example, she had picked a surface burner arrangement that was physically or practically impossible to build in a range that would have the size and type of oven she wanted, she then decided between the top and the interior—or a modified model.

In the fifth and last room, she selected additional features such as clocks, timers, thermometers, and made a final decision on price.

New Thoughts

The Nowland study turned up some new and significant design ideas:

1. The housewife, whether she realizes it or not, almost invariably uses each surface burner unit for a particular kind of cooking: left-rear for unattented cooking such as boiling, stewing, and simmering; left-front for things she has to stir; right-rear for hot beverages; and right-front for frying.

2. Most people consider the oven more important than the surface arrangement of the burners. On the large ranges, with two ovens, the housewife would rather have the second oven smaller, designed for broiling and roasting meats with moist heat, rather than have two baking ovens. On the small medium-size range with room for only one oven, she prefers to have it wider and more shallow for convenience in reaching. Also, she doesn't want the oven too high or too low, but likes a sloping beveled edge with a window, so she can see into it.

End Results

These findings led to several recommendations—some of which are being put into effect now, some of which are still being worked over in the lab.

In its 1955 line, Norge came out with the wide oven concept for both gas and electric models. On the electric ranges, it split the traditional surface top cluster of burner units, keeping two on the left, moving the other two clear over to the extreme right edge of the range top (its gas models were already arranged that way).

In this connection, some manufacturers are going even further. Philco Corp., which had Nowland research some of its ranges after the Norge study had been completed, has adopted a new split burner unit arrangement. It moved the right-front frying burner back from the front edge of the surface top, and placed the right-rear beverage unit over on the extreme right-rear of the top—giving an inverted L effect. Philco did this because research showed that people don't particularly care where their surface space is, since they use it more for storage than for actual work space.

Norge—and now other manufacturers—are working on double-oven ranges with the second oven a moist-heat broiler and roaster unit.

Philco's Problem

Philco had a slightly different problem than Norge. Philco didn't have a medium-size range (30 in. wide) on the market, and wanted to know whether people wanted such a model with the features of a more expensive range—and if so, whether they would pay for it. Nowland found the answer to both questions was Yes. So Philco put a large oven on its new medium-size range, and discovered that Nowland had called its market potential within 0.1% of actual sales figures.

Two Schools

While market researchers agree on the basic scientific methods of probing the consumer's mind, they differ on technical details. For example, another market research company, Crossley S-D Surveys, Inc. (*BW*—Oct.9'54,p119), believes in getting a picture of the total market via a quantitative nosecount before it starts to go into the qualitative motivations aspect.

Crossley currently is running a series of tests for GE appliances. In this study, Crossley uses what it considers a more flexible method: It carts its models around the country in a trailer, so that researchers can interview the housewife right outside her door. Crossley believes it can cover more ground this way, though Nowland holds that the forum is more thorough.

Another innovation of Crossley S-D's is the use of Stereo-Realist viewers (three-dimensional picture slides) to help the customer visualize the product being tested.

Nowland, too, has some new techniques. He has his interviewers wire or phone their findings back to the home office daily. This way, a line of questioning can be changed if any significant changes develop.

··{ 12 }··

S. C. Johnson Builds Hot Market for Coolants*

BY MURRAY CRAIN

S. C. Johnson & Son, Racine, Wis., has made Johnson's wax and other household products famous with many years of successful advertising and merchandising.

And now Johnson has moved into the industrial field. In approaching the great markets represented by industry demand, the company has fol-

* Reprinted by special permission from *Industrial Marketing*, December, 1956. Copyright, 1956, by Advertising Publications, Inc., 200 East Illinois Street, Chicago 11.

lowed the same policy of aggressive merchandising and advertising which proved so successful in the consumer field. While exact figures on industrial and institutional sales are not available, it is believed that these new markets and the business developed in them have added many millions of dollars to the company's volume and a substantial sum to its net profits.

Thus far Johnson's industrial division is promoting business in three directions: coolants for metal-working, finishing products for furniture manufacturers and protective wrappings for citrus and vegetable growers.

All of this does not take account of business in the institutional field, where floor wax and other maintenance items have been repackaged and promoted for use by schools, hospitals, hotels and other large institutional users. Here too, the methods which have succeeded in selling to the general public have been used effectively, with distributors backed by vigorous merchandising and advertising addressed to their customers, the institutional buyers.

How It's Done

A good example of how Johnson has successfully invaded one of the most difficult and important industrial markets is its development of coolants for use in metalworking. The product, the result of intensive study by Johnson's industrial research department, was tested successfully before being introduced to industry. Thus, the company had a record of successful use before it tried to pioneer a brand new type of product for machine operators.

The men who buy steel in one of its common forms and convert it into useful products have been plagued with the heat problem from the beginning of the industry. Coolants were developed to assist them in fighting this costly phenomenon, oil being the basic ingredient until recently. With the advent of automation and higher machine speeds, generation of temperatures of 500 degrees became commonplace and the life of costly tools shrank.

Johnson stepped into this picture with wax coolants and some claims that seemed extravagant in the light of past experience—claims that were, however, backed by that well-tested consumer technique, the money back guarantee. Because a reduction in heat of only 50 degrees multiplies the life of a tool five times, it was not difficult to induce metalworkers to give the new product a trial. This despite the fact that the wax coolant costs more. The higher initial cost of wax, claims Johnson, is offset by increased production and reduced scrap.

Supports Distributors

Johnson's industrial wax is sold exclusively through 124 distributors and the company's field men are cautioned not to call on plants unless they are accompanied by a distributor salesman. This policy not only pleases the distributor, but it gives his men the opportunity to see how technical problems are met by experts in wax cooling.

A key man in the Johnson sales set-up is the salesman in each distributor organization selected for special training. This sales man is frequently called on for help by his colleagues in solving tough technical problems.

The company's primary educational effort, therefore, is the factory training school, where salesmen who have shown special interest in wax coolants may broaden their knowledge of the product and its applications. The usual school term is three days—Tuesday through Thursday—giving salesman travel time without interruption of week ends. Expenses for travel and lodging are borne by the distributor. Meals and texts are provided by the company. One course is devoted to lubricants, one to cutting tools and a third to abrasives.

Six-Point Promise

Johnson acknowledges its responsibilities to distributors with this six-point promise:

1. To train your sales people as effective and articulate representatives for Johnson's wax lubricants.
2. To provide special assistance on complicated technical problems.
3. To provide a factory training school for your wax lubricants specialists and key salesmen.
4. To assist in your sales promotion activities.
5. To provide competitive prices, adequate packaging and uniform quality.
6. To sell through you, rather than merely to you.

In return, Johnson requires distributors to keep up adequate stocks and maintain suggested resale prices.

Ads Get Credit

Cutting oils are sold direct to metalworking plants. And, since Johnson previously had no direct contact with these users of its coolants, it is fair to give advertising the lion's share of the credit for the company's success in the industrial field.

Johnson began its campaign with modest pages in monotone. A second color was added later. The stepped-up tempo proved so effective that inserts were tested, frequently in four colors, with gratifying results.

Because wax coolants are more costly than cutting oils, Johnson's greatest success has been in large plants where coolant reclamation systems are in use. These big plants represent the major segment of the market. However, the company has secured enough business from small plants to indicate that their skepticism has waned appreciably.

Johnson's advertising schedule includes *American Machinist, Automatic Machining, Grinding & Finishing, Machine & Tool Blue Book, Metalworking, Mill & Factory, Modern Machine Shop and Production.* Needham, Louis & Brorby, Chicago, handles the account.

·{ 13 }··

How Special Products Built Volume Business*

BY PHIL SEITZ

If you can't sell shovels, then sell left-handed shovels.

That may not make sense (and may be entirely fallacious so far as the shovel industry is concerned), but the theory—somewhat over-simplified—worked for Reuland Electric Co., Alhambra, Cal.

Reuland makes and sells electric motors. But it didn't sell very many of them so long as it concentrated on its line of standard motors. Reason: the giant electric equipment makers had the market pretty well sewed up. No place for a new company like Reuland.

But Reuland has made the grade despite this discouraging situation. It has succeeded by first specializing in producing special electric motors and than expanding the toehold thus gained into sales of its standard motors.

The company got into the manufacture of electric motors during World War II. When the war ended, the two owners, Frank and Howard Reuland, decided to market standard electric motors instead of returning to their prewar repair and service organization for electric motors.

Sub-Standard Sales

To start, they made one standard design motor. Finding it difficult to sell against established competition, gradually more standard motor units were added in an effort to get the mass production volume possible in this field. The broadening of the line of standard motors did little to help in cracking the market.

It actually took four years of experimentation to learn that specialization was the key to getting established. This principle was established in 1950, and since that time sales have increased by at least 25% each year over the previous year. The company now occupies 40,000 square feet of plant for the manufacture of motors.

Through the 1946–48 period, sales efforts were backed with publication advertising featuring a straight product line of electric motors. Sales

---

*Reprinted by special permission from *Industrial Marketing*, September, 1956. Copyright, 1956, by Advertising Publications, Inc., 200 East Illinois Street, Chicago 11.

results were not outstanding. Plugging hard for sales, Reuland began to take on special and difficult motor jobs, where standard motors could not be used. They found they could get sound prices, and competition was much less keen.

The first inkling of the way to get solidly established in the field came with the development of a fluid-shaft motor, the first such motor to have an integral fluid drive. The new motor was "special" in the sense that it was superior to the jerry-build set-ups formerly used where fluid couplings were required.

Taste of Success

The new motor was introduced through publicity, several small ads and the distribution of literature.

Contrary to the company's experience when advertising standard motors, the promotion of the new motor, for the first time, brought evidence of results. Advertising was continued, and for the next two years, through 1950, ads featured either the fluid-shaft motor or other special motors. Although a relatively small schedule was used in just a few publications, results were tangible.

From this experience, Reuland concluded that, initially at least, a new company without national distribution couldn't hope to compete with established companies on their own ground—mass-produced standard motors—but they could compete in the field of special motors.

They did, however, begin to get business on standard motors from customers who had only been sold special jobs.

Analyzing these results it was decided the company's most effective approach was to go after business as specialists first, then to expand into sales of standard design units.

Help from Competition

Such an approach is practical because while the major volume of purchases by O.E.M.'s (original equipment manufacturers) is of standard units, just about every manufacturer has need for special motors for special purposes.

Reuland actually was helped during this period by the conventional selling done by the established companies. These companies pitched hard for the volume orders on standard units, and tried to avoid the special jobs and attendant problems. Another factor was that being geared to special jobs, Reuland could promise and deliver motors in less time than competition.

With these experiences in mind, Reuland adopted the principle of specialization as a basic policy. Both sales presentations and advertising were slanted in this direction.

Advertising and literature hit hard on the same theme: special motors for special jobs.

Reuland sales representatives began asking customers: "What are your problems?" They never pass up a potential motor sale no matter how impossible the job may look. Such "impossible" jobs are passed on to the home office for decision as to whether or not they can be handled.

Advertising's Job

Having proved it could get results when it has an idea to sell, advertising was placed on a firm and continuing schedule. The principal job assigned advertising was to establish the Reuland name among O.E.M.'s and distribution people as a specialist in the design of unique types of electric motors.

The advertising has established the company name and given salesmen valuable extra selling time. They no longer need to dilute their selling time to explain "who" Reuland is, or establish the ability of the company to perform.

Establishing the company name in the distribution trade has made a vital contribution to expansion of distribution. When Reuland set out for national distribution in 1949 it had the usual difficulty in getting desirable manufacturers' representatives. Today, the company name is known and accepted and this is no longer a problem.

Since 1949 the company has established an eastern factory at Howell, Mich., and sales offices in Oakland and Chicago. The company now has either its own salesmen or manufacturers' representatives in all principal cities.

Two New Ideas

The advertising program set up in 1951–52 has been relatively unchanged. Emphasis continues on special motors. However, two very successful promotional ideas have been developed which serve to dramatize the Reuland sales approach.

The first, "Xpandable Design," is used to spotlight the fact that various Reuland standard assemblies can be joined together in a number of different ways to produce special drive characteristics. That is, its basic motor units are designed to combinations of drive equipment—motors, brakes, fluid couplings, gear reducers, etc.—can be assembled in a single frame. This is called a power package. The phrase "Xpandable Design" has served to dramatize successfully what is considered an existing product advantage.

The results obtained through the "Xpandable" theme than developed into another idea, a "Special Motor Library." This points up the fact the company has a card file of blueprints, dies and molds, and other pertinent data on more than 3,500 special motor combinations it has produced.

The file is promoted as the Special Motor Library and ad copy points out that if a manufacturer needs a special kind of motor, it will pay him to check with Reuland first, rather than starting from scratch with another motor manufacturer. This promotion is very effective in stimulating sales because when the library turns up a motor suitable for the manufacturer's needs he saves money and gets delivery much more quickly.

Almost all of the company's advertising is in publications reaching O.E.M.'s. Currently regular schedules are running in *Electrical Manufacturing, Industrial Equipment News, Machine Design, Modern Materials Handling, New Equipment Digest, Product Engineering* and *Product Design & Development.*

No Ad Department

A modest supplementary schedule in *Business Week* during the last four years has also occasioned traceable interest from people on the management level.

Reuland does not have an advertising department, only its agency— Van der Boom, Hunt, McNaughton, Los Angeles. Gorden Van der Boom has been account executive since the ad program's start.

In practice, ad plans are approved by an informal committee of Frank and Howard Reuland; A. G. Fournier, general sales manager, headquartered at Howell, Mich.; Wayne Johnson, western sales manager in the home office, and Mr. Van der Boom, representing the advertising agency.

Originally, the company's ability to fill special motor requirements created a complete new market for its products. Over-all, however, the integration of sales with advertising themes—resulting from the combined supervision of management and sales—is considered the basic factor in Reuland's successful use of specialization to achieve its good position in the highly competitive motor manufacturing industry.

Part Four . . .

CHANNELS OF DISTRIBUTION
RETAILING
WHOLESALING

Chicago's Red Hot Merchandiser*

BY DANIEL SELIGMAN

"It should be unlawful for women to work in the home when they can have mechanical appliances! It is definitely unfair to our future generations to take a woman today and have her, when she finishes her washing, go into the back yard in the mud and hang up clothes. It is wrong because it weakens her body! It tires her! It doesn't give her the necessary time that she must spend with her children!"

The voice belongs to Sol Polk, proprietor of nine Chicago appliance stores. And what he says should command attention these days, for he has recently emerged out of nowhere to become the country's biggest dealer in nationally advertised appliances.

This is a little hard to believe at first acquaintance with Polk. He doesn't look like a titan of the market place. He looks more like Bob Hope. He is a comparatively young man, just turned thirty-eight, which is a statistic confusing to Chicagoans, who have recently been blanketed by advertising about his twentieth year in business. (Sol went into business when he was seventeen.) Visitors also may be confounded by the informal, not to say chaotic, atmosphere of Sol's office. Distributors, salesmen, bookkeepers, kibitzers, pile into it steadily. They come to see Sol, but often remain to talk to each other while he merchandises over the telephone, pouring milk from a container, doodling on a large artist's drafting pad. Virtually no daylight penetrates to this room, which is cluttered with Sol's huge conference desk, a record player, a projection machine, and half a dozen bright red Fiberglas chairs, which frequently are not enough to seat all of Sol's visitors; as many as ten people may be standing around. A television set receives commercial broadcasts; another TV set, operating on a closed circuit, enables Sol to inspect the traffic in his main appliance store downstairs. On the walls are a framed three-by-four-foot blowup of a testimonial to Sol that was once read into the *Congressional Record* by Republican Representative Richard Hoffman, of Illinois; a scroll memorializing Sol's recent membership in the Young Presidents'

---

* Reprinted by special permission from the September, 1955, issue of *Fortune* Magazine. Copyright, 1955, by Time Inc.

Organization; a chart that shows sales steadily mounting from 1955 to 1963.

This year, though Sol would never admit it, his business is reasonably certain to exceed last year's $40 million. With the opening last year of a vast new Polk store in Southeast Chicago (estimated volume: $10 million), Polk entrenched himself as the country's foremost dealer in G.E., Westinghouse, Norge, Hotpoint, Maytag, and Whirlpool white goods, and in virtually every major line of television sets. He carries nothing but nationally advertised products. In the Chicago area, to which his operations are thus far limited, he sells more appliances than all the State Street stores combined, and maybe even more than Sears, which for decades was the unchallenged leader in the field.

Some of Polk's competitors, contemplating his price cutting and his readiness to bargain with customers on price, regard him simply as a discounter run wild. Polk indignantly disclaims the term "discount house"; he sees his stores as "merchandising supermarkets." Since the terminological footing in this area is notoriously treacherous, it may be well to discard labels and relate just how Polk works.

The Nervous Stomach

His firm is called Polk Bros. Central Appliance & Furniture Co., but Sol is the heart and brains of it, as well as its nervous stomach. Sol is the founder, president, chairman, and chief shareholder, with 30 per cent of the capital stock. The rest of the stock is divided among his older sister, three older brothers, and the estate of a fourth brother, Dave Polk, who died recently. Brother Sam is secretary-treasurer; Morrie is vice president and general manager of the Southeast store; Harry is assistant treasurer; and Goldie Bachmann Luftig, the sister, is assistant secretary.

Goldie and the three older brothers, who are in their forties and fifties, are amiable, easygoing people, with large families. Sol is single, jet-propelled, and totally preoccupied with merchandising. He seems to sense, at times, that other people think about dogs, children, baseball, and politics, and he may affect a polite interest in these. His tolerance for such talk, however, is no more than three or four minutes. "What would you say," he will briskly break in, "if I told you we could sell a twenty-one-inch television set with a contour rocking chair for $119.50 and make a profit?"

It is not exact to say that Sol tries to do everything. The furniture business, which he professes not to understand, he leaves to sister Goldie. The purchasing he leaves to thirty-one-year-old Lester Bachmann, his executive vice president and a distant relative. Since inventories at Polk's now run well over $2,500,000 (and are turned over about fifteen times a year), Sol's willingness to let Bachmann handle most of the purchasing job denotes a lot of confidence in him. Sol also occasionally accepts the counsel of two young public-relations men in his employ. Gerry Fitzgerald and Jim Cooke. But this counsel is limited to questions of taste and propriety;

so far as promotional ideas are concerned, Sol needs help the way Winston Churchill needs a ghost writer.

And the fact is there is no part of the Polk Bros. operation that Sol does not personally perform from time to time. Occasionally he picks out old customers from the 250,000 names the store has on file (each name represents a purchase of $100 or more) and personally phones them to ask, apropos of nothing at all, what they think of the service. Virtually all letters of complaint cross Sol's desk. Customers whom he recalls only hazily are allowed to barge into his office and ask, on the basis of old friendship, for an extra-special deal.

But what Sol preeminently contributes to Polk Bros. is an evangelical fervor. His conversations with friends and associates consist in large measure of impassioned monologues on the wonders of life with appliances.

Friend of the Family

"When we were kids, we didn't have much," Sol tells people. "Now that we're in a position to give good values, good laborsaving appliances that ease the burden of life, we feel we should do everything we can." That Polk Bros.' principal mission is the enrichment of its customers' lives is a recurrent theme in Sol's talk. "Basically, we like people. Basically, we want friends. And we think shopping should be a family affair. Example! I don't like it when a man comes in alone to buy his wife a refrigerator. They're going to have it for ten or fifteen years. The thrill of selection should be a family affair. We like children. Shopping together brings the family together."

He regards the "warehouse sales" (i.e., selling to retail customers right off warehouse floors, rented auditoriums, etc.) recently instituted by Field's, Carson's, and several other State Street stores with scorn and revulsion. "What's the effect?" he demands rhetorically. "The effect is that the little girl will remember that 'the big beautiful bedroom set that my wonderful daddy bought for me came from a warehouse.' Warehouses are a passing parade!"

Until last year Sol had no real home outside his office; he slept at a hotel or on a cot in a room adjoining his office. He still sleeps at the office occasionally, but he now has a three-room apartment on the North Side, which he usually occupies during non-working hours. Roughly, these are between 1:00 A.M. and 7:00 A.M. During most other hours, seven days a week, he is apt to be at the office or on the telephone in his apartment.

The most likely variant of this routine is a business convention; Sol finds these intensely stimulating, and when he is attending them he may stay on his feet twenty hours a day. On his last stay at Miami Beach he got the inspiration to call a friend at C.B.S. in New York and propose that the company furnish the lobbies of the big resort hotels, gratis, with color TV sets, which still had not been seen by many visiting New Yorkers and Chicagoans. When C.B.S. had bought the idea, Polk steamed around to several dozen hotels in Miami Beach and sold them on installing the sets. This whirlwind campaign was ultimately futile because of transmission difficulties between New York and Florida. But at least it kept Sol off the beach.

His visits to New York tend also to be strictly business. A friend who once went along on such a visit describes it as follows: "All day old Sol was zipping around to the manufacturers' offices or talking shop with the dealers. Then he got upset when it came to be six o'clock, and he found that everyone was closing his office. He can't understand why people go home so early. We ended up walking all over the streets of New York till three in the morning, window-shopping damn near every appliance outlet in town."

Sol's "Secrets"

What U.S. business still has to learn, Polk thinks, is how to sell. The State Street stores now meet Polk's prices pretty consistently, and a number of discounters in town will beat his prices from time to time. But Polk's prices are geared to some special selling techniques. The first price a Polk customer encounters is on a tag bearing the list, or "manufacturer's suggested," price. The only products for which this tag means business are those of companies with rigorous fair-trading rules. On other merchandise the Polk customer ignores the list (or the salesman tells him to), and inquires what the price is. Suppose he is interested in a refrigerator listing at $420. Polk's price on this model is, let us say, $310; but before disclosing this fact the salesman will ascertain whether the customer has an old refrigerator he wishes to trade in. If he has none, the salesman will simply quote the $310 price. If the customer has an old, near-worthless box that he wants to get rid of, the salesman will quote an allowance of $110, which again brings the price to $310. If the prospect's refrigerator is really salable for $40 or $50, a further allowance will be made. That may not be the end either. A customer who continues to register deep doubts, or who starts to walk out, will probably find that Polk's can be reasoned with. The salesman himself may invent some reason why a slightly larger trade-in is feasible; or, more likely, he will flag one of the store's T.O.'s (take-over men), who will try to close the sale with a final concession— perhaps a few more dollars or a great big teddy bear for the kid. About one-third of Polk's sales are on installment.

This technique was not devised to circumvent fair trade. Sol Polk believes that it is good for the customer's morale to feel that he is being paid something for his old refrigerator. At the very least, Polk Bros. is helping him get the dirty thing out of his kitchen. In any event, the company gets enough secondhand appliances on an average weekday to fill two trailer trucks. About 60 to 70 per cent are sold to exporters or to dealers out of town. ("We don't like to slop up Chicago with used merchandise," Sol Polk explains.) About 10 per cent are given, free, to vocational schools or prison workshops. The rest are junked.

Sol Polk is eager to dilate upon his methods for almost anyone he meets. He is even eager to lecture other dealers—several of whom have visited Sol to study his operation. A number of manufacturers and distributors have also sent promising young executives to Polk Bros. for training. (Ten from Westinghouse were there in July.) Sol takes great pride in his tutorial role, and works as hard on these trainees as on his own salesmen.

Despite Sol's eagerness to communicate his story, there is still considerable confusion in Chicago about the "secret" of Polk Bros.' success. This is partly because Sol's homilies ordinarily do not include any data from his books; the corporation is closely held, and Sol is cagey about the figures. As a consequence, a number of rumors about Polk Bros. have been floating around Chicago.

One canard is that inventories are largely on consignment. In fact, they have always been purchased outright. Another interesting misconception is the widespread belief that Polk Bros. is still operating in the $20-million league. FORTUNE's estimate of $40 million sales is unofficial but known to be near the mark. (The same may be said of the other financial data in this report.) There is also great confusion about Polk's gross margin. One manufacturer, a major supplier who has known Polk intimately for years, recently guessed it to be 25 per cent. In fact, it usually runs around 18 per cent—which is considerably higher than the margin a stripped-down discount house works on (about 10 per cent), though it is well below the department-store level (30 per cent and up). Polk's operating costs are currently running around $6,500,000, which is 16 per cent of sales. Sixteen per cent from 18 per cent gross leaves him 2 per cent profit before taxes.

This 2 per cent, or $800,000, is supplemented by a tidy $200,000 net from a subsidiary installment-buying business, the Appliance Credit Corp. The total, then, is about $1 million before taxes, and about half that after taxes. Five hundred thousand dollars on $40 million sales is 1.25 cents on the dollar—roughly what a supermarket chain might expect to earn (see "Grand Union's Super-Supermarkets," *Fortune*, June, 1955). Polk plays it very close indeed.

Polk Bros. performs seven days and six nights a week, a total of eighty-five hours, at three locations in Chicago. The oldest, and now the least important, of the stores is in Southwest Chicago, where a huge neon sign announces: "Central Appliance and Furniture," which is what Polk's was called until 1952. Volume at this Southwest store is only about $2,500,000.

Compliments of Polk

It is the $10-million-a-year store in Southeast Chicago, the newest Polk outlet, that represents Sol Polk's idea of what a retail store should be. Its parking lot holds 4,000 cars. The main selling area is roughly the shape and size of a football field (50,000 square feet). On the floor for all to see are as many as 125 refrigerators, 75 freezers, 150 washers, dryers, and combinations, 85 air conditioners, 300 television sets. TV sets, washers, and dryers are connected and operable. Prospective customers may even plunk their own laundry into Polk's washers and dryers to test them.

Another feature of the Southeast store is a $25,000 bowling alley running the length of the huge front window. The alley is covered over during shopping hours. On Sunday nights Polk Bros. sets up a grandstand seating 300 bowling fans inside the store, runs off matches for midwest city championships, and sponsors a televised show of the events.

But the Polk carnival atmosphere is seen at its brightest in Northwest Chicago, in an agglomerate of seven stores stretching over most of two blocks, called Polk City. Here Sol's offices are situated. On an average weekday about 7,750 people pass through Polk City; on an average Sunday about 9,500. In the summer of 1953, Sol installed a portable ice rink at Polk City and persuaded the Ice Capades to stage a Sunday-night rehearsal for their Chicago opening. That Sunday, 21,000 people trooped through the Northwest stores. For the rest of the summer Sol offered free evening ice skating on the rink. To celebrate his firm's twentieth anniversary, Sol bought out the Chicago Stadium (some 15,000 seats) for an Ice Capades performance that was telecast as part of the Ed Sullivan show, and gave away tickets to his customers. Lincoln-Mercury, which sponsors Sullivan, got only a few tickets for its exasperated dealers, but for Polk Bros. the production was an enormous success.

At Polk City the children are commonly met at the doors by clowns bearing lollipops, balloons, Good Humors. A recent attraction was a band of genuine Sioux Indians. Inside the store, any prospective customer can have a Coke on the house. A Polk promotion also offers customers five, ten, or twenty-five cases of the new king-size Coke with purchases of varying magnitude. Polk figured that no one would want twenty-five cases of Coke on hand at one time; he lets the customers pick up the cases in several trips, over a period of months—which brings them back into the store.

Polk's has also given away toy trucks, copies of the book, *This I Believe*, and Smokey Bear dolls, 20,000 of which went to kids who duly registered themselves as junior forest rangers. During several recent Christmas seasons Polk's gave away Christmas trees with every purchase of $5 or more—and Sol himself, with some of his executives, stood at the doors to inquire of every departing customer whether his tree was big enough. If it wasn't, he got a bigger one; sometimes he got a bigger one anyway. Cowboys, Davy Crocketts, ladies in bathing suits, etc., are always wandering about on promotional missions. Sol wants people to have fun at his stores.

To make sure that no one ever forgets him, Sol spends something like $1,500,000 a year for newspaper, radio, billboard, direct-mail, and

TV advertising; he is the biggest TV advertiser in Chicago. The advertising is virtually all cooperative, with half the outlay, if not more, recovered from distributors and manufacturers.

Polk's services to his customers are as good as those offered by most department stores: deliveries are free and prompt; customers can get almost any major appliance the day after they buy it; anything can be returned.

They Come to Work in Cadillacs

One of Polk's most startling departures from orthodox discount-house procedure is in the caliber of his salesmen. They number 478. Some of the newest were recruited from colleges; Polk now has a man working full time at such recruiting. Before his salesmen go out on the floor, they are subjected to a stiff two-week training program, the major part of which is conducted by factory representatives who drill them on the products. Polk's salesmen know their lines inside out, and know how to sell them.

Their base pay is $55 a week. Layered upon this modest sum is a 1 per cent commission on sales, and on top of that there is a "spiff"— bonus for moving merchandise that the house especially wants to move. For the Polk sales force the formula is good for an average income of $8,700 a year. Some salesmen are hitting $15,000. In the parking lot for salesmen there usually are eight or nine Cadillacs.

In recent years the selling job done by the floor men has been supplemented by twenty-five outside men. These "captains," as they are called, range over wide areas of Chicago, looking up prospects. Any moderately prosperous home that has a clothesline in the yard is reasonably certain to be visited and lectured on the wonders of electric dryers.

While his promotion and selling techniques propel his volume upward, Sol has pushed his operating costs down. His warehousing operation and his bookkeeping are thoroughly mechanized. A single machine bookkeeping entry cost Polk's .035609 cents in 1953; last year the cost was down to .031135 cents. It is sure to drop further.

Sales Executive, Age Eight

Sol Polk's compulsion to sell is regarded with stupefaction even by his brothers and sister. They recall that at eight, while living on the West Side of Chicago, he had five other boys peddling magazines for him. The historic dawning of Sol's interest in appliances is described by Sol as follows: "I was very interested in growth. When I went to Manley High School we had the project of laying out a store, and the store I picked was in the appliance field." When Sol graduated, he got a selling job with Commonwealth Edison, and peddled irons, vacuum cleaners, and lamps from door to door. In less than a year his commissions, plus savings from his boyhood magazine business, added up to $1,000.

With this and another $1,000 supplied by a partner (who soon sold out), Sol rented a store on the North Side in 1935, and built up a small appliance inventory. He was then eighteen. Nights he put as much stuff as he could handle into a car and rang doorbells. This persistent selling enabled him to replenish his inventories without calling on the banks. His own "salary" from this business was $15 a week.[1]

Brother Sam joined Sol in 1937, and by 1940 the whole family was in with him full time. Sol's ability to get on with his older brothers and sister is a tribute to the closeness of the Polks. Sol was, after all, only twenty-two at the time. Sam had been manager of a Postal Telegraph office; Morrie had been a refrigeration-service man; Harry had worked for the Post Office; Dave had worked in a minor capacity with an investment firm; Goldie had been a housewife.

During World War II, Sol, Sam, and Harry were off in the Army. Sol was an Army sergeant serving in the European theatre. The rest kept Polk Bros. treading water.

In 1946 Sol returned from service, and converted the company into the soaring enterprise it has been in recent years. His first move was into Polk City, erected on lots that he had bought before the war. He was so eager to get started that he acted as his own contractor on the building job. The result had its ludicrous side: the building that went up in the center of Polk City didn't have any downspouts. These were later installed *inside* the store, where they are still visible, a perpetual monument to Sol's passion to get on with life's main business.

How to Zoom

What are Sol's plans for the future? Whether they will involve stores in other cities, a mail-order business, a branching out into soft goods is not yet clear to Sol Polk. His *rate* of expansion will certainly have to slow down. In 1946 the company did about $1 million gross; in 1950 it did about $12 million; in 1952 it did about $30 million; and this year the total could go as high as $45 million. Polk Bros.' net worth, which was $1,500,000 only three years ago, is today slightly under $3 million (not including the company's installment subsidiary and a realty holding company, worth together around $1 million). These whopping increases have been accomplished without borrowing a nickel from the banks. In the next few years Sol Polk does expect to put up one or more stock issues for sale; but he is hopeful that, as in the past, much of his expansion can still be financed from earnings.

Since Sol is still a young man, and still devising new gimmicks, he may

---

[1] Today he pays himself $15,000—a figure that one of his top salesmen may match. It is not known how much Sol takes out of his business, other than his salary. His 30 per cent stock interest would be about $150,000 in "dividends," but earnings have been plowed back. Obviously Sol Polk doesn't have very much time to spend whatever money he makes.

even end up in some variety of retailing now completely unknown to the trade. One idea began cooking as Sol thought about the way retail stores are pushing into the suburbs. Suburban stores are definitely limited in their operations, he believes, particularly in the appliance business; no one of them can ever grow large enough to carry the huge inventories to which customers (Polk's customers, anyway) have grown accustomed. The problem is to bring the suburban customer into a store at which he can inspect a wide variety of goods, without forcing him to travel great distances. A solution, Polk is thinking, might be a large number of suburban crypto-stores, operating without any inventories, but serviced by closed-circuit television.

The customer would come in and be led to a television screen. It would be more than thirty inches in breadth, utilizing color and 3-D. Zoomar lenses would propel the customer to a dramatic showing of any appliance he wanted to inspect. This would be located at a central supply depot. A two-way audio system would allow him to question a salesman at the other end, who could also whip around to other models upon request. The sale would finally be closed by an order-taker at the customer's side. Sol has had some encouragement from television engineers to whom he has communicated this exciting vision.

Speedboat King

If the future of Polk Bros. is uncertain, the future of Sol is about as predictable as the affairs of mortals can be: Sol will be in there moving merchandise. "Until the day God says 'Turn off the switch,' I'll want to be associated with new products," is the somewhat orotund way he puts it. Will Sol, after he has made a few more million, leaven his life with some other interests outside his stores? His associates are unanimous in thinking he will not, although Sol professes some fugitive thoughts along that line. Recently, he mentioned to an acquaintance that he had a new hobby.

"You have a *hobby?* What's that?"

"Well, I've been going in for speedboating."

"No kidding! What kind of boat do you own?"

"I don't exactly have a boat myself, but I have friends I go out with."

"Have you been out this year?"

"Well, to tell the truth I haven't had much time." And Sol added with a happy gleam in his eye: "You know, we've been pretty busy at the store."

··{ 15 }··

Auto Dealer Franchises in Peril*

During the past few weeks, William F. Hufstader, General Motors vice-president (distribution), has been barnstorming state capitols by Cadillac in defense of the auto industry's cherished system of franchise agreements with some 40,000 new-car dealers. It's a sign of the industry's mounting concern that he was assigned to the task.

The worries aren't for nothing. Last week, Arkansas' General Assembly passed a stringent law regulating the franchise system—despite testimony from Hufstader and representatives of Ford and Chrysler. Similar proposals keep popping up in other statehouses, even though last year saw the development of a new amiability between dealers and the factories.

Changes Made

That new mood, heralded at January's annual meeting of the National Automobile Dealers Assn., was a real improvement over the time, little more than a year earlier, when Hufstader had stated flatly to a U.S. Senate Antitrust Subcommittee: "The manufacturer must be in a position, based on his judgment and his judgment alone, to retain a franchise, to grant it, or to withdraw it." Thereafter, the dealers won from Congress legislation giving them a day in court against manufacturers who fail to act in good faith.

Then, at the NADA meeting in San Francisco (*BW*—Feb.2'57,p25), GM Pres. Harlow H. Curtice hailed a "new era in factory-dealer relations throughout the industry." But Curtice cautioned: "In point of fact, the relationship can be distorted to a degree that it no longer serves a useful purpose. Or it can be destroyed completely."

LETTER OF THE LAW

With laws affecting the system already on the books of 18 states, the manufacturers are rallying to prevent its destruction. Most of the existing legislation can be lumped into three broad categories:

1. Licensing laws, most of which require manufacturers to obtain a license to do business in a state.

---

2. Anti-coercion statutes.
3. Stiff regulatory measures, controlling the business from franchise agreement through to final retail sale.

In most cases, the statutes prohibit forcing a dealer to take delivery of vehicles, parts, or other commodities he didn't order, or attempting to do so; threatening a cancellation of the franchise to force an agreement or unfair act, or canceling an agreement without due regard to the dealer's equities or without just provocation.

Company View

"We can live with the anti-coercion and licensing laws," says an official of one of the Big Three. "But the full regulation and control proposals jeopardize the very franchise system."

And counsel for one of the major producers says: "The basic legal concept of the laws is a restriction of competition. Many of them would convert the franchise system from a contract to an 'in status' basis and place control of the industry in the hands of the dealers."

Arkansas Story

The bill just passed in Arkansas sets up a State Motor Vehicle Commission with six dealer members to pass on applicants for dealerships and decide their location. Besides forbidding coercive tactics and "unfair" cancellations of franchises, the measure declares it unlawful to refuse delivery of any vehicle within 60 days after receipt of the dealer's order. And if a manufacturer willfully doesn't comply with the act, or with the commission's rules and regulations, his license can be denied, revoked, or suspended.

Similar legislation was approved by the Arkansas General Assembly in 1955, but the State Supreme Court declared it unconstitutional.

Tests to Come

The crucial states now are Iowa, Nebraska, and Colorado. The first two, both with laws already in force, are considering amendments to beef them up. In Colorado, GM is leading an assault with the industry's heaviest guns on a proposal termed by Hufstader "completely without precedent in the history of this country." Besides stiff clauses on coercion and on cancellation and non-renewal of franchises, the Colorado bill would:

1. Designate the State Director of Revenue (appointed politically) to name a five-man dealer advisory board, issue licenses, and oversee the business in general.
2. Define the relationship between manufacturers and dealers as a fiduciary one.
3. Provide cause for a dealer to file suit for treble damages if a manufacturer violates the rules applying to termination and non-renewal of a franchise.

The manufacturers are particularly exercised over the provision declaring that their relationship with dealers is fiduciary. R. C. Somerville, assistant to the vice-president (dealer relations) of Chrysler Corp., told the Colorado House Judiciary Committee: "We assume this would mean that the manufacturer would be, in effect, a trustee for dealers. In such circumstances, the manufacturer would have to subordinate the interests of the buying public, its stockholders, and everyone else in the automobile industry to the dealers."

The Big Three agree that the bill would probably spell the end of the franchise system in Colorado because, as one executive put it: "We would have to sell our cars to everybody and his brother."

Why the Fuss?

It's hard to specify the reasons behind this legislation. James Moore, general counsel for NADA, thinks it's a feeling at the state level that the federal statute doesn't do enough for the dealers. The Arkansas Automobile Dealers Assn. and other advocates of that state's new law cited the forcing of unwanted cars, parts, advertising, and accessories on dealers by the manufacturers. In Colorado, one dealer in favor of the bill defined it as "a continued attempt to get some equality into the damned unequal situation."

Last week, the board of directors of the Colorado Automobile Dealers Assn. joined the Big Three in opposing the measure—although many members had previously favored it as individuals. This action substantially dims its chances for passage. When one Colorado dealer learned details of the bill, he telephoned Detroit to say: "If I'm going to be told when to go to bed and when to get up, I'd rather be told by the company than by a so-called advisory board of dealers."

IN THE MIDDLE

The position of the auto dealer is almost unique in retailing. In testimony before the Arkansas Senate Judiciary Committee, Hufstader contrasted it with two extremes—the independent merchant on the one hand and the agent on the other.

The merchant buys clothing, furniture, groceries, and the like from a wholesaler for resale. He's independent, both practically and legally, from the manufacturer, who's nothing more than a source—and frequently one of many interchangeable sources. A retail agency, on the other hand, is managed by a direct representative of the manufacturer, of which it may be either a branch or a subsidiary.

In Between

As for the auto dealer, Hufstader said: "Legally, he is not the agent of the manufacturer. Yet in his community he is looked upon as the manufacturer's 'representative.' The good will and degree of business success he is able to earn in his community depend importantly upon the quality and value of the product that the manufacturer has provided him. Conversely, the good will and success the manufacturer enjoys in all markets, throughout the country, are determined in substantial degree by how well his 'representatives'—the dealers—perform their functions."

In the franchise agreement, says Hufstader, the dealer is obligated to buy only when he places an order, "although a commitment to purchase is undoubtedly implicit in the agreement." And the manufacturer has no obligation to sell until he accepts an order—again, however, with an implicit commitment to do so.

Chaos Ahead?

This system is the envy of many another industry. And the auto makers want to keep it that way. Says one top executive: "Bills like that proposed in Colorado would only lead us to the type of situation now prevailing in the appliance industry—chaos."

This obviously refers to repeated statements from men such as Hufstader that Colorado-type legislation would force the auto makers to sell cars directly to all comers. This would lead to the auto supermarket foreseen by so many observers. A forerunner may be the non-franchised dealerships in the Southwest and West, even now selling cars of competing makes. These operations got started when freight differentials between various regions were high and factories were pumping out cars regardless of dealers' wishes.

Now, though, the situation is different. Freight charges have been distributed more equitably, and auto production is more carefully geared to orders received from the dealers. But if state laws make it legally dangerous for the manufacturers to issue exclusive franchises, the auto supermarket may spread.

·{ 16 }··

Korvette (The Discounter) Goes Elegantly Suburban*

By 1958, American manufacturers may be selling an additional $100 million worth of merchandise (and by 1959 $150 million more) to E. J. Korvette, Inc.

* Reprinted by special permission from *Sales Management*, November 2, 1956. Copyright, 1956, *Sales Management*.

And if the hopes of 36-year-old Eugene Ferkauf and his youthful associates materialize, Mr. & Mrs. Consumer will pay Korvette some $118 million for that merchandise. That's an average markup of only 18%—which contrasts with the 40% conventional department store markup, with which Korvette competes.

Korvette, as millions of consumers in the greater New York City area have been made aware in the past eight years, is a discount house. Ferkauf does not object to the description discount house, which Korvette plainly was when it opened for business in a former office at 6 E. 46th St., just off Fifth Avenue. But the Korvette store at Carle Place (Westbury), Long Island, New York, which represents an investment of a million dollars in fixtures, stock, and initial working capital, bears no resemblance to its predecessor.

Korvette has gone suburbanite in a big way in the past two years. And Korvette sees its big growth coming from new stores in and around metropolitan New York, and far beyond, too.

In a few weeks, when the annual audit is completed, Korvette expects that its sales will have hit $55 million in the year ended September 29. That will be an increase of $19 million in one year.

In matter-of-fact tones, Korvette's managers speak optimistically about sales of $225 million within two or three years. Six leases have been signed, and plans drawn for them. The present nine stores, together with six new leases and five other leases being negotiated, would make Korvette a 20-unit chain.

All this is a far cry from the tiny price cutter which opened shop in 1948 in a 1,000 square foot second-story loft just a few doors from its present mid-town offices. Ferkauf, with a $10,000 investment partly supplied by his father, ("a wonderful salesman") employed six salesmen, each of whom is still with the company and in a high position.

Korvette dealt strictly in traditional discount house merchandise—luggage, jewelry, and small electrical appliances. At first business was done in the secretive manner of the early discount house through a membership card.

Korvette differed from its price-cutting colleagues; it offered liberal return privileges and merchandise guarantees. Korvette did not extend credit; all business was done on a cash and carry basis.

Soon fame of Korvette's merchandising bargains sifted through shopping-conscious Manhattan; the cards were dropped and Korvette opened its doors to all prospective buyers. Business boomed and within six months Korvette had taken over additional offices on the same floor. Three years later, in a frantic weekend of work, Ferkauf and his loyal salesmen moved all stock and opened for business Monday morning on the street level. Each of these men, now Korvette executives, earned more than $50,000 in 1956.

That was just the start. In 1952, the mushrooming Korvette established its second Manhattan store and in 1953 took over a former super market for a store at Hempstead, Long Island, N.Y. The following year it opened its first department store in the $3,500,000 Korvette City Shopping Center, Carle Place, (Westbury) Long Island, N.Y.; and in 1955 set up two apparel shops near Rockefeller Plaza in Manhattan. In 1956, the ninth outlet was opened in West Islip, Long Island, N.Y. Both the Carle Place and the West Islip stores represent investments by Korvette of $1 million each for store fixtures, stock, and initial working capital.

Sales in the Korvette City store reached $27 million in fiscal 1956. This volume was produced in 90,000 square feet of department store space, plus 30,000 square feet of super-market space, and 20,000 square feet for toys, juvenile furniture and sporting goods.

With its big expansion program geared to $225 million annual sales within two to three years, Korvette is wasting no time in signing leases in shopping centers throughout the East. The firm's own architect, Aaron Kellner, is completing plans for stores in conservative, suburban Scarsdale, N.Y.; and in mid-state Poughkeepsie, N.Y.; as well as in North Plainfield, North Hackensack, and New Brunswick, all in New Jersey; Philadelphia; and Springfield, Mass.

From Korvette's point of view, the ideal high volume, promotional department store, should have no more than 100,000 square feet, in contrast with the typical department store's 300,000 square feet, which requires more stock, more salesmen, and more supervision.

A Discount House!

Korvette's stores will have chandeliers, attractive display areas, and perfume bars. One building may even sport a baked-in relief on its facade; another will have a fountain in its courtyard, even at cost of parking space for 28 cars. In March, 1957, Korvette will open a store in the old Oppenheim Collins building in Brooklyn, N.Y. It is expected that this store, consisting of 150,000 square feet will produce annual sales of $25 million. Korvette is now waiting the final acquisition by a developer of some property in the Grand Central Terminal area of Manhattan, where it can consolidate some of its Manhattan outlets into a department store.

Ferkauf is quick to defend the new artistic bent of Korvette: "I think people are insulting the average customer's intelligence if they think he should not shop in attractive surroundings." So strong is Ferkauf's aesthetic flare that salesgirls in the apparel stores wear corsages.

Although Korvette currently operates two profitable super markets with a combined annual volume of $11 million, Ferkauf has no plans to build any super markets in the near future. Reason: "Locations are hard to come by and the investment in a department store is smaller and the profit possibilities are better. Besides, you can only be an A & P or a Sears, Roebuck once in a lifetime, not both."

Is Korvette like a sprouting child prodigy? Is it growing too fast to build solid muscle? The answer appears to be "no." In fact, quiet, mild Ferkauf and his more ebullient associates, radiate a confident toughness which give no indication that they are personally awed or impressed by their accomplishments in the past eight years which they refuse to have described as "fabulous." For example:

Cubby-Hole Executive Offices

The Korvette executive offices are located on the fifth floor of a non-descript office building. Visitors get off the elevator, walk across a bare floor to a plain green door market, E. J. Korvette. From the outside, it is just another off-the-elevator door. Once across the threshold, the visitor immediately steps into a large room where the atmosphere is punctured with the clatter of computers, jangling telephones, and scurrying feet. At the far end of the central room, set off by a glass partition, is a modest cubbyhole which serves as an office for the top brass.

There is neither the space nor the desire for the executives to appear elegant. So they have no plush offices. They do not have secretaries. In fact, Ferkauf and his high school friend, former New York City fire lieutenant, William Willensky, have never dictated a letter, but both are avid users of the telephone. They wear suits ("Regular value $90; our price $57.97") bought in their own store; Ferkauf prefers a sport shirt and seldom wears a tie except to get into New York's restaurants.

Korvette executives have no objection to doing business in modern, well-equipped carpeted offices, which they frequently do, when they walk down a flight of stairs and borrow the office of Bernard Waltzer, their original accountant. Waltzer, who operates his own CPA firm, is Korvette's assistant treasurer and is a director. His last published Korvette income: $37,400.

In an earlier age, Ferkauf the founder, whose title is chairman of the executive committee, probably would have been described as a young tycoon. But in this age, he is properly described as a modern manager, who relies heavily on staff assistants. His six original salesmen, all boyhood friends, have made good in their own right. ("Some people think I am lucky," says Ferkauf, "but it never occurred to me that my associates might not be able to grow.")

The seven top executives have just taken a hefty pay cut. Commencing October 1, their incomes dropped to the annual rate of $20,800. Some 20 other executives have taken cuts, too. The savings, largely year-end bonus payments, are estimated at $250,000 to $400,000 for the 12 months. Now this interest-free money will be available for Korvette to invest in expanding the business, and to produce capital gains instead of personal income.

These young men, who worked their way up from floor salesmen, know what big returns they can make by a little temporary self-denial.

Ferkauf's income, as reported early this year, at the time $2 million worth of Korvette's stock was placed on the market for public offering for the first time, was $103,150. George Yelen, chairman of the board and the officer in charge of purchasing, was paid $58,667. Willensky, the president, who was Korvette's 15th employe, was paid $55,985. David Thorn, vice-president and director, received $58,667. Joseph Zwillenberg, treasurer, was the second highest paid official, with $66,197. Murray Beilenson, secretary, was paid $58,667, and Melvin Friedman, vice-president, received $56,467.

Seek Stock Gains

Each of these executives is an important stockholder and the group, quite frankly, anticipates appreciation in the value of his stock. The first stock issue was offered at $11, rose to a high of $26, and on October 22 closed at $17–19.

Korvette management's self imposed cut in personal income may pinch for 12 months, but the executives obviously have faith in the organization they have built. Sales have multiplied 27-fold since 1950. Earnings have risen from $27,000 in 1950 to an estimated $1,500,000 for fiscal 1956. Profits for fiscal '56 are estimated at just about fiscal 1955's 3.2%. This year Gimbels netted 2.1% and Macy's 1.6% on sales.

Korvette is proud of its ability to discount bills from the first day it opened and to operate so shrewdly on a low markup policy, enabling consumers to buy hard and soft goods at an average of 18% over the manufacturers price to retailers.

Sales currently consist of about 60% hard goods and 40% soft goods. The soft goods volume has been built up within the past two and a half years.

Soft goods offer attractive profit possibilities for Korvette. So the company is working to raise soft goods sales to 70% of total volume and let hard goods drop to 30% although both will represent a vastly increased number of units sold and dollars taken in.

No Secret: Loss Leaders

Ferkauf and Willensky make no bones of the fact that they offer occasional "loss leaders." For example, Korvette bought stockings for 42¢ a pair and sold them for 19¢, and stood ready to supply 5,000 pairs. Men and women's cashmere sweaters, and men's socks are also sold as loss leaders. Ferkauf places his losses on these below-cost sales at about $15,000 a year.

With its low markup and high volume policy, Korvette turns its stock at an average of nine times a year, or double the inventory turn in most department stores. Its turnover in food super markets averages 20 times. Although the food super markets are profitable, the company does not plan to place additional ones in operation because it can return a greater profit from its investment in money and manpower in department stores.

Now that Korvette, and the discount house, has more or less become of age, Korvette is able to offer a wider selection of brand names. The company does not stock the six or seven items which are fair traded and price-policed. Korvette, like other discount houses, still uses the gambit of marking merchandise with "manufacturer's list" or where there is no suggested price, it marks its merchandise "Regular value$—; our price$—."

Ferkauf and Willensky proudly declare that they have never paid one cent in damages in Fair Trade suits. Twenty-five suits have been disposed of short of final judgment; 28 suits resulted in judgments restraining Korvette from price-cutting; 34 suits are pending. The threat of Fair Trade action is now so remote that in 1957, Korvette will set aside no reserve to hire attorneys to fight cases. Company officials simply plan to talk their differences over with manufacturers and come to an amicable agreement.

Currently, Korvette carries nine major appliance lines, RCA-Whirlpool, RCA-Victor, General Electric, Emerson, Zenith, Motorola, Hot Point, Westinghouse, and Admiral. Two other big-name manufacturers would like to sell Korvette—now—after refusing to do so in the company's early days. There is just a trace of warmth of resentment in the voices of the executives when they talk about these two manufacturers, but they realistically point out that they have nine major lines, which is more than most retailers offer, and that they have no sound business basis for taking on two additional lines. To this extent, Korvette, like anyone who has suddenly hit the big time, is aware of its power to become an influential factor in merchandising circles. For example, Korvette in fiscal '56 placed an order for over $2 million in radio, TV sets, and washing machines with a single manufacturer. And only last month the company placed a $500,000 radio order for Christmas sales. Even the perfumers, who were among the first to protest discount house price-cutting, now are happy to sell Korvette. The company buys directly from Revlon, Chanel, and Coty, and is dickering for other name brands.

Hard-to-Get Soft Goods

Korvette finds it a little tougher to secure some soft goods lines, especially in ladies' sportswear. In many cases, department stores have close ties with apparel manufacturers and the stores can pointedly suggest the manufacturer limit sales to competitive outlets. So Korvette finds a number of ready-to-wear lines completely out of reach—now.

Korvette buyers strongly urge manufacturers to make an alternate line. They say, "If a manufacturer has five lines in blouses and it sells to Macy's, it won't put them out of business to sell to Korvette, too. They could give us an alternate line and change the label or make up a line for us."

At various times, Korvette has handled Arrow, Van Huesen, Mc-Gregor, and Phoenix.

Ferkauf candidly calls attention to his own share of merchandising failures. For example, he has not been able to sell art supplies or dietetic foods in profitable quantities. And in his Carle Place store, he thought early this year, he could do as much business by being open until 9 P.M. only on Monday, Wednesday and Friday nights. Apparently, there are a lot of people who can buy only on Tuesday and Thursday nights, because volume dropped off so much that Ferkauf restored five night a week openings.

For the first six years Korvette depended entirely on word of mouth advertising. But in 1955, the company invested over $1 million, the bulk of it in the *New York Daily News* and in Long Island *Newsday*. This year it has budgeted $1.5 million. Some of it may be spent in radio.

Since May, Korvette has offered a time payment plan on major appliances at two of its stores, which is carried by a bank without recourse.

Ferkauf and Willensky see a bright future, but even though they plan to quadruple sales in the next two to three years, they have a pretty good idea of what they would do if there is any downturn in general business. They have 85% of their personnel directly involved in selling, versus 50% for conventional department stores. They have no warehouses; merchandise is trucked directly to each store. They own only one building, which will be sold soon so that capital will be free for operation. And they are sticking closely to 100,000 square foot stores versus the conventional department store of 300,000 square feet. In their Carle Place store, for example, they have 350 employes, but they could cut back to 125 employes, and still "cover" the store adequately.

They respect the resiliency of conventional department stores, but they assert "If department stores try to match our prices, they will become losing operations." Most of all, Korvette counts on youth, aggressiveness, and enthusiasm. And one of the reasons for the enthusiasm is the fact that the chairman of the board *must* spend at least five days a week visiting every one of the stores, the president *must* devote at least two days and the founder and executive committee chairman *must* be in each store at least one day a week. These are executive committee *orders*.

He's "Branch Rickey"

The merchandise does not get moved in Korvette stores because the manager tells an assistant who in turn tells his assistant and who tells the floor salesman "increase your sales 10%!" Ferkauf points out "the floor salesman can't do that because he may not have the creative ability of a manager, and he doesn't have control over the tools to produce that 10%."

Ferkauf has the drive of a Mickey Mantle, but he would much prefer to be thought of as Branch Rickey with lots of able young fellows coming up from the farm teams. He is making plenty of room for them. Today there are 100 managers and 1,200 employes.

·{ 17 }··

City Store in Country Pays Off For Chain*

Here . . . is . . . what Edward W. Carter, 45-year-old president of Broadway-Hale Stores, Inc., considers "the most significant trend in department store business of the decade: the growth of regional chains." It shows, too, why he thinks they are booming.

Since 1947, when he joined what is now the Los Angeles—or Broadway —half of this West Coast retail business, Carter has been forging the links in a chain of department stores that fit this rapidly emerging concept.

Two Types of Chain

A look at Broadway-Hale's structure today shows you the pattern that has developed under Carter, as chief executive officer, and his partner, Prentis C. Hale, board chairman, who operates out of San Francisco:

1. The Los Angeles regional chain, which has grown since 1947 from a downtown store with two branches to its present string of suburban stores. Sales have climbed from $31-million to about $100-million.

2. The northern California string of six Hale stores centered in San Francisco, which was merged with Broadway in 1950.

3. The Dohrmann Commercial Co., a hotel supply and hardgoods specialty store chain in California, which Broadway-Hale purchased last year for $10-million. This gave Broadway-Hale a big interest—16%—in the highly profitable Emporium Capwell Co., northern California's leading regional chain, which just this week announced its eighth store in the San Francisco Bay area.

Los Angeles Deal

A week ago Carter and Hale wrapped up a deal that adds another link to the Los Angeles chain. Along with Sears, Roebuck & Co., they

---

agreed to build a new store in the 85-acre Del Amo shopping center in the southwestern area of Los Angeles. With a planned 1,150,000 sq. ft. of building area, this will be one of the region's biggest shopping centers.

In a sense, this latest addition to Broadway-Hale will cap one phase of Carter's big plans. For the time being, at least, it will be the final link in the Los Angeles area chain. Carter is still thinking about new locations for the time when population figures will support them, but he can now concentrate on some of the other ideas he has about modern department store retailing.

THE REGIONAL CHAIN

It is the regional chain idea that's at the heart of all the other schemes. In today's spreading metropolitan areas, Carter thinks this concept is the most certain, if not the only, avenue to successful department store merchandising.

"Regional chains are the coming thing," he says, "because they have the strength of size that a big chain has, yet are responsive to local demand."

Carter defines such a chain as a group of department stores located in one market area, operated under a single name, with merchandising, promotion, goods handling, accounting, and financing all centralized.

Evolution

First signs of the regional chain concept were the branch stores of major downtown department stores. Somewhere in mid-passage, says Carter, the idea emerged that each of these units should be a strong outpost in a ring around a marketing area.

In Carter's view, even the downtown store becomes just a part of this chain, rather than remaining the central "mother" store. In effect, Carter's thinking eliminates the "downtown" concept—although as a community leader in Los Angeles he remains a big booster for the city. Broadway's central city store actually is becoming another regional shopping center store.

Surefire

It's this view of modern department store retailing that distinguishes the regional chain from simply a branch store operation.

Carter doesn't exclude some of the big national chains—like Macy's, the May Co., Federated, and Allied—from developing in this pattern. Macy's, for instance, already has its ring of New York stores, its Bamberger chain in New Jersey, Davidson-Paxon in Georgia, La Salle & Koch in Ohio.

But, modified to suit local conditions, this trend Carter sees as being effective locally in any large urban-rural area. Such regional chains have one goal: the complete development of a natural market area. It gives the local groups like Broadway-Hale or Emporium Capwell the advantages of national chains, which Carter calls simply "loosely federated groups of regional chains."

Los Angeles is particularly suited to the concept, says Carter. It is big and is probably the most suburbanized city in the world. Growing as it did with the use of the automobile, it fits nicely into multi-store planning. Just as importantly, it is a region where tastes and buying habits are fairly uniform. As a result, it supports not only one but two other regional chains—Bullock's and the May Co.—in addition to Broadway.

Similar chains, according to Carter, are developing in Chicago, Detroit, St. Louis, Milwaukee, Boston, Cleveland, and Denver.

STRENGTH IN UNION

It is Carter's opinion that a whole list of advantages will assure the continued growth of regional chains. Citing Broadway's own experience, he ticks off such things as more merchandising and buying power, more efficient promotion, better command of prime money markets, the ability and size to afford more and better executives, better help from suburban areas.

Bigness Helps

Take merchandising. Says Carter: "Broadway possesses the market advantage of large-scale buying but preserves the flexibility inherent in single-store operation. It can offer manufacturers large orders and good coverage of the trading area and thus be in a strong position to negotiate favorable prices, rapid delivery, individual styling."

This bigness, too, ties in with manpower. Broadway has six merchandising executives and 60 buyers—each controlling big volume. Each buyer is responsible for $1.5-million worth of goods, merchandise managers for about $15-million. They have their counterparts in each store, to take care of local variations in demand.

Homogeneous Market

As for promotion, there is the obvious advantage of being able to advertise throughout the marketing area in one set of newspapers. This helps, too, in opening new units. The new Del Amo store, for instance, will benefit from advertising already circulated there—and at virtually no extra cost to Broadway-Hale.

Bigger advertising campaigns can be budgeted, too—and at a better rate per inch. What's more, says Carter, "We find that manufacturers tend to channel substantial amounts of their own cooperative advertising budgets through regional chains like ours."

Access to Money

The financial advantages are also clear. It is costing $12.5-million for Broadway to develop its Orange County shopping center in Anaheim, Calif. Carter points out:

"We are getting that money on favorable terms from the Prudential—a single-unit operation could hardly expect to command that kind of money or the rates we get."

Lower operating costs are made possible. For one thing, the help is better and there is more of it, since stores are adjacent to pleasant living areas. Providing parking space—important consideration today—is cheaper, delivery costs are less, land values more moderate, taxes not so high.

Besides this, a chain can build stores that give far more merchandising display per square foot than older downtown units.

Last year, Broadway-Hale took a major step to increase the operating advantages it already had. It completed a 600,000-sq.-ft. central service warehouse to serve all eight stores. Located on Los Angeles' freeway system, it consolidates receiving, marking, storing, and processing of merchandise, as well as the inventory accounting for all stores.

HOW BIG CAN IT GET?

As you might expect, Carter has definite ideas on just how big an area a regional chain should try to cover. His chief guiding rules:

1. No store should be more than 35 miles from the chain's central service warehouse. He doesn't think, for instance, that Broadway could operate a store in San Diego out of the Los Angeles regional chain.

2. All stores in each area should be blanketed by the same newspapers.

3. There should be some similarity in buying demand in the region.

After Broadway merged with Hale Bros. (at Carter's urging), it became apparent that the Hale part of the business in northern California didn't fit this set of rules completely. Not all Hale stores can be covered by a single newspaper, and the trading area doesn't have uniform characteristics.

As a result, the Broadway chain has jumped far ahead of the Hale group. It does three times the business in its eight stores as Hale does in its six stores in San Francisco, Oakland, Sacramento, and San Jose. And it nets 7.5% on sales, compared with 6% for the combined organization's owned retail stores.

New Interest

That may be one reason why Carter was especially interested in getting a foot in the door of the Emporium Capwell Co. through the Dohrmann Commercial Co. purchase. Emporium neatly matches Carter's ideas of a regional chain—four Emporium stores on the San Francisco side of the bay and, by the end of 1958, four Capwell stores on the Oakland side.

Carter refuses to discuss any plans involving Emporium Capwell. But since he and Hale are now on the board of that company, it is a safe bet their influence on future plans will be felt.

THE FUTURE

Whatever lies ahead, Carter thinks that his job is, as he puts it, "to break down the low-profit barrier typical of department stores, so we can command the capital with which to grow."

The regional chain idea, he believes, has already proved its value. This week he and Hale are preparing to release figures for the annual report. It will show sales of 137-million for the year ended Jan. 31. That's 22% higher than the year before. Earnings, at $4-million, were 38% higher. Part of that gain comes from the Dohrmann Commercial purchase—but Carter thinks a large part can be traced to his profitable chain operation in Los Angeles.

Improvements

But Carter thinks there are other things for department stores to do besides using chain operations to pull profits upward:

"We've gradually got to change the customers' notion about the department store so that they no longer look upon us as a depository of goods but an instrument of service." Then, he adds:

"We can gradually begin charging for those services."

He wants margins raised, too. That probably means elimination of basement stores. Broadway's downtown Los Angeles basement store was closed "because there was no economic demand for it." According to Carter, it costs just about as much to operate such a department as an upstairs floor, the markup is lower, fewer people need this kind of operation, and, besides, "it is more and more difficult to sell merchandise at prices that really compete with discount houses and other outlets."

Finally, Carter thinks there will be a continuing trend toward department store mergers because of (1) need for new capital for expansion and (2) a breakup of old family-held units under the blow of inheritance taxes.

··{ 18 }··

Old Style Selling For New Carriage Trade*

The name Hammacher, Schlemmer & Co. has held a special magic for several generations of customers. To a smallish, top-income group in recent decades it has been the quietly elegant first resort for the extra-special in gifts and home furnishings. Its customers expected—and got—the last word in quality and service, and willingly paid for it.

To John Gerald, new president and owner, this is the way retailing should be. Gerald, who had had his own interior decorating firm, brought with him a name he had built up as head of B. Altman & Co.'s interior decorating department. A man who loves retailing, he ardently advocates the old Hammacher, Schlemmer formula of top quality merchandise, and luxury service.

Quality was basic to the formula a hundred years ago, when Hammacher, Schlemmer meant hardware. In the days when there were no hardware stores, founder William Schlemmer filled a gap by selling the best, much of it at wholesale. When his son, William F. Schlemmer, moved uptown to New York's 57th Street in the 1920s and added luxury gift and household items, he polished up the formula for a pampered clientele.

In 1953, the last Schlemmer owner, widow of the founder's son, sold out to a group of investors. For a while it looked as though the old formula might go down the drain. The carriage trade had changed. A new, better-heeled middle market was moving in. The new Hammacher, Schlemmer management, like some other old-line retailers, tried down-grading and price selling to shore up sales. Last April, it sold to Gerald.

Gerald, too, hopes to cash in on the new money—and keep his old customers happy as well. But his strategy is to go back to the traditions that gave the store its magic in the first place.

One of the first things John Gerald did when he became Hammacher, Schlemmer's president, was to put the dwarfs to work again. These small creatures, emblem of Hammacher, Schlemmer's earlier heyday, had been in exile for 30 years. Gerald, who remembered them from his own boyhood, dusted them off and lovingly reinstated them in a post of honor in the store's windows and its advertising.

This single gesture tells a great deal about Gerald's approach to his new venture. He has made many changes in the old store. Some have been

---

simple physical alterations to modernize the layout. His most important changes, though, have not been innovations but reversions to the concepts on which the Schlemmers had built.

Details Add Up

Item by item, the changes don't loom very large—a liveried doorman to let customers in, "our Mr. Skinner" just inside the door to greet every customer; the addition of a service department, or the expansion of an old one. But they add up to a real atmosphere. Once more Hammacher, Schlemmer wears the unmistakable air of the carriage trade.

It is perhaps not quite the air of extravagance that the old Hammacher, Schlemmer had. Today's rich live different lives—at once more strenuous and more casual—from the ones their grandfathers lived. In making changes, Gerald has kept this sharply in focus.

Besides, Gerald, like every other retailer, knows that the movement of wealth in the postwar years has been toward the middle—down from the top, up from the bottom. Thus, a carriage-trade store has a brand-new market potential: the newcomers to prosperity, who would have shied off from such shops a quarter of a century ago. Gerald wants his share of that new money. This, too, calls for some different slants in merchandising.

Ways to Do It

Many old-line stores share Hammacher, Schlemmer's problem. All prestige retailers have felt the change. Most of them have tried, one way or another, to cope with the shifts of income and the new living patterns.

W. & J. Sloane has made a direct bid for the middle-income market with its Penny Wise Shop (*BW*—Oct.20'51,p137). Exclusive specialty shops such as Bergdorf Goodman (*BW*—Nov.17'51,p46) and Henri Bendel, Inc., have broadened their middle-priced lines. Even Tiffany & Co. last fall announced that it was overhauling its merchandising policies and advertising its sales for the first time (*BW*—Oct.29'55,p64).

Such shifts don't come easy. Sloane, Tiffany, and Bendel have all been through management changes in the past couple of years. Lewis & Conger, another old-timer, has recently given up the ghost. Whether or not the stores succeed in their efforts, it's plain that they have had to face a vital problem.

Keep What You Have

Gerald's solution sounds refreshingly simple. If you have the carriage trade, keep it.

"In this day of gimmicks, something-for-nothing mechandising," he holds, "there is still a good market among those who want to buy quality with confidence." Not only are the prestige customers worth holding in their own right—they also provide the glamor that will help draw the new money in.

Setting up such targets involves some shifts from Hammacher, Schlemmer's recent past. This store, too, has known the stress of changing times—and changing managements.

Change of Hands

By the time William Schlemmer's widow sold out in 1952 to David Berdon & Co., which buys and sells companies, the first flush of postwar selling was over. Sales were slipping. Maybe, suggests a veteran Hammacher, Schlemmer official, the new management was more frightened than it needed to be. At any rate, it took to such merchandising devices as advertising the $3.98 special, trade-ins, bargain-day selling. When Gerald bought it, it was a house divided against its traditions, and was losing money.

Gerald can cite businesslike reasons for his strategy for reversing the downtrend. But it is obvious to an observer that, in calling up the old merchandising graces, he is doing what comes naturally. The marriage of Hammacher, Schlemmer, carriage trade shop par excellence, and John Gerald, retailer, interior decorator, merchandising consultant, was more than a marriage of convenience. It was a marriage of love.

FROM THE PAST

If William F. Schlemmer could return to his store today, he would doubtless recognize and approve much of what he saw. Hammacher, Schlemmer is a smallish store; its volume ran around $3-million last year. It draws a faithful clientele from New York society and upper-crust customers the country over. Crowned and uncrowned heads of Europe, big theatrical people are its devotees. A flourishing catalog and mail order business comes in from well-heeled families the world over.

Genesis

Of course, Hammacher, Schlemmer wasn't always like this. William Schlemmer, the founder, fresh from Germany, started to work in his uncle's little hardware shop in New York's Bowery in 1853 at the age of 12. He developed the store into a top-notch supplier for both industry and consumers. In 1859, he persuaded Alfred Hammacher to invest in the concern.

Hammacher, Schlemmer became a name to conjure with in hardware. It's mammoth catalog was the Bible of the industry; it covered everything from nuts and bolts to piano parts.

Exodus

His son succeeded him in 1916. Unlike his father, William the younger disliked hardware. He moved the store to its present uptown site in

1926, relegated the hardware to the basement, and blossomed out into a retail merchant of costly gifts and housewares.

Shoppers looking for the exotic can still find it at Hammacher, Schlemmer: a gold-leafed eagle weather vane, priced at $245; a Lucite coat rack for $99; duck presses; a Wok shrimp fryer ("We're the only store in New York that carries a Wok," says Gerald). There's hardware, too, but nowadays it is the elegant, decorative kind.

As in Schlemmer's day, Gerald and his aides take pride in goods made for the store's own label—though it carries some brand merchandise, Wastebaskets embroidered especially for Hammacher, Schlemmer (at $55), little hand-hooked rugs at $100, hand-woven blankets from the Shetland Islands—items like these are the store's special joy.

Schlemmer invented some of the products he sold; he masterminded the martini mixer and the wooden valet stand. Gerald and his staff, too, take delight in devising items of their own, or in improving on the manufacturers' samples.

Stress on Service

If the merchandise spells carriage trade, the service says it even more clearly. "Women yearn for service," Gerald believes. "I want every woman who comes into the store, even if she spends only a dollar, to feel that there's nothing we won't do for her."

So Gerald has added to the service departments. Besides the new interior decorating department, he has expanded the carpenter's shop so that his staff can do cabinet work in a customer's home. He has restored the repair shop that had been allowed to lapse. Customers can bring anything to it, no matter where they bought it. Sometimes it's a favorite knife with a broken handle, or a metal meridian that is minus its globe.

The Little Niceties

Small graces all through the store aim to tell the customer he is important. Besides the doorman and the official greeter, Gerald has established six floaters, who have no fixed station. But Gerald says, "I want any salesclerk to go anywhere a customer asks her to."

In the old days, Hammacher, Schlemmer made a fetish of getting anything a customer wanted, whether the store carried it or not. Dominic Tampone, star salesman recently made a vice-president, recalls the maharajah who trustingly ordered a horse from Hammacher, Schlemmer —and got it—and the wealthy Brazilian who sent a mail order for an elevator to get his guests from his cliff house to the beach.

These days are back again—and Tampone is on the job. When the Duchess of Windsor wanted a pasteurizer, Tampone ordered it for her. The Duke wanted a greenhouse; Tampone got it.

In the mail order department, the same personal touch prevails. "Our Miss Susan Clay" handles this correspondence. She, too, is kept hopping with special requests: a Lucite cane, for example, for a woman who thought wooden ones didn't go with evening clothes.

Personal Attention

Watching Gerald roam through his store is a good way to understand his idea of service. He gives the air of being a pleasantly solicitous host in his own home. If the doorman is ill, Gerald unobtrusively steps up to let a customer in. He stops a woman in the aisle to ask if he can help. "I wouldn't ask any employee to do anything I wouldn't do myself," he says —and proves it by straightening up a mussed-up display bed.

In still another important respect Gerald is harking back to the old ways of retailing. He knows his store. "I know every piece of merchandise we carry, and I usually know its price," he says. Twice a week he inspects the merchandise as it comes to the receiving room. He wanders around the floors periodically.

"If a problem comes up with a customer, I want a salesgirl to say, 'You should meet our Mr. Gerald,' and I'll come right down," he says.

Big Small Decisions

If an important new item or line is to come in, Gerald looks it over— and is quite likely to have some thoughts on how to improve it. A glass shrimp-dip dish had proved popular—but all too breakable in shipping. Why not the same dish in Lucite? Gerald asks. A manufacturer has a telephone stand to sell. Gerald approves—but it should have room for two phone books, not one.

He sits in on the final choice of articles to be featured in the catalog— which accounts for a sizeable share of sales, though Gerald isn't saying just how much. He has a hand in all final decisions in the interior decorating department. He spotchecks all complaints that come in; when they are serious, he takes pains to answer them himself—and to see that wrongs are righted.

SOMETHING NEW

Gerald knows that the past hasn't all the answers. The most obvious change was the physical shakeup he gave the store's layout and decor. He made over the stodgy first floor, redecorated it, broke up the rigid German arrangement of counters. He added linen and antique furniture to the store's lines.

For Easier Living

To accommodate his old customers' changed living patterns, Gerald puts heavy stress on goods that make for "easy living." Gone are the cooks, he says, so we sell a lot of cookbooks. He wants products that are not only distinctive but useful: a waste basket with a disposable lining, a luggage bag that fits over a suitcase handle.

"This is real Hammacher, Schlemmer," he'll say—perhaps of a German knife that is screw driver, can opener, fish scaler, and flashlight all in one. "We don't want to be nifty-gifty," he explains.

To make clear the need for the changes, he tells of a wealthy woman who came in recently to buy a tray. Did she want silver? No, thank you, she wanted something she didn't have to polish. Hammacher, Schlemmer had it: a tray of stainless steel. It is significant, too, that the "never-out list" (which the store must keep stocked) includes such humble items as dish mops, furniture polish, paper napkins.

Matter of Taste

What works for the clients of long standing will appeal to the new market, too, Gerald is convinced. He has "unbounded faith in the average homemaker and her taste," regardless of her income bracket. Manufacturers and retailers tend to underrate her, give her inferior quality and styling, he feels.

The new money often has less assurance than the old carriage trade. That's where services such as the interior decorating department can help—and where the prestige of the store's name gives confidence.

Pricing, in fact, is not a paramount matter in Gerald's book. "I don't want just the best coffee maker for $50," he says. "I also want a coffee maker for the woman who pays $3.50. But it must be the best possible at that price."

OLD PROBLEMS

In a sense, Gerald is walking the same tightrope that other carriage trade merchants are walking. There is always the risk that a bid for the new market will offend the old. There's no doubt that the run-of-the-mill Hammacher, Schlemmer customer is special.

Tampone tells of the woman who called to order an item by phone. He told her the store was going to have a sale the next day. "Thank you for telling me," she said. "I'll stay away."

With that kind of thinking among customers, it is easy to see why Gerald quickly dropped the bargain-sale kind of promotion when he moved in. "I will not run an ad that says, 'Hurry, run, rush, get our special with a free attachment,'" he says.

Prices and People

Since its customers don't cry for bargain sales, the store doesn't have to mark down so many items during the year. That improves its average margin for overhead and profit. But it also means that the price and the merchandise must be right in the first place.

This is one reason that new merchandise gets such a careful going-over. Such an operation, too, puts a premium on new ideas, exclusive new products.

By far the biggest headache, though, is one that Gerald shares with other retailers: to get employees to give the caliber of service he wants. For many Hammacher, Schlemmer veterans, this comes as naturally as breathing. But newcomers to retailing haven't lived through the hard-sell days. Because he expects more of his help, Gerald pays better than average wages. Most of his sales clerks average over $50 a week (in many stores their pay starts at $38). Despite all this, the problem persists.

OLD LOVES

If Gerald succeeds in his new venture, it seems likely that his own enthusiasm will be a major factor. Gardening and fishing are his hobbies, but "my work is my pleasure," he says.

He was born and educated in South Carolina. His first jobs were interior decorating work for family friends. Three years' study in Europe brought him an acquaintance with famous homes in Europe; five years in Canada gave him decorating jobs there.

Breaking In

His first retailing experience was with W. & J. Sloane. In 1936, he moved to B. Altman, built up the interior decorating department there. After 12 years, he branched off, and, as John Gerald Associates, did both interior decorating and merchandising consulting—for such clients as James Lees & Sons Co., Kittinger Furniture Co., and Waite Carpet Co.

With Katharine Kinnane, one of his associates, he was consultant to the Planning Board of Henry Ford Museum and Greenfield Village of Dearborn, Mich.

Hammacher, Schlemmer appealed to him because he had loved the store as a boy, and he had a "healthy respect" for its name and clientele. It was just the right size: small enough for the personal operation he enjoys, big enough to have real buying power. With a group of investors —and a substantial sum of his own money—he took over.

Out of the Red

The high cost of the first year cut into profits in 1955. But the company was in the black in December, and by next fall "we'll be rolling," Gerald says.

Once the New York store gets its feet firmly under it, Gerald plans other Hammacher, Schlemmers. He feels he could handle perhaps a $5-million operation in his present shop without losing its flavor. After that, the West Coast, Chicago, maybe Dallas and Kansas City are possibilities.

·{ 19 }··

Consolidation Adds up to Fatter Profits for Safeway*

The radical reduction of its own private brands by Safeway Stores, Inc., is the obvious change any customer could notice in the big food chain's operations since Robert A. Magowan took over a year and a half ago.

But this reduction, a sharp reversal of former Safeway policy, is only one of a lot of differences showing up as Magowan attempts to re-mold the nation's No. 2 supermarket chain—second only to A&P—so that it can return a profit commensurate with its almost $2-billion sales figure.

The Sole Aim

His changes affect basic policies in pricing, purchasing, merchandising, advertising, real estate, administration—all of them aimed at one thing: keeping more of a bigger sales dollar.

Historically, of course, any retail food chain operates with a smaller margin of profit than almost any business—less than 2% after taxes.

But of all the major food chains, Safeway Stores has had the doubtful distinction of being low man on the totem pole—as low as 0.45% in 1952, and only 0.7% as recently as 1955.

Turn for Better

Next week in Del Monte, Calif., Magowan, Safeway's chairman and president, will assemble his top executives and retail division managers for conference.

At that meeting, he will confirm with hard figures what the financial statement for 1956 operations has already established: The profit margin corner has obviously been turned.

Magowan will tell his executives that earnings in the first 12 weeks of 1957 passed those of the same 1956 period by 46%—$1.61 per common share versus $1.10 last year.

What makes that 1957 improvement stand out is that it's a leap ahead of the biggest and best year the food chain has ever had—1956. Sales last year of $1.9-billion, up about 3%, returned a net of $25.4-million, up

---

* Copyright, April 13, 1957, *Business Week*, McGraw-Hill Publishing Co., Inc. Reproduced with permission.

87%. After taxes, that figures out to a profit margin of 1.28% and puts Safeway again in the running with other big food chains.

NO MORE VENDETTAS

Safeway had no magic formula for these gains. It did acquire new management, and to the extent that the new management has called a ceasefire in the vendettas that sapped the company's strength for years, you can credit Magowan for the new look. But the financial comeback can be traced primarily to the homespun policy of spending less than you earn.

New Replacement

Magowan stepped into the picture in August, 1955 (*BW*—Sep.3'55, p30). He had been sales manager of Merrill Lynch, Pierce, Fenner & Beane, whose senior officer, the late Charles E. Merrill, owned the largest single block (about 6%) of Safeway stock. He also was Merrill's son-in-law.

The shoes he was to fill at Safeway were occupied by Lingan A. Warren (*BW*—Dec.26'53,p90), one of the most controversial figures in merchandising since the late George Washington Hill of American Tobacco Co.

Unprofitable Crusades

Warren had the touch of genius that put Safeway in the big time. But he also had a jaw that could have been chiseled out of granite, and a will to match it. With this, and the resources of the second largest food chain to back it up, he waded with religious fervor into a succession of crusades —against trading stamps, premiums, coupons, advertising allowances, direct deliveries to stores, the retail milk pricing system.

Although his boxscore fails to show a single triumph, his zeal never flagged. He poured untold millions of dollars into his campaigns. His wrangles with the Grocery Manufacturers Assn. of America became epics at food trade conventions.

For all of his crusades, Warren found himself a lonely Don Quixote tilting at a forest of windmills.

High Volume, Low Profits

It's a glowing tribute to Warren that in the last 10 years of his presidency—the years of his fiercest fights—he more than doubled Safeway's sales and more than tripled the average sales per store.

Profits were another story. Anxious stockholders could see the sales curve running over the top of the chart and the profit curve skittering out at the bottom, and that didn't make sense. So Charlie Merrill lowered the boom. Warren was retired with the euphemistic title of consultant and a tidy percentage deal that runs for eight years. Magowan took over, first as chairman, and this year as president, too, when Milton L. Selby retired.

Fresh from Wall St. and its paneled shrines, Magowan shuddered at the gloomy old warehouse on the fringe of the wholesale district in Oakland, Calif., that serves as home to this national corporation with assets of $238-million. He knew it from a three-year stint he once served with Warren after a seven-year stretch with Macy's in New York. But 17 years in the cloistered luxury of Wall St. had clouded his memory of the frugality that awaited him in the West.

If Magowan shuddered at the building, the people who occupied it trembled at the invisible ax poised above them. They knew that nothing less than an earthquake could unseat Warren. With him gone, they wondered how safe they were.

Their fears were well-founded. Magowan turned out to be just as scrappy as Warren. The big difference is that Magowan doesn't fight the same people or the same things Warren did. With a securities dealer's perspective, he fights expense.

Penny Pinchers

Magowan is the first to admit that he knows nothing about the grocery business. And he has gathered around him a corps of top-level executives, all but one of whom are Safeway veterans, who know little more than he about how to peddle groceries. Of the six, three are accountants, one a lawyer, and one a public relations man who earned his spurs with J. C. Penney Co. The sixth came up through the store system, now is in charge of real estate and construction.

All the merchandising knowhow resides in the 18 retail distribution division managers and in the 27 zone, 122 district, and 1,981 local store organizations that fan out from them in 25 states, the District of Columbia, and five Canadian provinces. These people, constituting about 75% of the corporation's 54,000 employees, are the pampered darlings of the Magowan regime.

Ax Falls Often

The poised ax fell again and again. It landed in high places, it landed in low places. In some cases, at the upper levels, the blade abruptly settled some irreconcilable policy difference. Others who felt its edge were ready to retire anyway. The rest were victims of a sweeping consolidation of supporting services.

Magowan's first job, as he saw it, was to put out the fire—to arrest the decline in profit margin and, if possible, to fatten profits a bit. This would still the angry voice of the stockholders.

Strategic Withdrawals

His second job was to call off Warren's pet wars. Instead of fighting trading stamps as Warren did, Magowan decided to give them where competition forced him into it. He doesn't like premiums and coupons any more than Warren did, but if his customers and the grocery manufacturers want to use them, that's enough for Magowan.

He abandoned Safeway's resistance to direct deliveries of soft drinks, potato chips, packaged nuts, rack merchandise. If his division managers want to permit direct deliveries, it's their affair. Warren had wanted these products delivered to Safeway distribution centers.

Warren also had fought advertising allowances from manufacturers. He wanted to buy at the best prices with no strings attached. Magowan feels the same way, but not to the point of going to the mat with the manufacturers. "We're not going to prostitute our advertising merely to collect allowances and fill up a newspaper page," he says, "but we are going to conform to industry practice."

It may come as news in California, Utah, Idaho, and Washington, D.C., that Safeway has given up the retail milk price fight. In these areas, the chain opposed state floors under retail prices, offered to sell milk $1\frac{1}{2}\cancel{c}$ per quart cheaper, and was stymied at every turn.

"We're through with do-good causes," says Magowan. "However valid, they've made few friends for Safeway and lots of enemies. The company spent millions of dollars in opposing trading stamps, cutting prices, and issuing its own 'Cash-Saver' coupons, but we didn't put one dent in the solid front of the stamp givers. We learned the hard way that you can't combat stamps by cutting prices. If it takes stamps to hang on to our business, we're going to give them."

Advantages of Peace

There were two advantages in abandoning outside conflict. One was a welcome improvement in relations with the rest of the food distribution industry, the grocery manufacturers, and possibly the public.

The other advantage was purely financial. Drummond Wilde, vice-president and general counsel, doesn't reveal how much has been spent on lost causes, but admits it was a substantial sum and estimates that Safeway reduced its expenditure for outside counsel fees by 35% or more last year. Magowan says total legal expenses were cut in half, public relations expenses by 25%.

LOCAL AUTONOMY

Decentralization and consolidation were the tools Magowan used to effect the turnabout. Acknowledging his limitations in grocery merchandising, he turned over the merchandising function to his 18 distribution division managers. Nobody at the top level tells them how to sell groceries. He also made them accountable for their performance.

At Safeway, that's revolutionary. Warren held the division managers accountable, of course, but gave them little latitude.

Surprising Changes

Before Magowan had even warmed his chair, he called all the division managers together in Atlantic City—the first time the managers had met, incidentally—and told them, "You don't have to sell Safeway brands."

He warned them that Safeway would try to make its private label wares so attractive that customers would demand them. But it was up to division managers to decide whether they stocked or ignored Safeway brands. At the time, the company was imprinting its label on 210 different products in a variety of sizes that called for 600 different labels.

The bombshell, though, was his announcement that the division managers henceforth would buy national brand wares through established wholesale channels—no longer through the central buying office in Oakland. Furthermore, it was up to each division manager to assess the demands of his customers for national brands and to meet the demands.

"Our job," he said, "is to give the customer what she wants, not try to tell her what she should want."

Buying Freedom

Home office pressure for Safeway brands had been a thorny issue with the men who had to promote them. They were fine products. But there was such a profusion of them that promotion was both expensive and confusing, and the pressure from Oakland ignored the big consumer demand for nationally advertised merchandise.

Central buying of national brands, too, was a major bone of contention under Warren. Say the Kansas City Div. wanted a carload of Del Monte peaches. The manager sent his order to Safeway in Oakland. The Oakland office processed the order to California Packing Corp. (Del Monte) against Safeway's volume purchase. Del Monte delivered the peaches to the Kansas City warehouse, but billed Safeway in Oakland. The Oakland office in turn billed the Kansas City Div., adding an "upcharge" of perhaps 2¢ a case for handling.

The division people were appalled at the paperwork involved in this process, but they screamed in agony at the upcharge. In some cases they could have bought the merchandise from a broker for less than they had to pay the home office.

Although the fury of their complaints probably didn't reach Warren, some of the division men were outspoken in accusing the home office of operating an "extraction industry."

Now Magowan was telling them that all this was in the past. They were on their own. All that was required of them was to sell a whale of a lot of groceries and return a good profit. As an incentive they had a bonus system that would scale their own return to the results they produced. Elimination of the upcharge was, under the incentive system, like money from home.

BRAND CONSOLIDATION

The biggest upheaval at Safeway was in the supply and service divisions. Magowan took William S. Mitchell out of the controller's chair, made him vice-president in charge of supply operations. This is the division responsible for manufacture, processing, and promotion of all Safeway-branded products, as well as the purchase of all meat, fish, and produce. With supply no longer operating under the protective umbrella of front-office favoritism toward Safeway brands, it was up to Mitchell to make the distribution divisions clamor for his products.

Consolidation

By combining and consolidating, Mitchell trimmed the 14 supply divisions down to seven, and he reduced the 50 manufacturing, processing, and buying companies in those divisions to 29. He sold a butter plant in Muskogee, Okla., a soft drink bottling plant in Seattle, a meat slaughtering plant in San Francisco, a meat handling plant in Kansas City, a wine bottling plant in Fresno, Calif.—and still had 125 plants left. Others may be lopped off later.

A year ago Mitchell and his division managers tackled that great profusion of Safeway brand names. In canned goods alone, they pruned a list of 40 brands down to six. A check last week of the 210 brand names that were in use in 1954 showed that 71 have been eliminated. This doesn't mean necessarily that the products have been dropped, although some were. It means only that Safeway is using a smaller variety of labels and getting better mileage out of the dollar spent to advertise and promote those that survived.

The consolidation process is still going on. Mitchell hopes to wind it up substantially by June.

The Savings

Was it profitable? From 1955 to 1956, consolidation cut 38% out of the expense of management, accounting, advertising, and supervision in his supply operation. Advertising expense for Safeway brands—apart from local consumer advertising—was slashed from $7.7-million to $4.1-million. (Local consumer advertising in newspapers, radio, and TV rose from $14.9-million to $15.8-million.)

Magowan echoes Mitchell's performance figures with a good deal of pride. And he points out that although total sales of Safeway brands were about the same in 1956 as in 1955, the profit on them hit an all-time high last year. That makes it obvious that Safeway has no thought of giving up its private brands.

A similar, if less dramatic, result was produced in the service divisions—accounting, finance, advertising, personnel, research, legal, industrial relations, real estate, and construction. A. Russell Griffith, vice-president and controller, estimates the saving at 20%.

This year could produce some spectacular additional savings in the Real Estate and Construction Div. under vice-president George T. Burroughs. To keep pace with an obsolescence factor in old stores and to serve growing markets it's been necessary to add around 100 new stores every year. Last year Safeway opened 93; this year Burroughs is shooting for between 160 and 175.

NEW MANAGEMENT POLICY

Magowan has two outstanding characteristics that would endear him to the professional management man. He doesn't hesitate to make decisions, and he doesn't hesitate to delegate authority. And he expects those who report to him—the six members of his operating executive committee—to cultivate the same habits.

Pricing

Take pricing policy. How you price your merchandise is the very guts of retailing. Under Warren, the distribution division managers had a standing order to meet the lowest competitive price, city by city, day by day, regardless of who the competitor was.

Under Magowan, they're obliged to meet only valid competition, and they may exercise their discretion. And they're held accountable for the results over both the long and the short term. Russell Griffith credits this "realistic" pricing policy for last year's 15% jump in gross profit.

Warren used to screen the advertising budgets of the distribution zones. Magowan bucked the job over to Hugh Frost, the young man he promoted from controller to vice-president in charge of advertising, personnel, and research.

Sizing Up the Boss

One of the vice-presidents had a significant thing to say about the boss last week:

"He expects us to make decisions. When we make a bum one, we never hear a whisper of criticism. The only time he chews anybody out is when he hesitates to make a decision. In Magowan's book that's bum management."

··{ 20 }··

Hibbard, Spencer, Bartlett & Co.: Helping Hardware Dealers for 100 Years*

At approximately 8:20 A.M. any business day in Evanston, Ill., a slender, graying man of medium height enters a sprawling, one-story concrete and marble building, strides briskly through its lobby and up a curving flight of marble stairs, then moves quickly past a dozen or more glass-enclosed offices to enter his own spacious private office.

Within 10 minutes, another 314 men and women stream into the 850,-000-square foot building—some to occupy those offices, others to seat themselves behind desks in the vast open-office area. Fifteen minutes before, 216 warehouse employees have taken their places alongside a tremendous snake-like assembly line or have been engulfed in a jungle of merchandise and open-shelving.

All are destined to spend that day, as they and their predecessors have spent every working day for 100 years, striving towards a common goal—making hardware retailers remain a vital, dynamic factor in American marketing.

For the soft-spoken executive who occupies the mahogany-walled corner office, as it has been for the 6 men who preceded O. W. Ahl as head of Hibbard, Spencer, Bartlett & Co. of Evanston, Ill., it is a day to plan—and a day to fulfill plans of previous days.

It is just another working day in which to express, by both words and actions, the philosophy which has permeated the Hibbard organization and motivated its management since the company was founded in Chicago on March 22, 1855.

When you ask about their "philosophy of business," O. W. Ahl and other members of Hibbards' top echelon peer at you with quizzical looks.

That, they assert, is far too much of a high-brow phrase to describe correctly their basic beliefs. It echoes too much ideology and not enough good, sound business practice, which at Hibbards is concerned only with *helping independent retailers progress—and prosper.*

In Touch with Reality

Among Hibbard personnel, from O. W. down, there is a rare understanding of the small businessman and his peculiar and provocative prob-

---

* Reprinted by special permission from *Hardware Retailer*, January, 1955. Copyright, 1955, *Hardware Retailer*.

lems—rare because of Hibbards' own massive plant, its complex materials-handling facilities and its sales figures well up in the millions. Despite all this, however, management chooses to consider the operation nothing more than a gargantuan "small business."

Serving 5,000 or more mainstreet merchants in approximately 28 states, Hibbards is never more than moments away from the economic heart of America.

The flow of dealers' orders into Evanston acts as a series of economic impulses racing along an intricate network to a highly responsive nerve center. Hibbards' customers and its 144 salesmen are like sensitive outlying nerve cells which relay information to the firm's executives so that they keep tab simultaneously on business progress in industrial areas, agricultural territories, resort country, dairy lands, etc.

Leading the Way

Probably in no way can Hibbards' close relationship with retail customers be better pictured than by journeying behind the impressive concrete and marble facade which fronts its mammoth warehouse-office to see exactly how this intricate organization functions.

In a business where beauty of office and maximum degree of mechanization for a warehouse were practically unheard of, Hibbards paced the wholesale hardware industry 7 years ago by erecting a tremendous one-story warehouse on the outskirts of Evanston to supersede its 25-year-old, 14-story building in downtown Chicago.

Since then, an increasing number of wholesalers have adopted the principles of one-story warehousing. Invariably, in the planning stage these wholesale executives have looked to Hibbards for help, touring the concrete acreage in Evanston for ideas, and then revising, adapting and perfecting Hibbards' pioneering effort to suit their individual needs.

Faster service—getting merchandise to the dealer at less cost, and passing those savings on to him—with fewer "shorts" to confound him and hamper his buying efforts—those were the underlying objectives behind one-story warehousing for Hibbard, Spencer, Bartlett & Co.

The mechanics of drag-lines and the innermost operational details of such warehousing have been reported in *Hardware Retailer* so frequently that it would be needless repetition to review them again.

At any rate, the story of Hibbards and its century-long devotion to independent dealers is more a story of people, planning and personalities, than it is of mechanical marvels.

Dealer's Partner

Corporation progress can be measured many ways. Stockholders evaluate it by the size and frequency of dividends. Dun & Bradstreet and bankers rate it financially.

But to the most important group of judges—customers—the measure always is taken in terms of service and assistance—by evaluating a wholesaler's activities beyond the mere taking, filling and shipping of orders.

Years ago, before the words "Dealer Service" had been conjured up by some imaginative individual, Hibbard management conscientiously began seeking and finding ways to make its dealers more competitive.

Nowadays, when virtually every dealer is visited by dozens of traveling salesmen and his office is stacked high with want-books from their houses, it seems strange to consider Hibbards' first salesman as the forerunner of a Dealer Service department. Yet that's really what he was.

In Hibbards' early days, wholesalers didn't have drummers on the road. Travel was difficult at best, more often than not, impossible. But transportation improved as the country became more settled. And then, too, competition among wholesalers was getting keener.

Hibbards' first salesman went on the road way back in the company's infancy. His addition to staff evidently was not considered a very momentous occasion, for it was not recorded for posterity. Old records show only that he antedated by a number of years the regular sales force, which began activities about 1870.

From store to store he moved, showing and selling his lines, his primary function. But, in even those years, he established an operating pattern which thousands of Hibbard salesmen were to follow later—of gathering, sifting, evaluating and passing along promotion and display ideas from one customer to another so that each might benefit by the experiences of others on whom he called.

Consolidating Services

In 1932, with the country in the midst of a paralyzing depression, and with dealers suffering from the most serious shortage of all—that of customers Hibbard management concluded that right then, more than at any time in previous history, dealers needed managerial guidance and promotional assistance, and that, if financially feasible, the wholesaler should provide help.

Thus it was that the Dealer Service Department officially was created and given its title. Under this heading, the various dealer-service activities which had been entered into in previous years, one by one, were coordinated and improved upon. (New ones are still being added, such as the recent compilation of basic stock lists.)

1932 also was the year Hibbards set up its first model store. An expensive venture as far as money outlay goes, it paid off in the final analysis. In it, the company's salesmen, dealer service people, buyers and even top brass could pre-test ideas and merchandising theories in settings identical to those in which dealers eventually would put them to use.

Continually modernized in keeping with changing merchandising techniques, the model store served countless dealers as an inspiration for their own store-improvement programs. It gave them many new ideas to incorporate in their stores in Home Town, U.S.A.

For example, when the hardware industry first began considering *Quick*-service, the model store in Evanston was converted to a self-serve method of operation. Lessons learned there by trial and error are saving many Hibbard customers time and money when they, in turn, make the decision to go *Quick*-service.

Such helpful data reach dealers 2 ways: via salesmen, or through a monthly sales-promotion guide called, "Planned Selling," a comprehensive publication which pictures suggested window and interior displays, previews newspaper ad mats which are available, and points out tie-in promotional stunts.

In addition, "Planned Selling" is the vehicle Hibbards uses to offer specially-priced "hot" items which have been procured as traffic-builders for each monthly sales period.

The company always has worked closely with the state and national hardware associations. In recent years, cooperation has advanced to the hand-in-glove stage, allowing a free interchange of information between the 3, thereby helping improve their services to the dealer.

Keeping Up with the Times

Last year, dealer-support kept pace with developments in mass communications and advertising. Fourteen full-page ads were run in Chicago newspapers for True Value stores, which were listed in the ads. Timely specials were bargained-priced to bring customers into retail outlets.

Television was added to Hibbard promotion last fall with a unique tie-in arranged for True Value stores in Chicagoland. Sponsored by Portable Electric Tool Co., "Dr. Fixum," a well-known home-fix-it show, directed viewers to True Value stores for their hardware and housewares needs.

The Buying Function

Few functions in a wholesale hardware operation have received as little publicity as that of buying, yet upon the ability and wisdom of these men rests much of the responsibility for the firm's success and that of its dealers.

If merchandise is bought wisely, dealers can sell at competitive prices. If the buyer keeps his stocks up, dealers won't be plagued with "shorts" and back-ordered items.

However, if he fails to detect new merchandise preferences and trends at the earliest moment, his firm's dealers lose sales and they, in turn, look elsewhere for their needs.

In reality, John Q. Consumer is the only person a wholesale buyer has in mind when he makes a buying decision. He personally may like an item, admiring the profits, style, packaging, etc. The salesman likewise may become enthusiastic about it. And the dealer, in turn, might also take a fancy to it.

But unless a Hibbard buyer is convinced from his firsthand observations and experience that the ultimate consumer will like the item, he does not purchase it.

Hibbards divides buying responsibility among 14 major departments, all of them operated under direct supervision of Ed Kantowicz, vice president, E. L. Mackey, R. A. Brandt, merchandise managers, all of whom are former buyers. They are:

Heavy hardware
Mechanics' tools
Power tools—industrial supplies
Builders' hardware
Toys, wheel goods and giftware
Plumbing supplies
Agricultural supplies (2 divisions)
Sporting goods
Electrical and auto supplies
Guns and ammunition
Paints and drapery supplies
Major appliances
Housewares

Hibbard buyers are responsible for the buying and the sale of the merchandise in their department. This requires a thorough knowledge not only of dealer requirements but also consumer preference, both of which influence his buying decisions.

Naturally, too, Kantowicz points out, Hibbard buyers make it a habit to visit personally with dealers at every opportunity to acquire retail experience. They are encouraged to become acquainted with as many dealers as possible in their home neighborhoods and around suburban Chicago so they can obtain reports on public demand for their respective lines.

No phase of a buyer's job is more important than keeping abreast with design trends and product improvements. Dealers from outlying areas and salesmen rank as 2 important sources of this data. Pre-printed slips requesting merchandise tips and suggestions are supplied liberally to make it easy for opinions from the field to reach buyers.

Trade shows constitute a third way in which Hibbards' buyers keep tabs on developments in their fields. They spend considerable time at trade shows, trudging up and down exhibit aisles examining new items and, in general, acquiring a broad outlook on the basic style improvements being made.

Contributing the final balance for a buyer's good judgment is studious reading of trade publications.

Buying New Goods

Retailers and wholesale buyers can sympathize with each other on one count. Both spend a good portion of their busy lives talking to salesmen.

On an average, 25 "vendors" make their pitches in a buyer's office during the course of a week. This includes regular suppliers as well as hopeful manufacturers' representatives or salesmen with new lines to offer.

An exacting procedure, designed to minimize bad guesses, is followed in selecting new items. When a buyer feels that a new item is worthwhile, he attends a weekly meeting of the Promotion and New Goods Committee, composed of the sales manager, merchandise manager and general sales manager.

He comes to the meeting armed with pertinent information on the product and its merits, and in addition gives a source report on the manufacturer. This latter includes the manufacturers' sales policy, profit margins, freight terms and a list of other wholesalers being sold.

In committee, the buyer is asked how many items of like type or quality he already carries in stock.

"For the dealer's sake, we strive to avoid duplication of lines," Kantowicz explains. "This also helps us keep our own inventory in hand, but more important is the fact that it simplifies the dealer's buying job."

Before a buyer can add a new item which closely duplicates one already carried in inventory, he must dispose of the old item. Consequently, retailers are continually offered merchandise which is priced right and properly styled.

Packaging bears heavily on the acceptance or rejection of items, according to Kantowicz. If a new item is offered in a display carton, or as part of a "deal" that won't fit into an average store's layout, it is turned down because Hibbards feels that dealers will not accept it readily. It might be salable, but the item must be packaged to fit existing fixtures and floor space allotments.

The number of new items which get as far as the New Goods Committee remains somewhat constant between 1,500 and 2,000 yearly.

Inventory—King-size Headache

Only by strict control on new items is Hibbards able to keep its inventory around 30,000 items without sacrificing flexibility sufficient to satisfy dealer demand. Even so, counting inventory at year-end winds up as a 2 day job for the entire warehouse crew.

Considering that Hibbards' crew consists of more than 200 men and women, inventory-taking adds up to 3,200 work hours—the equivalent of one man working a 10-hour day, 6 days a week for 52 weeks—and no vacation.

Dealers who have recently completed their own inventory can shed a sympathetic tear for an inventory control problem of this size.

Hibbards' buying philosophy is best summed up by Ed Kantowicz: "From the buying standpoint, we are trying to offer our dealers the broadest selection of quality merchandise—priced to be in line with their competition, whether that competitor be a chain store, a syndicate operation or a super market or drug store trying to skim off a little cream.

"We are working closely with manufacturers supplying the hardware trade in the matter of packaging, keeping in mind the growing trend to self-service. This effort, we believe, is helping the retailer.

"When wholesaler and retailer work together, as we work with our dealers," Kantowicz concludes, "they will comprise a team that can't be beat."

Selecting Items for Sales

As its name implies, the Promotion and New Goods Committee does more than pass judgment on new items. It also selects merchandise for Hibbards' consumer circular and catalogs. The committee depends heavily on dealer experience in making selections.

Immediately after each promotion has been concluded, the Dealer Service Department surveys dealers in all parts of the country who represent all types of trading areas. The dealers grade individual items in that promotion as good, fair or poor sellers.

When tabulated, these surveys are an accurate barometer of the buying preferences of the public.

Each buyer compiles a list of items which he feels will fit into the particular promotion being planned. First consideration is given to seasonal appeal and Hibbards' ability to provide special prices. Next step is to review the item's cost to Hibbard, comparing its regular and suggested sell with its regular and suggested retail, how the item sold in the past, and finally, the buyer's expectations on the quantity that will be sold.

Admittedly, because of the very nature of the hardware business, a good many items repeat from year to year, simply because lines do not change very much.

New life is injected into each promotion, insofar as possible, by drawing upon the new goods added to Hibbards' inventory each year.

What Items Sell Best?

Housewares items are among the most successful products for consumer promotions, dealers report. Women respond more readily to bargain appeals than men. Hence, Hibbards directs most of its bargain-priced leaders to the female of the species.

For instance, during 1954's Fall True Value Sale, a small enamel roaster priced at 39¢ brought women into stores in droves. An ironing board, carrying a much higher price tag but still representing a mighty good bargain, likewise demonstrated remarkable pulling power.

In order to guarantee that its broadsides and catalogs will develop extra traffic for dealers, Hibbards slashes its margin on leaders. Not all of the cutting can be effected at wholesale level, however. Some reduction in dealers' margins must take place.

By bearing most of this burden, however, Hibbards' circular merchandise still manages to show the dealer a very satisfactory markup.

The Salesman's Job

Once a manufacturer has convinced a buyer and the New Goods Committee that his item should be added to inventory, disposition of the merchandise becomes the responsibility of a relatively young man (37) whose entire business career has been within the Hibbard organization.

It's up to George McIntyre, vice president and general sales manager, to see that it sells.

"My background is not too colorful," McIntyre asserts. "Because my early training was taken during the depression, it was necessary to immediately create habits of attending to very little but business. I now find myself with no hobbies of which I can brag."

Keeping 144 salesmen enthusiastic as they range far and wide servicing 5,000 customers, keyed to the high pitch that Hibbards requires of its field force, is the way "Mac" spends his days.

A few of those 5,000 dealers are situated in some far-off places—from Vancouver, Wash., to Brownsville, Texas, and Miami, Fla. Orders even come in from a dealer located in Nassau, Bahama Islands.

McIntyre shudders noticeably if the word "selling" is applied to the men under his supervision. He much prefers the word "servicing" to describe their activities.

A Hibbard man, he says, *services* approximately 30 retail hardware stores per month. In addition, each calls on some sporting goods outlets and specialty stores.

The time a salesman spends with a dealer depends primarily upon the cooperation the dealer gives him. For a Hibbard man to service a customer adequately, McIntyre considers half a day the minimum requirement. In that time, he will cover promotional helps which are available, review dealer service activities emanating from Evanston, and pass along any worthwhile ideas gleaned from other customers.

And, unless he's fond of tersely worded home-office memos signed, "McIntyre," he'll secure an order before departing.

McIntyre points out, though, that a salesman's first responsibility is to assist the dealer with his merchandising problems.

A good salesman, as McIntyre describes him, acts as a dealer's merchandising specialist. Drawing upon the experiences of other retailers on whom he calls, and adding that to what is drummed into him in sales letters and at sales meetings, he possesses a vast storehouse of information which he can translate into display and merchandising improvements for his customers.

"We supply him with a sales promotion guide and expect him to help decorate windows, re-arrange counter displays, and do anything else that needs attention. We don't want want-book writers.

"I like to think that a Hibbard salesman is not as concerned with the immediate order as much as he is the dealer's over-all welfare," McIntyre says. "The order automatically follows.

"For instance, a few months ago our salesmen were advising dealers that orders for steel goods would earn an extra 5% if entered by Nov. 15. They were attempting to save that dealer 5% on his purchases, a 5% which he would lose if he waited until February or March to do his buying."

Similar savings, he says, are continually being passed along to retailers. As a result, Hibbards' men expect to supply a major portion of dealers' requirements.

"The independent hardware dealer today is faced with a real challenge in effectively competing with syndicate stores for the consumer dollar," he says. "Not only the chain stores, which usually have handled many of our hardware lines, but now many food and drug chains are adding hardware items in an effort to increase their profit margins.

"The hardware dealers' syndicate competition has a distinct advantage in practically all lines with their gigantic purchasing power, professional display and advertising service." However the independent hardware merchant can successfully meet this challenge if he will cast his lot with an aggressive, forward-thinking wholesaler who is equipped to furnish him with comparable sales promotions and bargain-price trade stimulators, such as are made available to the syndicate store by their headquarters.

A Two-way Responsibility

"Hardware wholesalers must recognize their responsibility to their dealers and provide them with the same professional services that are being supplied to the individual chain store outlets," McIntyre continues. "This can be accomplished if the retailer and wholesaler will accept their individual responsibility and develop a high degree of co-operation. The job cannot be done by one alone. I believe a hardware wholesaler salesman has a very definite responsibility if he is to justify his position in a method of distribution such as this," he says.

"On the other hand, if the wholesaler's salesman is to devote a greater portion of his time in assisting his dealers with merchandising problems, then the hardware merchant should select that wholesaler as headquarters for a large share of his requirements. In the past, many independent hardware dealers have exercised their independence to too high a degree and have purchased their requirements from a great number of sources.

"This has resulted in devoting a great deal of time to duplicate interviews with many salesmen performing identical functions.

"If the independent dealer will recognize that it is possible for him to concentrate the majority of his purchases with one source," McIntyre concludes, "then the detail involved in placing his orders will be reduced considerably. Thus it becomes possible for his salesman to profitably spend a great amount of time with him."

Fast Service Assured

When Hibbards moved from downtown Chicago to the 18-acre Evanston warehouse, a remarkable speedup and simplification of order-handling took place.

Nowadays, same-day or 24-hour service is standard operating procedure. For instance, an order received Tuesday morning normally is on the shipping platform that night or, at the lastest, Wednesday noon.

Processes necessary for such speedy handling and order-filling are quite fascinating.

Orders are first handled in the mail department, then quickly transferred to the Order Entry department, where they are entered, numbered and split into 2 parts for faster handling.

One portion is routed to the Broken Package section of the warehouse; the other goes to Full Package. Both parts are filled simultaneously.

When completed, the filled orders are merged at the shipping dock, but not before each part has been double-checked after warehouse employees have scampered or roller-skated through the maze of shelving to fill it. At the shipping dock, the sheets are referred to the Bill of Lading department, where shipping receipts are completed so the shipment can be turned over to a trucking concern.

Order sheets then are dispatched to the Pricing department where prices are checked, extended and totaled. This process completed, the order is fed into a Bruning machine which makes invoices photographically for mailing to dealers.

Low-cost Distribution

"After we have the right merchandise (which we never quite achieve), and have housed it in a low-cost warehouse, our job is to supply it to dealers at the lowest possible cost. It is our responsibility, I feel to reduce distribution costs wherever possible.

"If the dealer desires to operate from check-lists, pre-printed order blanks, etc., and has the necessary personnel to do the work, then much of the work normally done by the salesman can be eliminated. This is exactly the method used by successful chain store operators, and there is no reason why an independent hardware retailer cannot operate in the same manner. Savings can be realized, and these should be passed on to the retailer.

"I feel also that our retailer should be offered the opportunity to make additional savings in distribution costs by factory shipments direct to the dealer whenever they can be set up on an economical basis, from a quantity and weight standpoint, by the manufacturer. This saving, where it can be realized, must be passed on to the retailer.

"Also, many items can be purchased on a pool-car or pool-truck basis by securing orders in advance and distributing direct from the incoming car to the dealer, without having to put them in the warehouse. This is another means of savings that can be passed on to the retailer.

"The aggressive dealer of today is searching for a program of hard-hitting promotions and merchandising ideas. It is Hibbards' job to help the dealer move merchandise at the retail level."

··{ 21 }··

How Nabisco Reshuffled Its Marketing Setup after 57 Years*

Since it started baking and selling Uneeda Biscuits in 1897, National Biscuit Co. has grown into one of the larger U.S. food marketers. During all those 57 years, Nabisco stuck faithfully to its policy of distributing direct to retailers through its own sales and delivery force. Now, after thinking about it for seven years, Nabisco is making its most radical distribution change—it will start full-scale use of wholesalers for non-perishable products.

What this means, actually, is that Nabisco has finally joined the army of other companies cutting down or eliminating direct-distribution. Nabisco will continue to distribute its perishable foods directly through its 3,500 salesmen and 1,900 trucks, but the company will switch to wholesalers for its cereals and dog foods. At the same time, the change will allow Nabisco to add new products to its line, something it found difficult under the direct-distribution system.

To build a new marketing organization for its cereals and dog foods, Nabisco has divorced them from the rest of the firm's operations, put them under a newly-organized Special Products Division and departed

---

* Reprinted by special permission from *Tide*, November 6, 1954. Copyright, 1954, *Tide*.

from a 57-year-old direct-distribution tradition. Its main reason for the move:

1. Unlike most of Nabisco's other products, dog food and cereal aren't perishable. Therefore there is little need for the speedy (and expensive) delivery from bakery to retail outlet required for the company's other products—mostly crackers (200 varieties) and bread (Nabisco has 15 cracker bakeries and 16 bread bakeries across the U.S.).

2. Where each Nabisco salesman sold the complete line of products in the past, some lines—specifically dog foods and cereals—got only secondary attention. Under the new Special Products Division, its sales-men can devote their full energy to its products and, by the same token, salesmen elsewhere in the company will be able to concentrate their efforts more effectively on a smaller line. Nabisco's sales vice-president Lee S. Bickmore explains that "We thought it advisable to set up direct responsibility for these products and divorce them entirely from the thinking of a cookie and cracker house." Adds Hal M. Chase, general manager of the new division: "Biscuits always dominated the house."

3. As an almost self-contained operation, no longer restricted by the former direct-distribution system, the new division enables Nabisco to expand horizontally into food products beyond its present fields. "If we were just interested in continuing our present set-up," Bickmore points out, "we wouldn't have taken this step." Two companies pur-chased by Nabisco early this year indicate something of the company's plans: it bought Ranger Joe Cereal Co. (Chester, Pa.), maker of Wheat Honies and Rice Honies, and Schooley & Son (Luzerne, Pa.), maker of Blue Streak Dog Food.

Backed to the Hilt

Nabisco is backing its new division with a greatly expanded ad cam-paign. Last month the company made its first foray into network tele-vision with a half-hour Friday evening ABC-TV show featuring a latter-day Rin Tin Tin. The dog will also star on a half-hour Sunday night Mutual radio network show beginning in January.

To give the new division complete autonomy, Chase has full control and authority over all its operations. The division will share the com-pany's legal, personnel, purchasing and publicity departments, but all other phases of its operation is in the hands of specific departments within Chase's division.

The decision to form the new division was by no means sudden. Nabisco has been racking up record sales each year for the past eight years (1953 sales: $359 million), expects to reach a new high this year also—and, with insignificant exceptions, it's been done by distributing directly through retail outlets. However, for about seven years the com-pany has considered making a change in anticipation of diversifying into other lines. Another factor is that most new supermarkets ask for

How Nabisco is changing its distribution methods

FROM THIS . . .

SHREDDED WHEAT		BRAN	DOG FOOD	
Oakland, Calif. bakery	Niagara Falls, N. Y. bakery	Battle Creek, Mich. bakery	New York N. Y. bakeries	Los Angeles, Calif. bakeries

BY COMMON CARRIER
(RAIL OR TRUCK)

250 NABISCO-OWNED REGIONAL SALES AGENCIES AND WAREHOUSES

1900 NABISCO-OWNED TRUCKS

500,000 U.S. RETAIL FOOD OUTLETS

TO THIS . . .

SHREDDED WHEAT		BRAN	DOG FOOD	
Oakland, Calif. bakery	Niagara Falls, N. Y. bakery	Battle Creek, Mich. bakery	New York N. Y. bakeries	Los Angeles, Calif. bakeries

BY COMMON CARRIER
(RAIL OR TRUCK)

CHAIN STORE WAREHOUSES AND FOOD WHOLESALERS

CHAIN STORE AND WHOLESALER TRUCKS

500,000 U.S. RETAIL FOOD OUTLETS

delivery to either their warehouses or through wholesalers so their ordering and bookkeeping is simpler.

More than four years ago, Nabisco set up a "task force" of key personnel from every department in the company to study the problem with
some outside management consultants and come up with a report. After
an 18-month investigation which ended in February, 1951, the group
recommended the setting up of a separate division using a tailor-made
marketing system. A second Nabisco task force explored the idea more
thoroughly and laid out plans for starting up the new division: they
analyzed such things as costs of operation, sales and profit potentials from
both a short and long range view, methods of distribution and expansion
possibilities.

Fragility & Freshness

Nabisco had been in a comparatively poor competitive position, cost-
wise, just because of its expensive distribution methods for its cereals
and dog foods. The firm's salesmen call on nearly 500,000 U.S. retail
food stores, visit most of them at least once a week. Most other major dog
food and cereal companies sell through distributors. The Nabisco task
force found it unnecessary to give these products the daily attention
crackers and bread require; they are not as fragile, and freshness isn't as
much a day-to-day sales factor. Consequently, they can be handled in
larger units with more efficiency.

In talking about the formation of the Special Products Division,
George H. Coppers, Nabisco president, explains that "We are enthusiastic about this step. It places the products involved into the form
of distribution utilized by our major competitors and, more important,
the distribution greatly desired by many of our major accounts."

Jobbers Clamoring

Nabisco either doesn't know or at least isn't saying how much will be
saved in delivery costs through the new distribution system. Bickmore
does concede that "It will make a difference for the U.S. as a whole.
We don't know what the area-by-area change will be."

On August 1, Chase was moved up from his job as director of marketing for Nabisco's sales department to take over the new division.
The second task force had set up a table of organization and Chase's
first job was to "fill in the slots." Almost all the newly created jobs
were filled from within the company.

To insure a complete divorce (and to stimulate a fresh approach) Nabisco even removed the cereal and dog food products from McCann-
Erickson (which still has all other Nabisco products) and turned it over
to Kenyon & Eckhardt (under account executive William King, Jr.).
The ad budget for cereals and dog foods (Pal Wee-Bits, Milk-Bone, Nabisco Shredded Wheat and Nabisco 100% Bran) has been increased

"substantially" without cutting elsewhere (Nabisco's total ad budget this year will hit about $9,000,000). The new division will advertise in consumer magazines, newspapers, spot radio and television (besides the Rin Tin Tin shows), food trade publications, medical journals and dog publications. It will also distribute point-of-purchase displays and continue supplying film and educational material for school children.

However, by far the heaviest emphasis will be placed on network radio and television. Some of the impact of the expanded mass media campaign is expected to "spill over" and pep up sales of the company's other products.

A Lot on the Nose

Just a few weeks ago, the Special Products Division started distributing in the San Francisco area; it will move into Southern California and the Pacific Northwest any day now. Chase hasn't decided where the next move will be, but he's aiming for national wholesaler distribution as fast as possible. He's got a tough trade relations problem on his hands, what with food brokers in every area of the country clamoring to handle the lines, but he isn't hurrying with any decisions. Nabisco marketing specialists are choosing wholesale outlets with special care to insure that the company's expensive new venture pays off.

In any event, general manager Chase and his staff anxiously await the reaction to Nabisco's two Rin Tin Tin network shows. Quips Chase: "Never did so much ride on the nose of a dog."

·{ 22 }·

The INCO Distributor—a Partner in Sales*

Distributors for International Nickel products are located in 36 cities in the U.S. and in Canada, United Kingdom, Argentina, Chile, Peru, Brazil, Mexico, Uruguay, Belgium, France, Germany, Italy and Switzerland. They sell the 50 different INCO alloys.

One of the oldest and largest of these distributors is the Whitehead Metal Products Co., Inc., New York, with annual sales topping $50,000,-000. Company has branches in Philadelphia, Buffalo, Harrison (N.J.), Cambridge, Syracuse and Baltimore. It is the only distributor in the U.S. that is a wholly-owned subsidiary of INCO.

---

* Reprinted by special permission from *Printers' Ink*, December 16, 1955. Copyright, 1955, *Printers' Ink*.

Whitehead has been handling INCO products since 1917. Only two other distributors predate Whitehead—Williams & Co., Pittsburgh, the first of the company's distributors (1909); and Steel Sales Corp., Chicago (1917).

The New York representative for International Nickel is a healthy giant. Its main headquarters on lower West 10th St. include 188,000 square feet of space. An additional 30,000 square feet is being added. In its warehouses Whitehead stocks 20,000 different items . . . products of INCO, Alcoa, Anaconda and other big names in corrosion-resisting metals and plastic. Whitehead's monthly pay roll is more than $250,000. It has 25,000 active accounts, 100 salesmen—and business has never been better. In October Whitehead chalked up more than $5,000,000 in sales —its largest single month.

But times weren't always rosy for Whitehead. The early years were rough. At the turn of the century, Judson J. Whitehead, Sr., was manager of a brass warehouse in Boston. Working with him was a spirited young man, Thomas M. Bohen, who is now chairman of the board of Whitehead. Mr. Whitehead opened up his own shop in Boston in 1914, bringing young Bohen along as a salesman. The baby organization, which was handling the products of Detroit Copper & Brass Rolling Mills (later absorbed by American Brass Co.) had 3 salesmen. Their books showed total sales of $100,000 for the first year.

Whitehead Metals was having its problems in 1926. In that year, International Nickel stepped in and made the distributor a wholly-owned subsidiary. An executive at INCO says the move was made "because of financial reasons."

"Busted and Broke"

Outspoken T. M. Bohen, with a twinkle in his eye and the assurance that comes from knowing that sales now are better than ever, puts it more bluntly: "We were busted and broke."

But even as a wholly-owned subsidiary of International Nickel of Canada, Whitehead gets the same treatment as any independent distributor in INCO's chain. INCO has no favorites, nor can it afford any. Whitehead gets its allocation of nickel products just the same as the other distributors. Relations between the distributor and its parent company are scrupulously unbiased.

And Whitehead sells the metals of other companies with the same intensity that it peddles nickel alloys from International. It, too, can ill afford to be partial.

"We do not sell INCO products where other materials are better suited," says Mr. Bohen. "Our job is to help the customer select the best material for the job at hand."

These days, nearly half of all Whitehead's sales are in INCO products. But, like International Nickel, Whitehead has problems of supply.

The bulk (considerably more than 50%) of total nickel orders comes from priority sales. There's no question that Whitehead could sell more nickel than it is now getting, but so could any one of the other INCO distributors.

Problem of Supply

The problem of supply is pinpointed by Whitehead president Clayton D. Grover: "Sometimes a customer will use a substitute. He may go back to nickel alloy in a few years when supply will be plentiful. But the risk we take is that the customer might decide to make a permanent change in his choice of metals. Then we risk the loss of a customer."

It's not unusual for Whitehead to work for 3 or 4 years on a future order, only to be frustrated by lack of supplies. Take the case of large architectural jobs. Whitehead officials are in on discussions even before the blueprints are created. Throughout the blueprinting and planning stages, Whitehead executives are available for counsel. But when the customer wants to place the order for the nickel products, Whitehead may be stymied. Not enough material for the order!

Years of investment in service go down the drain if the customer decides he can't wait for supplies to come through. If some other suitable metal is available, both Whitehead and International Nickel risk the loss of future business. The constant fear of all nickel interests is that a customer once lost may never return.

"There's no answer yet to this problem," says Mr. Grover. "As long as the government is stockpiling nickel and big defense requirements continue, the problem will exist."

Meantime, Whitehead and other INCO distributors aren't sitting on their hands. They're out selling hard, with major emphasis on solutions of customers' production problems, both present and future.

For the job of present and future selling, Whitehead keeps its staff of 100 salesmen on its toes. Company maintains an active advertising program designed to help its salesmen in the field. The distributor's advertising investment is about $180,000 a year. Direct mail to some 66,000 customers and prospects, some advertising in the metal trade papers and a slick catalog brought up to date every few years combine to provide the backbone of the company's advertising efforts.

Promotional Help from INCO

A major advertising assist comes from the extensive industrial advertising of International Nickel itself. The company's sales and advertising slogan, *Help your customer and you help yourself*, takes form in INCO's trade advertising. Distributors' names are included in the promotional material, and case histories highlight the constant attempt to help the distributor solve his customers' problems.

In addition, Whitehead and other INCO distributors get a hefty assist in the form of cooperative advertising allowances. The large mass of technical and sales literature furnished by INCO is all at the disposal of the company's distributors.

The widespread activities of INCO's research and development department dovetail with the technical needs of Whitehead. The research and development staff spends about two-thirds of its time on metallurgical problems. INCO metallurgists, engineers, physicists and industry specialists are continually at work helping the distributor's customers solve their problems.

Technical Services

The development and research department works not only for the consumer of nickel and nickel alloys but of all other metals as well. There are welding forums and clinics, corrosion engineering activities and extensive field tests of heat-resistant alloys. International Nickel's marine test stations at Kure Beach and Harbor Island (both N.C.), and its research laboratory at Bayonne are other centers of service to the metals consumer.

Staffs of INCO's development and research field offices are experienced consultants who help users choose the proper alloys to solve their materials selection problems. These staffs offer an excellent complement to Whitehead's own technical staff.

Another outlet of INCO's development and research activities involves the technical meeting—a recent innovation. Meetings are held throughout the country to help solve metals consumers' problems. During the past 5 years, technical meetings have been held with 1,382 companies.

What does the metals consumer get out of these meetings? There are at least 5 objectives of these meetings . . . and they generally pay off:

1. To answer consumers' specific problems.
2. To review applications of various metals, including INCO alloys in industry.
3. To discover industries' needs as a guide to the development of new information and new alloys.
4. To demonstrate the competence of INCO's staff, the resources of data upon which they can draw and the value of the help they can give.
5. To promote good relations between INCO engineers and the engineering staff of the metals consumer.

Whitehead recognizes the need and the value of this kind of complementary activity on the part of its supplier.

Whitehead's salesmen are experts in their own right. The average outside salesman has about 9 years' service with the distributor. But even at that, Mr. Bohen figures that his distributorship averages about 2 or 3 calls a day to International Nickel for the purpose of getting the answers to a customer problem.

Unique Problems of Telephone Selling

Whitehead's total selling staff includes both inside and outside salesmen. The inside man is a service salesman who handles most of his business over the telephone or by letter. His task is neither easy nor mechanical.

This inside man, according to the Whitehead selling plan, is faced with 8 major problems. He is unable to see the buyer. He must rely solely on hearing him clearly and understanding him correctly. He must ignore interference of extraneous noises at both ends of the wire. He must do his job within a limited time. He must determine quickly what the buyer wants to know. He must get the needed facts. He must know where to find the necessary technical information. He must adjust his speed of conversation to the buyer's speed of comprehension.

For these reasons, Whitehead has a great deal of respect and admiration for its effective inside salesmen. Both Mr. Bohen and Mr. Grover are quick to assure you that by no means are these inside salesmen mere order takers. They're hard-selling service salesmen. 60% of Whitehead's business is handled by inside salesmen.

Four Duties of Outside Salesmen

Outside salesmen are in the field calling on customers and prospects. Twelve of these outside salesmen deal largely with INCO alloy products.

The average Whitehead field salesman has 4 types of duties: (1) He must plan his work; (2) sell all of the Whitehead products; (3) record and report on his activities; (4) keep up with his job and with local industries.

Within the scope of these main activities, Whitehead's field salesmen are concerned with 3 types of sales—competitive, expansion and conversion sales.

There's no room for passivity in any of this. Whitehead salesmen must get the prospect to buy from Whitehead the same material he is buying from another source—or they must convince a customer to use more of what they buy from Whitehead.

Perhaps the most difficult job is to convert the prospect from the material he is using (and with which the prospect's engineer, designers, technical men and production staff are familiar) to the use of a material (one handled by Whitehead) with which these various groups are not familiar.

Two-Man Teams

Whitehead field salesmen work closely with supplier representatives. It's quite common for a Whitehead salesman to consult a specialist from International or for one of Whitehead's other suppliers to get help in planning for the Whitehead salesman's future calls.

Strategy for these two-man planning teams is carefully worked out for utmost effectiveness. Before the Whitehead salesman hits the road, he confers with the specialist so that he clearly understands his selling objective. The Whitehead man contributes his knowledge of the buyer's attitudes, opinions and problems. Or he may tell the specialist that there are still other problems to be solved—technical, competitive or relating to a material specification.

With all the facts from the salesman, the INCO specialist on the industry of which the sales prospect is a part is then able to give the Whitehead man the information that will help him get his order.

At INCO district meetings with Whitehead's main and branch offices, considerable time is spent in discussing the problems of individual customers and prospects. In fact, the Whitehead salesman gets specialized help and advice from International to help him do a more effective selling job with his present customers and to help him develop new ones.

Branch Managers from Management Committee

Whitehead runs an efficient shop. Each of its 7 branches (including home base in New York) has its own sales force. The branch manager is general sales manager of his organization. Each branch keeps its sales activities current via monthly meetings. Once a year Whitehead gathers all its salesmen for a general meeting.

Whitehead's operating policies grow out of its day-to-day activities, guided by the efforts of a management committee consisting of all branch managers and the officers of the company. In addition to Mr. Bohen and Mr. Grover, other company officers are: E. W. Silver, vice-president and treasurer; E. W. Lothman, vice-president and secretary.

More formal policy is laid down by the board of directors. In addition to Whitehead executives, it includes 8 executives from International Nickel.

Whitehead makes its biggest margin of profit, according to board chairman Bohen, by selling small lots. "We make our living by buying cases and breaking them into small lots," he says. The board chairman would like to have all small orders doubled in weight. Whitehead's average order—and this probably holds for most INCO distributors—weighs about 200 pounds and comes to about $160.

Whitehead customers include such big names as Firestone Industrial, Scott Paper, Armstrong Cork, Pullman Standard Car, Bates Mfg. Co., General Electric, Raytheon and Westinghouse. On the other hand, on a typical day's order sheet you might find such customers as the First Church of Christ Scientist, Harvard University or a retail hardware store in Pawtucket. The small order to top them all came in one day from the Ritz-Carlton Hotel—it was for 6 half-inch Monel machine screws.

Regardless of the size, Whitehead fills every order and performs the traditional service role of the industrial distributor. "An industrial distributor is interested in service more than any one thing," says president Grover. "His goal is to have the material in the warehouse when the customer wants it."

Like its supplier, International Nickel Co., Whitehead finds it difficult to have material on hand to fill every order. That's why service more than ever dominates INCO's operating policy and that of its distributors.

··{ 23 }··

The Confessions of an Industrial Distributor*

BY R. G. DEVRIES†

To sell me, a manufacturer has not one but two problems. First he has to sell me personally about the values of his product. And then he has to help me do a selling job on it.

I am an industrial distributor, and there are more than 2,500 other industrial distributors, or mill supply houses, in the U.S. plus maybe another 2,000 supplementary distributors. We do a business of about $4 billion a year and many companies rely on us almost entirely to handle their direct selling to industrial users and consumers.

As for me, I do about a half million dollars' worth of business a year and maintain a constant inventory of around 10,000 different items worth more than $100,000. I specialize in cutting tools of all kinds, fasteners, precision tools, and transmission material such as V-belts, sheaves, and so on. I market nothing under my own brand but sell everything under the brand name of the manufacturers whose products I distribute. For this reason I am deeply concerned with their selling and marketing programs.

Altogether I handle the lines of ten major suppliers and about 40 other suppliers. The advertising, promotion, sales and marketing programs of these suppliers have a direct effect on the amount of business they do—therefore on the amount of business I do, and I will explain why.

---

* Reprinted by special permission from *Industrial Marketing*, November, 1955. Copyright, 1955, by Advertising Publications, Inc., 200 East Illinois Street, Chicago 11.
† President, Northern Industrial Supply Co., Chicago.

Ways to Keep Me Happy

Of all the lines I handle, I would say that the Cleveland Twist Drill Co. does the best over-all marketing job. The company manufactures drills, reamers, tool bits and the like; and I am best pleased with it, of all the companies whose lines I sell.

1. It maintains engineering counsel and advice in Chicago equal to that in its own factory.

2. The quality of its personnel is outstanding.

3. Its men make industrial calls entirely on their own and assist in the engineering problems of our customers.

4. It has a teletype service direct to its plant, which gets action in the shortest possible time.

5. Whatever it sells must be sold through an authorized distributor.

6. It supports its price structure.

7. It advertises strongly in industrial publications directly to users of its supplies with mention of buying through authorized distributors.

8. Its catalog is outstanding in its method of publication and in its descriptive material. The catalog is complete, printed in two colors, and the company is generous with giving us enough copies for our customers with our firm's name imprinted on the cover in gold ink.

We're Not Alone

We are by no means exclusive distributors of Cleveland Twist Drill Co. products. In fact the company has seven authorized distributors in Chicago alone. But it favors no one distributor. When its sales engineers go out, they do not go with the sales engineers of any distributor, unless the customer specifically requests it. It takes something special, I would say, to keep seven competing distributors in one city happy but the company does.

The engineers of Cleveland Twist Drill save sales for us constantly. One of our customers manufactures large quantities of precision valves. The heads are die cast and the metal is extremely abrasive. In this material the drills wore out too fast and there was extreme breakage. A sales engineer of Cleveland Twist Drill studied the problem at our request and was able to recommend a change in the point of the drill, in the lead and in the flutes. The redesigned drill had an increased service life of 500%.

We sold fewer drills for this one job, of course, but we have the satisfaction of solving this problem and of delivering a satisfactory product. And both our own services and Cleveland Twist Drill products have risen considerably in the esteem of our customer.

Don't Do This

Let me contrast this example with that of another company whose products we distribute. The company is a tool manufacturer with a nationally-known brand. Its products are excellent. It advertises fairly well in trade publications. Its catalogs are good and complete. Yet it is erring.

1. The caliber of its men is low.

2. Its engineering service does not approach the quality of that offered by Cleveland Twist Drill. If it did, its sales would certainly increase to a point justified by the high quality of the product.

3. The company is failing to adhere to its established price structure and appears to be allowing certain distributors to undermine the structure. This is hearsay, but the evidence seems pretty conclusive. For example, we are losing a lot of orders because our customers ask us for quotations on this particular brand and when we don't get the orders they tell us that our prices are not competitive.

The company's attitude toward customers is indicated by the fact that when I challenged their representative on this point he demanded that I dig up the proof. Proof would be extremely difficult for me to get and relatively easy for him.

Spend Time with Us

There are many ways that manufacturers can help distributors sell their products. A fine example is that of the Lufkin Rule Co., precision tool maker.

Lufkin is interested in our problems and in the men selling their tools. Their representative in Chicago has learned the art of instilling in our sales engineers an intense interest in the tools made by Lufkin. Whenever new tools are out, their sales engineer spends time with each salesman demonstrating how the tools operate, what their advantages are, and somehow inspiring them with enthusiasm for Lufkin products. He also conducts classes.

As a result of these special selling efforts our sales of Lufkin tools have increased more than 400% in four years.

As I write this we are participating in a direct mail campaign planned and organized by Carborundum. They have printed seven four-color direct mail pieces which are going out in the next 14 weeks. One of these is mailed every two weeks to customers all over the country, imprinted with the name of the industrial distributor sponsoring the particular list of names.

We have submitted to them a list of 600 of our own customers and we pay $1.84 per hundred for typewriter addressing of the mailing pieces to these customers plus 2¢ postage for each piece. Carborundum pays for the printing, paper and envelopes and handles the program. They have gone all out on this campaign and I think it is excellent. I believe it will click.

A direct mail campaign of a different kind in which we are participating is sponsored by Bausch & Lomb. They have released to us folders on card stock containing a postcard and imprinted with our firm name. The folders describe a booklet they have prepared called "Industrial Magnifiers, How to Choose and Use Them." And they invite the customer, in our name, to tear off the postcard and mail it to Bausch & Lomb requesting the booklet.

The postcard also contains our imprint so that Bausch & Lomb will know how many of our customers have responded.

Advice to Manufacturers

If I can give advice to manufacturers selling through industrial distributors it is that they have to help us sell. We have to sell directly, and often in very competitive situations. And we also have to give service.

1. Trade publication advertising is extremely important. Most of our customers ask for specifically branded products. They can only know about those brands by some form of advertising.

2. Direct mail is also important in establishing identity of products, and even more valuable to us if it ties our name in with the manufacturer's brand name.

3. Direct calls and direct selling is essential for many products. We have to sell directly and our efforts are aided by manufacturers' direct selling efforts. This is especially true for technical products that require a high level of engineering know-how, ability to answer technical questions, and help in solving technical problems.

4. Service calls are important. Our salesmen are also engineers but usually they cannot compete in engineering know-how with the sales engineers of a particular line who have specialized in its problems. Just as we have to stand back of the products we sell, so the manufacturer has to stand back of the products he sells. And one of the best ways he can do that, if the product warrants it, is to provide a service organization.

5. Complete catalog data is absolutely essential for most industrial products. It is necessary for us in ordering and selling, and for the customer in ordering and buying.

6. Envelope stuffers have a certain potential, but I don't think they're No. 1 on the list by a wide margin.

7. Point of purchase material is of minor interest to us. We have to have some counter service but we really don't want to pick up business from the street. We want to take orders by telephone or mail and make our own deliveries.

8. Participation in trade shows, demonstrations, sales courses, and any other sales aids that help us sell are welcomed. Of course, manufacturers cannot do everything, but the essentials cannot be neglected.

Ideal Time for a Drive

But in most cases, gaining general acceptance is a long haul. For example, we deal with a company which makes a fine drill chuck. We sell some of them because they could make deliveries at a time when we couldn't get Jacobs chucks, which are our regular line. That probably would have been an ideal time for this company to put on a strong selling and merchandising campaign. But they didn't and now Jacobs chucks are again in good supply. We sell many more because our customers ask for them by name.

That's what a strong marketing program can achieve for any industrial producer. Selling is easier and better for both us and the manufacturer.

·{ 24 }··

What a Good Co-op Can Do for its Members*

BY JOSEPH J. TROUT

"Today, our biggest problem is fighting the battle of location," says Willard Rhodes, manager of Associated Grocers of Seattle, Washington.

By fighting the battle of location, Mr. Rhodes means that his organization, owned by some 412 State of Washington grocers, names as its number-one problem in 1956 that of learning about the development of new locations with good potentials for super markets, sewing them up for members, and providing the wherewithall for members to build on those locations. Retailers throughout the country will agree that this is perhaps the biggest two-sided problem of the day: the availability of good locations, the financing needed to develop those good locations into going stores.

Five years ago, Rhodes might have singled out entirely another problem as his members' most pressing need; five years from now, it will probably be another one still unheard of. The point is this: the important attribute of a successful wholesale house is successful members, and to have successful members, the house must anticipate and furnish whatever services its retailer-customers require in order to be on an equal footing with—even one step ahead of—their competition.

Cooperatives have had an up-and-down history, just as have other factors in the food business. They are by no means a new element in retailing; in 1892, the Frankford Grocers' Assn. was formed in what was

---

* Reprinted by special permission from *Progressive Grocer*, November, 1956. Copyright, 1956, *Progressive Grocer*.

then a suburb of Philadelphia. At the time, the specific need of the founding grocers was an agency for bill collections and the clearance of credit information. Successful at these functions, the grocers decided to use their jointly-owned organization as a buying agency for basic food store staples. Eventually, this blossomed into a full-line wholesale organization, which flourishes to this day.

During the intervening sixty-odd years, other cooperatives have started all over the country, all of them designed to help their founding grocers to overcome cooperatively pressing competitive problems that they couldn't best as individuals. Some of them, having accomplished their original aims, rested on their laurels and withered, often becoming millstones around the necks of some of their more progressive members. Others kept pace with the changes that developed in the business, and have been the means of bringing their retailer members into the front ranks of today's retail food business. Today, there are more than 200 retailer-owned wholesale houses in the country; they serve more than 50,000 retailers, who represent a good cross-section of the industry: small stores, superettes, super markets and chains (companies operating 11 or more stores).

Associated Grocers of Seattle is one of the outstanding co-ops. Behind its success is an ability to discern the problems of its members, to offer service that will promptly provide the answers. This is why AG of Seattle is now engaged in 'fighting the battle of location' for its members; why five years ago its aim was to become a one-stop wholesale shopping center (AG members can buy groceries from their warehouse, of course; they can also buy meats, produce, frozen foods, even toiletries); why 22 years ago it was concerned only with providing its members with groceries at competitive prices. This is why AG members have faith in the future and in their ability to meet whatever competition it may bring.

Service Builds Success for AG

Whether from personal memory or hearsay, many readers will remember the business climate of 1934. The worst of the big depression was over, and conditions had started a turn for the better. While this would ordinarily have meant a brighter future for the small independent grocer, there were two additional developments peculiar to the grocery field that darkened his prospects somewhat: the growth of the chain store, and the introduction of the super market. Most of the independents of the day still had much to learn about the advantages of group buying, group advertising and concentration of buying with one wholesaler. For that matter, so had most of the wholesalers.

In that year, J. B. Rhodes, father of present manager Willard Rhodes, seeing the need of grocers in Washington for a good cooperative buying setup, established Associated Grocers of Seattle. In that first year, the total investment of the new members in the co-op was $8300, and the group's total wholesale volume was just $1 million. In 1955, sales to members exceeded $53 million, and so far in 1956, indications are that wholesale volume for the year will be close to $65 million. In terms of retail sales, this will amount to more than $160 million. In the past ten years alone, Willard Rhodes estimates that members of Associated have increased their share of the total sales in the market in which they operate from about 8% (in 1946) to close to 30%, today.

What is behind this remarkable growth? The basic reason—the co-op's ability to anticipate its members' needs—has already been advanced. But this is oversimplification of the case.

The rock upon which any successful business is built is good management. In a co-op, management may mean many things. Some houses rely on active, day-to-day participation in management of the retailer members. These members are usually elected to serve on certain committees (buying, advertising, warehousing, merchandising, etc.), and these committees report to a general membership meeting which is held at frequent intervals. This is a splendid, down-to-earth, town-meeting type of management, but it can often become bogged down in personality clashes; and impasses—damaging to the overall effectiveness of the group—can result.

Another type of cooperative management is the hired manager, who is given by the co-op complete authority over the day-to-day operation. He is hired by the board of directors, who are retailer-members elected by their fellow members, and he is responsible directly to them. He is on a straight salary basis (he may, of course, have a bonus or commission arrangement but he owns no stock in the co-op). This is the arrangement at Associated of Seattle.

Retailers Spend Their Time Selling

What in turn do the members get from such a manager? Freedom from the burdens of operating another business, and the benefits of competent, professional full-time management. Retailers can spend their time selling—which is their primary function—and leave the problems of buying, warehousing and delivery to the manager. The management of the co-op then becomes his responsibility; he engages his own staff, and supervises the entire operation.

At Associated, this is quite an operation: there is a nine-acre warehouse building at Seattle, a smaller one at Yakima; there are ten cash and carry depots scattered throughout the territory, and all told, more than 400 people employed by the group. Among the services that this operation supplies to its retailer members are these:

Grocery Buying. This is the basic reason for the existence of most co-ops. At Associated, the availability of groceries at good, competitive prices is only the beginning of the service rendered for the members' grocery departments. New products are introduced here, slow movers discontinued. Deals are considered; those that are accepted are coordinated so that they are in member stores when manufacturer promotions break. Members are provided with competitive pricing information, and with a set of suggested retail prices on items that will assure them of meeting competition, and still earn a satisfactory margin.

Advertising.   This is another basic service that is of assistance to members. There are two groups of stores in Associated: Thriftway Stores, the larger (minimum 7000 sq. ft.) stores, and AG Stores, the smaller ones. A complete advertising campaign is conducted for both groups of stores: for those stores that belong to neither group, hand-bills and other advertising accessories (window posters, etc.) are prepared.

Meats, Produce, Frozen Foods, Toiletries.   Complete lines of all of these product groups are available to members through their warehouse, making it a complete one-stop shopping center for members. Availability of product is one thing, supplying members with the merchandising know-how to move that product is another—and a complete merchandising and advertising service on these products is supplied.

Accounting.   A complete retail accounting service is available to members; this provides them with analytical studies of store performances, crews for taking store inventories, and, of course, keeping a complete set of books for the stores, with a minimum of work on the part of the retailers.

Financing Assistance.   This is one of the newest services made available to members of the Associated Group. Under arrangements made by headquarters with a Seattle bank, financial aid for building new stores or remodeling existing ones can be made at advantageous terms for the members. Details of this plan will be set forth in a forthcoming article.

New Locations.   The importance attached to new locations by Associated has already been indicated. The group has an active real estate division that is constantly scouting good new locations. When one appears, headquarters itself will option that location, often even start the building before a member retailer definitely commits himself to operating the store. Some might feel this to be overstepping the bounds of the wholesale house; actually it is a fairly common practice among both retailer-owned and privately-owned houses.

Why? Again it's a matter of meeting the challenge of the times. Today, the most likely super market locations are to be found in new shopping center locations or on highways in quickly developing communities. Developers of these properties want a responsible tenant whose name on a lease is an asset when negotiating financing for the construction of buildings. Since speed is essential, most often, these developers will go to the group that can act fastest in committing itself to the lease. If the wholesale houses couldn't act fast, these developers would probably approach the chains—and thus preclude the possibility of independent merchants securing good shopping center locations.

As it is, because of the reputation built up by Associated's real estate department, real estate developers come to them with offers quite frequently. Thus in another—and timely way—membership in Associated or a similar group is putting the independent on an equal footing with

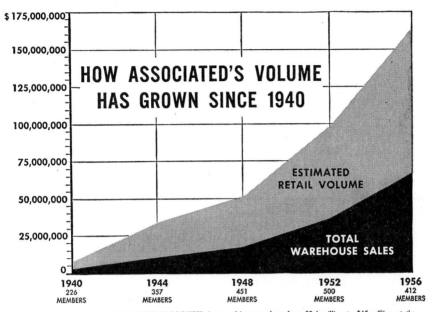

HOW ASSOCIATED'S VOLUME HAS GROWN SINCE 1940

ESTIMATED RETAIL VOLUME

TOTAL WAREHOUSE SALES

| 1940 | 1944 | 1948 | 1952 | 1956 |
| 226 MEMBERS | 357 MEMBERS | 451 MEMBERS | 500 MEMBERS | 412 MEMBERS |

Growth Proves Merit of Policies

VOLUME HAS SKYROCKETED in past 16 years alone from $2.6 million to $65 million at the wholesale level; note too that while membership is declining from peak of 500 in 1952 to 412 in 1956, average annual sales per store have gone from $195,372 to $395,000 in the same time. AG's margin on all products handled (including perishables) is 5.16% from a dead-net cost.

the competition. More than 90% of the new AG or Thriftway locations are developed by headquarters, and to indicate the frequency with which realty people approach the group, they turn down about 90% of the offers they get.

Goal Is Assisting Members to Become Larger

Membership in Associated is evenly divided between the large Thriftway Stores and the smaller AG Stores. The trend, of course, is toward larger stores, and it is expected that there will soon be a larger number of Thriftways. The goal of Associated's membership isn't the addition of new members to the group, but rather assisting present members to become larger. This, after all, is the trend of the entire food business— fewer stores, larger stores.

The Retailer-Owned Wholesale House

A co-op—as the retailer-owned wholesale house is commonly called—is, according to the dictionary, an association of retailers organized to provide. advantages in buying and selling for its members. Historically, grocers' co-ops have been regarded as organizations primarily for buying merchandise at terms that will permit them to retail that merchandise at competitive prices. Realistically, many of them have become more than that. The more progressive houses have taken to heart the phrase in the dictionary definition 'advantages in buying *and selling*' and provided a well rounded selling and merchandising program for their members.

The range in size covered by the more than 200 retailer-owned houses is as vast as the range in size of stores in the retail food business. There are houses whose total annual wholesale volume is less than $1 million—and there is at least one house whose annual volume—at wholesale, again—is over $200 million. The average volume of these houses in 1955 was $7.8 million. Spokesmen for the 50,000-plus cooperative merchants in the U. S. claim a total retail volume of $9 billion in 1955.

As the size of the house varies, so, too, do the services provided by the house to its members. Some sponsor voluntary groups (an apparent contradiction to the usual trade practice of crediting voluntary groups only to privately-owned wholesale houses) with complete advertising and merchandising programs; others do not sponsor advertising groups.

Some might consider the greatest advantage of membership in a co-op the low margin at which it can distribute merchandise to its members. In 1955, retailer-owned houses operated at an average gross margin of 4.3%, compared to an average of 7.0% for the privately-owned wholesalers. Just as any alert retailer could point out, however, that low prices are not the end and all of successful retail merchandising, so can any member of a retailer-owned wholesale house tell you that low prices are not the great asset of membership in such a group. Perhaps Willard Rhodes, manager of Associated Grocers of Seattle, whose story is told on the following pages, can best sum up the feeling of the co-ops on this point: "The co-op," he says, "has no advantage that isn't available to other groups. What is important is what is done at the retail level for the retailer; helping him to grow is no longer a matter of price so much as it is service, and the ability to think in his terms."

Because of the great range in operating methods the story of Associated on these pages cannot be taken as typical of the entire retailer-owned industry. It is typical, however, of the advanced thinking characteristic of the most progressive of these groups, and of the type of operation that has been responsible for the remarkable regeneration of all wholesalers, both retailer-owned and privately-owned, in recent years.

··{ 25 }··

Which Channel Will Win?*

BY WILLIAM G. RAOUL†

It is a waste of time to talk about the immense size of an industry, or its wonderful growth prospects, without considering who must sell the products—and how he is going to make money while doing so.

Too often, in considering the future of our own businesses, we fail to realize the position of the other man. Perhaps he is our customer, and we wonder why he is so slow to see and act on things which are obvious to us. Or perhaps the other man is our supplier, and we can't understand why he is so blind to the need for a new kind of merchandise.

The truth is that every business is different; a life and death situation for me may be only one of a thousand problems to my customer. This is especially true in the field of electric heating. Our product is all-important to my company, as a manufacturer, but it is only one of literally thousands of products which the electrical distributor must handle, and sell at a profit.

Search for Distribution

There are a lot of pitfalls in size and growth of various industries. Take room air conditioners, for example. There we have an industry measured in hundreds of millions of dollars—maybe billions—I haven't looked it up. Perhaps a good many of you have sold window units, or are still selling them. I think you will admit that the profit possibilities are not as great as the mere size of the industry would lead us to believe.

Then there was another glorious rat race when television first reached volume sales. Everybody in the country needed a set, didn't he? So there was an unlimited market, and anybody could try his hand at being a television dealer. Nearly everyone did, and again the business opportunities of the new industry were considerably clouded over in the confusion.

The other day a group of us were sitting around in my office and moaning over the latest outrage committed by our credit manager. The man who had sold the order asked this question: "Why is it always the man who sees this opportunity, who wants to take a new idea and run

---

† Vice President, Cavalier Corp.

with it, why is that man always the one with no credit"? It's a good question, too. We decided finally that the successful electrical wholesaler stays in business as much from the lines he is wise enough to turn down, as from those he has found it possible to sell at a profit. The easy prospect is too often the man who hasn't found his place in the industry, or who tries to ride so many different horses that he falls off all of them.

The lesson for us as a manufacturer is clear. We must think more about our customers' business, and find the channel of trade, or the way of selling that is logical, economical, and profitable to all concerned. We must constantly search out the man who has the right kind of business for selling our products.

Some of you have been in electric heating for years, and it may come as a surprise to you to learn that many electrical distributors expect heating to sell through entirely different channels. And perhaps to people from localities where there is very little installed electric heating, it will be a surprise to learn that the business is already firmly in the hands of electrical wholesalers in all the areas where the industry has progressed to the point of volume sales.

The distribution of a new product is by no means fixed from the beginning. If sales prospects are sufficiently bright, we find several kinds of wholesalers, dealers and even manufacturers all competing to control the distribution of the product. A period of comparative chaos may result before the most efficient method of distribution wins out over the other. The best method may not even win. The industry may continue to grow in a direction which was established almost by accident.

Electric heating began in a very small way, and since the job had to be connected by an electrician, it was natural that the first sales went through electrical wholesalers and contractors. Of course, the business grew, and in many wholesale houses today electric heating is the largest single category of business. But for the nation as a whole, the industry was still microscopically small. So small it wasn't noticed by big capital or big distribution. It was a small and thrifty tree growing up in the shade of the forest, but reaching toward the sunlight and with it a fiercer competition from other industries.

The Specialty Selling Game

In parts of the country other than the Southeast, the first sales did not follow normal electrical channels. Oddly enough, they didn't follow heating industry channels either; they sprang up as a new specialty selling game. The manufacturer of heating equipment would have welcomed sales to the distributor, with his established credit, his wide list of customers and his financial strength. But the distributor, looking at things realistically, saw that there was as yet no established sale for electric heating, and hence no profit for him. He turned it down, and from the short term point of view, it was probably a wise decision.

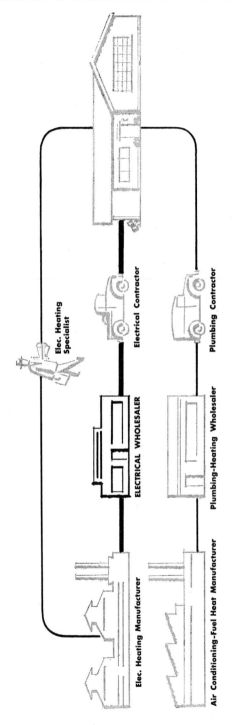

Elec. Heating Specialist

Electrical Contractor

Plumbing Contractor

ELECTRICAL WHOLESALER

Plumbing-Heating Wholesaler

Elec. Heating Manufacturer

Air Conditioning-Fuel Heat Manufacturer

So the heating manufacturer established a small scale specialist in the field. That man had to do the whole selling job, often on an almost house to house basis. The total volume of business was extremely limited in such areas, and still is. The heating dealer needed a long markup to survive. So he came to insist on buying as a "distributor." Actually he distributed to no one but himself in most instances. The point is that he not only needed the markup, he had to depend on a blind item. He could not afford to let the lines of equipment which he sold become known to the public through published price lists of any kind, because the markup which he needed to do business was more than people could understand.

There is in my mind nothing reprehensible in this method of doing business. Pioneering a business is a high cost undertaking, and those costs have to be recovered along the way. These early electric heating dealers sold a new product and a new idea against every kind of opposition, beginning with the power companies. The best of them insisted on adequate insulation and did an excellent job wherever they possibly could. And they were wonderful salesmen.

Some of these specialist firms are still growing, and in some areas (especially in the Middle West) they have almost established the pattern of distribution. They buy lines on an exclusive basis to avoid price comparison and to protect their markup. They do a wonderful job. Why aren't they the logical, sensible way for this business to grow? Perhaps they are, and perhaps they could adapt their operations to a greatly increased volume of sale.

Our Preferred Channels

But they have certain limitations, and my company, in common with the majority of manufacturers in this field, is trying to sell in a different way. We have heard all the arguments about how poor a salesman the electrical contractor makes, and how indifferent the distributor is about selling our product. Griping about your customer's performance is just normal manufacturer's behavior.

The crucial question for the manufacturer is this: "How can my product reach the public everywhere at lowest cost?" There isn't much argument about the cost in our preferred method of distribution. The contractor often shades his markup on the heaters in order to get the wiring job. Sometimes he fails to realize his own need for profit as a merchandiser. The total markup on our product is slightly less than standard department store practice for most articles (and I don't exclude Sears; they know more about marking it up than we realize). And our contractor often sells for less than the list, because of his interest in the whole job. So we know that we have found a low cost method of selling.

We also know that in the hands of a full-line wholesaler, our products are available to all electrical contractor-dealers in an area. Nobody has a lock on the sale. We can be sure of very wide distribution under competitive conditions.

There might still be some doubt as to whether we have chosen the right course in selling to the electrical industries, but in answer to this question we can point to proven success in all the volume areas. We can also note what plumbers have done with water heaters and similar appliances. Because of their interest in the installation they have proved able to sell successfully against all other types of dealers. Plumbers have within the past 20 years moved from the service category into the merchandising, and whatever a plumber can do, an electrician can certainly repeat. It is a business development which makes sense.

Many Distributors Cool to Heating

Having proved (to my own satisfaction, at least) that regular electrical distribution channels are the right one for this industry, can we conclude that this is the way things are going to be, and that everything is taken care of? I do not think so. There are some very thorny problems to be overcome.

In the "new" areas, where electric heat is just barely starting, we face the fact that the distributor himself often refuses to sponsor the business. He reasons that where there is no established sale there is no place for a distributor, and he sees himself not as a pioneer, but as a man who gives definite services on things which move regularly in trade. He is right, but the situation is one in which the established rules don't always apply.

If the electrical distributor cannot take on the job, a specialist of some kind must be established. Yet every electric heating job must be installed by an electrical contractor, and all the articles that accompany the sale —wire, panels, conduit, etc.—are found on the distributor's shelves. The electrically-heated house yields from two and a half to three times the dollar sale in electrical supplies of the house heated by other means. Can the electrical industry let this business escape into other channels?

We face this problem every day when we call on distributors in the undeveloped areas. We are asking them to become partners in a pioneering enterprise. Too often, they cannot see it. They tell us to establish the dealers first, and then talk about stocking the line.

The trouble with that approach is two-fold. If we establish a dealer who succeeds, he will want to buy direct. And he will lock us out of a free market, by controlling our product in his area. We don't want the exclusive dealer; we want the product to be available to everyone.

What's more, we feel that the distributor is the natural leader of the electrical industry. I think you men often discount your own importance to the contractor. As manufacturers, we see it more clearly. When you hold a sales meeting, the contractor attends, and when you stock a line, he believes in it. We call on contractors all the time, and the questions they ask reveal the importance of the distributor.

Will the "Scrub Pine" Take Over?

The nature of the electrical industry demands a wholesaling link between manufacturer and dealer. This is not true of all industries. It is true for us because of two facts: the enormous number of items involved in the trade, and the fairly irregular pattern of demand for them.

Our first problem, then, in any new area is to enlist the support of distributors. As soon as electric heating equipment is in the stock of full-line electrical distributors, the specialist heating man with his exclusive control of the market is out. He cannot compete in cost with regular electrical trade channels. This is happening today. Heating specialists are going out of business, and some of the manufacturers who have followed this pattern of trade are already in trouble.

When you abandon a field and let the forest take it over, one of the first things that comes up is scrub pine, because it can thrive under the easy conditions of full sunlight. It grows for a few years, becomes overcrowded, and after a few more years you find the tougher hardwoods (which can grow up even in shade) taking over. A similar transformation is taking place in our own field.

The Trends in Tennessee

So far we have talked mostly about the problems of early growth in electric heating. I think it is time to look at some of the old timber, to see what is happening.

Electric heating has flourished in the Tennessee Valley for the past ten years, but it is interesting to note that the market is entirely undeveloped in more than half of the state, populationwise. Memphis has discouraged it, until the growth of air-conditioning finally forced them to take a new look. Now the load is getting some encouragement, and a tremendous new market is opening up. Distributors from other parts of the state, with their long experience in the field will compete with local firms for this business. The heaviest saturation in electric heating which I know of is in Clarksville, Tennessee, with 33 per cent of the heating market. Chattanooga is close to the same figure. But consider how far we are from a declining market—the future is still much greater than the past.

Important trends in the distribution of electric heating will be noticed first in the Tennessee Valley. When the business was truly in its infancy there were few lines. Established markups were fairly easily maintained. Now the field is crowded with new contenders. There are 16 manufacturers making one identical type of electric heating equipment, and since the family bed is getting a bit crowded, some of them are trying to get into bed with others among us who never made that particular type of equipment. From having an inadequate choice of lines, the distributor has come in a few short years to the position of having more lines available than can be sold through existing houses.

There are dangers on both sides. The house that carries too many lines cannot operate profitably on any of them. But on the other hand, the manufacturer who can find no place in the distribution picture must establish something of his own, usually a dealer who calls himself a distributor. In the long run such arrangements may not succeed, but they are powerfully upsetting while they last.

We saw a striking example of that in one city in the Northwest. Two or three well-established heating lines had all the distributors in the city. It was a cozy situation. Then along comes a new heating line, and he couldn't find a home. Nobody would take him on. He established a contractor as his exclusive distributor. The last comment on the situation which I heard came from our sales agent in the city. He said, "If we have new competition, and I know we will, I would much rather see that competition come through legitimate distributors." This will be a perpetual problem in the next few years, there will be more lines than distributors.

One of the aggravating factors in the situation is the fact that manufacturers of electric heating equipment have introduced few really worthwhile innovations. I make an exception in the case of electric baseboard, which is now available in a number of lines and which has literally created new markets. In general we have tended to stay with what we had, instead of pioneering improvements. This is a natural consequence of the small size of our industry, and it will become less of a problem in succeeding years.

We have volume today which will permit heavier tooling costs and real engineering development. Lowered margins are the inevitable results of sticking too long with an unimproved product. We can see much of that trouble today in areas where electric heat is first in public acceptance. It has become so easy to sell that we all overlooked the need to improve it constantly. Only a new product can produce real profits. It takes the right mixture of established volume business and new products to give a satisfactory markup.

Still More Competition

There is one more great and unknown factor which will appear not only in the areas of volume sale, but everywhere, and that is the entry of fuel heat manufacturers into the electrical heating industry. Today they appear to be fast asleep, which is the normal situation of a business when it is losing its future. Their industry is so immensely larger than ours that they can't see any particular threat.

It is rather surprising to me that they have been so slow to wake up, however, and I know it cannot last. There have been mergers between heating and air-conditioning manufacturers, and the resulting firms will be very powerful indeed. They are likely to approach electric heating through the combined heating and air-conditioning central system. They are central heat manufacturers and they naturally think in those terms.

Some of these combined systems will be heat pumps, others straight resistance heaters plus air-conditioning. The heat pump, as you know, has been and still is being heavily promoted by power companies. They picked up the idea several years ago, before summer cooling had become a dominant load. In those days it made sense for them to sponsor a year 'round load which used somewhat less current for heating than would straight resistance heating.

Now, of course, they are riding the wrong horse for their own interests. Their heat pumps create just as much peak demand in really cold weather as resistance systems, but produce far less revenue. Furthermore, in spite of growing sales, they cannot hope to sell enough of these year 'round systems to balance off the summer increase. It is time for a new look, but power companies move slowly.

Regardless of disadvantages in heating (and there are some definite drawbacks), central systems of combined heating and cooling will be a factor in the future. They may bring new opportunities to you as electrical distributors; they are certain to bring new competition. The heating manufacturers sell in a number of ways, and mostly outside the electrical industry as we know it. As they move into our field, you will find your business in electric heating under a serious threat.

Outsiders are always surprised to find how we sell. They cannot understand how the electrical industry can expand into a new field. This is heating business, why don't we utilize the experience, the knowledge and the skills of the established heating industry? Perhaps a considerable part of our industry may eventually go that way, but there are still reasons why we as manufacturers can expect to sell through the electrical industry, and means whereby you can meet the competition of other distribution channels.

The first factor in our favor is the simplicity of decentralized electric heating. No sheet metal ductwork is required, there are no water connections. An electrician can do the whole job.

Then there is the question of economy. The man who has to connect the job can certainly afford to handle the business for less. It has been proven in plumbing; it is being proven every day with electric heat.

We can also expect efforts to sell electric heating equipment direct to builders. This may be either through builders supply houses or direct from the manufacturer in many cases. We must remember that as this industry grows people will be attracted into it who are accustomed to sell through channels other than ours. They will try to establish their sales through the trade they already sell. All of this means new competition from every side, and new threats to your interest in electric heating.

Distributor's Answer?

It is wise to start into a field which poses so many potential problems? That is the question which each man must answer about every new product which is offered to him.

In conclusion, I can tell you what one distributor told me. He was a man who had spent his life in the electrical industry. His business is in a state where all the electric heating has been sold by a single specialty sales outfit. We had been unable to establish distributors; nobody in the electrical industry seemed to take any interest. They said that heating was out of their line.

This man listened to all our arguments without indicating his feelings one way or the other. I was beginning to think we had lost him when he finally said something. He pointed to one of these built-in range tops and said:

"You know we are about to lose that one. We sell some, but more and more are going to the builder by other routes. Maybe we could have held that business, maybe not. It has some problems that the electrical contractor can't handle too well—the cabinets to go with it, for example. We've lost a lot of other ventures through the years too. There may have been reasons—it's hard to say. But I see no reason why we should lose electric heating, unless we let it go by default. It is all electrical work, and it carries a lot of other sales with it. We can't afford to lose it, and I don't intend to. We are going to do something about electric heat." And he did. He put in a stock, arranged sales meetings, and as a result we have a sales outlet in a new territory.

There is no sure way—indeed, there is no way at all—to guarantee having the upper hand over all competition. But if a product which electricians can install is freely available through full-line electrical distributors, is advertised and promoted adequately, and is fairly priced, it will reach the public at less cost than through any other channel. And if there is genuine competition among contractors, the builder can save nothing by buying his heating equipment through other channels.

What about the contractor or dealer who reaches such a powerful position that he can dictate to both manufacturer and distributor? Situations of this kind arise occasionally, but if the best lines of the industry are available to all contractors, you have the best possible insurance against domination of the field by any one interest or group of interests. This is still a new business, even in those areas where electric heat gets 98 per cent of the new housing, and—in my opinion—a business opportunity for electrical distributors.

Part Five . . .

ADVERTISING AND PERSONAL SELLING

·{ 26 }··

Florida Citrus Account Is Recaptured by B&B*

BY JAMES V. O'GARA

Lakeland, Fla., June 2—Benton & Bowles, the agency which lost the Florida Citrus Commission business in 1950 to J. Walter Thompson Co., tonight was named to succeed Thompson on the $3,500,000 account.

A presentation that consumed two hours and 22 minutes impressed the 12-man commission with its brisk, businesslike, confident qualities. It won out for Benton & Bowles over Thompson, Grant Advertising, Cunningham & Walsh and Dancer-Fitzgerald-Sample. It cost the five agencies an average of about $30,000 each to come here and pitch.

The citrus commission awarded its business to Benton & Bowles 80 minutes after hearing the last of the presentations made during the past two days. Industry advisory committees indicated that they favored B&B over J. Walter Thompson, though there was momentary pressure to name two agencies, one to handle fresh fruit and the other to handle processed fruit.

The commission decided there would be one agency, that it would be Benton & Bowles, and that the commission would go along "generally" with B&B recommendations.

The first presentation yesterday morning was preceded by the statement from Robert C. Wooten, new chairman of the commission, that he had "no candidate as to an agency, nor do the other commissioners; the agency will be selected after the presentations rather than prior to them."

This was obviously a reply to rumors that citrus politics had already dictated which agency was to get the account.

There were two reasons why B&B strongly wanted the account. Robert E. Lusk, president, told the commission: "We want the business—though we're not starving to death—because (1) the account represents one of the few grocery-produce opportunities open to us and (2) it's a matter of pride. We had this business for seven years prior to 1950, and regaining it would make us all proud."

* Reprinted by special permission from *Advertising Age*, June 6, 1955. Copyright, 1955, *Advertising Age*.

A factor that seemingly registered with the commission at agency choosing time was B&B's emphasis on the arrangement calling for two teams inside the agency to handle both the fresh and processed aspects of the citrus business. Mr. Lusk said these teams would "compete with each other," much as do similar teams working on various General Foods and Procter & Gamble accounts handled by the agency.

Where Thompson was committed to ad copy that would leave the consumer free to "select" whether she wants fresh, canned or frozen concentrated citrus, B&B advanced the theory that different ads should sell different forms of citrus.

B&B built a typical ad for the commission that read like this: "After school—after play, refresh them with Florida Vitamin C—the vital vitamin your body cannot store."

Next came "a buying impulse illustration," showing orange juice being poured from a pitcher for two laughing youngsters. Then came "one form at a time" sell: "Get extra-juice oranges . . . get fresh Floridas: they're sweeter, they're plentiful now."

The demonstration ads shown by B&B retained the hand and glass symbol pioneered by Thompson. B&B men described it as "a really memorable, wonderful device." The hand and glass is usually accompanied by the line: "At least this much every day." B&B ads carried these words: "Better for you—any time you're thirsty—fresh Florida oranges."

Benton & Bowles proposed that the commission's $3,500,000 advertising budget be divided about like this: $1,875,000 for television, $650,000 for magazines, $400,000 for newspapers and $375,000 for radio. These total $3,300,000, allowing a balance of $200,000 for production and contingencies.

The tv tab would go for "a bold and unorthodox" plan of "hard-selling" ten-second station breaks. All these would stress the health value of citrus. They would plug the specific form of citrus the public should buy, as well as the particular advantages of that form.

B&B's Gordon Webber said that the ten-second station breaks for Maxwell House instant coffee ("amazing coffee discovery") have done a highly successful job for General Foods. The citrus spots would run thrice weekly in 68 markets for 52 weeks.

In addition there would be 60-second daytime participations in 68 markets for a year, at the rate of three every two weeks. In the East and Midwest there would be one-minute participations on the "Today" program in 52 markets. A $375,000 budget was suggested for 10 radio newscasts a week.

B&B, which said it will do "somewhat over $60,000,000 in billings this year," told the commission that $30,300,000 of that figure goes into tv and radio for its clients. It added that any tv advertiser will get more for his money at Benton & Bowles.

A chart titled, "Agency tv performance comparisons," gave cost-per-thousand commercial minutes as follows: Average nighttime show, $3.31; ten top rated programs, $2.05; Agency A (five shows), $4.39; Agency B (12 shows), $4.06; Agency C (two shows), $3.96; Agency D (four shows), $2.79; B&B (8 shows), $1.96. The unnamed agencies were B&B competitors for the citrus account, and their nighttime shows were here considered.

On the 15-man B&B team here, in addition to Atherton W. Hobler and Mr. Lusk, were Al Whittaker, research; Ted Steele, tv and radio; Harry A. Warren, v.p. on the Maxwell House account, who now becomes manager of the agency's new Lakeland office; Otto Prochazka and Annette Talbert, both creative; Dave Crane, media, and Mr. Webber.

Mr. Lusk told the commission that General Foods and P&G account for somewhat more than half the agency's business. He also said that of the agency's last $30,000,000 increase, $20,000,000 came from the growth of present accounts. He said only eight of B&B's 20 clients spend $1,000,-000 or more, that 72% of the agency's volume is outside New York and that of the 31 products handled for 20 clients, "27 are in first or second place in their classiffcations."

J. Walter Thompson Co., which made its appearance after all other agencies had been heard, spent just seven minutes less than three hours on its pitch to keep the citrus account for the sixth year.

The world's biggest agency sent a 13-man team on the Lakeland mission, with nine of them talking before the commission. These included Don Francisco, account supervisor; O'Neill Ryan, member of the agency's review board; Dr. Arno Johnson, research boss; Dr. Herbert Fisher, research; Wallace Elton, creative; Albert Cameron, who presented a magazine campaign proposal; Robert Urban, promotion aspects; Arthur Porter, media, and Robert Ballin, tv-radio commericals.

Mr. Francisco told the commission right off that "if we ran separate campaigns for each form of citrus we would end with a crazy quilt campaign, in which each part would be competing with the other."

Mr. Elton presented a series of magazine ads which would have made repetitious use of the phrase, "The true fountain of youth"; would have repeated the Vitamin C story in each ad; treated specific health problems and told a success story by showing that more people are discovering the benefits of orange juice.

A magazine drive for grapefruit would have aimed at (1) arousing desire by overweight persons to return to trimmer figures, and (2) making the product desirable to all for delicious flavor. The campaign would have repeated in each ad, "Have grapefruit instead."

Typical headlines included, "Go back to your just married weight" and "Help him back to his G.I. weight."

Thompson proposed the use of network tv and network radio, newspapers and magazines. A budget breakdown went like this: tv and radio,

$1,709,813; magazines, $650,899; newspapers, $667,824; Canada, $150,000; trade, $50,000; export, $60,000; outdoor, $7,000, and preparation (including rate increase reserve), $254,464.

Mr. Ryan told the commission that the Thompson agency handles 39 food products, which have been at the agency an average of 16 years each. It also has 28 non-food grocery products and 20 industry and association accounts. "No agency in the world has so much experience in these categories," he said.

He added that the commission's $3,500,000 account would rank 11th in size at Thompson. Bigger ones in Chicago, he said, are Swift, Libby, Kraft and 7-Up. In Detroit, he said, Ford is bigger. Six accounts handled in the New York office also are larger, he added, but he did not name them.

"You may think of J. Walter Thompson as a little old and a little rich," said Mr. Ryan, "but we got that way by hard work."

First agency to pitch for the $3,500,000 Florida citrus account was Dancer-Fitzgerald-Sample, which was represented by its president, Clifford Fitzgerald, and Will Huse, Paul Keenen, Dr. Lyndon O. Brown and Victor Pietrowski.

The five-man D-F-S team concentrated largely on (1) a recital of its successes with Gold Medal flour, Cheerios, Oxydol, Pink Dreft and other products, (2) a swingy, infectious singing commercial and (3) a promise to increase the commission's present advertising from its present 1.5 billion messages a year to more than 7 billion messages, while purchasing the same media as currently used.

The media proposal—"not a recommendation, but a demonstration"— was described to the commission as an "action media plan." It would increase the one message a month currently being delivered to each of the 130,000,000 Americans "making decisions" to 4.3 messages a month.

"This isn't a bargain counter thing," said Mr. Fitzgerald. "We will streamline the copy story, so you will need smaller space. You can buy these space units more frequently, thus delivering more messages.

"As for tv and radio, it is not enough to have a fancy star. You have to give the public something that rewards them for their time.

"On television," he said in answer to a question, "instead of just a 60-second shot, you should also be using a shorter idea.

"You should buy a low-expense show with a high audience.

"The 'Lone Ranger' is a perfect show for the use of one of our clients," he said.

He also explained that only half pages would be used in magazines "instead of some full and some half pages," as he characterized present practice.

Mr. Fitzgerald added that these half pages would deliver on an "equally effective" basis; the gain would be in more frequent insertions.

Mr. Pietrowski outlined the merchandising angles for D-F-S. He is a former Kroger Stores merchandising executive. At Kroger he apparently was acquainted with Frank D. Arn, now merchandising director of the citrus commission.

Mr. Fitzgerald said a big problem for citrus is that production will shortly increase three times as fast as the U.S. population.

To solve this problem, continued Mr. Fitzgerald, "we need to build up habit sales" of citrus. "No one says Coke or coffee is good for you. They are habit drinks. They are the ones that get the volume."

Another worry, said Mr. Fitzgerald, is that media rates are bound to continue their upward spiral. Still another is the fact that "$170,000,000 is being spent yearly against citrus."

This was a reference to promotional funds being used to influence various beverage decisions. D-F-S' president broke the figure down as follows: $75,000,000 on soft drinks; $63,000,000 on tea and coffee; $27,-000,000 on milk and $5,000,000 on non-citrus fruits and vegetable juices. He said that $11,000,000 was being used to promote citrus products of all kinds.

Mr. Huse, slated to be account executive if D-F-S won out, said that only one out of 20 beverage decisions made by the American public each day favors a citrus drink. "The potential for citrus," he added, "is tremendous."

Mr. Fitzgerald, who said his agency bills $50,000,000, told the commission that D-F-S has 21 stockholders, "all of them working partners." They average 46 years of age, he said.

He said the citrus account, at $3,500,000 annual billing, would rank after Gold Medal flour, General Mills' Cheerios, Oxydol and Phillips Milk of Magnesia, Pink Dreft and Bayer Aspirin.

He said it would rank ahead of such products as Bab-O, Hellman's, Tums, Nucoa margarine and Mounds candy bars.

He explained that "Mr. Dancer and Cliff Fitzgerald have alternated the titles of board chairman and president for 16 years."

"We're in the office at 8:35 A.M.; we're hungry, alert and having fun doing a great job," he said.

Following D-F-S to the rostrum was Cunningham & Walsh, which sent a nine-man team from New York. Unlike D-F-S, Cunningham sent "no slides, no movies, no charts." In the words of John P. Cunningham, president, C&W sent "just men."

With Mr. Cunningham were account men Russell K. Jones, William Mulvey and John Burns; Anthony Chevins, creative; Harry Vosburg, research; Newman F. McEvoy, media; John Sheehan, radio-tv, and H. W. Grathwohl, marketing.

Mr. Cunningham had each of his colleagues introduce himself, give biographical data, and tell, generally, how he would help C&W handle the citrus account. Mr. Cunningham wrapped up a 60-minute presentation in these words:

"If you forget everything else we have said, nail these points down. We have stated that our major over-all objective would be to make the American family regard citrus as a necessary staple—like bread or milk.

"To do this we must:

1. "Turn non-users into users, chiefly by penetrating the lower income masses, the minority groups (Negroes and others).

2. "We must pick up lagging markets, by research and copy testing.

3. "We must be wary of big one-shot expenditures, such as a glamor tv show. We must buy mass—perhaps on a tailored, sectional basis (tv spots, newspapers).

4. "We must appeal to self-interest, to desire for health. People must be given a strong reason to buy. People think they can't live without bread, the staff of life. Milk, too. Citrus should be up there.

5. "We must remain flexible—for local conditions, inventory situation, seasonal variations, etc.

6. "We must cultivate the child market extensively, using proven juvenile techniques.

7. "We must increase the between-meal pick-up habit, with something like the coffee break."

Typical of the "rather staccato, all oral approach" employed by other men from C&W were remarks made by John Sheehan, who said:

"You need a strong selling idea repeated over and over again. Radio and tv are ideal for such a job. We have the know-how to make radio and tv work hard for you. We have the men with broad experience and enthusiasm."

Mr. Cunningham left a leather-bound volume with the commission. He said it contained pictures of his team, the substance of what each had to say, and their biographies. He said that his agency was "different" because of "these men—you can't get them anywhere else.

"C&W is on the way up. We have vitality. We have unusual creative ability, vigorous marketing know-how, and creative field work planning.

"There are no Madison Ave. dilettantes at Cunningham & Walsh," he said. "We work behind retail counters one week a year. Our men get back, once a year, to the grass roots of selling. They learn why customers buy this product and reject that one."

Mr. Cunningham said 43 stockholders own C&W and that he does not own a controlling share. He added that the agency's billings increased from $26,000,000 to $44,000,000 in five years. Personnel increased from 250 to 400 in that time, and payroll went up 100%, he added.

He said the citrus account would rank in terms of billing, after Chesterfields and Texaco—about on a par with Sunshine biscuits.

Last, longest and largest of the Wednesday pitches was tossed by Grant Advertising. The *Tampa Tribune* told its readers that Grant's was the only full-scale pitch because the other agencies called in to bid for the citrus account "are members of the American Assn. of Advertising Agencies, which forbids its members to offer a full-scale presentation in bidding for an account held by a member of the Four A's. Grant is not a member of the organization."

In any case, Howard Jones, exec. v.p. in charge of Grant's central creative group, who was introduced as a "technical man whose forte is not public speaking," seemed to score with the commissioners with a wry wit, a fine command of language and an apparent knowledge of the politics surrounding the citrus business.

Mr. Jones presented a detailed budget for the Florida group's promotion money. Grant, he said, would spend the $3,500,000 like this:

Magazines—$644,692, Sunday supplements—$277,420, newspapers—$652,590, radio and television—$1,381,798, tangerines and Temple oranges—$180,000, outdoor boards—$13,500, trade papers—$55,000, rate reserve—$50,000, and production (all media) $245,000.

Grant said it was scheduling $800,000 for the Tom Moore "Florida Calling" show via Mutual. Mr. Jones commented briefly, "If you want him, we don't intend to let that detail wreck what we want to do for you."

Also scheduled was a 39-time participation in the "Dave Garroway Show." These would come over a period of 26 weeks on 52 stations. This, it was figured, would cost $185,000. Grant also proposed to spend $780,000 on more than 85 radio spots a week for a year on the Mutual network's 528 stations. In addition, $208,000 would go for ten-second identification spots in Class A television time.

A "booster" radio and tv fund would come into play in "emergencies" caused by, say, an oversupply of citrus in the Cleveland market, or elsewhere.

Grant's presentation also included showing (1) a score or more of glossy print ads in color and b&w and (2) showing a symbol for Florida citrus (an orange with the outline of the state superimposed). Mr. Jones assured the commission that it "can stop advertising for Sunkist" by adopting such a symbol, which would appear on Florida oranges and in all advertising.

Grant also showed specific plans for Florida grapefruit copy. Typical headlines were: "Florida grapefruit every day . . . will help keep colds and flu away," "Fight the 'cold war' with Florida grapefruit," and "The health fruit—from the Health State."

The Grant agency began its pitch—via Will C. Grant, president; John A. Dey, v.p. in charge of Florida operations; and Palmer Tyler, v.p. and manager of the Miami office—with a "native-son" angle. Mr. Grant told how the Miami office would provide "on the ground service" and give "complete creative service."

Mr. Dey showed pictures of the Miami personnel of "Florida's largest advertising agency." He dwelt on the length of residence in Florida of each staff man. Finally, he showed a picture of the children of all Grant's Miami people.

Mr. Tyler assured the commission that Grant, Miami, was big enough to take on the job and urged it to follow "the trend in other states to keep the big jobs at home." Now, he added, "it's time for Florida to do the same."

Other members of the Grant team in Lakeland were Lee Heagerty, v.p. in charge of merchandising, and Wally Capel, copy supervisor in Chicago.

·{ 27 }··

Continental's New Ad Strategy*

When Ford Motor Co. introduced its luxurious new $10,000 Continental 14 months ago (*Tide*—Oct. 22, 1955), it set an annual production goal of 4,000 units—and expected demand to be considerably greater than available cars. And to give its new prestige car a running start, Ford spent almost $1,000,000 in advertising during the last three months of 1955.

Today, Ford Motor Co. executives are probably wondering who pulled the plug. For the first nine months of this year, exactly 1,182 Continentals were sold—hardly a 4,000-a-year rate. Further, Ford has modified its sales objectives, now has reduced Continental production to 1,200 cars a year. In fact, Ford only starts building a Continental when a dealer orders one—and the dealer doesn't order until a customer has signed up to buy.

What made the Continental fizzle out after such tremendous demand following its unveiling? There's probably no one single answer. Certainly price isn't the problem, because GM's Cadillac Eldorado brougham costs upward of $12,500 compared to the Continental's $10,-000 (or $11,000 with air conditioning)—and GM will probably have little trouble disposing of every Eldorado it makes.

Part of the answer may lie in the general sales slump suffered by auto makers this year. Another part of the answer may lie in Chrysler Corporation's promotion of its Imperial as a prestige car. And a final clue

---

* Reprinted by special permission from *Tide*, January 11, 1957. Copyright, 1957, *Tide*.

may lie in the fact that Continental isn't changing its styling each year —a practice that runs contrary to all Detroit's marketing theories.

Probably the biggest reason for Continental's failure to live up to expectations, however, lies in Ford's advertising approach. Ford now thinks that it aimed for the wrong market in its Continental advertising, and has already moved to correct that. Explains James M. Woodman, Jr., assistant general sales manager in charge of advertising, sales promotion & training of the Lincoln division (which now includes Continental):

"Our first advertising was coldly formal. Though some of it was in color, the colors were virtually monotones. The backgrounds in most of the ads were more important than the car. They typified the backgrounds of most of the people we thought we wanted to appeal to—the people in the big mansions.

"Now," continues Woodman, "we have turned our advertising around. We are trying to make it more personable, more human, and to get it off its pedestal."

"Now we are humanizing the ads; the car is more important. There are people in them. There is warmth."

"We are using a horizontal mass group of media for the ads, with a limited budget. They are appearing in the *Wall Street Journal, Time, Newsweek, Town and Country.*"

Adds Woodman: "When the Continental first was announced, we were pioneering in a new market. No other car as expensive has been sold since the Duesenberg back in the 1920's. No one knew what the market was. Until the Continental came out, only about 144 cars a year were sold in the $10,000 class, and most of them were foreign makes."

"First we acquired a list of people with a quarter million dollars net worth and worked on them as prospects. But we have found that this was an unproductive list. In the first place, they were old people; they were cautious spenders; they were perhaps not prestige conscious because their positions in the social structure were already assured."

"Since then we have found there is a great deal of difference between net worth and income," Woodman explains. "The first list, for instance, had a death rate twice that of average lists. So we moved into the group of people with a proved ability to pay—proved income—and who had the fine car habit. They're what we call the 'shoot-'em-up' boys, the all-American livers. They are, for the most part, active in industry. They are the mink coat and yacht buyers. They want a good car, they are proud to own the finest, and they can afford it."

"We thought at first that the Continental was the social car, the mark of social distinction," concludes Woodman. "But we have found our buyers among this other group, the younger people, active in business, willing to spend for the finest."

Actually the Lincoln dealers handling Continental (originally 650 but now fewer after many withdrawals from the sales agreement) could sell the car by pushing hard. But, says Woodman, "This might result in discounts and some other trade practices we wouldn't like. Discounts alone would lessen the prestige of the car."

Continental executives have made other interesting discoveries over the past 14 months. They discovered, for instance, that its biggest sales areas have been, in this order, Los Angeles, New York, Florida, Texas, and Detroit.

They also discovered that selling a $10,000 car requires a different sales technique. A prospect comes in, looks the car over, borrows it for a weekend. Then there is a period of incubation, when the salesman sits back and waits. After two or three months, the customer decides. If the dealer is lucky, the prospect decides to buy—lucky, because for every Continental sold, the dealer gets 26% of the purchase price.

··{ 28 }··

Two Jobs for INCO Advertising: Sell The Trade, Influence the Public*

International Nickel advertising works both sides of the street. It sells to the trade and influences the public.

Long-running and consistent trade and consumer institutional advertising does the trick. In the trade, INCO has been a consistent advertiser for 32 years. From the start, its advertising in industrial publications has sold nickel by selling its applications in all kinds of industries.

The institutional advertising, which started in Canada in the early 1930s and in the U.S. during World War II, sells ideas and builds goodwill among customers and the general public. This advertising largely holds out hope for future progress with nickel—"your unseen friend."

How $3,000,000 Budget Is Split

U.S. advertising of all kinds comes to $3,000,000. Of this, about 50% goes into trade advertising efforts, and the other 50% into institutional endeavors. Canadian advertising, trade and institutional, all handled by Cockfield, Brown & Co., Ltd., is close to $1,000,000. C. E. Macdonald, manager of Canadian sales and development, directs the advertising there.

---

* Reprinted by special permission from *Printers' Ink*, December 16, 1955. Copyright, 1955, *Printers' Ink*.

For its institutional advertising in the U.S. (coordinated by Fred Wood, assistant vice-president and assistant to Herbert Fales, vice-president and assistant to the chairman of the board), International Nickel uses 9 full-page insertions a year in 4 general magazines and 5 executive news magazines. In addition, it runs 6 insertions of 1,000 lines in each of 30 newspapers in 19 cities. News programs—most are 15-minute, 3-days-a-week—are carried on a spot basis in 13 cities. In addition, plant-city newspapers are used. Industrial films are also the responsibility of Fred Wood.

For its total advertising in the U.S., INCO allots 25% of its ad budget for magazines, 5% for newspapers, 10% for spot radio. Business-paper advertising makes up 15% of the budget, promotional material accounts for 35%, and films 10%.

INCO's industrial advertising is under the direction of Robert Lloyd, who reports directly to L. R. Larson, vice-president and general sales manager. A look at the 1955 trade advertising budgets for INCO alloy, nickel, precious metals and ductile cast iron shows this breakdown:

Item	%
Direct mail and publications	41
Trade and business papers	35
Consumer magazines	8
Customer and distributor cooperation	8
Shows and exhibits	7
Advertising research	1
	100%

Steady Use of Business Papers

As an industrial advertiser, INCO has been one of the most consistent. The company started using the industrial trade press in 1923 with an initial budget of $23,000. Over that 32-year stretch, INCO has seldom faltered in its steady use of business publications.

In 1955, it is using 902 insertions in 112 trade papers in 44 vertical and horizontal fields for its industrial advertising. That's a lot of industrial advertising spread over a big, broad area.

Mr. Lloyd's department and the Marschalk & Pratt division of the Mc-Cann-Erickson agency turn out more than 400 trade ads a year. In addition, an extensive direct-mail department maintains a mailing list of 250,-000 names. Currently, INCO is receiving 50,000 requests for 170,000 pieces of literature. Four gadget mailings of 100,000 each also go out as part of the direct-mail coverage. These are for distributors who pick up the tab for half of the bill.

Extensive activities of INCO's industrial advertising department include producing 6 periodicals: *INCO Magazine*, circulation, 35,000; *Nickel Topics*, 125,000; *Process Industries*, 47,000; *Mechanical Topics*, 64,000; *Nicklore*, 28,000; *Nickelsworth*, 158,000. All of these are quarterlies except *Nickel Topics*, which is published 11 times a year.

Working with Bob Lloyd is a staff of 67. Robert A. Wheeler is assistant general manager of advertising, in charge of pure nickel advertising and Maurice J. Phillips is assistant to the advertising manager in charge of INCO nickel alloys.

Ad Research

A great believer in advertising research, International Nickel uses Starch, Readex, Gallup & Robinson impact studies in addition to periodical readership surveys. As a result of some of its testing, International is generally convinced that color in its industrial advertising doesn't pay. The company is happy with the results it gets from its industrial advertising, which is 99% black-and-white.

"If there is an explanation for this procedure," explains adman Lloyd, "it may be that engineers skip the froth and devour the meat when served news of developments in their field."

For effectiveness in turning out industrial advertising that attracts readership and brings results, INCO has worked up an effective system of cooperation with its advertising agency.

A recent case in point concerns an ad that appeared in 4 industrial publications. A. E. Woehr of Mr. Lloyd's department was assigned the job of going out into the field to dig up material for the ad. Woehr called on the Bullard Co. in Bridgeport to get a service report on Inconel furnace retorts used in their heat treating department.

Mr. Woehr made his report and summarized his findings: "Rapid failure of original retorts led the Bullard Co. to search for better materials. Final selection was Inconel, which gave twice the service of second-best material and 3 times the life of the original equipment."

Worksheet for Ads

An advertising worksheet was prepared for the agency. The worksheet detailed size of the ad, publications on the schedule, subject matter, principal purpose of the ad, secondary objective and readers' reaction desired.

Purpose of the ad: To show that Inconel retorts give long service life consistently, and can even be reconditioned for additional service whenever necessary.

Attached to the worksheet was the complete field report. From this raw material, the agency created an effective case-history ad: "Inconel triples life of pit carburizing retorts at Bullard plant. . . ."

INCO has been a trade advertiser long enough to have either fallen into or deliberately planned a number of advertising techniques that were rare when created but are common procedure today.

Early Use of Inserts

Probably one of the first inserts in trade publications was an early ad for International, a 4-page, two-color insert that blossomed into about a

30-page insert as a result of customer participation. Not only did INCO pick up impact and excitement, but the device undoubtedly opened the eyes of more than one publisher of industrial publications to future advertising possibilities.

INCO's industrial advertising, like its institutional efforts, is concerned with future business. Says Mr. Lloyd: "Basic material advertising like ours is different than consumer product advertising which demands immediate results. We're not shooting for quick results. We're advertising today for future business."

The old shortage bugaboo has touched the company's institutional program. When INCO started its *Just and durable* peace campaign during the war, the ads were completely institutional. After the war when nickel was plentiful, the emphasis was almost completely on product. These days there appears to be a 50–50 balance between the two. Some of its consumer advertising is downright "tradey."

Prospecting through Consumer Ads

A recent full-page ad in one of the national magazines is a strong-selling advertisement on behalf of one of INCO's developments, ductile cast iron. The ad contains very little copy and includes 5 pictures. Purpose of the ad is to show that INCO-developed ductile cast iron has exceptional ductility and can be bent like mild steel. Like most of its consumer advertisements, this one offers a booklet.

Other advertisements in the general magazines are apt to describe dramatic and interesting uses of INCO nickel alloys or cover some facet of INCO research or describe some specific company activity in the fields of mining, refining or other International Nickel operations.

Another facet of the consumer campaign is the series of ads appearing in the executive-type magazines. During this period of government stockpiling and rapidly expanding demand for nickel, these ads aim largely at providing news of progress being made in expanding the supply of the metal.

INCO's top management often has a direct hand in the institutional advertising. It's not at all unusual for board chairman Thompson and president Wingate to be in on meetings where themes and general policy to be expressed in the ads are discussed.

Management Is Represented in Ad Sessions

Management is specifically represented at all times by vice-president and assistant to the chairman Herbert Fales. Fred Wood reports directly to Mr. Fales. Actually, all advertising, including trade insertions, is carefully checked for company policy before any ads are published.

Top management of the advertising agency, in the person of Marschalk & Pratt president Sam Meulendyke, is represented in practically all company conferences on the institutional program. However, inclusive advertising meetings with Robert Lloyd, Fred Wood, Sam Meulendyke and

Herbert Fales represent part of the coordinated procedure International Nickel employs to give all of its advertising consistency and substance in relation to top management policy.

Publicity and Public Relations

Under Fred Wood comes a group of publicity and public relations functions in addition to institutional and plant-town advertising. Publicity for the trade is coordinated here and so is the publication of the company's New York employee magazine, *Pen and INCO,* and the editing of horizontal external publications to management groups in the U.S. and Canada.

INCO executives have an aversion to the term "institutional advertising." They would prefer the phrase "company advertising." This, in their opinion, is a way of differentiating between advertising directly to the trade and the public.

But no matter what it's called, the company's consumer advertising has at least two tough jobs to accomplish. It must: (1) tell what part INCO is playing in the production of nickel; (2) tell what nickel means to the man on the street.

For the first objective, the company often talks in terms of production, exploration, ore reserves, new mining methods, new plants. The second job is a bit more difficult. Here, INCO has to get over the hurdle of advertising a product the layman knows little about and rarely sees. INCO may talk about the application of nickel to television, electric heating units, appliances. It might cover the vast contributions INCO has made to the aeronautical industry or in rayon or in cellulose or in the building industry. It certainly has a wide field of industries to talk about, because nickel is used in food processing machines and in the extensive equipment of the petroleum industry. You name the industry, and the chances are nickel is used in it. The job of the institutional advertising is to translate all of this to an exciting message for general consumption.

Regular Review of Ad Appeals

Periodic review of the company's institutional advertising is always a subject on the advertising agenda. If INCO officials begin to feel that a change is in order, the usual procedure is to have a confab which will include agencyman Meulendyke. With his own staff, he later transforms suggestions and recommendations into specific advertising appeals.

The agency may make up several different basic approaches to a theme. Each approach will include roughs of several ads. From here, the job is one of pre-testing the thematic approaches.

In the past, INCO has used the Psychological Corp. and Gallup & Robinson for testing possible consumer ads. In a testing operation, a panel of 500 or 600 may be used. The initial purpose may be to select the basic theme. The next step is to write copy and run a comprehensive test on copy readership to determine if the consumer understands what the company wants to say.

This same basic procedure is used for every campaign. INCO has been pre-testing its ads for the past 7 or 8 years. The agency probably prepares 4 to 6 rough layouts for every ad run.

On the justification for the cost of advertising research, this answer is given by assistant to the board chairman Fales: "One advertisement may cost $70,000 or $80,000. Certainly it's worth a small percentage of that if we can get at least some assurance that we're on the right track."

International Nickel is conservative in its investments in advertising. The increases over the years have been the result of increased marketing problems with broader fields to cover. However, in recent years the increases have largely been the result of increased costs.

But advertising is considered an important and worthwhile ally of sales. INCO has been a pioneer in trade advertising and in industrial institutional advertising, and all signs point to the continuation of strong, consistent and fruitful advertising in the future.

Dr. John Thompson, chairman of the board, sees it this way: "If you're going to run a developing business, you've got to have a rounded business. You must develop a sound marketing and distribution system. Advertising is part of all that."

·{ 29 }··

Keen Sales Sense Gives New Vitality to a Homely Utility Product*

The J. Marie Martin Co., San Francisco, has transformed the ungainly table pad into a styled item, slimmed it down, adapted it to modern needs, made it handier, more functional—and promoted it to the furniture department of home furnishings, department and interior decoration stores as a selling mate to a wide variety of contemporary tables. Within the last six years it has increased its outlets from 500 to 1,500, and doubled its sales volume.

True, it classifies as a small business, with its volume of a quarter million, but for sales executives with a "stepchild" product, this is an

---

* Reprinted by special permission from *Sales Management*, December 15, 1953. Copyright, 1953, *Sales Management.*

encouraging story. It shows what can be done with such an item when, as in the case of the Martinbestos table pads, sharp sales sense and creative imagination are put behind it. In Martin's case the product was:

1. Made more attractive to modern tastes with contemporary materials.
2. Functionally improved.
3. Given extended uses that increase its market.
4. Offered to appropriate dealers with a merchandising package (including a smart demonstration setup).
5. Proved a plus profit item for dealers.
6. Made so easy to sell that the most inexperienced salespeople can add it to each table sale.

It was considered an improvement in appearance when the flannel covering of table pads was changed to green felt on one side and white fabric on the other. Then, as Sales Manager Vi Littell puts it, "We began to realize that table pads could—and should—be styled like other articles of home furnishings."

The firm began to add what it calls "correlated tones" to harmonize with woods of contemporary tables. At first the available materials were similar to oilcloth in texture. Not satisfied, the company began to look for more handsome coverings. It purchased fabrics embossed to give grainy surfaces, or the appearance of a variety of leathers. Constantly studying the newest furniture styles, it was able to offer, for example, "black lizzard" to go with a modern interior having Chinese or Oriental touches, or an embossed gilt fabric for a high-style decorative scheme. Fabric tones such as "Spanish mahogany," "maple," and "Spanish ivory" began to be included, with harmonizing felt undersides.

While surface appearance was enhanced and harmonized with changing trends in interior decoration, functional improvements also were studied. The pads were made easier to handle, use, and store. The functional changes culminated in the total conversion of the insulating material from asbestos to aluminum foil. This made it possible to offer a pad that was thinner, and lighter (by about 10%), but with improved insulating properties to provide better protection for fine table surfaces.

Next, the management realized that it had a large, untapped market in dining and entertaining habits. In today's casual living buffet suppers are growing in popularity. Doesn't the householder require protection for other dining and living room surfaces than the family table? Television has changed eating customs radically, with meals served on trays, or on coffee tables. There are also cocktail tables and glass-topped tea wagons.

"We asked ourselves what we could offer, in the way of protection for the surfaces of these many functional tables which have constant use," says President Ben Morden. "We also made a mental note of the obvious fact that these small tables sell 15 to every one of the larger dining room tables."

With that realization, J. Marie Martin began to offer neat pads to protect any shape or size of coffee, cocktail or other chairside table, in fabrics to harmonize. It introduced an unstitched pad, which did not resemble a table pad, but looked more like a leather-top surface. Its multiple layers and the felt and fabric materials surfacing them were put together with a non-warp adhesive glue which gave equal or better strength than stitching. The product thus became a custom item.

The merchandising program behind it is strictly a packaged deal.

"Actually," Morden points out, "we never sell a thing when we go into a store. We offer a service. We show the store owner or manager of the furniture department that he is losing business every day if he does not offer his customers table top protection for every table in the house, and if his salespeople fail to sell surface protection with every type and size of table sold in that store."

Many retailers are surprised when asked if they offer table-top protection in terms of changing eating habits. "Why, I never thought of it," is the too frequent reply.

J. Marie Martin does not place its table top protectors in the linens department only. Mrs. Littell points out: "The reason a housewife has to go hunting in the linens department for a table pad is, more likely than not, that the salesperson in the furniture department or store who sold her a table, any sort of table, failed to sell her a custom-made pad to go with it. The time to sell table-top protection is when the table is purchased—when it is new."

To encourage the dealer to sell a modern Martinbestos table pad with every table, J. Marie Martin Co. has a well-rounded dealer aid program.

First item is a counter display box containing: samples of the three qualities of the pad, made up as miniature facsimiles of actual pads to show materials, workmanship, hinging for folding and storage; color swatches and an established number code for ordering attached to each sample; paper patterns with full instructions for measuring all types of table tops ("Our pads are as accurate as the pattern received from the dealer."); sales features for each quality of pad.

This kit (Cost: $5) is furnished free to dealers. Smaller stores receive a single kit; a large department or furniture store receives one for each appropriate section. For example, the "modern" department would receive a display kit and so would the "maple" or other specialty section.

To point up and dramatize the use of aluminum foil for the insulation, the price sheets included with each sample are printed on aluminum coated sheets. These sheets indicate simple ordering rules; list six sales features for each quality.

The company does not expect dealer's salespeople to know how to sell its table pads. It makes every effort to aid in their training. The selling points, given in brief sentences, can be used verbatim or can be re-worded. For example: "Tailored by expert craftsmen for perfect fit" . . . "Liquid and heat-resistant washable pyroxylin-coated fabric by du Pont" . . . "Choice of 10 attractive colors to harmonize with the finest tables."

Morden points out: "An inexperienced salesperson need only glance at these as he displays the samples and swatches and discusses them with the customer."

To better prepare a dealer's salespeople to sell Martinbestos pads the company conducts sales training meetings in the store. "We go in before the store opens," Morden explains, "and show the salespeople, as well as department heads, buyers, store managers, owners if it's a small store, that this is a plus sale, surprisingly easy to make whenever a table is sold."

The salesman is taught to say at the strategic moment: "I would feel guilty if I did not recommend insurance against mars, scratches, burns, liquid damage, of this beautiful table. We have a firm that makes a particularly fine, and beautiful, table pad for our customers. . . ."

It is emphasized that table pads are suggestion items: "Not a single pad is ever sold unless the customer is *told*." In their training of store personnel the company uses a simple demonstration device which is adaptable for the store itself.

A small stand lamp with a 100-watt bulb has affixed to opposite sides of the light a miniature asbestos and an aluminum-insulated pad. The lamp is turned on, the demonstrator shows how a heat spot forms in the asbestos pad, and how heat is dispersed in the aluminum one. It is further shown that as soon as the heating agent is removed (turned off, in this case) the aluminum pad cools, whereas the asbestos pad retains the heat up to 15 minutes.

In the training program, this demonstration includes placing the salesperson's hands on the aluminum and then on the asbestos pad after the lamp has been on for a few minutes. A mildly burned skin surface serves as a memorizer when the palm is held against the old-type pad.

When the aluminum insulation was first used the new pad was introduced to and through the dealers with the aid of samples of both asbestos and aluminum pads with corners cut off the former, and an oval cut-out in the latter down to the foil, to demonstrate the difference in construction. A cut-back strip showing the successive layers of materials in the pad and the covering fabrics is now used in selling dealers, and provided to them for their store displays and selling operations.

Despite all these aids, there are salesmen who will not figure out the cost, nor extend the price on pads to fit a given table. This proved a stumbling block to salesmen until Mrs. Littell hit on another useful aid. She developed a tag to be attached to each table which would supply all necessary price information for a pad to fit the table. Tags are supplied to the dealer and, under the direction of a department head, are filled in and attached to tables displayed on the floor. The salesmen need only consult it to give a quotation on a pad.

A store does not have to handle the finished pad if it prefers not to. The company will ship direct to the customer, the dealer taking his profit.

Morden sums up: "We are making it so easy for the department store, furniture dealer or interior decorator to handle our pads that practically no effort at all is involved. There's plenty of grief in selling tables, the larger ones in particular. It isn't difficult for us to show a dealer that one of our pads sold with each table almost pays for his problems in handling the table."

The company does a small amount of advertising in merchandising publications. Dealer advertising is much more extensive. No retailer ever receives any advertising allowance from the company. But department and furniture stores that handle Martinbestos pads have done and continue to do an excellent job of newspaper promotion in their regular space, often running large display copy. The company provides cuts, suggested layouts, copy.

This well-rounded program has achieved:

Growth from 500 active accounts, mainly in California, to 1,500 over the 11 western states, representing the cream of the available outlets, all within a five- or six-year period.

Sales volume has been increased in the same ratio as the number of accounts, and continues to grow.

The business is now a steady year-round one instead of being concentrated in the last three months of the year.

The company has put out a place mat to be used with a linen doilie for casual service. Also aluminum-insulated, offered in six standard sizes— round, oblong and rectangular using the same fabrics as the Martinbestos table pads, this will be a production-line item. Manufactured in volume, stores will stock the individual place mats and merchandise them like any other product. With no promotion as yet, the company receives a demand for 1,500 mats a month.

Says Morden: "We expect this item to become as important sales- and profit-wise as table pads."

··{ 30 }··

This Year—$100,000,000 for Electrolux?*

BY LAWRENCE M. HUGHES

"Ninety-five percent of the people who will become the proud owners of a new Electrolux today," says Walter Dietz, "had absolutely no idea of buying a new vacuum cleaner when they got up this morning."

As president of Electrolux Corp., New York, Dietz directs an army unofficially reported at 7,000 door-to-door salesmen across the U.S., whose ingenious and indefatigable ability to put ideas in heads and order books in hands builds 7,000 "individual businesses."

The fact that for 22 of its 32 years in this country Electrolux has led all other vacuum cleaners in sales suggests that its door-openers find plenty of pay dirt in the parlors of the nation's 46 million wired homes.

How much all this adds up to in corporate volume is still a well-kept secret. But some statistics may show the trend:

Since 1934 the factory's floor space at Old Greenwich, Conn. has been expanded eight times.

In the year ended last December 31 working capital ($26.1 million) had multiplied three times and net worth ($22.1 million) more than twice since 1946.

Customer instalment accounts receivable, or "easy payments," came to $25,488,587, or 31% more than a year before.

In 1947, when the company was still struggling to meet "pent-up demand," combined commissions to salesmen totaled $22,320,787. At the long-established Electrolux rate of 35% this meant a $78 million volume.

Probably, 1956 sales will be around $100 million—every unit of which will have been sold at full list price.

This volume is being done in vacuum cleaners and the service of them; in such accessories as attachments to scrub and polish floors, and in such home products as waxes, rug shampoo, dusting brushes, moth crystals, a mothproofer, Garment-Aire bags.

Current sales are being stimulated by a new Automatic Electrolux. This features lighter weight, 20% more suction, and a "brain" that shuts off the cleaner and pops open the cover when the dust bag is full.

But direct selling itself cannot be automated. Walter Dietz calls it

---

* Reprinted by special permission from *Sales Management*, December 7, 1956. Copyright, 1956, *Sales Management*.

"creative selling in its purest form." And one of his associates adds: "We don't wait for the cow to back up to be milked."

Creative selling, incentive compensation, recognition, and a lot of latitude, under aggressive management, all help the salesmen to grow in direct proportion to their ability to sell.

Whereas in other companies "your opportunity depends on the next man," Dietz emphasizes that "in Electrolux *everybody sells himself ahead*."

Every officer—including Elon V. Ekman, chairman, who brought the business over from Sweden in 1924; Walter Dietz, who joined in 1925 and has been president since 1942; Harry A. Strong, San Francisco, v-p for western operations; Paul R. Boggs, v-p for sales—started upward from door-to-door.

The 30 division and 300 branch managers all sold themselves into their jobs. Their income, on a commission basis, grows with their ability to get their men to sell.

Some of them today can count their "worth" in six and even seven figures.

But in endless rounds of contests, for managers at all levels and their men, Electrolux comes up with handier and showier symbols of sales success. Two perennials among them are pachyderms for lapels: a Silver Elephant for selling 50 vacuum cleaners in one month; a Diamond Gold Elephant for 100 a month.

These worked out fine until Laurier B. (Larry) Bazinet really started spreading ideas. For his achievements Electrolux had to produce a special Platinum Elephant: In October 1955 Bazinet sold 300 vacuum cleaners.

This mark made Roger Bannister's four-minute mile look like slow motion. It was 51 more than the previous Electrolux record which had stood since 1949, and nearly double the record 186 established in 1947.

Bazinet made it in Maine's northeastern Aroostook and Washington counties, the 10,000 sprawling square miles of which grow a great many more potatoes than people.

The new Automatic Electrolux sells for $89.75. Thus, at 35%—not including "extras" and other home-maintenance products—Bazinet's commissions for that month came to about $9,300. Could he have kept going for a year at a 300-a-month clip, he would have earned $111,000. Actually, last year, he sold a total of 1,000 machines, on which his commissions exceeded $30,000.

Would Rather Sell

Electrolux thought such skill should be shared, and appointed him manager of the Worcester branch. But Bazinet discovered that he would rather sell than manage. After three months he went back to his beat. Monday mornings find him loading the gray sedan with 20 vacuum cleaners. He has arranged with Frank Briggs, his branch manager at Portland, for replenishments on the road. He says good-bye to his wife and two boys at their home in Lewiston and is off to his self-chosen territory, which starts 100 miles away. Often his family won't see him again until Saturday night.

But Larry's life is not all toil. He likes to see his family oftener. He likes to fish. And he also enjoys taking time out several times a year for all-expense-paid shindigs which Electrolux throws for last month's elephant-winners and their wives.

For the annual spring get-together for "Easterners" and wives Electrolux has taken the tab for as many as 3,500, who overflowed the Waldorf-Astoria into nine other hotels. Diamond Gold Elephant salesmen may bring their branch and division managers and *their* wives. Varying with sales records, the couples stay from three to five days.

Similar meetings are held for western winners and wives at Phoenix or Palm Springs.

These affairs now are informal. But not long ago Electrolux was paying $5,000, just for the New York meeting, just for pressing dress suits. With theater tickets and other entertainment (but no liquor), and fashion shows where wives are asked to "pick your own gowns," and miscellany, Electrolux foots an annual "recognition" bill for six fat figures annually.

Mr. and Mrs. Diamond Gold Elephant Joe Doakes arrive at the Waldorf on Friday. Their days start with a continental breakfast in the Astor Gallery or Jade Room. Saturday night they attend an Electrolux dinner and then a Broadway show. Monday through Wednesday they attend business meetings, to which the wives are invited. Each evening the company provides entertainment.

To its 25th birthday party in New York in 1949 Electrolux even invited competitors.

Average eastern attendance is now 2,500. About half as many get to the western meeting. Next spring, for the first time, western winners may go to the Waldorf, and eastern winners to Phoenix.

Meanwhile, at other seasons, star salesmen in both sections are winning free weeks for themselves and families in faraway sun spots, or are getting the cash equivalent from the company. Divisions and branches are holding shindigs to celebrate awards or simply to set out to sell.

Every Electrolux invitation embraces a woman. The men are told: "If you're not married, bring your mother. If you're widowed bring your daughter." The women, it seems, appreciate the full life which strong selling can create. They won't let their men relax.

But whether a man sells 10 a day or only one, it's his business. And he may sell where and to whom he wants. "Our only map," says Walter Dietz, "is the U.S." If Maine's Bazinet should make a sale in San Bernardino County, Cal., or Broward County, Fla., he would not be encroaching and he would get his full commission. But wherever he sells, he must assume responsiblity for instalment accounts.

At Electrolux the " 'Close' Is Just the Beginning"

Electrolux salesmen are not slow about bringing out the order book. They know that "the 'close' is just the beginning."

Analyzing 2,341 demonstrations that produced sales, by new and experienced salesmen, Electrolux Corp. finds that 44.1% of all of them used a "standard close." Then ranked the "early close, 28.4%; contest close 28.1%; trade-in breakdown 19.4%; operation close 16.1%, and other closes 11.1%.

Men with less than two months' experience use primarily (53.8%) the standard, and then the trade-in and early closes. With veterans of 10 years and more the early slightly outranked the standard (39.3 to 37.6%) but all other closes stood higher.

When the prospect starts thinking of costs and terms, the salesman pulls the standard close: "Most of our good customers give us $20 or $25 down. If you will give me $20 today, that will leave a balance of $———. Would you rather have your first payment fall due on the 18th or the 19th? (If no answer, "Will the 18th be OK?") That's fine, just OK this order."

If the prospect says, "We are paying for so many things now that we simply can't buy anything else," the salesman (still busy demonstrating) stresses "the overwhelming importance of a clean home."

If she asks him to come back in the fall, he uses a contest close to get her to buy today. If that fails, he takes "decisive action." Some men gather all the dirt piles into one big pile. Others ask, "What is your hardest cleaning problem?" He then tackles it, and shows her the order book.

In the early close he cleans a small area of one rug: "See how simple. No bending, no work to it. Notice how quiet it is. You can even listen to the radio or watch television while you're cleaning." He watches for "red light signals," or any suggestions about her particular problems, and tackles them.

One version of the operations close is: "Mrs. Jones, if we find as much dirt in your davenport as we found in your rugs, floors and in this other furniture, you want your Electrolux today, don't you?"

The trade-in breakdown: If the prospect asks, "What will you give me for my old cleaner?" the salesman takes hold of it and says: "Mrs. Jones, if I came here to sell you this machine, and went over your rug with it many times, and then you got out your Electrolux cleaner and went over your rug and got all these dirt piles . . . you wouldn't honestly pay me $5 for this machine. Would you?" (He pushes the old cleaner away.)

The salesman may suggest that the old cleaner be used in basement or garage or be given away. If pressed, however, he checks the old cleaner's price with his Blue Book and makes an allowance.

Electrolux does not rebuild or resell such old cleaners. Not long ago the company dumped 40 truckloads of them into the Atlantic Ocean. This was one way to create sales opportunities.

"We don't object to three or four men calling on the same family," Dietz adds. "One of them might make a sale. Every man should regard every home as a prospect.

"We don't build fences around the branches, either."

Any man, young or old, of morals, manners and reasonably good appearance may sell Electrolux. The company does not mind open collars or broken English. But Dietz emphasizes: "Every man must be honest. He must be a gentleman. He must use no liquor on the job . . . We never let our men forget that, to our customers, they *are* Electrolux.

"To protect our customers and all our people we cannot even give an individual the benefit of a doubt.

"Not long ago I learned that, in spite of all precautions, one branch had hired an ex-convict, a check forger. The governor of his state and three clergymen begged us to 'give him a chance.' But we could not. Soon afterward this man was back in the penitentiary for another crime.

"One salesman was suspected of being 'involved' with an Indian girl. We released him promptly. A few weeks later we found that he was *really* involved."

He is proud of "the stability of our personnel. In field management we have almost no turnover. In selling, as we grow older, we get a terrific number of father-and-son combinations." A son cannot inherit the "business," but he can learn a lot from his father. The president's own son, Raymond, discharged from armed service last September 1, won his Silver Elephant in Kentucky and is now branch manager at Lansing, Mich.

Men and managers learn and grow together. And by daily bulletins to both groups, the weekly 12-page *Electrolux News* to the entire force, and otherwise, hq. keeps them on their toes. Primarily, in all these communications, "the men tell each other"—and learn from them.

Trained in Field

The branches hold meetings every weekday. But sales training now is confined largely to letting prospective salesmen "go out with a successful salesman and watch him make money . . . If a man plays according to our rules, he can make a lot."

Rule 1 contradicts the old foot-in-the-door theory.

"The first thing a successful salesman does when he comes to a home," says Walter Dietz, "is to see which side the door is hinged on. When the door is opened, he takes off his hat, says 'good morning' pleasantly, and *takes two steps backward*. This proves to the housewife that he's not trying to crash in."

During his demonstration he listens to everything she says and watches her every move for clues that will help him close the sale. Should she ask, "Will it clean upholstered furniture?" his answer is not, "We'll come to that later" but, "Will it?—watch *this!*"

He also tries to keep himself at a higher level. She should be seated while he stands and sells.

The corporation introduces its own little touches of "psychology." Men need not report calls—only sales. Thus, Dietz explains, "all they see is a record of accomplishment."

Electrolux News of Nov. 19, 1955 carried a full-page picture of Larry Bazinet setting out to sell, and the headline, "ELECTROLUX HAS A NEW CHAMPION."

Months earlier, it seems, Bazinet "knew he was going to break the record sometime in 1955." In May he had sold 100 in order to join other Diamond Gold Elephant men and families the next month for a company-paid outing at Delray Beach, Fla. To come out ahead in the Home Furnishings Contest in June, he sold 100 in 10 days—and in one day, 17 in a row. He and Manager Briggs decided on October for the all-out attack.

"Bazinet sells suction," Electrolux tells the sales force. He sells more with words than demonstration. But he can demonstrate.

While nearly all the homes he visits have vacuum cleaners, "a modern Electrolux" is something else again. In his record breaking month, he would show how the machine would suck up three half-pound steel balls. "Show me another vacuum cleaner that will do this," said Larry, "and I will give you this cleaner." If the ball demonstration did not roll them over, he tried the Dirt Detector, a plastic holder which some salesmen use with dirt-revealers. With the detector on the business end, he picked up stove lids, chairs, tables and miscellany.

The new Automatic will do much more.

An ancient embarrassing moment in this business concerned the salesman who walked into a farm home, dumped a pile of dirt on a rug, and then learned that the home was not wired for electricity. While nearly all of Bazinet's homes are now wired, he goes easy on the dirt: "just enough piles to be convincing—never more than three . . . on bare floors he used just one swipe of the brush."

Each sale takes about 10 minutes. Often he works "wholesale." In his record month he sold 300 units on fewer than 300 demonstrations, before family groups. He figured that if he could win mother and father, married sons and daughters would buy too.

Satisfied Users Help

His customers even helped in the record breaking. Many arranged family-group demonstrations. (About half of all Electrolux sales are made on "referrals" from satisfied customers.)

Hillary J. McCrossin, Boston, New England division manager, has said that Bazinet's record "will never be broken." Bazinet disagrees: "If I can do it, someone else can."

President Dietz set out to prove to *Sales Management* that "we have the highest paid specialty sales organization." He spiced our interview with telephone calls to Electroluxers in several states. Then I cut in for personal proof of profitable selling.

We talked, for example, with Victor Polity, Union City, N.J. Victor had just wed when he lost his job as bellhop in 1925. Then he started selling Electrolux. During the depression he made enough to save $15,000. In 1936 Dietz, then vice-president, "talked him into management." He became a "team manager" (which, Dietz explains, "is no different from a branch manager") and now has 20 men with him. In his best year Polity earned $40,000. He figures his current "worth" at $100,000. He still makes sales calls.

We failed to reach Frank Briggs at Portland. He was in Boston, at a meeting with other branch managers under McCrossin. With the Bell System's help, we barged into it.

Briggs had been a potato farmer, when he joined Electrolux in 1930. He "didn't know anything" about vacuum cleaners, but in his first week sold nine. As assistant branch manager at Pittsfield, Mass., he pushed his annual earnings to $60,000. As manager at Portland, since 1938, he has done somewhat better. He told about his 700-acre farm, where he grows apples and potatoes, his sawmill and other interests. His assets: $300,000—"all due to Eloctrolux."

1,000 Yankee Salesmen

Portland, boasts Briggs, can "outsell the big cities. We've built the largest direct-selling organization in Maine, and our business continues to grow, across the whole state." He says some nice things about Larry Bazinet, who "works Aroostook County, 425 miles from Portland."

McCrossin points out that "we used to have 1,000 salesmen in New England, and we hope to have that many again. Lots of opportunities in our area haven't been scratched." The division runs want ads in newspapers and is hiring several salesmen a week, from all business backgrounds and of all ages, including retired people.

(A tight labor market now cramps direct-selling forces.)

After selling stocks and bonds, McCrossin went to Electrolux in 1925. In his best year he earned $140,000. A little prodding produced the fact that, "thanks to Electrolux," he's now a millionaire.

Walter Dietz finds "opportunities everywhere: When we first opened a branch at Hempstead, L.I., the population of that village (not to be confused with the *town* of Hempstead, embracing various villages) was less than 10,000. But this branch has sold more vacuum cleaners than any other." It still ranks among the top 10.

"Generally, we start in larger cities and reach out." Rural penetration could be deeper. But a study by *Progressive Farmer* among its southern farm subscribers still shows Electrolux far ahead in vacuum cleaner ownership, with 27.8% of the total—followed by G-E 8%, Air-Way 7.7%, Hoover 6.3%, Sears, Roebuck's Kenmore 6.0%.

Industry vacuum cleaner sales in 1955 were 3.3 million. After Electrolux (which has not yet achieved an ambition of selling as many as all the rest combined) the national leaders are said to be Hoover, G-E, Westinghouse and Lewyt. Air-Way and others sell door-to-door. Hoover sells both to homes and through stores.

Electrolux claims to "open the doors for the industry."

Its early machine, Dietz explains, was the "first in the United States with an enclosed bag. While our men did a terrific job of selling it, they did not succeed with thousands of people to whom they demonstrated. Yet those people were so impressed with the enclosed bag type that they demanded one like it from their local stores. In 10 years every other vacuum cleaner had an enclosed bag."

The four keystones of the company's growth, he says, are "(1) the product; (2) our method of selling; (3) our concept of the sale (including service responsibility *after* the sale), and (4) our treatment of *non-buyers*."

Electrolux does not merely "assemble": It builds nearly all the parts for its machines. And it assumes full responsibility for their effective operation.

On one early vacuum cleaner, Dietz recalls, "something wasn't quite up to par. We changed 200,000 of those parts without expense to any customer—even before most of them had any trouble."

Not long ago, just after introducing the Automatic, "we came up with a radical new development—the dial. We changed thousands of machines which people had purchased without a dial. This also meant changing front covers—which sell for $18.75 each.

"Our customers had bought a good product. But the dial made it so much better, in some areas, that we wanted them to have the benefit of it."

All 300 branches offer company-maintained service. On special problems, however, Electrolux has been known to send an engineer from Connecticut to Dallas, without cost to the customer.

Dietz warns the salesmen: "Some customers complain that 'I never like to call Electrolux for service because when the man comes, he always tries to sell me a new cleaner.'" A salesman should "make an honest estimate of the cost to put that cleaner in first-class condition. The customer is then in a position to decide whether she wants a new machine or not."

Like Happy Customers

Making friends counts in making sales: "The product makes part of the sale. The salesman himself makes the rest of it. The customer has to like both." The salesman should not be "aggressive to the point where it blocks us." After the sale he should make sure the customer is happy with her purchase. (And in the process he can get her to think of him as a steady source of various home-maintenance products.)

Because its own people sell all its products to the consumer, Electrolux does not have to worry about discount houses. And whether a customer buys one vacuum cleaner or 100, every unit of the same model sells at the same price. Not long ago, Bell Laboratories tested various vacuum cleaners, decided on Electrolux, and were somewhat miffed to learn that it couldn't buy them "wholesale."

And on every sale an employe gets a full commission.

Customers seem to approve both Electrolux products and policies. Walter Dietz cites findings in one independent survey, which showed that "out of every 100 Electrolux buyers today, 59 will buy another Electrolux. For all other makes together, the average brand loyalty was only 12%."

Electrolux in fact to some extent "pre-insures" loyalty. The Automatic was field-tested in 13,000 homes. Of 1,900 of these users who wrote in their opinion of it only 29 were "not fully happy." Within a month the company saw to it that all but three were happy.

Over the years this company has gone out of its way to make friends. When the nation's banks closed in March 1933, salesmen were authorized to accept checks from customers. (The losses were almost zero.) During World War II the salesmen who had not gone into military service worked to keep the cleaners cleaning. Although its own plant was devoted entirely to war work, the company still could boast that "no Electrolux cleaner for which service was requested remained inoperative."

Under a "preferential contract" plan, on payment of a $25 down payment, the company promised the purchaser delivery of a cleaner within a year after production of civilian goods was authorized. The certificate also guaranteed a ceiling on price. The contract, to which Electrolux was able to adhere, brought an avalanche of sales.

Through 28 years Electrolux expanded without national advertising. Since 1952, however, it has run a modest campaign in magazines (through Batten, Barton, Durstine & Osborn), which it credits for "opening many doors." Salesmen leave reprints of ads with a reminder:

"PLEASE READ THIS: AN IMPORTANT
MESSAGE ABOUT A WONDERFUL
CHRISTMAS PRESENT—
INSPIRING TO GIVE—
THRILLING TO RECEIVE. I
WILL BE BACK—(he inserts date) . . ."

Some salesmen hand a reprint to the prospect and say, "While you read this I will go to my car and show you this wonderful new cleaner."

The campaign, which may be expanded, is running in *Better Homes and Gardens, Ladies' Home Journal, McCall's,* and *Parents'.*

Currently, the company spends $215,000 a year for advertising.

In the month when Larry Bazinet set the 300 record, 106 men won Diamond Gold Elephants for selling 100 machines. Production per man was the highest ever attained.

But when one record falls, Electrolux goes after the next one. Paul Boggs wired all the men that "never do I remember a November starting in such a high pitch of excitement. At one branch meeting today men . . . threw their chairs around the room."

In the first month after the Automatic's appearance the West shamed the East by coming through with six times as many Diamond Gold Elephants. Recent leaders among branches for the Sales Cup, Supply Cup and Service Award, respectively, were Portland, Me., Kansas City, Little Rock. Gulf Division was out front in cleaner sales and Western Division in supply sales. Supplementing a continuing silver bowl award for assistant branch managers and their groups, Electrolux was offering a sterling silver tray, "sponsored by Vice-President Paul Boggs." Ten of the 16 assistant managers who won the bowl once or more have since been advanced to branch manager.

In Daily Touch

Every Monday and Thursday hq. knows how a half-week went across the country, up to the night before. Daily, words of praise—and otherwise—go out through Electrolux Press Service to the men and bulletins to the managers. "Our job," says Walter Dietz, "is to relay the thoughts of the men in the field. We help them to talk to each other."

Electrolux News is a whole jungle of elephant symbols and other stimulations and recognitions: Contest batting averages; pictures of award winners and award meetings; letters from satisfied customers. And slogans: "There's DANGER in Dust and Dirt;" "If you can make your prospects know what you know, you'll hardly ever lose a sale;" "Timid heart ne'er won fair lady's name on the contract book."

And human interest: While attending last spring's elephant-award meeting in New York, one branch manager was stricken with appendicitis. Electrolux taped the five-day proceedings for him and reproduced them in Roosevelt Hospital.

A cartoon character called Elux reminds the salesmen: "Hundreds of thousands of homes today still are without benefit of an Electrolux cleaner. Electrolux Selling is OPPORTUNITY UNLIMITED."

How much all this pays the stockholders, however, may be another matter.

In the postwar decade after-tax profit started at $3.1 million; reached $4.1 million in 1948 and in 1950; declined to $1.8 million in 1952, and since has risen to $2.8 million in 1955. Then in nine months of 1956 profit dipped, with higher wages and steel costs, to $1.7 million, or an annual rate of $2.2 million.

Dividends per share fluctuated between a low of $1 in 1953 and 1954 to $2.20 in 1947, and last year were $1.25. Over the decade total earnings per share were $25.99. Of this $15.15 was declared in dividends and $10.84 retained in the business.

Walter Dietz is not worried: With the products and the people to sell them, he is sure that the profits will climb.

A lot of doors are still to be opened by Electrolux.

··{ 31 }··

"I'm a Low-Pressure Salesman"*

You tell James Fiorentino that you are thinking of buying a radio-controlled garage door operator, and suggest, "so go ahead and sell me one."

"Very possibly I wouldn't know where to start," says Fiorentino. "I don't have any high-pressure talk on the tip of my tongue. I don't know who you are, what friends of yours have our doors, or what feature interests you most in a radio-operated door."

"I," Fiorentino adds, "am a very low-pressure salesman."

That, from the Minneapolis man who was top salesman in the nation in a two-month campaign conducted by Crawford Door Co., Detroit, national distributors for the General Motors Delco-matic Garage Door Operator, which costs about $235 installed.

In the 60-day contest, Fiorentino sold 50 units. He said he could have sold more, but sales were running too far ahead of installations. Fiorentino and his two brothers, Antonio and Orlando, who own Garage Door Operator Service, believe in careful expansion.

Interested Neighbors

"I get most of my leads from satisfied customers," he says. "We see to it that they are satisfied by checking back a time or two following installation. Those return calls usually net us a name or two of a neighbor or a friend who will be interested. That keeps our file of prospects alive."

So Fiorentino goes to see the satisfied customer's friend.

---

* Reprinted by special permission from *Sales Management*, May 1, 1956. Copyright, 1956, *Sales Management*.

"I'm no High-Pressure Pete," he says, "I figure a man is being high-pressured practically every time a salesman comes to see him at his home or at the office, or calls him on the telephone.

"I figure a prospect appreciates a change from that routine."

So Fiorentino, having the satisfied customer's consent to use his name, tells the prospect who sent him, how the friend likes his automatic door, how little trouble it was to install.

They look at the garage, and Fiorentino soon knows whether the prospect is interested chiefly in reliability of the device. His child or dog might run under the door as it was closing: He would be interested chiefly in the light touch halting the door's operation.

"Sometimes we back out of a sale where proper installation is impossible," says Fiorentino. "We place that much importance on satisfied customers."

That happened a few weeks ago, with an attorney who had ordered one of the operators. He had a cement basement garage—and had been given a poor cement job. It crumbled during the drilling for the installation and obviously would not support even the lightest operating unit.

"I told him I would prefer not to sell him one of the units, and I told him why," says Fiorentino.

Impressed by Honesty

"Within the next two weeks, two new prospects were referred to us by the attorney, who apparently was impressed by our honesty. We sold both of those prospects."

Then Fiorentino went to the attorney's garage, probed around until he found a beam where it should not have been, had an extension rigged to the unit so that the distant beam could be used, and got the door properly installed. It's working fine, and Fiorentino won't be surprised if more prospects are referred to him by the attorney.

Fiorentino and his brothers take a booth at building shows and do a little other advertising. If things slacken, Fiorentino gets on the telephone, calls up and down streets in a neighborhood he has selected, often completes the deal without having seen the buyer. One sale in a neighborhood frequently sets off "chain reaction" buying from neighbors who see the door being operated from the transmitter in the buyer's car.

"But mostly I depend on satisfied customers," Fiorentino says. "I like to come highly recommended."

All of which makes R. A. Hackathorn, president, Crawford Door Co., a very happy man, and glad to have had his sales promotion manager, G. W. Messer, award Fiorentino for contest prizes a Hoover vacuum cleaner, a Daystrom kitchen set and other products worth some $400. Both Crawford Door and Fiorentino like the profits they made from low-pressure salesmanship.

·{ 32 }·

Industry Tries Selling By Seminar*

Nobody needs to be told that the heavy machinery that is putting so large a part of the verve into the U.S. economy is getting more and more complex. But as this is happening, the selling job that heavy industry has to do is getting more and more complicated, too. So much hard cash, so much advance planning, so much heavy betting is involved in purchases of heavy machinery nowadays that the men who make big and expensive equipment are having to work up new marketing methods if they're to sell their products.

Right now, they think they've found one answer to their selling problems: Don't send your salesmen to your customers, bring your customers to your own plant.

In one form or another, this is a time-honored device. It may turn up as a "casual" (yet carefully timed) invitation to "drop in and see us when you are in our neighborhood." It may be an open-house to show off a new plant, or a tour designed for supervisory personnel. A research plant—Purina Ralston's Research Farm is a case in point (*BW*—Mar.13'54, p48)—may make special bids to customers to bring their problems with them and find their solutions in the host's products.

Refined Approach

More and more companies find that when they refine these occasional invitations they gain an important selling pitch. The refinement is the regularly staged seminar, lasting one, two, three, or more days, put on for the customers' technical men, the design and product engineers. Some of these seminars, like Westinghouse Electric Corp.'s Machine Tool Electrification Forum, give experts from a number of companies a chance to pool their knowledge. Other companies—especially in the aviation field—use such seminars as their prime sales tools.

One of the newcomers at the seminar game is Electro-Alloys Div. of American Brake Shoe Co. Over the past two years this outfit has held nearly a dozen seminars on the manufacture, metallurgy, and engineering of alloy at its Elyria (Ohio) plant. Guests come from such blue-chip operations as Chrysler Corp., International Harvester, Bethlehem Steel, Oliver Iron & Steel, U.S. Steel Research, Pickands Mather, Link Belt.

They spend two days touring the facilities of Electro-Alloys and getting down to brass-tacks discussions of design principles for trays, rails, retorts, hearth rolls, chain belt testing, and the like.

No Sample Cases

There are plenty of reasons why this kind of selling is growing. The sheer bulk of much of heavy industry's product makes it an unlikely package for a salesman to tote from door to door. And a customer who is sinking tens or hundreds of thousands of dollars in new equipment wants to be sure what he is getting, and wants to know a lot about his supplier before he lays down his money. The quickest way for him to get the answers is to visit his supplier's plant.

Twin Coach Co., in Buffalo, tells how it operates before it bids for a subcontract supplying components to large aircraft manufacturers. Before it gets an invitation to bid, Twin Coach has a team of six to 12 experts come in to visit its plant. The team investigates nook and cranny: finances, cost accounting, engineering and technical personnel, traffic management, packaging, even water supply and cost and supply of power.

Customers, of course, have always wanted to know these things. But today—in an era of huge industrial expansion, calling for new equipment that daily becomes more complex and more expensive—there is extra pressure to have all the answers before signing the purchasing contract.

Equipment Race

It would be dangerous for a customer to buy much of today's heavy industrial equipment from a catalog or a salesman's description. Innovations and improvements of old techniques and a constant flow of new processes and machinery keep customers hopping to stay abreast of the times. Seminars at which the beauties of these new industrial babies are expounded are a good way to introduce the new machines and new processes.

It's no accident that the aviation industry has gone in heavily for seminars, that International Business Machines has set up a Computer College for potential customers at Elmira, N.Y., or that Taylor Instrument Co. holds special demonstrations of its gasoline refinery automation equipment at its Rochester (N.Y.) headquarters.

Customers are responding enthusiastically to these seminars. They're sending representatives from all over the U.S. and Canada, and some even from overseas.

The host company usually picks up the tab for incidental entertaining, but the guests usually pay for their own transportation.

There are some exceptions, especially when the host company has its own airplane. And the NesTier Div. of Charles William Doepke Mfg. Co., near Cincinnati, finds that hiring a helicopter to fly potential customers from the airport to its plant pays off in good customer relations.

Costs

It is hard to say whether this form of selling costs more than the old doorbell-ringing technique. Some concerns believe it is much cheaper than keeping up a field sales force. In some cases, they can cut out the field force altogether. This is what happened when a group of three companies set up Alden Research Laboratory, in Westboro, Mass. The laboratory is a promotional demonstration center for Alfax Paper & Engineering Co., Alden Electronics & Impulse Recording Equipment Co., and Alden Systems, Inc., and these companies keep no field sales forces. All their selling is done when prospective customers visit their laboratory demonstrations.

The new technique hasn't been pushed quite so far by most other companies. Westinghouse's electronic and X-ray divisions in Baltimore, for example, give their prospects a complete sales pitch, but they do have a field sales force as well.

Soft-Selling

For the most part, though, selling at seminars is held to a very muted key. Most companies emphasize that the salesmen who follow up the seminars are the men who write the orders. Of course, the salesmen are able to write their orders far more readily if the customer has seen the product and has had a detailed explanation of its accomplishments.

One reason for the difference in the intensity of the sales pitch is that in many cases seminars serve more than one purpose. General Electric Co., an old pro at the seminar game, makes a distinction here. "Developing a market is quite different from developing sales, although the two complement each other," says J. J. Heuther, manager of GE's Market Planning & Development Section of User Industries Sales Dept. For companies seeking market development rather than immediate sales the sales pitch at seminars is soft.

Results

Few companies care to make any estimates of the practical dollar returns in sales of such programs. Electro-Alloys believes there has been enough increase in orders from its older customers to warrant continuing its new program. But company after company points to the fact that it has no difficulty in filling its roster for a seminar.

There are certain pitfalls, some companies admit. One problem, says Bendix Aviation, is to get together at the right time the correct composite group from all over the country. Occasionally, companies have stubbed their toes by forgetting to include some concern with a stake in their products—and have made enemies instead of making friends. Worse yet, one extrusion supplier ruefully notes, customers sometimes will come in, watch an extrusion process, and after soaking up all available information, will buy presses of their own so they can turn out extrusions for themselves.

Gains

But the overwhelming vote among manufacturers who put on such shows is favorable. Whether the effort aims at developing new markets—which may entail product development—as in the case of Monsanto Chemical Co. (*BW*—Jun.16'56,p185)—or immediate sales, they cite these advantages:

1. There's nothing like a captive market, and a customer under your own roof is a complete captive.

2. Customer-supplier understanding improves significantly, says Electo-Alloys' sales manager, William D. Raddatz. Customers, with their new understanding of the processes involved in turning out the products they buy, are less likely to ask the unnecessary—or the impossible—from the equipment they buy.

3. The feedback of information works both ways. Companies that hold seminars often get tips from their customers. One seminar guest at Electro-Alloys asked the host company's engineers, "Why do you use such a high nickel content in the alloy on that unit?" The engineers discovered they had no good answer—and that there was no good reason for using so much expensive nickel. Joy Manufacturing Co., Pittsburgh machinery producer, is another one that reports customers often come up with ideas. From Joy's viewpoint, this has the pleasant result that the customers are apt to buy equipment when they feel it embodies their own ideas.

4. Seminars open doors for salesmen who have had trouble getting to see potential customers. They establish the personal contacts that count for so much in this kind of custom selling. Electro-Alloys thinks this is significant: In its two-year experiment with seminars, it has watched the caliber of its visitors move from engineers and metallurgists to chief engineers and top technicians.

Sales managers in many heavy equipment companies feel that the whole selling approach in their industry is changing. The older "seat-of-my-pants" salesmen who are low on technical knowhow and strong on selling are disappearing fast. Replacing them are the younger engineering graduates, perhaps less qualified from the sales point of view, but with more factual knowledge and a better understanding of the customer's problems.

·{ 33 }··

What It Takes to Make a Sale*

BY GEORGE D. FARLEY

Ever wonder why you're successful—or unsuccessful—in making a sale?

If you could take just one of your sales—one that you consider typical—and break it down step-by-step—you'd probably uncover a multitude of revealing and helpful information.

That knowledge could be invaluable to effective self-improvement of selling performance. You could put it to work immediately. But it's hard to come by. Why? Because you're too close to it. Every day, you live with it. You can't get outside for a good, long, objective look.

This article—the story of one sale from start to finish—may help you take that look. The sale is not typical, nor is it unique. You may never be called on to provide the extent or the kinds of service salesman Joe Gavenda furnished his contractor customer and Pine Chemicals, Inc.—but then again, you may.

Joe Gavenda's not the greatest hotshot electrical distributor's salesman in the world. But, as Tab Electric Supply's Sales Manager Jerry Madden says, "He uses his head. Anything that will increase Joe's effectiveness—he'll try. He's like a thoroughbred. I'm just along for the ride."

Gavenda came to Tab nine years ago after earning a certificate in electrical engineering at the Trenton School of Industrial Arts. He's been selling ever since. He's a member of the executive committee, Central Jersey Electrical League, and was recently elected president of the Industrial Maintenance Association, a division of the league.

You may agree or disagree with many of Gavenda's selling ideas. But one thing is certain. He's not an order-taker. He's a creative salesman—one you can learn a lot from.

FINDING THE LEAD

On a sunny Sunday afternoon in early summer, 1955, salesman Joe Gavenda's eyes came to rest on a 5-line item in the Trenton Times.

It said that the first commercial processing plant for the continuous distillation and refining of pine oleoresin in the U.S. would be built in

Fieldsboro, N.J.—a few miles south of Trenton on the east bank of the Delaware.

Just what "... processing ... distillation and refining ... pine oleoresin" meant, Gavenda wasn't sure. But he was certain that a good prospect was locating in his selling territory and that meant new business.

Jots Them Down

So he made a note of the item. After nine years of selling, it was a habit —a profitable habit. He added the new lead to pages containing dozens of fragments of information gleaned from many sources—satisfied customers, fellow employees, manufacturers' salesmen, trade association meetings, yes—and even tips on hot prospects picked up from his competition.

What to do next? Easy. He made it number one on Monday's selling agenda. The lead was tucked away; the salesman was ready to move.

MAKING CONTACT

Early Monday morning, Matthew Rue, Jr., received a visit from Joe Gavenda in the downtown Trenton sales office of Filtered Rosin Products, Inc.

Rue, vice president and general manager of Pine Chemicals, Inc. (an affiliate of Filtered Rosin) was glad to discuss the groundwork he was laying for the new plant and pleased to receive Gavenda's offer of service on behalf of Tab Electric Supply.

No Sale

Pine Chemicals hadn't reached the buying stage yet, he explained, but would be in the market soon for a large quantity of electrical equipment. Gavenda asked for more details and got them.

He also learned that Pine Chemicals planned to bring in a local electrical contractor for the construction and maintenance of the new plant's electrical system.

On Right Track

When he left Rue's office, Tab's top outside salesman headed straight for the office of one of his oldest customers—contractor Frank Blanche. Joe learned Frank was being considered for the job and offered to help him get it. They talked over what it would involve, planned for it and Blanche got the contract.

CREATING INTEREST

To sell an industrial on a contractor is one thing; to sell yourself and your company as the supplier is another.

That's how it was for Joe Gavenda at this point in the sale. While he wasn't exactly out in the cold, there was no guarantee that Pine Chemicals would buy any electrical apparatus or supplies from Tab Electric.

His immediate goal was apparent: he had to stimulate and maintain interest in the mind of the customer.

Head Start

How did he do it? In several ways. To begin with, he had an "in" with the contractor. Though Tab was not Blanche's primary source of supply, Joe had been building toward that goal for a long time. He'd worked closely with Blanche on many jobs, never drawing the line on service, engineering aid, layout assistance or trouble shooting.

Because of the secrecy that generally characterizes the chemical business, there were no blueprints, hence no specifications for the contractor to work from on this installation.

What's more, the plant would be using an unique chemical process—making security all the tighter.

Suggests Survey

Gavenda saw his chance and grabbed it. Basic construction of Pine Chemicals' new plant had started. Why not, he suggested, permit him to make a survey of the site with Blanche?

Rue could go along and briefly describe where processing equipment was to be placed, what power was needed and where, what controls were required, etc., for the whole operation.

His offer was well received and the physical survey began. Gavenda obtained as much detail as permissible and drew up a rough floor plan and a preliminary general materials list for the contractor's use from his survey.

The distributor's salesman explained to Rue that he would now draw up a thoroughly detailed plan for the job based on the physical survey. There were many points to be explored, he stressed, especially those involving hazardous areas of the plant.

Runs into Resistance

Rue questioned his designation of some areas as requiring explosion-proof equipment. Joe emphasized the roughness of the survey and the difficulties of making snap judgments about the areas. But he repeated his belief that they were correctly labeled as hazardous.

When the conversation made it plain that similar areas in the company's Baxley, Georgia, plant were considered non-hazardous, he promised to check up on the whole question.

Once the verbal review of the survey was completed, the real work began for salesman Gavenda.

Sales Research

That night—before he did anything else—Joe began checking his survey against the National Code and the New Jersey Underwriters' regulations.

Just as he'd thought, the areas in question were hazardous and did require many explosion-proof items. He carefully researched the survey until he was certain, then prepared for the next step—drawing up a complete list of materials.

But before he went ahead, Gavenda contacted Rue. Explaining what his own research had revealed about the explosion-proof areas, he recommended calling in the local inspector for the Underwriters' Association.

Heads Off Error

That way, he explained, Rue could get the final word on the questionable points, before any mistaken purchases were made.

Joe went on to say that he'd worked closely with the Underwriters many times before and he'd be glad to help arrange the pre-installation inspection. The salesman scored. Rue thanked him, asked him to go ahead.

Now the distributor's salesman took up the task of drawing up a complete list of materials from the general list and survey.

Heavy Homework

For several nights, Gavenda worked hard checking catalogs and codes, doing his own engineering. Since this list was to be the basis for this job's specifications, he wanted to be absolutely certain of each detail, especially on the explosion-proof items.

Working at home is nothing new to Joe Gavenda, but it isn't a regular thing, either. He always has his reasons.

Good Points

For one thing, it frees him to make more selling calls during his working day. He doesn't find himself trapped inside with pricing, layouts, phone calls, etc.

For another, he can always weigh the potential value of a customer far beyond the immediate sale, and adjust his after hours work accordingly.

A job might require a maximum of personal effort with a minimum of sales return, at first. But it's the repeat business Gavenda is always aiming for—from contractors and industrials.

But let him explain it: "In this case, I recognized that a lot of responsibility rested on my company and myself. The job could gain us prestige. It could also bring us most of the future business of the contractor doing the work."

Price Less Important

"As far as the engineering, special applications and specifications went, I didn't mind the extra effort. I've always found that when you and your firm really show that you're interested in a customer and his problems, he's a lot less likely to quibble about price and a lot more likely to go along banking on your word in the future.

"Sincerity goes a long way. But it's your own foresight and judgment that decides how far you go with extra service."

Clear for Action

With his complete list of materials finished, Gavenda was ready to ask the Underwriters' inspector, Jim Glendenning, to tour the Pine Chemicals plant site with Blanche and Rue.

He felt that this step was vitally essential before any materials ordering could be done. "You may have your own pretty sound opinion on what's right in this business, but that doesn't make it the law," he explains.

Several pieces of processing equipment were not yet in place when Glendenning looked over the plant with the manufacturer and the contractor. The verdict: no determination was possible at the time.

Bad Tidings

Gavenda heard the news the next day. "That was a real rough day," he recalls with a smile.

CLINCHING THE SALE

Selling's tough enough without extra problems, but to Tab Electric Supply's Joe Gavenda, they make the final sale all the more satisfying.

At this point in this sale, he was heading into more than his share of headaches.

First—and painfully foremost—was the question of designating hazardous areas in Pine Chemicals' new plant. Then, he had to remember the need for many special and unusual items and think about how to get them.

Joe also kept delivery scheduling in mind. And on top of all that, he really had two customers to please—Blanche and Rue.

Speed Vital

He had to move fast. Checking with Rue, he determined the date that all the major pieces of non-electrical plant equipment would be placed at the job site.

Then he contacted Jim Glendenning and arranged for another inspection tour.

This time Gavenda was on hand. The group—industrial customer, electrical contractor, inspector and distributor's salesman—made a complete and detailed analysis of the approved electrical requirements. Joe asked plenty of questions and took many notes.

The tour had a happy ending for him. Rue was pleased. His questions were answered. Gavenda had gone to a lot of trouble. And Rue appreciated that, he said.

High Pressure

Joe asked permission to go ahead with his planning and the resin manufacturer agreed.

"I knew I'd clinched the sale then," says Gavenda, "but we were still a long way from home. I learned long ago not to ease up on your own pressure until the installation is completed."

Following Glendenning's inspection and clearing up of all hazardous area questions, the distributor's salesman was ready to draw up the final list of materials.

It included everything needed—control equipment, special lighting, switches, weatherproof and explosion-proof items, special cables, connectors and junction boxes, motors, panelboards, etc.

Detailed Data

One copy of this list went to the contractor for his on-the-job guidance. It contained pointed information on the regular and special items, advanced data on later installation problems and complete engineering on the many special applications involved in the plant's electrical systems. But there was more.

Every item was identified with catalog numbers and its exact location in the plant.

Another copy went to Tab Electric's sales manager, Jerry Madden. Gavenda and Madden reviewed the list carefully. They started checking with manufacturers by phone on availability of special items, so as to arrange for timing of deliveries.

Inside Backing

Madden alerted Tab's inside personnel on the new account. The object: "To get all of us to give the extra push necessary to securing and holding onto new customers."

From the final materials list, Gavenda drew up his own specifications for the job. With Madden, he began to order all the equipment and supplies.

This was done tightly, with a sharp eye on a minimum of leftovers. "Frank Blanche was depending on us for the right materials at the right time in the right place—and no troublesome overages," Tab's sales manager explains. "And we were just as anxious to please him as the new industrial. The payoff would be the bulk of his business if we stayed on the ball."

Real Challenge

Drawing the specs was the most interesting part of the sale to Joe. "I was faced with a real application challenge," he says. "I had to be sure that the plant had exactly what was needed, but at the same time I was thinking of standardizing.

"Pine Chemicals has more than 100 acres and is looking forward toward continuing expansion. So what I was drawing up were really specifications for the future, as well as the immediate sale."

More Rewarding

"Selling's more satisfying if you don't have to burden manufacturers with problems. And knowing what you're doing goes a long way with your customers."

FOLLOWING THROUGH

"Winding up a sale is just like bowling to me," declares Joe Gavenda. "Even though you're sure you're a shoe-in for a strike—you still put body English into it."

That's how Tab Electric's salesman approached sewing up this sale to Pine Chemicals, Inc.

All deliveries had been scheduled. All special item orders had been placed with plenty of time to spare.

Inside Teamwork

Tab's service organization—busy with its top speed daily operation—still found time to give a little extra attention to this job.

Inside men made sure that special products would arrive on time. They contacted Gavenda when Blanche ran into trouble, and generally provided the kind of back-up service that only a full-functioning electrical distributing firm can come up with.

Most of the material was in the house, but there were a few hold-ups along the line. Sales manager Madden kept a finger on the order flow—prodding now and then to make certain of key deliveries including items that could put Tab's service reputation in a dim light if not secured and delivered when needed and where needed.

Profitable Sales

"We're not volume-hungry," Madden says, "because volume has an ugly twin called price. We're not interested in that kind of business. But we are out tooth-and-nail for the smaller, repeat business such as this, that we can nurture, build and then grow big with. That's why we gave this sale special handling."

To Joe Gavenda, time is money. Every day's a selling day—with no compromise. But he still found time to visit the Pine Chemicals job two or three times a week.

Sells Confidence

On most of these visits, he wasn't needed but he knew his call was re-assuring to Blanche.

"I've never believed in sell-them-and-vanish," he says. "That's for the order-takers. If they're right, more power to them. But I just don't feel right if I can't make a non-selling call occasionally to maintain a little customer confidence.

"Take Frank Blanche, for instance. I've worked with him before. He's a good contractor—always does fine work. Who cares? I do. Why? Because you don't do electrical work in a sloppy way—and you don't sell electrical supplies in a sloppy way—not if you want to do either one profitably for 30 or 40 years."

Four Debts

"Don't get me wrong," he continues. "I didn't take this job to bed with me. But every now and then I'd remind myself that I had four obligations. To Frank—to Pine Chemicals—to Tab—and to myself."

So, many a night found Joe taking a call from the contractor, making a call to a night superintendent in a plant a hundred miles away, calling another Tab employee and arranging to deliver an item himself first thing the next morning. But it paid.

Daily Checks

Gavenda visited the job daily when a particularly difficult application phase in the installation work came up. He and Blanche checked prior work and tackled immediate problems together. If he needed an item in a hurry, a phone call to Tab would bring it in a matter of minutes.

Manufacturers cooperated wholeheartedly. Their expeditious supplying of unusual products oiled Tab Electric's service clockwork. Their offers of engineering assistance were appreciated but "totally unnecessary with a salesman like Joe," says Madden.

As the new plant neared completion, Gavenda intensified—rather than relaxed—his efforts. He wanted to keep the customer sold—with a view to future expansion sales. "Why build a chair for someone else to sit in?" he reasons.

When the installation was finished he invited the Underwriters' inspector back in for another tour. Rue was well satisfied with the job; the contractor was satisfied with Tab.

Customer's View

What does Pine Chemicals, Inc. think of the service provided by the electrical distributor and his contractor customer?

Here's what Matthew Rue, Jr., vice president and general manager, says:

"When we decided to open a plant here—close to our market area—we weren't certain how we'd accomplish our over-all construction. Even though our equipment would be new and our process primarily automatic, we decided against bringing in our own engineers and electricians from Georgia.

"I'm glad we made that decision—especially on our electrical construction. What Frank Blanche, Joe Gavenda and Tab Electric have done for Pine Chemicals to provide satisfaction and service has been more than we expected.

"They've helped make a transplanted industrial more welcome."

Distributor's View

And what does Tab Electric Supply think of salesman Joe Gavenda and his methods? Here's what sales manager Madden says:

"Tab—as an electrical distributor—is always anxious and pleased to find salesmen who use their own initiative in locating, cultivating and building possible sources of additional business.

"Joe Gavenda is this kind of salesman. I don't have to act as a bird dog or tell him the points or places where he should call. He concentrates; he knows where potential business is to be found—and how to take it from there.

"These same thoughts apply to initiative taken by a salesman such as Joe, in acquiring, improving and developing his own knowledge and then applying it to customer service.

"These characteristics are extremely beneficial to a distributor who looks for—and tries to develop—sales personnel of this type, rather than be satisfied with the innumerable ordertakers who finally become the sands that undermine any full-functioning distributor's operation."

Around Again

The last time salesman Joe Gavenda and contractor Frank Blanche talked with Pine Chemicals' vice president was a few days after the installation was completed and inspected.

"What's next?" asked Gavenda.

Rue smiled. "See me in about two months," he replied.

Joe grinned at Frank Blanche. Then he took out his "little black book" and made a note of the new lead.

Part Six . . .

PRICE STRATEGY

·{ 34 }··

GE Fights for "Volume" Prices*

Last December 22 General Electric Co. suddenly set in motion what will doubtlessly develop into an historic marketing milestone. On a closed television circuit, W. H. Sahloff, GE vice-president and general manager of its housewares & radio receiver division, told distributors that, effective January 1, 1956, list prices on all GE small appliances from toasters and irons to blankets and vacuum cleaners would be cut 5–30%.

The cuts pared distributor margins from 15% to 13%; pared dealer margins from 36½ to 32% (both discounts are figured on list price); and pared the price the manufacturer gets (see chart). For example, the list price on one GE vacuum cleaner dropped from $69.95 to $49.95—much nearer the discount house price (in non-fair trade states) of $39.95.

GE's move, however, is not primarily a move to meet discount house competition (GE's effective fair trade policing by & large has the discounting problem under control). It is primarily a way to increase small appliance sales, which are not keeping up with ever-increasing production ability. Small appliances, incidentally, broke through the $1 billion sales mark last year for the first time, double 1949's volume.

Said Sahloff in stating the thinking that makes GE's move historic: "We strongly feel we are building a monument to the foresight which we, together, have had in doing voluntarily today that which we would have been compelled to do tomorrow."

What Sahloff did not discuss is this: implicit in the "volume" marketing pattern GE presses for is "supermarket" selling even in the smallest retail store. It's obvious that despite ever-increasing manufacturer aids (e.g., bigger co-op budgets, increased field sales forces), there's a physical limit to the amount of additional traffic many small distributors and dealers can build. Volume is doubtlessly the key to survival in electrical appliances from now on, and doubtlessly lower prices are the key to volume. But will that concept eclipse the small businessman?

GE's move followed an 18-month study of small appliance marketing trends. That study, said Sahloff, disclosed first & foremost that consumption is not keeping pace with rising productivity. There is "a definite need to broaden the base of the marketing pyramid," to penetrate more deeply the middle and lower income brackets. It's obvious, declared Sahloff, that lower price is the way to do this.

---

* Reprinted by special permission from *Tide*, February 11, 1956. Copyright, 1956, *Tide*.

	GE CLEANER		GE STEAM IRON		GE TOASTER	
	OLD PRICE	**NEW PRICE**	**OLD PRICE**	**NEW PRICE**	**OLD PRICE**	**NEW PRICE**
Manufacturer's price to distributor	$33.93	$27.23	$8.71	$8.15	$9.68	$9.79
Distributor's price to retailer	44.42 *(distributor's margin: $10.49)*	33.72 *(distributor's margin: $6.49)*	11.40 *(distributor's margin: $2.69)*	10.09 *(distributor's margin: $1.94)*	12.67 *(distributor's margin: $2.99)*	12.12 *(distributor's margin: $2.33)*
Retailer's price to consumer	69.95 *(retailer's margin: $25.53)*	49.95 *(retailer's margin: $16.23)*	17.95 *(retailer's margin: $6.55)*	14.95 *(retailer's margin: $4.86)*	19.95 *(retailer's margin: $7.28)*	17.95 *(retailer's margin: $5.83)*

"The more we studied," Sahloff continued, "the more we realized that mass marketing means mass distribution and mass pricing, and retailing as an arm of mass distribution was dynamically changing."

One such change is the growth of manufacturer participation in the entire marketing process. Through national advertising, through packaging, through taking over much of the product servicing job, manufacturers "have shouldered more & more of the functions historically assumed by retailers." Since manufacturers do more such selling for retailers, it's clear to GE at least that retailers can stomach a cut in their traditional unit margins.

Sahloff made it plain what GE has in mind: "Realistic pricing, cutting costs of operation & selling, increased unit volume, doing business with dollars instead of percentages, acceptance of lower margin competition MUST be the general order of the day."

Sahloff also made it plain that he holds little hope for those retailers who don't harken to his advice: "Merchants who seek to perpetuate high margins of gross profit will find themselves consistently undersold by the competitor who has found means of reducing selling costs and overhead."

Sahloff, incidentally, hopes the new lower prices will help GE promote new products (for instance, it has a new cordless electric clock) "at more realistic prices . . . and enhance our position in gift buying in competition with non-electrical merchandise."

If the need for the price cuts is clear enough, how exactly did GE work them out? Sahloff explained it this way. Consumer price is the result of three things: cost of the product itself; distribution & selling costs; the profit that goes to the manufacturer, distributor and dealer. Assuming that operating cost are held down with maximum efficiency, there's only one way to pare the consumer price: cut the profit of manufacturer, distributor and dealer.

"The burning question then," Sahloff admitted, "is how to maintain a healthy, growing business if profits are reduced." The answer is this five-point "credo" which already is beginning to affect small appliance marketing:

1. "We must change our way of operating.

2. "We must adopt merchandising techniques which will exploit to the fullest extent possible the lowest consumer prices which we can establish.

3. "We must be able to move physically the larger quantities of merchandise the consumers will buy at lower prices.

4. "We must learn new ways of controlling expense.

5. "We must change our thinking from the old concept of percent profit, to the new concept of greater dollars of profit, which comes from selling larger volume."

GE's housewares & radio receiver division this year will spend well over $15,000,000, the largest advertising & promotion budget in its history. Field sales forces, which help distributors with key accounts, will be increased. GE expects both distributors and dealers to do much more local promoting, with increased company assistance.

GE's competitors are hardly happy over GE's pricing move. Not one reduced prices on every product, as GE did. Sametime, only the biggest dared to reduce distributor and dealer margins. Here's what other manufacturers have done so far:

1. On the same day GE's move was announced, Casco Products Corp. cut retail price of its steam iron from $18.95 to $15.95 (GE's competitive iron was cut from $17.95 to $14.95). Casco, however, did not slice distributor or dealer margins.

2. Landers, Frary & Clark cut retail price of its coffee maker, followed on January 5 with reduced prices on irons and one toaster. It, too, did not cut distributor and dealer margins.

3. Toastmaster division of McGraw Electric cut the price on its largest selling toaster from $19.95 to $17.95 (GE's competitive toaster was cut to $17.95). It cut both distributor and dealer margins on that toaster. But, sales vice-president William O'Brien says Toastmaster will go no further.

4. National Presto Industries cut the price on one iron from $17.95 to $14.95 (comparable to a GE model), pared distributor and dealer margins to the GE level. But it, too, indicated it would go no further.

5. Then Westinghouse Electric Corp. cut a steam iron and a dry iron to comparable GE prices. It cut distributor and dealer margins, but also indicated that was the end of its compliance.

6. Hoover Co. chopped prices of two iron models and its coffee maker, paring distributor and dealer discounts.

7. Sunbeam Corp., which held out for a month, finally reduced a "jun-

ior" mixer to $18.95 (still $1 above GE's comparable hand mixer), announced trade-in allowances on a steam iron and on a combination mixer-blender. Sunbeam told its distributors and dealers that it would retain "historic trade margins," but hedged the statement this way: if retailers sell competitive lines on which prices & margins have been reduced, "they will have proved by their actions that historical margins are not necessary (and) to remain completely competitive we would have no alternative but to adjust profit margins accordingly."

Clearly, GE's move squeezes manufacturers, particularly the smaller ones, between rising production costs (price of metals such as stainless steel, copper and others used in electrical appliances rose 17% between July and October of last year) and the apparent need for lower price tags. About all the manufacturer who is operating efficiently can now do is bid for more volume by increasing productivity and forcing more effective distribution.

"We're not crusaders. We're businessmen," complained Casco Products executive vice-president John J. Reidy recently. "Anything that affects our distributors adversely affects us. When profits are cut, salesmen's commissions are cut. We don't intend to sit idly by and see that happen. GE has no right to 'expert' on the distributor and dealers. They have no right to set up . . . how much the distributors and dealers can make. Nobody is that big."

Nonetheless, you can expect most manufacturers to follow the GE trend—that is, eventually cut margins on their full lines. Possibly, the manufacturers are better equipped to meet the new marketing need of volume sales, as opposed to high profit sales, than distributor or retailer, particularly the smallest of those.

Certainly, the distributors are hardly happy at the moment. Distributors, contends Arthur W. Hooper, executive director of the National Assn. of Electrical Distributors, are limited in power to cut operating costs, which is the only way they can survive under lowered margins. Hooper has called on manufacturers for improved packaging and labeling, reduced distributor contributions toward cost of co-operative ads.

The real worry, if GE and the industry care to worry about it, is the small retailer who exists virtually everywhere and has probably not even heard of the volume marketing trend. It can probably be argued that if he survived a couple of years of discounting, he's probably indestructible. But that avoids the long-term issue, which GE's move has now made inescapable: volume or "supermarket" marketing in as many product fields as possible (even autos) is all but here. The auto manufacturers are pressing for it (*Tide*—January 14). And GE is forcing it on the small appliance field.

There's some hope for the small retailer, but it's hardly enough to spur you to open an appliance store. One hope is that fair trade will get a new lease on life as prices become more realistic. That, of course, would protect smaller retailers against loss leading by larger stores. Another hope is that expanded manufacturer sales teams will be able to reach retailers and teach them to market better (as American-Standard hopes to do, *Tide*—January 28). A third hope is that markets will grow big enough to include small retailers. GE's Sahloff, for example, sees annual small appliance sales at $3 billion by 1970—80% of which will come from new products not yet marketed.

·{ 35 }··

The Lure is Price, Not Glamor*

Across the U.S., plain, box-like structures crammed with piperacks full of men's, women's, and children's apparel, are popping up with amazing speed. Robert Hall Clothes, Inc., which calls itself the A&P of apparel retailing, is intent on carving for itself a sizable piece of the cash-and-carry market.

Two things are remarkable about Robert Hall. First is its beanstalk growth. In 1940, it was a single loft store in Waterbury, Conn. Last week, an opening in Paramus, N.J., brought the 194th store under its wing; it has added 15 new stores this spring. Its fastest growing has been in the last few years; since 1951 it just about doubled its shops. By September of this year, it will have 200. And management has no thought of stopping there; it has just announced that it aims to keep on expanding, at the rate of 25 or 30 new stores a year.

Bucking a Trend

The second outstanding aspect of the operation is that it has grown by bucking a dominant trend in today's market—the trend to upgrading. Retailers of all kinds—Ohrbach's, supermarkets, variety stores, the mail order houses—have followed the rising income by adding style, fancy specialties, glamorous buildings and equipment, higher-priced goods. Robert Hall has stuck by its original premise that you can merchandise by saving people money. It has kept its sights strictly on the group with incomes of under $5,000. That's the group that buys on price, and Robert Hall sells primarily on price.

Not Talking

To these two dominant aspects of the business, you might well add a third: Nobody knows much about how Robert Hall operates.

The smiling, quiet president, Harold Rosner, has little to say on the subject. Sales and profits are buried in the consolidated figures of the parent, United Merchants & Manufacturers, Inc., which owns a string of textile mills and finishing plants as well as the retail chain. The trade guesses that Robert Hall accounts for from $80-million to $100-million of United's $340-million-odd total sales, and the $100-million figure is probably too high. (By comparison, the Lerner chain of women's apparel stores had a volume of $147-million last year.) With no supporting data, one can argue success only from the rapidity of the chain's expansion. That may not be an infallible test, but it at least indicates confidence in the chain's merchandising formula.

From the start, the management has operated on a let's-try-it attitude. "We play by ear," Rosner says. The trade tends to shrug off the enterprise as opportunistic, takes a severely wait-and-see view of its future growth. But so far the Rosner ear seems well tuned to the wants of its unpretentious market.

HOW IT WORKS

Go into any one of the Robert Hall stores today and you'll find the same picture: a large, bare selling space, chock full of dresses, suits, coats, hanging on clothes racks. There's no spare space on the floor—the buildings run from 7,000 to 15,000 sq. ft., and into that area they pack an average of 15,000 garments. There are three to six fitting rooms apiece for men and women, and from 10 to 20 sales people wandering around unobtrusively. There's a cashier's desk. That's about all—no display windows, no stockrooms, no attempt to glamorize the surroundings.

The service is as Spartan as the shops. Robert Hall dispenses with charge accounts, deliveries, alterations on women's wear (it does alter men's clothing free of charge). Sales pressure is very low; families wander around in slacks, thrashing out the merits of one garment against another. The chief merchandising gimmicks within the store are a guarantee on all the suits, and a liberal returns policy.

Savings

In its advertising, the constant theme is how Robert Hall saves its customers money. It makes a virtue of its lack of merchandising style. "You can't wear show windows and fancy fixtures," its promotion literature reads. "You can't wear overhead. Why pay for it?"

Robert Hall picks its locations on the same general theory. It's a cardinal principle at Robert Hall to keep rentals low. Except for the big central headquarters on New York's 34th St., its sites lie outside the heart of downtown, maybe two or three miles away. Or it settles in a neighborhood location convenient to several smaller communities. New housing developments—where children are likely to abound—are Robert Hall's meat. It won't go into a shopping center for two reasons: It would have to conform to the center's architectual style and lose its own trademark of simplicity; more important, the rents are too high. But it has no qualms about settling on the edge of a successful shopping center.

This policy has several advantages. In a low-rental area there can be plenty of room for parking space. Furthermore, by reaching into the fringes of growing industrial communities, Robert Hall gets close to its customers. The net result, says Frank Sawdon, vice-president, is that the chain's rentals come to around 2% of its sales; for some retailers they come to as much as 6%. As do most chains, Robert Hall works on a lease-back arrangement with real estate owners.

Of course, Robert Hall gets the benefits common to all chains of buying in huge quantities. Orders for 25,000 dresses at once are not uncommon, with 10,000 reorders. The entire 35,000 may disappear in three or four weeks. Centralized buying in New York and centralized warehousing make for efficient operation.

Big Stocks

Since Robert Hall advertises that it has "racks and racks" of clothes, big stocks are an essential to its program. This calls for speed in shipping; and the chain is proud of its new "Monorail" warehousing equipment, unveiled last week. An International Business Machines installation tells the buyers by Tuesday of each week just what dresses have sold in what stores, to make reordering easy.

All this, the chain's officials say, means a lower markup on Robert Hall goods than other stores offer. It is Robert Hall's secret what the markup is. One guess puts it somewhere under 30%, against the usual 45%. The highest price you can pay in Robert Hall's today is $46.95, for a man's topcoat. Women's dresses range from $3.89 to $14.89; boys' coats from $9.95 to $26.95.

How Much Quality?

The trade is divided on the degree of quality that can be bought with that kind of money. Some believe the prices are slightly better for the goods than you would find in the average bargain basement. A couple of years ago the chain ran afoul of the Federal Trade Commission on the basis of its advertising claims of comparable values and prices. Since then, it has apparently kept its skirts clean, though its competitors are irked by Robert Hall's hard-hitting advertising claims that it undersells everyone else.

Robert Hall management, of course, insists that it undersells. It points out that it has its own testing laboratory, that every garment is inspected when it comes to the warehouse, that it rejects some 20% of the goods it buys. Rosner concedes that in one respect he has had a break: The difficulties of the textile business of the last few years have enabled him to offer better quality at a price. This applies particularly to men's wear, he says. In women's wear, style is so important that pricing advantages are harder to come by.

Another point works in favor of the men's lines. Since 1946, Robert Hall has owned its own men's topcoat and men's suit factories. The women's lines it buys in the open market—either as finished goods or made to order.

The First Loft

The operation is a glorified extension of the idea behind the first Robert Hall store. It was in 1939 that Rosner and founder Louis Ellenberg, who together operated a chain of 50 stores, noted that a clothing manufacturer lured a stream of retail cutomers to his unprepossessing loft. Why not see, they argued, how rock-bottom you could get in merchandising and still win a market.

They picked a loft in a Connecticut town because it was a tough market, and a most inconvenient site. It took them six months to believe they were on the right track. Throughout the war, they expanded, sometimes into other lofts because new building was scarce.

"We didn't know till after the war whether our policy would work," Rosner comments. "Anyone could sell then." But with the war's end, they decided they had the answer. They moved into new buildings, because "we had to get respectable." Now 85% of their first outlets have been relocated.

There have been some changes along the way. At first it was entirely a men's wear store. Early during the war it added women's; since the war, children's wear has grown fast. Now its merchandise is split about 50–50 between the sexes.

But basically the same concept holds as in the early days. Robert Hall is eager to expand its stores. But it isn't keen on adding many more lines. There is more air to squeeze from markups in the big-ticket items, Rosner points out. Furthermore, in a semi-self-service operation there is danger from pilferage in accessories and smaller items.

WHY IT WORKS

The trade sums up the Robert Hall formula as "price and promotion." The chain's management says they advertise no more heavily than other retailers as a percent of sales. But they do blanket the market with radio, TV, and newspaper spots when they open a new store.

The question remains: Why does a price appeal have such strength in today's market?

Rosner has his own answer. The upgrading of income has made so many things necessities that used to be luxuries that the market—particularly the cash market—has to save somewhere. And clothing, which has taken a steadily declining share of disposable income for some years, is a logical spot to save.

Casual

It is possible, too, that for many of its customers Robert Hall represents an upgrading of sorts—from the bargain basement or the small local store. Further, there is evidence that people in the higher-income group are being squeezed into a lower-priced market for some clothing. That seems to hold especially for families with children. The whole trend to casual living has brought a stress on the kind of clothing—slacks, sportswear, and the like—that a low-priced store can offer.

Again, Robert Hall is riding right with the trend to one-stop shopping. Robert Hall calls itself a family store, makes a big point of being open from 9 to 9 so that the man of the family can come along. It has taken full advantage of the mobile, car-riding population to get to its customers, watches population shifts carefully.

·{ 36 }··

No Price-Cutting on Beautyrest:
How Does Simmons Do It?*

BY ALICE B. ECKE†

At a time when discount houses are forcing many a manufacturer to abandon the principle of Fair Trade, Simmons Co., America's No. 1 mattress maker, is militantly maintaining a Fair Trade policy. And making it stick.

Sales, in 1955, hit a new high of $156,333,729, an increase of 12.4% over 1954.

---

* Reprinted by special permission from *Sales Management*, June 1, 1956. Copyright, 1956, *Sales Management*.

† Senior Associate Editor, *Sales Management*.

The Simmons sales record under Fair Trade is all the more significant because of the higher price—$69.50—of its bellwether product, the Beautyrest mattress.

Fair Trade works for Simmons because Simmons makes it work, says John W. Hubbell, vice-president in charge of merchandising and advertising, through its long-standing selective distribution policy, protection of the integrity of its product, and steadily expanded national advertising which has made "Beautyrest" a brand name known and respected by millions. Simmons management sincerely believes that Fair Trade is a two-way street and that the manufacturer has as much responsibility in maintaining Fair Trade prices as the retailer. The advertising budget for the current year will run over $4 million.

Simmons main competition, Hubbell explains, comes from literally hundreds of local manufacturers who produce conventional open coil type mattresses and enjoy the advantages of local marketing flexibility. Simmons fights this competition with higher quality standards on all mattresses, plus the unique Beautyrest with its costly independent pocketed coil construction, and 65 branch warehouses, or service stations as the company prefers to call them, where merchandise is readily available.

Simmons is the largest manufacturer of mattresses, ranking No. 1 in the industry. Several other companies are neck-and-neck as the next largest, but any one of them would be a poor second. Simmons estimates that it outsells the second largest manufacturer by at least 4 to 1. Approximately 24% of the mattresses sold last year were sold by Simmons.

"Our Fair-Trade policy," says Hubbell, "has the dual effect of giving the consumer the most for his dollar in terms of better sleep equipment and of protecting our dealers by insuring them a reasonable profit on our products.

"Only Simmons has been able to move in volume top quality mattresses in the upper-price brackets. These are Beautyrests. And to make a monthly check on uniformity of quality, Beautyrest mattresses are bought on the open market by the United States Testing Co. for testing purposes. The other big Simmons edge is advertising, promotional and merchandising support. Simmons believes that a successful business is built backwards from the consumer to the factory. Every Simmons move revolves around a retail-minded approach to the consumer. We enjoy the reputation of being 'the friend of the retailer.' Here Simmons holds top position."

Proof of the soundness of the Simmons retail-minded sales policy is the fact that net sales through the years have consistently increased. In 1941 they totaled $62,692,928; in 1942, $65,392,002; in 1944, $67,797,332; in 1946, $92,924,877; in 1951, $154,020,191. Sales during the first quarter this year were up 16% over the like period last year.

Advertising, which has top position in the company's sales operations, has also increased over the years. For example, in 1945 the appropriation was approximately $1 million all told. For the current year it will be in excess of $4 million.

Over the past 10 years Simmons has done about 50% of the industry's advertising. Almost the entire amount of the advertising budget is given over to Beautyrest, the company's top quality mattress, thereby creating consumer acceptance for the top quality item in the line.

The Simmons retail distribution policy, Hubbell explains, might be defined as one of "selected broad distribution."

In major markets, generally speaking, all important dealers carry and support the Simmons line. As Hubbell points out, most of the Simmons competition is local. When contrasted with some local brands, it is found that local manufacturers have up to four times as many dealers as Simmons in certain given major markets. Management believes in selecting dealers who can be important to the company and in restricting distribution to the extent that the Simmons line can be important to the dealers.

While there is no formal franchise agreement between Simmons and its dealers, retail distribution arrangements are generally based on a reciprocal support policy wherein Simmons supports each dealer to the best of its ability and, in turn, expects each dealer to support Simmons merchandise, particularly the quality items: Beautyrest and Hide-A-Bed.

Simmons marketing policy goes back to 1925 when the management initiated a bold retail-minded program which changed the course of mattress marketing. This was built on five marketing principles:

1. High unit sale.
2. Excellent net profit.
3. Price and profit protection.
4. A new and super product.
5. Powerful, continuous consumer advertising.

The company's Beautyrest marketing program today is based on these same proved principles. The Beautyrest mattress at $69.50 represents a high unit sale. The Simmons 30-year program of consistent advertising has created an assured acceptance of this top-price line—only the Beautyrest mattress sells in volume in the over-$60-price range. The average department store does some 20% of its unit sales in this price line, and the average furniture store obtains slightly over 30% of its total unit sales in this top-price bracket—a price line created by Beautyrest advertising.

Simmons marketing policy has always advocated a top retail net profit, with the result that today the bedding department is one of the top-profit makers in a retail furniture or department store. For example, in department stores, research has demonstrated that, while the bedding department represents only about 1.4% of total main-store sales, it contributes 3.3% of total main-store profit. This is due to the profit contribution of the over-$60-price-line mattress—Beautyrest.

In furniture stores, National Retail Furniture Association estimates indicate that, because of the contribution of the over-$60 mattress sales, the bedding department represents 12% of total stores sales, contributes $50 in sales per square foot and from every dollar of inventory will produce $7.24 worth of sales and $3.09 gross margin.

The over-$60 mattress price line represents in the average department store 20% of unit sales but 33% of dollar sales and a walloping 64% of net profit. One Beautyrest sale is worth eight $39.50 promotional mattress sales in terms of the net profit contribution.

The Simmons sales organization is decentralized and sells direct to the retailer. The company is organized into four operating divisions: Atlantic, Southeast, Central and Pacific. Each division is headed by a divisional general manager charged with the full responsibility for the operation of all manufacturing facilities and for directing all sales operations for his division. He is responsible for increasing profits within his assigned area.

Within each division there are district managers responsible for sales and manufacturing conducted within their districts. They, in turn, report to the divisional managements.

There are 223 salesmen in the field. From the time they join the sales staff they are continually told to "think retail." This is a basic Simmons policy in defining the relationship between the salesmen and their customers. The salesmen spend most of their time working with their dealers, planning and developing retail promotions to move Simmons products to the consumer. They are trained to solve their dealers' problems.

Quotas for all Simmons products are established for each salesman. There is an over-all incentive program set up for members of the sales organization, in the form of a contest—the All-American Contest. Winners and their families are given substantial awards such as vacation trips, etc. This year top prizes will be Pontiac automobiles.

Policing Fair Trade price maintenance is a must duty for each member of the sales organization. Wherever it is legal to do so, the company vigorously polices the maintenance of Fair Trade prices for its products. Each salesman is charged with the immediate responsibility for seeing that Fair Trade prices are adhered to by his retail accounts. Where necessary, legal action is employed to bring about compliance.

The advertising support behind the retail distribution policy and the sales organization: Simmons management believes that the principal objective for its advertising is to develop mattress and sofa bed prospects and condition them favorably toward purchasing Beautyrest or Hide-A-Bed, thereby creating a sales opportunity for the retailer.

To reach today's market with the impact and consistency needed, most of the company's advertising is aimed at the consumer without diverting funds for cooperative retail advertising which Simmons management feels is primarily a retail responsibility. Adequate retail advertising is made possible through generous and protected profit margins on Beautyrest.

The 1956 $4-million-plus advertising appropriation, through Young &

Rubicam, Inc., is divided into three functional budgets: a basic consumer budget, a promotional budget, and a tactical budget.

The basic campaign involves only Beautyrest mattresses and Hide-A-Bed sofas. The media employed are 100% magazines, both mass and selective. They include *Life, The Saturday Evening Post, Reader's Digest, Farm Journal, Living for Young Homemakers, Bride's Magazine, Modern Bride, Guide for the Bride, The American Weekly, Ladies' Home Journal, Small Homes Guide, Home Modernizing, Better Homes and Gardens*, and *This Week*. This basic campaign is built on a very high frequency. For example, in *Life* alone 18 pages will be scheduled this year.

The promotional campaign is designed to stimulate timely retail promotional activity and to provide an element of excitement and urgency in behalf of Beautyrest and Hide-A-Bed. Media used for this campaign are *Life, Parade, Family Weekly, The American Weekly*, in the case of Beautyrest. Hide-A-Bed promotional advertising is scheduled in *The Saturday Evening Post* and *House & Garden*. These promotions are heavily merchandised and surrounded with complete dealer aids in display, advertising mats and sales training.

The tactical campaign is a new activity aimed at markets of opportunity as defined through an analysis of sales figures, a familiarity with local competitive conditions and a study of the Beautyrest consumer position. These facts, together with intensive field work, have resulted in the isolation of major markets where it is believed that additional advertising and local promotions can substantially improve Beautyrest sales. This campaign is based primarily on TV spots supplemented by newspaper, radio and outdoor advertising.

With its trained sales staff and its three powerful advertising campaigns Simmons then gives its dealers the opportunity to sell quality by:

1. Giving over almost the entire amount of its advertising appropriation to its top quality mattress—Beautyrest—thereby creating consumer acceptance.

2. Concentrating, through engineering and research, on development of unique and distinctive product advantages in the Beautyrest mattress, setting it apart from all others in the Simmons line and from those produced by competition.

Continually Improved

For example, when it was introduced in 1925 Beautyrest was looked upon as a radically different mattress. Throughout the years it has been continually improved. In 1927 a new patented crush-proof border was added. In 1932 the shape of the coils was changed to increase durability. In 1933 new construction warranted a five-year guarantee. In 1939 it was made deeper and thicker—a more comfortable mattress. In 1940 a 10-year guarantee was announced as a result of increased durability. In

1951 a choice of firmness was offered through the introduction of an extra-firm model Beautyrest as well as the standard. In 1955 the independent coil action was increased some 19% through a new manufacturing process known as "floating action coils."

Today Beautyrest is distinguished from all other innerspring mattresses by independent coil action. Coils are not tied together, do not sag together, thus giving body-fit comfort. Recent tests made by United States Testing Co. on 20 competing mattresses priced between $59.50 and $79.50 indicate that Beautyrest outlasts the second best mattress by three times.

3. Establishing a stabilized distribution, selling direct to retailers, Fair-trading prices and policing them.

4. Establishing top profit margins on the quality product, Beautyrest.

Simmons accomplishes this by first analyzing the profit opportunity for the retailer in selling $69.50 price line mattresses. An independent organization, Russell W. Allen Co., is retained to direct this retail research.

The Beautyrest profit margin for retailers gives a maximum of 48.9%. This percentage does not include freight charges which generally average about $1 per mattress and is based on carload shipments from the nearest Simmons plant. For smaller retailers who do not purchase merchandise in mixed cars, there are 65 service stations or local warehouses equipped to give immediate delivery on Beautyrest. Profit margins for Beautyrest deliveries from service stations are: one only, 43.2%; twelve, 43.9%.

Payoff in Retail Profits

Although profit margins are necessarily lower on single unit deliveries from a service station, nevertheless, it is possible for retailers to achieve a substantial turnover with a minimum inventory investment through this service. Simmons management recognizes that, after all, return on inventory investment is the payoff in retail profits.

5. Scheduling periodic promotions to arouse retailer enthusiasm and encourage retailer support—usually once every six months. These promotions are built around a concentration of dramatic, offbeat national advertising designed to serve as a promotial springboard for the retailer's use. There are no premiums or price concessions on Beautyrest during these promotions.

For promotions Simmons provides retailers with floor and window displays for Beautyrest, plus display ideas. Newspapers, direct mail, radio and TV advertising props are available for all retailers.

6. Establishing a Retail Sales Training Institute because Simmons management considers the floor salesman to be crucial to the success of any manufacturer in selling quality. From the Institute training material is sent out periodically to the homes of 40,000 retail salesmen. This training program is planned to improve the level of retail selling of Simmons products and aims to accomplish this in three ways: (1) providing

product information; (2) improving selling techniques; (3) providing sales incentives for retail sales personnel.

The retail training program is supplemented by frequent sales meetings conducted by Simmons salesmen. Each salesman is provided with a full kit of props for staging the meetings.

7. Planning two types of retail incentive programs to assure maximum support of floor sales personnel to Beautyrest.

A National Contest

The first program is the Beautyrest Band Wagon Contest. This is a national contest broken down into regions and districts, offering prizes totaling around $128,000 in value. For example, the first prize this year will be 16 Buick automobiles, one for each of the Simmons 16 sales districts, and the second prize will be 16 Chevrolets, one for each district.

To qualify for this contest, a retail salesman must sell eight Beautyrest units—mattress or box spring—and answer a few simple questions. He may enter as often as he sells the eight units. Judging is done by an independent organization, The Reuben H. Donnelley Corp.

As an aid for retailers themselves, Simmons has a number of planned contests for store use. This is important, Hubbell explains, during promotion periods since there is no price reductions on Beautyrest. Contests run from simple punch boards to complex programs involving accelerating compensations based on a salesman's personal sales. Simmons provides plans and other material such as record-keeping charts, but does not contribute to salesmen's pay.

"Thus," Hubbell concludes, "despite the popular trend to price-cutting, discounts and rebates, Simmons has consistently maintained a firm price policy based on the principle of a quality product at a fair price. Simmons has been and will continue to be a leading advocate of Fair Trade profit protection. This is achieved through our direct controlled distribution methods, together with policing and strong national advertising. Simmons cannot and will not live with discount retailing."

·⟨ 37 ⟩·

How Detroit Figures Auto Prices*

Chances are that no automobile dealer, busy as he is trying to attract the attention of the bashful spring buyer with the lure of falling prices

---

* Copyright, April 6, 1957, *Business Week*, McGraw-Hill Publishing Co., Inc. Reproduced with permission.

Here's What the Dealer Pays for 1957 Models

FORD CUSTOM, V-8:

$1506.32

CHEVROLET 210, V-8:

$1571.16

PLYMOUTH SAVOY, V-8:

$1595.24

DODGE CORONET, V-8:

$1747.24

BUICK SPECIAL:

$1833.37

MERCURY MONTEREY:

$1836.92

will quote a tag as low as those you see above. For those prices are just about what he pays the factory for the V-8 four-door sedans shown. He tries—but hardly ever succeeds—to get a price one-third more.

So those prices are the absolute floors, below which dealers will go only at peril of bankruptcy, even if the market situation turns a lot more desperate than it is now. And even in the search for a big spring market, the manufacturers most likely will not cut their own prices to the dealers to give the retailers any more trading room.

That is one of the characteristics of the automobile pricing system that sets it apart from other industries.

Confession

Factories in the past have changed wholesale prices during the model year—Chrysler cut a few years ago—but it is an exceedingly rare thing, for such action generally connotes a miscalculation of such proportion as to endanger a company's future. The only other explanation for a factory price cut in midyear would be a gigantic change in the nation's economic status.

Factories do, in effect, cut their wholesale prices—but as a normal rule only toward the end of a model year and only after a magic barrier has been crossed. That barrier is something called the "standard volume." An understanding of those two words is an understanding of the automobile business and how its unique distribution setup functions.

Such an understanding, too, makes it clear that there is a rigidity about Detroit's pricing system making it imperative for auto companies to defend like grim death their factory list prices—up to a certain time of the year—and then engage in some wild fluctuations in the market place. In part, this rigidity stems from (1) the heavy investment costs of making autos and (2) the seasonal and cyclical swings in production schedules peculiar to the industry.

STANDARD VOLUME CONCEPT

The concept by which factories set wholesale auto prices hasn't changed in more than 30 years.

The "base price" of automobiles at General Motors' factories, for instance, means the same thing today as it did when Donaldson Brown and Albert Bradley created the standard volume concept in the early 20s. Volume in this context has nothing to do with a sales manager's estimate of how many cars he will sell in a year. Volume to Detroit's pricing people is related to the capacity—ability to produce—of the manufacturer's plants.

Hypothetical Case

Assume you are just entering the automobile business. The first step in determining standard volume is to plot the total auto market for some years back and some years ahead (there is no commonly accepted span of years). This gives you a curve representing the trend of market demand over the years. Then you determine what percentage of the market you should have and plot your own average market through the years to come.

Now you have to assume that at some point during those years the market peak demand will be above that curve. But by how much—10%, 15%, 25%? That is where you have to use judgment arbitrarily. Assume the peak demand is set at 25% above the average trend of demand. That means you build a plant with capacity for 125% of the production as it will average out over the years. Accordingly, your average production— again over a period of years—will be 80% of the plant's practical capacity. That 80% becomes your standard volume.

Starting Point

Here's how it would work out: You want a plant that will give you a practical capacity of 1-million cars a year. Your standard volume then would be 80% of that, or 800,000 cars. This average figure of 800,000 cars a year becomes the basis of your pricing system. Your problem is to set prices so that you will cover all your direct costs, plus the cost of the plant if it operates at an average rate of 800,000 cars a year over the course of its usable life. Some years, of course, it will turn out more than 800,000 and some years less. But by pricing on the basis of 800,000 you insure that you will (1) make the return you want over the life of the plant and (2) have enough margin of extra capacity available to handle the peaks of the market as they occur.

Totting It Up

You figure your costs exactly on the basis of producing 800,000 cars a year, including what you would have to pay for all materials and all direct labor, plus overhead, allowance for depreciation, amortization, and taxes. Assume your total bill for the 800,000 cars comes to $800-million. Each car actually costs $1,000.

You have to have a return on the money you used to establish the facilities to build the cars. GM's goal always has been a 20% return on investment.

At this point, you have a factory cost of $800-million. Then you have to figure out how much working capital you need and what your fixed investments are. This is the figure to which you apply the 20%. You then calculate your selling expense on 800,000 cars. Together all these things might add up to 25% of the factory cost.

Then your "base price" would become 125% of the factory cost—or $1,250—just as long as you don't change your profit goal.

A Gamble

But this $1,250 is not necessarily the wholesale price of your car. You have to consider the competitive factors.

THE DILEMMA

The mythical $1,250 factory price is what you would like to get in order to yield your 20% return. But your competitor has a car that seems equivalent in value to yours. And he sets his price at $1,200.

In theory, of course, you could sell your cars for $50 more than your competitor. Both you and he are selling to a captive market—the dealers. Your dealers may think your price is too high—but, if they want cars at all, they have to pay it. In practice, though, your dealers would either die of financial malnutrition or switch their franchise—because their customers are not a captive market, and they would have to absorb the difference.

Avoiding a Giveway

Your choice then is deceptively simple. At a price of $1,200 per car, you are giving away $40-million—$50 on every one of the 800,000 you need to make your standard volume. You have to figure on selling about 33,000 more cars to get it back, or find some way to squeeze $50 out of the cost of your car.

Competitive pressures in pricing can work in reverse. Last fall Ford announced its 1957 prices before Chevrolet did. Ford prices, on the average, were something less than 3% higher than in 1956. Chevrolet prices turned out to be about 6% higher. So Ford—in one of the few examples of a company changing a price already announced—revised its scale upward. "We found," says a Ford man, "that we were giving away $20-million to Chevrolet."

Counterbalances

The one significant thing to remember about the standard volume concept of pricing is that as long as your capacity—say to make 800,000 cars a year—is unchanged, your costs change only with changes in the costs of materials and labor. Over a given period of years, your standard volume would never change. Accordingly, you could weather changes in the economy. In a poor auto year such as 1954, you may fall below your standard volume and, instead of getting a 20% return, get only 10%. In a boom year such as 1955, you may shoot far above standard volume in output. Your price base would be the same, and the two years would balance out in return on your investment.

This is what makes the automobile business about as risky as a weekend in Las Vegas. If sales exceed your standard volume, you make extra profit at a fabulous rate; if sales fall short of the standard volume, profits dip disproportionately. For example, if you need to sell 800,000 cars to meet all expenses and get a fair return on investment, and you wind up selling 1-million, those extra 200,000 cars are all profit—except for the direct material and labor cost involved.

Look at it this way: Actual labor and material costs account for only about 75% of the sales dollar. On the standard volume alone, you net 8% of selling price; on all cars above the standard volume, you net 25%.

However, the reverse also is true. If you fall short of standard volume in sales, your profit slips at a fearful rate. Look at what happened to the Big Three in the past two years:

PERCENT CHANGE OVER PREVIOUS YEARS

	Chrysler		Ford		GM	
	1955	1956	1955	1956	1955	1956
Unit sales	+79	−32	+31	−25	+32	−19
Dollar sales	+67	−23	+38	−17	+27	−13
Profit	+440	−80	+92	−46	+48	−29

TIME FOR A CHANGE?

In a very good year, such as 1955, an auto company will sell its standard volume quickly—reportedly in that year General Motors had sold its standard volume by the end of July. After that, it customarily splits some of the extra return with its dealers.

Practices vary. To help dealers through the "clean-up" period (roughly August through October) before introduction of a succeeding year's models, some factories will run incentive contests among dealers, with a bonus for every car above a certain number. Other companies have a sliding scale of increase discounts, based on when the dealer orders from the factory. General Motors gives an extra 5% discount to dealers for all cars (and trucks) in their hands on the day the new models come out. For a Chevrolet dealer, as an example, this means a 29% discount, instead of 24%.

This isn't entirely altruistic. After the standard volume has been made, it is to the factory's best interests to keep production rolling until the last possible day before the plant must go down for model changeover.

Possible Modifications

There is, however, a feeling among the very small group of Detroit experts in pricing theories that perhaps some modifications in the standard volume, either in concept or in application, are due. This involves two matters: cost of adding capacity, and market potential.

First, take the cost of new capacity. No auto company will say what its standard volume percentage actually is. But there are indications that although it hasn't been revised for a considerable number of years, it is now being moved upward. In other words, auto companies are recognizing the facts of modern production life. The traditional standard volumes (as a percentage of capacity) were established when labor was relatively more important in total cost than capital investment. Thus, it made sense to keep your overtime labor costs down by spreading your capital costs over a lower percentage of capacity—the standard volume— than is feasible today. Up to now, a company found itself able to afford excess capacity of, say, 20% over the standard volume as a means of protecting its market position in all the seasonal and cyclical fluctuations. It could pay for that 20% of sometimes idle capacity by figuring the cost of it as part of the standard volume price.

Competitive Woes

Now, though, with plant and equipment costing so much more, you have to add so much more to the standard volume base price to buy that 20% protection that it throws your prices out of line with (1) a competitor who may have older capacity and (2) the general price picture of the whole economy.

So what you do is refigure your standard volume by changing the percentage—from 80%, say, to 85%.

This is risky, if you are determined to maintain your market share regardless of how auto demand swings in a season or over the years. It means that you are betting that such swings won't actually be so wide as the industry, using an 80% standard volume, has assumed. Both Ford and Chrysler in 1955 form good examples of what can happen. They were in a bind because they actually did not have enough capacity to take full advantage of a swing.

You have to remember that market position is important—it can affect acceptability of your car to the public and hence influence used car prices that give dealers room for trading.

More Buyers

But it may be that auto companies will have to live with that risk for still another reason. Total market potential is slowly creeping up for new cars—more slowly by a great deal, apparently, than Detroit had expected—but still it is moving upward. So new capacity is a must, again to maintain your share of the larger market. But with costs so high, it is difficult to get back your normal 20% return on investment. In figuring out your base price, older equipment still gives you 20% on the investment of 20 years ago. But on facilities built in 1957–58 extra efficiency isn't enough to make up the difference.

Thus some auto companies find themselves in a strategic squeeze. They have to raise their standard volume percentage in order to spread costs over more units (1) because of price competition with a more favorably situated competitor and (2) because the increasing market requires added capacity, which is out of line in cost under the old standard volumes.

·{ 38 }··

Retailing: It's a New Ball Game*

BY CHARLES E. SILBERMAN

One of the great discoveries of the late John Wanamaker, and for many decades one of the seemingly immutable laws of U.S. retailing, was the Single Price. Nowhere has it been more venerated than in the quality department store; to go into Marshall Field's of Chicago, say, and try to *bargain* was unthinkable. Not today. For some months now there have been no price tags on major appliances at Field's sedate State Street store. Field's appliance salesmen carry little black books bearing the current price quotations—quotations that vary as the competition demands.

In abandoning Single Price, Field's is running with the retailing pack. Discounting and bargaining now are endemic in the markets for cars, furniture, appliances, home furnishings, toys, cameras, drugs, sporting goods, gasoline, and auto accessories; the multiple-price system is spreading even to clothing. In markets that account for at least two-fifths of America's annual retail sales of $180 billion, list price is being reduced to little more than a point at which to start bargaining. In this vast area of the U.S. economy, price has become almost as fluid as in an oriental bazaar.

UP .....DISHWASHERS DOWN .....VACUUM CLEANERS STEADY .....REFRIG

The market quotations shown below do not appear on the financial pages of any newspapers, but it might be useful if they did. For twenty-nine appliances, and two makes of automobile, the quotations show a price structure much more fluid than that of the New York Stock Exchange. The "highs" and "lows" were reported by FORTUNE correspondents after shopping fourteen cities in June. "Par" is list price; "closing" prices are a rough average of the prices in all fourteen cities.

	Par	High		Low		Closing
ABC automatic washer 80G	$ 309.95	$ 309.95	Atlanta	$ 213.75	Seattle	$ 220.00
Ampro Hi-Fi tape recorder 757	239.95	239.95	Cincinnati	159.50	Boston	179.00
C.B.S. Columbia tape recorder 355	299.50	259.95	Dallas	220.75	Los Angeles	222.00
Chevrolet BelAir (a)	2,576.40	2,276.40	Toledo	2,126.40	Toledo	2,215.00
Cummins Do-It-Shop 440	79.95	67.00	Chicago	49.97	Seattle	63.00
Dormeyer mixer 4201 (b)	45.75	42.95	Los Angeles	27.89	New York	31.95
Dormeyer toaster 6500	19.75	17.79	Salt Lake City	13.03	Des Moines	14.92
DuMont 21″ TV console (c)	299.95	263.71	Atlanta	200.00	Boston	223.00
Fedders ¾ t air condit. 49MG	349.50	349.50	Atlanta	209.00	New Orleans	265.00
Ford custom (d)	2,395.00	2,200.00	Chicago	1,900.00	Chicago	2,050.00
Frigidaire refrigerator freezer (e)	469.95	469.95	Atlanta	310.00	Los Angeles	379.95
G.E. clock radio 578	44.95	44.95	St. Louis	27.00	New Orleans	34.95
G.E. dishwasher SU60M (f)	299.95	299.95	Washington	193.26	Dallas	249.95
Hamilton gas dryer 362G	279.95	235.00	New Orleans	171.45	Washington	191.00
Hoover vacuum (g)	97.50	87.50	Salt Lake City	54.95	Los Angeles	79.95
Hoover steam iron O11	17.95	16.95	Los Angeles	10.75	St. Louis	13.95
Hotpoint double oven RD23 (h)	499.95	450.00	Boston	316.00	St. Louis	404.96
Kelvinator electric dryer DE2	239.95	189.00	New Orleans	165.50	Washington	183.15
Kitchenaid dishwasher KD1OP (f)	345.00	344.00	Salt Lake City	237.00	New York	250.00
Motorola portable 55B1 (i)	34.20	32.95	Atlanta	23.95	Toledo	29.00
Norge refrigerator freezer C1280 (j)	429.95	350.00	Boston	274.63	Los Angeles	329.00
Osterizer 10W (k)	39.95	31.50	Chicago	24.89	New York	26.13
Philco ¾ t air condit. 84M	349.95	315.00	Boston	259.95	Cincinnati	257.92
Philco 24″ TV console 61-10	379.95	325.00	Salt Lake City	240.00	Toledo	320.00
Universal coffee maker 4410 (l)	29.93	26.95	Boston	18.00	Des Moines	19.98
Vornado desk fan 16C	26.95	26.95	Cincinnati	18.17	Boston	21.00
Waring blender PB5	43.50	39.75	Boston	26.89	New York	30.00
Westinghouse electric range FH (m)	259.95	240.95	Salt Lake City	185.00	Boston	208.00
Westinghouse Laundromat H1	229.95	229.95	St. Louis	160.00	Toledo	173.00
Westinghouse Mobilaire fan 4020 (n)	79.95	64.00	Toledo	43.98	New York	49.95
Westinghouse toaster TO542	19.95	19.95	Cincinnati	11.95	Dallas	14.00

(a)—8-cylinder 4-door fully equipped sedan, clean-deal basis, Toledo. (b)—Super Chef. (c)—"Winsted." (d)—8-cylinder 4-door, fully equipped, clean-deal basis, Chicago. (e)—Imperial 11.5 cu. ft. white, CIV-115. (f)—undercounter model. (g)—"Constellation" #82. (h)—de luxe with rotisserie. (i)—with battery. (j)—Customatic. (k)—white base. (l)—10 cup. (m)—30″ de luxe. (n)—with timer.

The breaching of Single Price is only one of a number of changes now taking place in the U.S. distribution system. But most of the changes are related to a simple central conviction, shared by consumers and manufacturers and, in growing numbers, by retailers: retail margins can be brought down.

Retail margins can be brought down in three ways: by shifting some of the burden of traditional retailing services backward onto the manufacturer, or forward onto the customer; by eliminating some of the traditional services altogether; and by performing the remaining retail services at lower cost—in other words, by true increases in the productive efficiency of retailing itself. Expressing itself in these three ways, the pressure on retail margins is transforming the U.S. distribution system.

Only 50 Per Cent

In the past twenty-five years, as related in previous articles in *Fortune's* anniversary series on "The New Economy," rising productivity has created a fabulous advance in U.S. income. Since 1929, output per man-hour in U.S. industry and agriculture has more than doubled. In the same period, productivity in distribution has increased only 50 per cent. Only in America would one call this "only" 50 per cent. The 50 per cent increase is in fact an impressive achievement; in the nature of distribution, productivity increases come harder than in manufacturing. Not all the big retailing changes of the past twenty-five years have necessarily enhanced productivity. Taken together, however, they have kept the U.S. distribution system tolerably well attuned to the immense changes in U.S. manufacturing and in the U.S. market. Certainly a vast amount of inventiveness has been invested in U.S. retailing in the past quarter-century:

1. Sears, Roebuck revolutionized store location and layout (as well as store management) by building stores with parking areas outside the established shopping districts. (Conceived by General Robert E. Wood, this development actually was begun in the 1920's, but the big momentum came in the 1930's.) In many respects, the postwar shopping-center boom has been built on Sears' foundations.

2. Sears' merchandise planning and research helped build the mass market for such products as refrigerators, washing machines, electric and gas ranges, and power tools. Sears redesigned these luxury or specialty-market products for mass production at a mass-market price, then found producers able to supply the mass market at the mass-market price.

3. Through national advertising and promotion, manufacturers have shouldered more and more of the selling function historically performed by retailers. Thus it is that big stores frequently refuse to stock a new product unless it has been elaborately pre-sold, and unless the manufacturer supplies a generous cooperative advertising allowance.

4. "Breaking bulk" was once the almost exclusive function of wholesalers and retailers, but manufacturers have been taking over more and more of the packaging function. By demonstrating the power of impulse buying, the supermarket has enormously stimulated packaging by manufacturers and the use of package design as a prime selling tool for anything from haberdashery to nails and screws. According to the Grocery Manufacturers Association, 70 per cent of supermarket purchases are made on the spur of the moment. Supermarket operators are now chafing for the day when they can slough off their butchering departments entirely, stocking on ordinary sales racks meat that has been preserved indefinitely by irradiation with gamma rays.

5. Manufacturers have been taking over the job of servicing more and more consumer durables, where servicing once was a major function of retailers and of distributors.

6. The consumer has also been assuming more and more middleman responsibilities, through cash-and-carry and self-service.

7. More important, the consumer has taken over more and more of the job of pre-selling himself (see "The Web of Word of Mouth," *Fortune*, November, 1954). Certainly the consumer is turning almost anywhere

but to the retailer for information and advice on what to buy—witness
the 750,000 circulation of *Consumer Reports,* up from 101,000 in 1945.

8. Stores have been getting bigger. The number of retail firms has
grown 38 per cent since 1929, from 1,330,000 to 1,840,000, while retail
sales more than doubled, from $86.5 billion to $180 billion (in constant
1954 dollars). Average sales per firm, consequently, have expanded 50
per cent, from $65,000 to $97,800. Since 1949, moreover, average sales
per firm have risen 18 per cent (in constant dollars) while the number
of retail firms grew less than 3 per cent. The retailing population, in fact,
has registered declines in each of the last two years.

The Widening Gap

But distribution productivity continues to lag behind the growing
efficiency of industry and agriculture, and in the past few years the gap
has been widening. Since 1947 output per man-hour has been rising at
a rate of 2 per cent a year in distribution vs. 4.3 per cent in production.

Distribution efficiency cannot lag so far behind production without
forcing either a relative increase in distribution costs or a decrease in
distribution services. The pressure is particularly strong because distribution wages are pulled up by manufacturing wage rates. Since 1947
labor income in distribution (including income of proprietors and unpaid
family workers) has risen 2.7 times as fast as distribution productivity.

As a result of the transfer of retailing functions backward to the
manufacturer and forward to the consumer, however, "distribution
costs," i.e., the costs chargeable to distributors, have *not* risen relative
to production costs since 1929. And so retailing and wholesaling last year
took almost precisely the same share—about 36 cents—of the consumer's
dollar as they did in 1929. Even the split between retailers and wholesalers
has remained stable at about 28 and 8 cents, respectively. The market, it
appears, has placed a firm ceiling on what it is willing to pay for the
services of retailers and wholesalers.

This apparent stability merely reflects a balance of power between two
opposing forces. On the one hand, consumers are refusing to pay the
traditional retail margins, and on the other hand, retailers are having
increasing difficulty just holding to the existing margins because of sky-
rocketing costs. The outcome must be a frontal attack on the entire
retail-wholesale cost structure.

Will Discounters Go "Legitimate"?

The discount house, more sharply than anything else, has dramatized
for both consumers and retailers the obsolescence of the old retail
cost-price structure. If history repeats itself, however, the discount house
ultimately will follow its predecessors' path to "legitimacy" and to
higher margins. Harold Barger, author of the forthcoming study, *Distribution's Place in the American Economy Since 1869* (National Bureau

of Economic Research), believes that a "law of increasing margins" operates in American retailing. Each new retailing type has started as a price
cutter. But with the coming of age and respectability the department
store, the mail-order firm, and the supermarket have taken on new
functions, added services, changed the product mix—and sometimes
grown soft and flabby. Supermarket margins, for example, have been
creeping up for several years, and growing numbers of stores are reaching
out for non-food product lines that carry much higher margins.

In the discount houses certain telltale signs already are visible. Despite their ostentatious displays of crude desks and unfurnished offices,
discount-house executives are already panting for the status of "legitimacy." In Manhattan's Masters Mart, for example, on a post in the
center of the main selling floor, there is a brass plaque engraved with a
message of "esteem and loyalty" to the head of the firm on the occasion
of the store's enlargement in 1949. The president, Stephen Masters—
brother of the founder, whose portrait in oil hangs on a balcony wall—
resents being called a discounter, insists he is simply a "retailer." The E. J.
Korvette chain, fastest-growing discount operation in the East (probable
1955 sales, $50 million), likes to have its seven branches called department
stores. And Sol Polk, head of the bustling and hugely successful Polk
Brothers Inc. of Chicago, bridles at the very mention of discounting,
denying the importance of price cutting altogether. "What the customer
wants," he insists, "is to be loved, to be reassured of the soundness of
his decision to buy."

Merchants to the Middle Class

For love or for money, the customers are pouring in. According to a
U.S. Chamber of Commerce study, discount outlets last year did an
annual volume of $25 billion—15 per cent of retail sales. The discounters'
market share, in the bigger cities, may run as high as 75 per cent in
certain lines—television sets, big and small appliances, housewares, outdoor furniture and accessories, sporting goods.

The discount house has become the supplier par excellence to the
new middle-income group—the $4,000-to-$7,500-income families who
account for more then 40 per cent of consumer expenditures. The discount house almost always sells for cash, and only the middle and upper-
income families are able to pay cash or to borrow directly from banks.
Many low-income families, on the other hand—whether from necessity
or from ignorance—continue to pay list price or more at "credit stores."
For the goods-craving, money-bearing, middle-income families, the merchandising techniques of the discounters have been beautifully tailored.
It's not coincidental that the discount house has specialized in appliances
and home goods. More than any others, these were the commodities
that suddenly emerged in the postwar as "necessities" while still bearing
their old "luxury" price tags (and markups).

Now the discounters are looking well beyond the appliance business. Last December, for example, the E. J. Korvette chain opened its first full-scale department store in 90,000 square feet of space in Westbury, Long Island. The branch is currently operating at an annual rate of $20 million, compared to an estimated $25 million for the nearby Hempstead branch of Abraham & Straus, one of the largest suburban department-store branches in the country. About one-third of Korvette's Westbury volume comes from sales of men's, women's, and children's clothing and of household furnishings. The store is adding 30,000 square feet to house a supermarket, luncheonette, beauty salon, and drive-in cleaning service. Korvette also has plans in the works for at least two more department stores in the New York suburbs and for a women's specialty shop.

The Counterattack

However much the discount house itself may change in time, it has profoundly changed the tone of "conventional" retailing. Discounting has spread to almost every standardized commodity in wide demand, and to some with limited appeal, e.g., Geiger counters, sold in Seattle at 20 per cent off the list of $139. And discounting is being practiced by almost every type of "legitimate" retailer in every part of the country. It takes a fine eye nowadays to distinguish the "discounter" from the "legitimate" retailer.

In Chicago, for example, Marshall Field's, Carson Pirie Scott, Mandel Brothers, and Goldblatt Brothers—the four leading department stores—are offering "discount prices" and frequent "warehouse sales." And the sales are being promoted with revivalist hoopla. On one occasion Mandel's helicoptered loads of tables, carpets, and appliances to a parking lot next to its warehouse, to dramatize the "freshness" of its merchandise. Field's, on the other hand, has successfully promoted warehouse sales merely by notifying its charge customers.

In Washington, D.C., weekend "warehouse sales" of furniture, appliances, and home goods have been so successful that one downtown store is building a new warehouse just for this purpose. George's, a large appliance chain that is credited with starting the fad, has successfully replaced nine of its twelve stores with two warehouses. These sales are not very different from the capital's traditional Washington's Birthday "giveaway" sales. The latter are avowedly one-shot, loss-leader affairs. But Hecht's, the city's largest department store, now advertises every day discount prices on page-long lists of merchandise.

Cincinnati's venerable John Shillito Co. labels appliances and toys with the legend, "This is the nationally advertised price, ask the salesman for our price." At least one Cincinnati store keeps its prices in line with discount-house prices through an elaborate system of espionage. In one instance, after its shopper was recognized by a discount house and barred from the store, the "legitimate" retailer sent back a pregnant

Mata Hari with accompanying small child, and the mission was completed.

In St. Louis the three major department stores, Stix Baer & Fuller, Famous-Barr, and Scruggs Vandervoort & Barney, are aggressively fighting the discount house. Consequently, a customer can shop a discount house first for housewares, appliances, silverware, jewelry, toys, or sporting goods, then trade against the discounter's price in the three "legitimate" stores.

New types of discount outlets are springing up in various parts of the country. Seventeen months ago a dry-goods store was opened in 20,000 square feet of floor space below street level in the vacant Hope Mills at Lonsdale, Rhode Island. Customers push supermarket baskets past crude tables heaped with shirts, socks, sheets, shoes, etc. Last year's sales were $2 million. "Everybody tells me I'm doing everything wrong," owner Martin Chase says. "All I know is, I have money in the bank." In recent months similar stores have been opened in empty mills in Springfield, Worcester, Fall River, New Bedford, and Brockton, Massachusetts, and in Pawtucket, Rhode Island.

Industrial "buying clubs" provide discount prices on a wide variety of items to an estimated seven million people. The Goodyear Tire & Rubber Co., for example, operates two company stores in Akron, Ohio, where employees can purchase products of Goodyear and of other manufacturers below list.

Automobile dealers, of course, are a special branch of the retail world and their problems are outside the main focus of this article. But many of the same forces that are squeezing the margins of department stores, appliance outlets, grocery stores, etc., are also pressing the auto dealers. Their effective margins have fallen from a national average of 19 per cent in 1949 to 15 per cent this year. And retail margins on tires, gasoline, and auto accessories have been shrinking, too.

Despite all the pressures on retail margins, it's still true that the product that requires intensive selling effort should and can carry a generous margin—certainly a bigger margin than the product in heavy demand can carry. And the biggest single reason for the postwar rise of the discounters was that the "official" margin system failed to make this distinction; a retailer earned as much on the sale of a refrigerator or washing machine, the virtues of which had long since been accepted by the consumer, as on a freezer or dishwasher, which the consumer was not yet persuaded he needed. Since the retailer kept busy dispensing the former, he felt no incentive to push the latter.

The New Realism

The manufacturers must accept some of the blame for this unrealistic margin system. At least one of them, General Electric, seems to be trying to remedy the situation. G.E. recently abandoned suggested national prices for major appliances and lowered the list price on its new electric coffee maker and electric mixer. For the record at least, the G.E. Small Appliance Division still believes in "fair trade" regulations. But one G.E. official believes the discount-house "problem" will disappear only when retailers' margins are brought so low that no one can profitably undercut them by more than 5 to 10 per cent. Consumers, he argues, will pay up to 8 per cent for the convenience of neighborhood shopping, congenial atmosphere, etc.

In addition to needing and deserving a higher margin, the seller who really creates a desire for a new product can usually command full list price. But the retailer who merely dispenses a product on which the consumer has already sold himself cannot expect to be paid for a "selling" service he didn't perform.

Bigger and Cheaper

The revision of the margin structure will produce a number of other changes in retailing. One will be an acceleration in the trend toward larger stores. The object of reducing margins and prices, after all, is to increase volume. A store too small to do a bigger volume on its reduced margins will be driven out of existence. The pattern is clear in food retailing, where the supermarket revolution is well advanced. And it is even visible in the discount houses: the smaller discounters are being forced out by the larger ones.

While lower margins increase volume, it's also true that higher volume makes lower margins possible, e.g., by reducing the required ratio of inventory to sales. According to one manufacturer's rule of thumb, inventory need increase only with the square root of sales.

A trend toward fewer and bigger stores can cut manufacturers' costs, too. Big stores, for example, project their buying requirements more accurately than small stores, which usually project only their current sales volume. The small stores either overbuy (and later cancel) or underbuy (and later demand rush deliveries). One big appliance manufacturer estimates that manufacturing costs could be cut at least 10 per cent by the better production scheduling that would result if the small franchised dealers were eliminated.

Selling, New Style

One way to increase the productivity of sales personnel is through "merchandising"—as distinguished from old-fashioned personal selling. Merchandising, in this sense, means building more sales appeal directly into the product or into the store through attractive styling, design, color, assortment, display, promotion. Because of lagging productivity, personal selling is becoming prohibitively expensive except for large-profit items. In the absence of great new products like the auto or television, or of great catalysts like war or inflation, manufacturers and retailers can maintain a high level of consumer expenditures only if they speed up replacements of their existing products through slight but appealing improvements, i.e., by merchandising. The auto manufacturers have shown this year how effective merchandising can be in stimulating buying, obsoleting a large part of the postwar fleet on color and style alone.

Refrigerator manufacturers are trying to speed up the ten to fifteen-year replacement cycle through the use of color and by developing flexible "built-in" units, and men's clothing manufacturers are changing color and fabric texture each season. Even the staid and functional American bathroom is being merchandised for all it's worth. American Radiator & Standard Sanitary Corp. has redesigned its bathtubs, sinks, and other bathroom fixtures with new styles, shapes, and colors in an effort to cut the bathroom-replacement cycle from forty to fifteen years.

What's Your Line?

Retailers will have to place even greater emphasis on merchandising, since they cannot indefinitely spin off old functions to the manufacturer or the consumer. Retailers, therefore, are re-emphasizing their fundamental role as a service organization built to provide the right merchandise in the right style, color, size, etc., at the right time and place. Recognition of the last two has already led to the growth of suburban stores and of regional shopping centers and to the revival of night openings.

There's nothing very startling, of course, about the suggestion that the retailer's job is to provide the right merchandise. But the job is getting harder. The sheer quantity of things to sell has grown enormously. The level of mass taste has improved, as in the replacement of "borax" furniture by contemporary design. These two factors are placing a premium on the retailer's ability to choose and display the most appealing merchandise.

The store that can do that—that can stock the most appealing merchandise and so save the customer's time and energy by narrowing the range of choice—can eliminate a lot of other "frills" or can command a higher margin. Witness the success of a discount house like Korvette, of a specialty store like Ohrbach's, and of a high-priced specialty department store like I. Magnin's.

The way the store communicates its superior selections is just as important as the way it buys. The first job is to bring people into the store through advertising and promotion. But then the customer must be induced to buy—preferably to buy a lot more than he had originally planned.

Do It Yourself

One of the hallmarks of the new merchandising approach is self-service. Conversion to self-service or self-selection almost invariably increases store volume. By bringing the merchandise out into the open where customers can see and feel it, and by forcing new attention to attractive display, self-selection multiplies the chances of impulse buying, especially by female shoppers whose browsing is rarely as aimless as it seems. Most customers prefer self-selection, in fact, since it simplifies the problem of choosing by putting all the choices in plain view. It also reduces the shopping time.

But while Americans, particularly of the middle-income group, don't have to be sold on the "necessity" of owning a refrigerator or a car, the question of which brand to buy is still open. And relatively few Americans have yet been convinced that they "need" *any* brand of air conditioner, dishwasher, electric dryer, leather luggage, power lawn mower, broadloom carpeting, encyclopedia, and so on. So the retail salesman is by no means obsolete.

There's no real conflict, however, between "merchandising" and the need for effective personal selling. It is highly uneconomical to have salespeople handle merchandise and wait on those customers who already know what they want and who resent having to wait for a salesgirl's attention. Properly used, self-service can *increase* the effectiveness of personal selling by reserving it for those products or customers that really need it.

Self-service also increases the effectiveness with which selling space is used—particularly important for department stores, whose occupancy costs average 6.1 per cent of sales. Stores are searching for other ways of cutting occupancy costs or improving space utilization. Federated Department Stores, for example, has built its most recent stores, e.g., Abraham & Straus in Hempstead, Long Island, and Foley's in Houston, Texas, with "perimeter stockrooms" i.e., stockrooms adjacent to the selling areas. This cuts materials handling and bookkeeping costs, and gives faster service to cash-and-carry customers. Marshall Field's "store of the future" in Park Forest, Illinois, embodies modular design. Since walls and "permanent" fixtures can be easily moved, the size and layout of all selling areas can be adjusted quickly and inexpensively to changes in buying patterns or in selling techniques. And the store is so laid out that any department can be opened independently of any other— e.g., a restaurant can be kept open during the evenings and on Sundays.

The Automatic Store

Technological change is speeding up, too. The greatest and most stubborn cost of the "legitimate" retailer is the "cost of assortment" i.e., the cost of maintaining the inventory of styles, colors, sizes, etc., that his customers expect.[1] Variety stores carry between 20,000 and

---

[1] One of the greatest irritations in the "legitimate" retailer's existence is his customers' willingness to accept the discounter's narrow assortment while insisting on ever bigger assortments from *him*.

40,000 separate items, not counting different sizes, colors, etc. And a large department store may carry as many as 400,000 items.

Determining how much stock of each style and color and size of each item presents a staggering task for the human brain. But it is a relatively simple one for the electronic brain. And so, after lagging far behind manufacturing in office mechanization, retailers and wholesalers finally are putting the electronic brains to work.

Wholesalers have taken the lead. John Plain & Co. of Chicago, wholesaler of gifts and housewares (annual sales about $30 million to $35 million), has been using a Remington Rand-built electronic data-processing machine, called the "Distribution," for nearly two years. This automatic brain tallies all incoming orders and can give instantaneous cumulative sales totals for 39,000 classifications of merchandise, making it possible to process incoming orders in less than three hours, and to give buyers daily sales reports.

And Remington Rand has over 100 orders for a newer Univac file computer, which can tally orders, prepare the invoices, and calculate inventory. One Univac, to be installed next year for Super Valu Stores Inc. of Minneapolis, a wholesale grocer supplying 560 midwest stores, will issue daily inventory reports and keep tabs on 3,000 items of stock, automatically typing a purchasing order when an item reaches a predetermined re-ordering level. The machine will also show, on request, the exact location of any product in Super Valu's new seven-acre warehouse.

Retailers are just beginning to catch up. Bloomingdale's in New York, Filene's in Boston, Berland Shoes in St. Louis, and Broadway Department Store in Los Angeles, among others, now calculate sales totals and breakdowns each day on punched-card machines. Price tickets in these stores are punched with a code showing price, color, style, manufacturer, etc., which is automatically reproduced on conventional punch cards. The cards are then run through sorting and tabulating machines. Both retailers and electronics manufacturers, however, expect to replace this cumbersome, "old-fashioned" electromechanical system with an electronic computer that will instantaneously calculate both sales and inventory from data fed it at the point of sale. This electronic wizard would also automatically process charge accounts and other accounts receivable. And it would provide new kinds of information; for example, breakdowns of inventory by age of merchandise. An experimental prototype, built by Telecomputing Inc., is already in operation at J.W. Robinson, Los Angeles department store.

What's It Worth

And so the years ahead should see a vast change in the appearance and in the substance of U.S. retailing and wholesaling. Productivity will rise, costs will fall, and so will margins on many products. But the over-all cost of distribution, as a share of all costs in the economy, is not likely to slide much below the present 36 cents of the consumer dollar. At best, distribution will hold its own against the pressure of rising productivity in industry and agriculture.

This, in itself, is cause for congratulations. The fact that retailing and wholesaling take no larger share of the consumer dollar today than twenty-five years ago—and that the share probably will not rise—is one of the most impressive achievements of American capitalism. Distribution has always been considered capitalism's soft belly. Americans, in particular, have been prone to moralize about the "high cost" of distribution and make it a scapegoat for their economic ills. The agrarian radicalism of the late nineteenth century, for example, was based in large part on the gap between the prices paid to the farmer and the prices the consumer paid for food. The attack on "excessive" distribution costs was particularly intense during the great depression, which many people blamed on high and rigid distribution costs. The conviction that distribution did cost too much was greatly strengthened by the publication, in 1939, of the Twentieth Century Fund's *Does Distribution Cost Too Much?*, which reported that distribution took 59 cents of every consumer dollar. The fund's study was addressed to the total cost of distribution, including distribution of raw materials, and transportation costs (not just the cost of retail and of wholesale distribution, as measured in this article), but the 59 cents became a much-quoted and, to many people, a scandalous statistic.

High Means Low

It's impossible, of course, to decide whether distribution costs "too much" without first deciding how much distribution is worth, how much distribution should be done, and who should do it. Distribution costs must be "high" in an industrial society because of extensive specialization and because more and more goods in more and more sizes and shapes are made available to more and more people. Distribution costs must be "high" if mass markets are to be created—a fact that has deeply impressed many envious European students of America's postwar economy. It is mass markets, not "low" distribution costs, that produce low consumer prices. And much of what passes for inefficiency in U.S. distribution is unavoidable, unless Americans surrender the convenience of being able to shop anywhere and at any time.

This is not to say that distribution costs can never be "too high." There are inefficiencies in U.S. retailing that can be identified and attacked. They are being attacked, and that is the big excitement in U.S. retailing today.

Part Seven ...

LEGISLATION

·{ 39 }··

Fair-Trade End at Kodak Gets Cool Reception*

BY CAMERON DAY†

Both the photographic industry and fair-trade forces are speculating this week on future effects of Eastman Kodak's abandonment of fair trade. Whatever may develop later, first reactions indicate that: (1) dealers generally don't like it and (2) other fair-trading manufacturers in the field won't drop fair trade just because Kodak did.

This hardly softens the blow to fair trade, already weakened by the loss of other major followers and plagued by a pattern of adverse state court decisions. The list of heavyweight backers of fair trade is thinning. With Kodak's defection, the familiar prediction that the policy is dying becomes more significant.

In its statement, Kodak gave routine reasons for forsaking fair trade. Kodak, as Westinghouse said in the same situation, still favors the policy in principle but says it is impracticable to enforce.

Kodak stated: "There are now 16 states plus the District of Columbia where it is no longer possible to have effective fair-trade agreements either because no fair-trade legislation exists or because provisions of fair-trade laws have been held unenforceable by the courts." Further, said Kodak, many dealers had complained of this situation.

Some observers, pondering other possible reasons behind the move, recalled the U.S. Supreme Court ruling affecting McKesson & Robbins, drug manufacturer. In a rebuff to fair trade, the Supreme Court held that a company functioning both as a manufacturer and a wholesaler cannot make contracts with other wholesalers, even on its own trademarked items, since this is not provided for in the federal Miller-Tydings and McGuire acts.

This decision, in principle, had implications for Kodak, a manufacturer that maintains retail stores. The question—whether a manufacturer may have fair-trade contracts with retailers when the manufacturer operates competitive retail stores—has long been argued. In 1953 the Federal

* Reprinted by special permission from *Printers' Ink*, January 11, 1957. Copyright, 1957, *Printers' Ink*.

† Senior associate editor, *Printers' Ink*.

271

Trade Commission, taking a negative stand on the question, attacked Kodak's fair-trade program on these grounds.

In January 1955, FTC reversed itself and said it was okay for Kodak to make fair-trade contracts even though its own stores competed for customers. Now, however, with the top court coming to an opposite conclusion, it seemed that Kodak inevitably would have been faced with dropping either fair trade or its retail stores. So, the speculation goes, this may have influenced Kodak to abandon fair trade now.

Dealers Not Elated

Whatever the prime reason for Kodak's decision, a quick check of dealer sources shows little elation. For many who have staunchly kept their fair-trade contracts, Kodak's new stand means they must up unit sales to maintain the same dollar volume. Accordingly, there was some surprise at Kodak's statement that many dealers had requested the move.

Malcolm L. Fleischer, New York attorney who represented the retail photographic industry in fair-trade enforcement, says dealers do not favor Kodak's action. He adds:

> The fair-trade picture is not as blurred as the recent Kodak release would have it appear. True, there have been setbacks in some of the state courts, but more than 70% of the total volume of fair-traded merchandise is sold within the borders of states where the constitutionality of the law is no longer assailable. As one who has had much experience in this field, I am of the firm conviction that a planned and uninterrupted enforcement program is feasible and well worth the cost involved to the manufacturer. There are few trademarks more valuable than Kodak's, and it is difficult to understand a policy that permits it to be thrown to the wolves.

Fair-Trade End Forecast

Stephen Masters, top discounter, says Kodak's move is no surprise, since he predicted fair trade eventually would be dropped by even its staunchest supporters. Noting that several major companies, formerly fair-traders, have left the policy, he sees Kodak's step as another advance toward the complete collapse of fair trade. He contends, as he has before, that "the right of the public to buy at the lowest price can't be interfered with." The public, he says, is learning every day that it can buy products without paying a premium for the cost of enforcing a "useless" fair-trade policy. And he applauds "the wisdom and courage" shown by Kodak in its action.

Willoughbys, colossus of camera stores, was credited with the early comment that it faced "a further shaving of our profits." Later, Stephen L. Sturz, president, commented: "We have always been strongly for fair trade and have been giving full and ethical support to Kodak agreements. However, when fair trade can't be maintained 100% down the line, a manufacturer may be fully justified in abandoning it. We will now find it possible to meet under-the-counter dealers and discount houses that have forced our customers to leave our store because of this unfair competition."

Another dealer didn't enthuse over Kodak's move. But he said the decision isn't really as important, to him, as the attention it's getting indicates. More significant, he believes, was Kodak's dropping fair trade for its color film in 1955 (this came about when Kodak signed a consent decree with the Justice Department's antitrust division, which had attacked Kodak's monopoly of amateur color-film processing and control of the film's resale price through fair-trade contracts). Further, he noted, except for its Retina camera (made in Germany), Kodak doesn't compete strongly in the top-grade film camera line, much of which is made in Japan and Germany.

Meanwhile, Samuel Krivit, president, *Photographic Trade News* (an industry publication), says: "We deplore what has happened but realize that Kodak felt it was the only decision possible." Krivit sees fair trade still far from dead in the industry. He urges dealers with fair-trade contracts to support them strongly. Kodak's decision, he says, points to more intense competition and "more aggressive promotion and increased advertising will be needed in the turbulent times ahead."

No Opposition Expected

Whatever dealer feeling, Kodak will get no overt opposition. The company is still the giant in the industry, and anyone in the business must stock Kodak products.

In the wake of Kodak's move, Willoughbys rushed out with discount ads, as did Davega and other stores. This was expected, since Kodak's action affects everyone in the industry. Same time, the company doesn't surpass competition as it once did. In the past decade amateur photography has grown at a dizzy rate and new companies with new products have jumped into contention. In 1953 amateurs shelled out some $400,-000,000 for photo equipment, accessories, development and printing. A year later the figure catapulted to more than $700,000,000 and, by now, may be around one billion dollars.

With Kodak a vital force in the industry, its new stand is being scrutinized all over. At General Aniline & Film Corp.'s Ansco division (probably number 2 in the field) the feeling is to stay with fair trade. Ansco has had the policy longer than Kodak, which had been with it 19 years. (Kodak did drop fair trade in May 1952 when it seemed that, because of the Supreme Court's Schwegmann decision, fair trade was doomed. With passage of the McGuire Act, however, Kodak resumed fair trade at once).

T. Matsui, executive director, Canon Camera Co., maker of a luxury 35mm. camera, says he visited many dealers recently in states without fair trade and found they still generally favor fair trade, even though it is out in these areas. He intends to "uphold fair trade even though

Kodak has abandoned it completely, since the bulk of our business comes from smaller dealers."

Right Move for Kodak

Henry Froehlich, president, Konica Camera, which imports medium-priced 35mm. cameras, says Kodak made the right move. He believes (as Konica operates) in giving dealers a price range with floor and ceiling prices. The dealer then may use the price within the range best suited to the area. In New York, which he calls a discount area, the price would be around the floor tag; in areas without discount houses, the price would be at the ceiling. At Tiffen Marketing Corp., filter maker, president Saul Tiffen says his company won't be affected, but he believes one reason for Kodak's move is increased competition from foreign countries, mainly Japan. He adds the action may anger some old-time dealers, but they won't stop stocking Kodak products.

Nat Kameny, partner, Kameny Associates, New York agency handling a batch of accounts in the field, believes a manufacturer is justified in dropping fair trade when it can't enforce its agreements 100%. Fair trade, says Kameny, protects dealers only when it is properly enforced. S. Nomura, vice-president, J. Osawa & Co., importer of Ricoh cameras, will stay with fair trade because it "allows dealers to order with confidence." Nomura says that with Kodak cameras so widely distributed, the company naturally found fair trade difficult to police. And, he adds, the situation bears close scrutiny to see just how far Kodak prices will fall.

Much of the industry will be watching developments for the same reason as Kodak's new policy takes hold. And there will be more comments on the situation. There's bound to be, following an action that affects an industry providing materials for cameras to click more than 5,000,000 times daily.

·{ 40 }··

FTC's Current Approach to Robinson-Patman*

BY PHILIP K. SCHWARTZ

In the past 12 months the importance of the Robinson-Patman Act has become more critical to advertisers and advertising agencies than ever

---

* Reprinted by special permission from *Tide*, October 12, 1956. Copyright, 1956, *Tide*.

before. The Federal Trade Commission, now with a Republican majority, is attacking with especial vigor what it considers to be violations of Robinson-Patman. Every advertiser, whether he pays his retailers for co-op advertising, or instore displays, or even offers them a demonstrator, finds himself involved with the complex and far-reaching provisions of Robinson-Patman.

Over the last year, FTC has indicated its attitude toward Robinson-Patman with a series of significant proceedings:

1. Against nine major grocery manufacturers in connection with their participation in network merchandising programs such as Chain Lightning (NBC), Supermarketing (CBS), Radiodizing (ABC) and Mass Merchandising (ABC).

2. Against 11 other food manufacturers in connection with their participation in the special anniversary cooperative promotions of Food Fair and Giant Food Shopping Center (Washington, D.C.).

3. Against United Cigar-Whelan Stores Corp., Products Advertising Corp. (Whelan's house agency operated as a separate enterprise) and four large drug & cosmetic houses in connection with the cooperative television programs sponsored by Whelan.

4. Against four large cosmetic houses in connection with their programs of furnishing demonstrators or granting advertising allowances.

5. In addition, the FTC has also instituted proceedings against many other cooperative advertising arrangements. And if all the above suits aren't enough, consider the statement of one FTC commissioner to the effect that this is just the beginning!

Then, too, there is the pending $3,000,000 triple damage action against A&P and three large food manufacturers based on the latters' purchase of advertising space in *Woman's Day*, a magazine distributed only in A&P stores but published as a separate commercial venture by a subsidiary of A&P. The theory of this extreme application of Robinson-Patman is that advertising purchased in *Woman's Day* is actually a special advertising allowance to A&P rather than the purchase of advertising space in a publication.

The two sections of Robinson-Patman especially pertinent to advertisers are described in the accompanying box. Before there can be a violation of either section, there must actually be competition between the retailer or distributor to whom a payment or service is given, and another retailer or distributor to whom a payment or service is not given. A special merchandising campaign can be conducted in one recognized trading area, therefore, and need not necessarily be conducted in another completely separate trading area.

However, while competing retailers must be involved, it is not necessary to show that the retailer who did not receive the payment or service was damaged by the discrimination! Section 2(a) of Robinson-Patman, the basic price discrimination section, provides that a discrimination in price between competing retailers is not illegal unless the effect of the discrimination is "substantially to lessen competition."

The advertiser is rare today whose marketing program doesn't involve merchandising promotion. Over the last 50 years, merchandising has tended more & more to involve some form of cooperation between the seller (or advertiser) and his customers in the marketing of his product or service.

Whatever form that cooperation takes, it usually is referred to as "cooperative advertising." As such, it is governed by a complex and often troublesome law known as the Robinson-Patman Act, passed in 1936.

The Robinson-Patman Act has two separate sections dealing with cooperative advertising. One section, 2(d), refers to services rendered by the buyer (or retailer) and paid for by the seller (or advertiser)— such services as co-op ads, special displays, etc. The other section, 2(e), refers to services and facilities rendered by the seller—for example, furnishing demonstrators, etc. Because of the similarity of these two sections they are generally treated together.

Section 2(d) provides that an advertiser cannot make a payment to a retailer for a service or facility furnished by that retailer unless the advertiser makes that payment available on proportionally equal terms to all competitors of that retailer.

Section 2(e), as currently interpreted, provides that an advertiser cannot discriminate in favor of one retailer by furnishing a service or facility to him without making such service or facility available to all competing retailers on proportionally equal terms.

The accompanying article was prepared to offer advertisers guidance in the planning of merchandising promotions, and to aid advertising agencies in advising their clients on the legal problems involved.

This raises the question of what constitutes "competitors." A simple rule of thumb would be to determine whether the retailers involved sell or attempt to sell the same product to the same customers. Thus a grocery store in New York City is not a competitor of a grocery store in Denver, obviously, because their customers are not the same. But a drugstore in New York City which sells a particular product is a competitor of a variety store across the street which sells the same product.

This point was involved in the Whelan case, as well as in all other proceedings under these two sections of Robinson-Patman. In the Whelan case, the FTC charged certain manufacturers with making payments to Whelan in return for promotion of their products on the TV shows involved, and that the manufacturers had not made similar cooperative advertising payments to their other customers who compete with Whelan. The competitors which FTC claimed it was protecting consisted of every individual or chain store which was a competitor of any Whelan store in any area covered by the commercials on the TV shows.

The same principle applies in the Food Fair and Giant Food cases where, as part of an anniversary celebration, the chains offered to perform special promotional activities to all their suppliers in return for fixed payments. The fact that the chain offered the deal to all its suppliers on proportionally equal terms did not deter this proceeding, because the FTC considered the fact that the manufacturers involved did not offer the same or similar payments to all of their own retailers who were competing with Food Fair and Giant Food.

An important point here involves the issue raised by one of the examiners. If an advertiser accepts a plan offered by one of his customers, he said, the advertiser then adopts the plan as his own, and he must make it available on proportionally equal terms to all his other customers competing with the customer whose plan he adopted.

The statute involved requires that a merchandising plan be "made available" to all competing customers on proportionally equal terms. For an advertiser, for example, this means that his payment or service must actually and openly be made known and available to all his competing retailers in such a manner that they can avail themselves of the service and facilities if they desire.

It is no defense for an advertiser to say that any customer who asks for it can get it; there is a positive obligation on the advertiser's part to advise all his competing retailers of the plan. It is not even enough for an advertiser to tell his salesmen, in good faith, to notify all retailers; the advertiser must make certain that the information actually reaches every competing retailer, even though the advertiser may know that certain retailers are not in a position to take advantage of the particular offer.

The payment made by the advertiser is not to exceed the amount spent by the retailer. This seems to be an obvious rule, but it was highlighted by the Trade Practice Conference Rules promulgated last December by the FTC for the corset and brassiere industry.

One of the rules relates to the widespread (but legally questionable) practice of paying at national line rates for advertising by a retailer, even though the retailer might only pay for the advertising at the lower local rates and pocket the difference. The theory behind this practice is that the retailer is entitled to receive payment for the value to the advertiser of the services rendered, and the national line rate represents such value. However, assuming these Trade Conference Practice Rules represent the thinking of the FTC, this method of computing payment may have to be changed.

A corollary of the preceding rule is that it is the obligation of the advertiser to see to it that a retailer actually does what he is supposed to do before the advertiser pays. For example, it may not be sufficient for the advertiser merely to accept a tear sheet as complete proof of performance; he should also have satisfactory proof that the ads appeared the requisite number of times.

The payments made by the advertiser should have a reasonable relation to the value of the services performed by the retailer—if it doesn't, the excess portion of the payment would merely constitute a price reduction. There should also be some system for establishing some value for the services performed by the retailer.

Now, a word about the phrase used in both sections 2(d) and 2(e): "proportionally equal terms." Until a few years ago, the FTC took the position that an advertiser had to have the exact promotion or merchandising program for all competing retailers. If he offered one retailer a demonstrator, he had to offer demonstrators to all—he could not offer the others newspaper advertising. If he paid one retailer for newspaper advertising, he had to pay the others for newspaper advertising—not for radio advertising or handbills.

But today an advertiser may have a promotional program in which alternate services are made available to his competing retailers. He can pay for newspaper advertising by some retailers, for radio advertising by others, for handbills by others, etc. Furthermore, it is not necessary that each service be exactly as good or as valuable to one retailer as an alternate service is to a competing retailer; nor is it necessary that every feature of the program be usable by, or even suitable for, every retailer. However, every competing retailer should be able to participate in the plan on some basis and should be reasonably able to take advantage of at least one of the alternates.

The basic test is that there must be no effort or intent on the part of the advertiser to favor one retailer over any competing retailer, and that the plan be "honest in its purpose and fair and reasonable in its application." If this test is met, it is also possible that the payment for each type of service can be different; for example, if payment is computed on a per case basis, a certain amount per case could be paid for newspaper advertising, a smaller amount per case could be paid for handbill and radio advertising, and a still smaller amount per case could be paid for store displays—provided, however, that there must always be a fair and reasonable relation between the alternates provided and the respective payments.

"How do my competitors get away with it?" you may ask. Unfortunately, it is no defense that "Everyone else is doing it." And you cannot say to FTC, "Why pick on me? Why don't you stop my competitors?" FTC alone selects the companies it wants to proceed against. In the Whelan case, for example, FTC proceeded against only four manufacturers as "typical" even though it admitted right in the complaint that 57 manufacturers had participated in the programs in 1954!

How important is the size or prominence of a company when it comes to possible action by FTC? Undoubtedly it is an important factor. The larger the company, the more people know of its practices, the more people are affected, the more likelihood of complaints being filed. And, from the FTC's point of view, the more likely a question of significant public interest will be involved.

What about FTC proceedings against advertising agencies and media? With only one exception, no case has ever been instituted under Robinson-Patman against an advertising agency: the current Whelan case. There, Whelan's house agency (a wholly owned subsidary) was joined as a respondent because it "planned, originated and promoted" advertising for Whelan and was the "agent and instrumentality" for Whelan in connection with the challenged activities.

In the normal course of events, an advertising agency will not be joined by FTC with its client in proceedings under Robinson-Patman. A house agency, even when operated as a completely separate venture, is more likely to be joined in a proceeding by FTC solely because of the close legal relationship to the advertiser, but even then FTC would first have to find that the agency was an "instrumentality" for carrying out the merchandising program.

The same principle applies with regard to media. If FTC can show that the medium is the instrumentality for carrying out a merchandising program, it could proceed against the medium under section 5 of the Federal Trade Commission Act, which in general terms prohibits unfair methods of competition. FTC claims that "knowingly to induce or receive" illegal discriminatory payments or services constitutes "unfair competition" under section 5. On this theory FTC could proceed against any firm which it considers to be instrumental in effectuating a discriminatory merchandising program. (Incidentally, it is under this section FTC is proceeding against Whelan, Food Fair, Giant Foods, etc.)

In the current proceedings mentioned above, involving "Chain Lightning"—(NBC), "Supermarketing"—(CBS), "Radiodizing"—(ABC) and "Mass Merchandising"—(ABC), FTC claims that the networks, serving as intermediaries, entered into agreements with grocery chains whereby, for free radio or television time, the chains agreed to give instore promotions to specific products in their stores located in the area reached by the network station used; with this additional promotion as an extra inducement, the networks then solicited the manufacturers to buy television or radio time at regular rates.

FTC claims that this tie-in was all arranged by the networks and indirectly constitutes the giving by the manufacturers of promotional allowances—free time—to favored customers. However, despite the fact that FTC considers the networks to be instrumental in effectuating these merchandising programs, one reason why FTC did not proceed against them was to avoid the separate issue at this time of whether FTC or FCC has jurisdiction; FTC first wants to settle the basic legal principle as to whether or not the program itself violates the Act.

The advertising agency and the advertiser should be very careful in considering such arrangements. They must be examined carefully from the point of view of the advertiser. If the advertiser participates in this arrangement (whereby certain chains or customers get free time or space or some other advantage) will he be offering any alternate service to all his other competing customers? If not, then consider carefully the known attitude of the Commission.

On the other hand, many advertisers still participate on the purely practical basis that FTC can't (and apparently isn't going to) proceed against everybody, and they might as well get the benefits of the arrangements while they can. Then again, there are a few advertisers who continue to participate because they do not think FTC will be successful.

One final point of general interest. In October, 1953, for the first time in 20 years, the Republicans attained a majority on the Commission. Since that time, has there been any noticeable change in activity, procedures, enforcement or interpretation as compared with the prior Democratic administrations?

Yes and no. With regard to procedure, the present Commission shows a much more businesslike approach. It has revised its procedures to eliminate a tremendous amount of red tape, delay and expense; it issues meaningful opinions with every decision, it has speeded up the processing of matters from start to finish; it has substantially reduced the necessity for extended trials and hearings; it more efficiently follows through on the enforcement of completed cases.

All these improvements have enabled the FTC to assume a larger case load, extend its investigations, institute more proceedings, and in general become much more active than most of its predecessors.

As for interpretation of Robinson-Patman, there has been no significant change which can be attributed solely to the present Commission. As shown by the previously discussed cases, the present Commission is still prohibiting certain activities even where no injury to competition is shown. It is still proceeding against one or a few violators where many others are known to be engaging in the identical practices—thus showing that FTC is not enforcing Robinson-Patman on proportionally equal terms (to use FTC's own words).

As a result, the business world can now say it has an FTC which is more businesslike in certain respects, but which is more "active" than previous Commissions. This raises the interesting question: which is better for business, a technical, un-businesslike approach by FTC, with inadequate enforcement, or an FTC with a more practical businessman's approach and more effective enforcement?

··{ 41 }··

Exclusive Dealing: Under Fire*

There's good evidence today that exclusive dealing—the method by which a manufacturer ties up a retail outlet as its exclusive sales agent—is on shakier ground than ever before.

The trend has shaped up quietly on a number of fronts. It is a glacial movement resulting from various forces, some legal and some economic. Here are some of the signs:

1. In the petroleum marketing field, oil companies have been affected by the famous Standard Stations case of 1949 (*BW*—Jun.18'49,p21). In that decision, the Supreme Court frowned on forcing retailers to sell exclusively Standard Oil Co. of California products. The influence of this and similar cases can be seen in recent statements by Socony Mobil Oil Co. reassuring dealers of their right to buy competing products (*BW*—Jul.23'55,p104).

2. In hearing aids, a series of antitrust cases has forced companies to cease their exclusive dealing practices.

3. In autos, a rash of private antitrust suits hinges on exclusive dealing. By hacking away at exclusive dealing, these suits may conceivably lead to revision of the whole method of distribution on which the car industry has been built. In autos, exclusive dealing has reached a more advanced state than in any other major industry.

Lost Franchises

The legal flurry in autos traces directly to the pressures of competition. Detroit is getting tough about the franchises of dealers who haven't sold enough cars or who haven't measured up to the auto makers' standards in other respects.

In the last few weeks, no less than 18 dealers for various divisions of General Motors Corp. were dropped in the New York City area. Their year's contracts came up for renewal but weren't picked up by GM.

This sort of thing makes it certain that there will be more suits against the auto companies in the near future—particularly in view of the fact that Congress this year passed legislation to aid private antitrust claimants. This permits federal judges to award less than triple damages in private suits. When triple damages were mandatory, judges and juries hesitated to award damages.

Down to Cases

Some recent cases filed by dealers have broadened the base of the attack on the auto companies' franchise systems. Three cases in particular are significant:

1. A Baltimore dealer—Webster Motors Co.—won a triple damage award of more than $570,000 against Packard-Studebaker. Webster charged—and proved to the satisfaction of a jury—that Packard, prior to its merger with Studebaker, illegally combined and conspired with another Baltimore dealer to drive smaller franchised dealers out of business in the area.

The case has been appealed. The industry figures that it's a dangerous precedent to let stand.

2. In Connecticut, Hathaway Motors, Inc., of Hartford brought suit against the three big car makers as well as a number of dealers in the area (*BW*—Mar.19'55,p68). Hathaway is an "independent" that bought new cars and sold them cut-rate as "used." It claims that a boycott prevents it from buying new cars from the manufacturers.

3. In North Carolina, a Greensboro dealer that used to handle Lincolns and Mercurys, Miller Motors, Inc., is charging Ford with a number of monopolistic practices (*BW*—Aug.13'55,p54). These include the tying-in of parts and accessory sales, and coercion through 60-day cancellation clauses in contracts.

The auto companies tend to poohpooh these suits, say that they always arise when economic conditions begin to squeeze the dealers. However, one thing seems clear: The dealer-company relationship has changed enormously over the years, and now once more it is changing in small ways as Detroit attempts to conform to legal demands. The franchise system is getting chipped around the edges.

AUTO DEALER SYSTEM

The present franchised dealer system in the auto industry has developed over a period of 50 years. Around 1920, it evolved into its present form of tight factory control over the dealer.

The industry has metamorphosed through several stages of distribution: first through manufacturers' agents, then through wholesalers, later through distributors, and finally to direct dealing with franchised dealers.

The present system arose through several needs. One was the necessity for some way of handling used car sales. More important, however, was Detroit's pressing need for cash turnover. The dealer took title to the car on delivery, and Detroit had the money in its pocket.

Strings Attached

As the manufacturers began dealing direct with retailers, there were two things either expressed or implied in the selling agreements:

1. The granting of exclusive territories to the retailers. This was written into the agreement—and primarily for the dealer's own protection.

2. The insistence that the dealer exclusively handle his factory's products. This sometimes was written in—it was in early Ford contracts—but more often merely implied.

Since the beginning, selling agreements have stipulated that the dealer will represent the manufacturer to the best of his abilities, or words to that effect.

Handling another make of car is interpreted as not conforming to that requirement. Auto men insist that if a dealer "adequately" represents his factory in his area, he won't have time to handle a second make of car.

Territories

The grant of exclusive sales territories, however, remained in the selling agreements until after World War II. It was generally enforced by compelling the dealer who sold outside his territory to pay a fixed sum to a dealer whose territory was infringed.

For years, says one highly-placed official of a big auto company, attorneys warned that territorial security was illegal under the Sherman Act. But the companies continued it in the selling agreements until the Standard Stations decision in 1949.

The Standard case actually dealt with exclusive franchises, not territorial protection, but it was a warning to the auto business. The auto companies decided that, if the government was going to begin looking at selling agreements between manufacturers and retailers, they had better move first. So they dropped the territorial provision from their contracts. As exclusive dealing in product wasn't written in the agreements anyway, no changes had to be made in this respect.

THE LEGAL SIDE

Section 3 of the Clayton Act outlaws exclusive dealing contracts where the effect "may be to substantially lessen competition or tend to create a monopoly in any line of commerce."

Over the years, lawyers have struggled over the meaning of this clause. While every exclusive dealing contract lessens competition, the law bans only those that "substantially" lessen competition. Defense counsel will argue that exclusive dealing contracts are often an aid to competition and that Congress acted with deliberation when it decided to ban only those that "substantially" lessen competition.

Some Upheld

In the many years of litigation, many different explanations have been offered for exclusive dealing contracts.

At first, the courts accepted various defenses from companies that used exclusive dealing contracts. In the Sinclair case, for example, the Supreme Court approved exclusive contracts after Sinclair pointed out that the public would be deceived if any brand of gasoline but Sinclair was distributed through Sinclair pumps.

Then, in 1949, a wave of panic swept over the marketing executives who relied on exclusive dealing contracts. In the Standard Oil of California case, the Supreme Court by a 5–4 vote said exclusive contracts were illegal if they involve "a substantial number of outlets and a substantial amount of products whether considered comparatively or not." In this case, the exclusive contracts outlawed by the court covered 16% of the gasoline outlets in the western area in question. These gas stations pumped 23% of the total gallonage in the area.

Retreat?

This case marked the high point of what the lawyers term the "quantitative substantiality" theory of proof. At the time, there were widespread warnings that it might virtually preclude any sizable company from using exclusive dealing contracts.

Subsequently, however, the Supreme Court has tended to make what might be called a "retreat from Standard Oil."

The Republican Administration, too, has been chary of using the Standard Stations decision in its antitrust prosecutions. It has applied the "rule of reason" approach to exclusive dealing. Said the Attorney General's National Committee to Study the Antitrust Laws:

"The heart of the matter is the ease with which rival suppliers can practicably secure consumer access in alternative ways."

Furthermore, the committee cited some of the benefits that can flow from exclusive dealing—for the buyer, assurance of a steady source of supply and protection against price fluctuations; for the seller, reduction of selling costs and a way for "new entrants to gain a foothold" in the marketplace against "powerfully entrenched rivals."

FTC Decisions

However, the boxscore of Federal Trade Commission decisions shows that the casualty rate for businessmen involved in exclusive dealing contracts has been just as high under the "rule of reason" as it was under the old, arbitrary "quantitative substantiality test."

In fact, the new doctrine may prove to be even more troublesome for the businessman. For one thing, it casts a cloud of uncertainty over all exclusive dealing arrangements. Besides, it is resulting in such fully documented FTC decisions that the commission will probably have less trouble defending itself when the reasonableness of its finding is challenged in court.

Maico Case

In its Maico Co., Inc. (manufacturers of hearing aids) decision, FTC said every company involved in an exclusive dealing case should have the opportunity to show that its exclusive dealing contracts were not lessening competition.

Despite this widened opportunity for proof, there is not a single instance where FTC has held that exclusive dealing contracts were being properly used.

After FTC had ruled out similar contracts used by two of its major competitors—Dictograph and Beltone—Maico decided to accept a consent order and drop the exclusive contracts.

Additionally, there is trouble brewing at the Justice Dept. for Philco Corp.—a suit that is clearly aimed at destroying all exclusive territory contracts. It would bar Philco from requiring distributors to sell only in their own territories, bar distributors in turn from making the same requirements of dealers.

The total effect of this and other suits may crack the facade of exclusive dealing even further.

··{ 42 }··

Quantity Discounts and the Morton Salt Case*

BY PETER G. PETERSON[1]

The requirements of the Robinson-Patman Act should be seriously considered in the formulation of many pricing policies. These requirements are in such a state of flux that any exposition of recent developments in the administration of the act seems desirable. The Morton Salt case presents an excellent opportunity for such an inquiry.

It is an obvious and yet significant fact that any antitrust case is at the same time a legal and a business matter and that it is not wise or possible to divorce the two points of view. This makes it necessary to straddle the areas of interest of the legal technician and the businessman. The

---

* Reprinted by special permission from the *Journal of Business*, Vol. XXV, No. 2, April, 1952. Copyright, 1952, University of Chicago.

[1] Associate director, Market Facts, Inc.

difficulty of this task is somewhat imposing, since what is "superficial treatment" to the antitrust lawyer may be considered "overbearing legal technicalities" by the business practitioner. It is hoped that sufficient attention to both points of view has been achieved in this paper.[2]

Within the past few years there has been unusual activity in the antitrust field. The surprising number and variety of cases seem to have resulted in a considerable degree of confusion on the part of lawyers, businessmen, and legislators. Some have gone so far as to suggest that a state of "chaos" exists.

In fact, nearly everyone except the Federal Trade Commission says he is confused. Corwin Edwards, chief economist of the FTC, has characterized this widely proclaimed state of "confusion" on the legality of pricing practices as "mere ghosties and ghoulies and six legged beasties and things that go hump in the night."[3]

It is probably safe to say that much of the confusion is less imaginary than Mr. Edwards would suggest. Some substantial confusion among members of the Commission itself is found in a Senate committee report which documents statements made by various Commission members on particular pricing practices that are considered illegal. That some of these statements are inconsistent is made quite obvious.[4]

If it can be assumed that the antitrust situation is characterized by something less than complete clarity, the cause probably rests on some recent antitrust cases. Two of them are the Cement Institute case and the Rigid Steel Conduit case, both dealing with the broad problem of the legality of geographic price differences. The crux of the geographic pricing problem is still that of the legality of competitive freight absorption when not accompanied by conspiracy.[5]

The now famous A & P case and its attack on vertical and horizontal integration is perhaps a third source of current confusion. Among other

---

[2] The author is indebted to many: to James Lorie, associate professor of marketing, University of Chicago, for his critical guidance of the entire project; to McBride and Baker, counsel for the Morton Salt Company, for their many helpful suggestions and their generosity in allowing access to the cases of Morton Salt and the Federal Trade Commission; to the FTC for sending a great deal of relevant material; to David Gooder, of the law firm of Lord, Bissell and Kaydek; and to John Jeuck, associate professor of marketing, and George H. Brown, professor of marketing, University of Chicago, for their enlightening comment. None of these is necessarily in agreement with the opinions expressed in this paper. And, of course, the author alone is responsible for the final version and for any errors in fact or interpretation that it contains.

[3] In a speech before the New England Council, Dixville Notch, N.H., September 18, 1948.

[4] Study of Federal Trade Commission Pricing Policies Interim Report (Washington: Government Printing Office, 1949) and Hearings on Competitive Absorption of Transportation Costs—S. 236 (Washington: Government Printing Office, 1949).

[5] The Georgetown Law Journal of January, 1949 (Vol. XXXVII, No. 2), is almost entirely devoted to the legal aspects of geographic pricing. It contains some of the most extensive and excellent commentary available on this matter.

things, this perplexing case is further evidence of the fact that the implications of price competition are not widely understood or accepted, particularly where smaller firms are affected.[6]

Finally, there is the question of price discrimination through the use of quantity discounts. The inherent complexity of this problem is well illustrated by the Morton Salt case. In view of this, it is somewhat surprising that this case, for the most part, has received relatively little attention. The quantity discount as a sales stratagem is undoubtedly far more prevalent than the basing-point price. Likewise, many firms other than those vertically and horizontally integrated grant and receive quantity discounts. Thus, the Morton Salt case, by virtue of its potential impact, would seem to merit more attention than it has received.

The plan of this paper is as follows: (1) a descriptive statement of the background of the case; (2) a discussion of the arguments presented with an evaluation of what appear to be the more crucial issues; (3) the Supreme Court's decision; and (4) some suggestions regarding the possible consequences of the Court's decision.

By and large, the discussion will center around the practical effects of the Morton Salt case and the Robinson-Patman Act upon the pricing policies of businesses. In so doing, it is almost inevitable that the attention be focused on the pricing policies of large businesses, since the statute, in its conception and implementation, seems to be aimed specifically at restricting the pricing alternatives available to these firms.

BACKGROUND OF THE CASE

The Morton Salt Company produces salt which it sells to wholesalers, retailers, and manufacturers. This particular case[7] related only to the sale of table salt. Morton's principal brand, "Blue Label," is sold in the well-known round blue package that contains 26 ounces, twenty-four such packages to a case. As an inherent part of its pricing policy, Morton's Blue Label Salt was sold only on the basis of a national delivered price. More important, however, was Morton's standard quantity discount system which lies at the heart of this case. A brief discussion of the discount structure seems necessary.

Carload Discount

When sold in carload lots, the delivered price of a case of Blue Label salt was $1.50, a discount of 10 cents per case. This discount was also allowed under the so-called "pool-car arrangement," where a number of customers would join in the purchase of a carload for delivery at a

---

[6] For an interesting statement of its economic implications see M. A. Adelman, "The A & P Case: A Study in Applied Economic Theory," *Quarterly Journal of Economics*, LXIII (May, 1949), 238–57.

[7] *Federal Trade Commission* v. *Morton Salt Co.*, 334 U.S. 37 (1948).

specific destination. The customer would then pay the delivery cost from that point to his own warehouse, and the Morton Salt Company, in turn, would bill each of these customers at the carload price. It is significant that 99.9 per cent of Morton's table-salt sales moved in carload lots.

5,000-Case Discount

Those customers who purchased 5,000 or more cases of Blue Label salt in any consecutive twelve-month period were allowed a discount of 10 cents per case. Where applicable, this was in addition to the carload discount. Certain "organizations," some of which appeared to be little more than groups of companies or retail outlets, were allowed to combine their purchases in order to qualify for this discount. One such group was the National Retailer-Owned Grocers, Incorporated, which acted as a purchasing agent for its retail members—in other words, a voluntary chain.

50,000-Case Discount

Morton Salt granted a discount of 15 cents a case to all purchasers of 50,000 or more cases of Blue Label salt in any consecutive twelve-month period. This included the five-thousand-case discount but was in addition to the carload discount where applicable. Clearly, both the 5,000- and the 50,000-case discounts were of the so-called "cumulative" type.

On the basis of the combined purchases of their branches, only five grocery chains qualified for the 50,000-case rebate. These were the American Stores Company, A & P, Kroger, National Tea, and Safeway Stores. The delivered prices on Blue Label salt, after making allowances for these various discounts, are shown in Table 1. It is of interest to note that the carload discount had been offered since 1922 and the five-thousand- and fifty-thousand-case discounts since 1927 or 1928.

TABLE 1
DELIVERED PRICES ON BLUE LABEL SALT

	Per Case
Less-than-carload purchases	$1.60
Carload purchases	$1.50
5,000-case purchases in any consecutive twelve months	$1.40
50,000-case purchases in any consecutive twelve months	$1.35

50,000 Discount

Table salt other than Blue Label was not sold on a delivered-price basis. Instead, such salt was sold at list price plus transportation charges from the nearest plant. On the sale of this other table salt, Morton maintained a unique schedule of discounts known as "unit discounts," each unit amounting to approximately 5 per cent of the list price. One unit was allowed on carload lots, and another unit was given to those customers purchasing $50,000 or more of table salt during any consecutive twelve-month period. While the system of unit discounts did not apply to Blue

Label purchases, those purchases were included in determining whether a customer qualified for this $50,000 discount.

By virtue of the quantity discount system, the Federal Trade Commission found that the Morton Salt Company was discriminating in price between competing wholesalers and retailers. The Commission also found that those price discriminations resulted in the competitive effects condemned by the Robinson-Patman Act. The Seventh Circuit Court did not agree,[8] and the Federal Trade Commission appealed the decision to the Supreme Court.

THE ARGUMENT

A reasonably thorough discussion of the argument before the Supreme Court is likely to yield some added insight on the key issues in price discrimination involving quantity discounts as well as the Commission's point of view toward these matters. In the attempt, however, to present the essence of a voluminous record in relatively few pages, it has been necessary first to select and then to condense what appeared to be the relevant issues. It is hoped that this process of selection and condensation has not seriously distorted the true importance or meaning of the arguments presented.

It would appear that the argument centered about three questions: (1) Was the general quantity discount system discriminatory within the meaning of the Robinson-Patman Act? (2) Did the burden of proving that any discriminatory prices were (were not) justified by cost savings rest upon Morton Salt (the Commission)? (3) Was the evidence sufficient, in quantity and quality, to support the conclusion that the quantity discounts had an injurious effect on competition?

1. *Did the Quantity Discount System Result in Price Differentials that Were Discriminatory within the Meaning of the Robinson-Patman Act?* Morton Salt argued that its quantity discount system was not discriminatory. The Commission had simply made the unfortunate error of arguing that all differentials are discriminations. In the words of Morton Salt, "The standard discounts have at all times been openly available on equal terms to all purchasers."[9] Thus, by definition, these discounts could not be discriminatory.

The Commission had a ready answer: Assume that a company had a

---

[8] FTC Docket 4319, U.S. Circuit Court of Appeals for the Seventh Circuit, No. 8703, October Term, 1946, April Session, 1947.

[9] Brief of Respondent, *Federal Trade Commission* v. *Morton Salt Co.*, No. 464, p. 6. In its brief before the circuit court, Morton Salt had referred to *Webster's New International Dictionary*. Since discrimination meant "to make a difference in treatment in favor (of one compared with others)," it was argued that the differentials produced by the standard discount structure could hardly be categorized as discriminatory.

list price for certain merchandise but made separate contracts with large chain organizations purchasing 50,000 units, allowing them a 50 per cent discount. This discount would be unlawful (assuming injury to competition and absence of cost justification). But, following Morton's reasoning, if the company were to offer the same discounts to all purchasers of 50,000 units (realizing that only the same large chains could buy these amounts), the discount would be legal. The analogy was a direct one, since only five chains qualified for Morton's 50,000-case discount. In the Commission's words, "An offer couched in terms which only a few can accept is clearly not as a practical matter equally available to all purchasers—and the Robinson-Patman Act was intended to deal with a practical problem."[10]

The Commission went on to conclude that no such "meaningless differentiation" was intended by the Robinson-Patman Act. To demonstrate this, the language, purpose, and history of the act were carefully explored. Numerous references to congressional reports were made in order to establish the original intent of the lawmakers. For example, Representative Utterback, who played a significant role in drafting the bill, had said:

> But the bill does not permit price differentials merely because the quantities purchased are different, or merely because the methods of selling or delivery are different, or merely because the seasons of the year in which they enable production are different. There must be a difference in cost shown as between the customers involved in the discrimination, and that difference must be one resulting from the differing methods or quantities in which such commodities are to such purchasers sold or delivered.[11]

The FTC also produced other House committee reports demonstrating that body's interest in the survival of independent merchants and its conception of the Robinson-Patman Act as remedial legislation. With this statement of legislative objectives, the next step in the Commission's presentation was a direct one:

> Congress was obviously not unaware of the patent fact that the large chain stores could obtain an advantage over their smaller competitors by means of a general quantity system allowing discounts to all purchasers of very large quantities of merchandise. To have excluded such transactions from the requirement that quantity discounts be related to cost savings could to a great extent have defeated the purpose of the statute.[12]

The FTC made still another major point in its attempt to reject Morton's contention that its standard quantity discount system was not discriminatory, since it was open and equally available to all. Reference was made to the second proviso clause of Section 2 as amended. Briefly, the

---

[10] Petitioner's Brief, *Federal Trade Commission* v. *Morton Salt Co.*, No. 4161, p. 26.

[11] *Ibid.*, p. 19.

[12] *Ibid.*, p. 20.

proviso states that the Commission may fix (and establish) quantity limits for particular commodities or classes of commodities where it finds that "available purchasers are so few as to render differentials in amount thereof unjustly discriminatory or promotive of monopoly in any one line of commerce." The point, and it seems well made, was that the only exception in the Robinson-Patman Act to the cost-savings clause was a restriction rather than an expansion upon the legal allowance of quantity discounts.

Thus, it is apparent that the FTC made several assaults on Morton's basic contention. The Commission's basic strategy makes sense. Laws are written to achieve certain purposes, and, rather than engaging in any sort of academic festival, a serious effort seems to have been made to discover the "real" meaning of the act by a careful review of its legislative history.

Morton, however, rejected the Commission's definition of the issues. First, Morton objected to the Commission's conclusion that very few Morton Salt customers could qualify for some of the larger discounts. The Commission had no basis for such a statement, they said. The criterion used, amount of actual purchases of salt, is an irrelevant one, since the total capacity to purchase salt is the only meaningful index. Quantity discounts are a merchandising device designed to reach the firm's total salt-buying capacity, and the testimony the Commission gathered from the witnesses was completely devoid of any statements as to their total salt purchases.

This argument seems somewhat lacking in substance.[13] As a practical matter, a given wholesaler could probably not buy all his salt from one manufacturer. His purchases of salt are geared to retailer demand which is not for Morton Blue Label salt alone.

Morton rejected another aspect of the Commission's case. The FTC had argued that the discount pattern favored the large buyer. Actually, Morton argued, the reverse is true. The small buyer purchasing 50 cases as a part of a carload shipment receives a 10 cents' discount, or $6\frac{1}{4}$ per cent. For an additional 10 cents', or $6\frac{1}{4}$ per cent, discount the customer must purchase 5,000 cases. Furthermore, the 50,000-case customer is required to buy ten times that of the 5,000-case buyer and yet receives only an additional 5 cents' discount, or $3\frac{1}{8}$ per cent. In effect, Morton

---

[13] A word is in order on the construction of legal cases. Apparently, the lawyer is often much more enthused about the validity of certain of his arguments than he is about others. He includes his less valid arguments, since he is essentially interested in winning his case rather than in presenting a completely defensible brief. A friend recently summarized this situation: "What you do is throw everything in the legal hopper that has any chance at all of being accepted. I have won cases where the decision hinged upon arguments that I felt were almost irrelevant." The point, of course, is that any criticism of the briefs in the case at hand would most certainly have already occurred to Morton Salt or the FTC. Thus, this criticism is a reflection not in any sense on the abilities of the respondent or the petitioner but only on some of their arguments.

seemed to be suggesting that the large chain stores were being discriminated against.

This argument is extremely interesting. It would imply that the rate of discount should be proportionate to the amount purchased. This is a unique criterion when one remembers that the act contains a cost proviso stating that price differentials (the discounts) must be justified by cost savings, assuming injury to competition.

2. *Did the Burden of Proving that the Discriminatory Prices Were (Were Not) Justified by Cost Savings Rest upon Morton Salt (the Commission)?* The argument at this stage appeared to be little more than legal shadow-boxing. In a highly generalized statement the circuit court had made a faint suggestion to the effect that the burden of showing cost justification did not rest with Morton Salt. The Commission became understandably concerned over the unpleasant prospect of having to show lack of cost jusification as part of its case. Justifying cost savings is a ghastly task, even assuming all the "facts" are available. For an outsider, such as the FTC, the task is perhaps impossible. The Commission, therefore, presented a barrage of legal precedent, all of which substantiated the well-accepted fact that the burden of showing cost justification falls upon the person claiming the benefit of the exceptions.

This, however, was not the point. The crux of the argument still centered around whether the standard quantity discount system was discriminatory. The legal dialogue might be summarized as follows: Said the Commission: "We have shown that the system is discriminatory. Since you have not presented any evidence showing that these price discriminations are related to cost savings, the verdict must be that the quantity discount system is illegal within the meaning of the law (assuming competitive injury)."

Said Morton Salt: "You have not shown that our standard discount system is discriminatory. While we both agree that differentials were produced, your error has been in arguing that discrimination results merely from the existence of these differentials. Thus, since you have not established that the system was discriminatory, it is immaterial that we have not presented cost evidence."

Since much of the legal argument at this point in the case seems overly circuitous, it would probably be worth while if some attention were to be directed to some of the more general implications of the cost justification issue. They are sometimes ignored.

At the outset it seems worth while to emphasize that the Robinson-Patman Act is permissive legislation; that is, it permits but does not require the manufacturer to pass along any or all of the cost differences (savings) in selling his goods to one group of customers as compared to another. Assuming that the price differential has the negative competitive effect specified by law, the manufacturer will find himself legally embarrassed only if the differential is larger than that justified by cost savings. Nothing prevents him from setting up price differences between the two groups of customers that are less than the cost differences, and, of course, the manufacturer is always perfectly safe (legally) in charging both groups the same price.

It is clear that the economist would consider this a somewhat perverted concept of price discrimination, since the act encourages a very real form of discrimination by allowing uniform prices in spite of cost differences. Since this would normally take place at the expense of the large buyer, it would seem more accurate to say that the Robinson-Patman Act is concerned with price discrimination only if the smaller buyer is adversely affected.

Another general, and perhaps obvious, point should be made. Elementary economic theory suggests that one should think in terms of marginal cost and marginal revenue when pricing products. It is not difficult to see that the cost standard of the Robinson-Patman Act restricts the application of this general principle, first, because one is generally forced to think in terms of average and not marginal costs and, second, because one is often forced to ignore variations in demand from one area to the next and from time to time.

In addition, the problem of implementing this cost standard is often minimized. The naïve assumption is often made that it is possible to isolate objectively the costs of producing and selling products associated with given customers. In the words of Corwin Edwards, "In selling to different customers, few costs are clearly segregable, and the allocation of the rest is determined by policy decisions which masquerade as mere accounting procedures."[14]

3. *Was the Evidence Presented Sufficient, in Quality and Quantity, to Support a Conclusion that the Quantity Discounts Would Injure Competition?* The Morton Salt case well demonstrates what has been called the "interpretative enigma"[15] arising from this short passage in the act which outlines the requirements of competitive injury, "where the effect of such discrimination may be substantially to lessen competition or tend to create a monopoly in any line of commerce, or to injure, destroy, or prevent competition with any person who either grants or knowingly receives the benefit of such discrimination, or with customers of either of them."

Morton Salt initiated its argument on the competitive effect of the quantity discount structure with a broad indictment of the Commission's case. "Any line of commerce" was translated to mean the whole-

---

[14] Corwin D. Edwards, *Maintaining Competition* (McGraw-Hill Book Co., 1949), p. 161.

[15] Edward F. Howtrey, "The Robinson-Patman Act and a Prima Facie Case," *Georgetown Law Journal*, XXXVII (May, 1949), 541.

sale grocery business. "Competition between customers" was interpreted to mean competition between wholesale grocers and between retail grocers who buy from Morton Salt.

Thus, the Commission was completely out of focus by concerning itself with "a particular line of products of a particular vendor, or competition with respect to particular products of a particular vendor as it exists or might exist between customers of that vendor."[16] The Commission had simply made the fatal mistake of confusing the act of selling particular items of a particular producer, the Morton Salt Company, with the flow of business in a line of commerce.

By this definition of competitive injury Morton Salt assigned the Commission the task of showing that the Morton quantity discount system stood accountable for past or probably future injury to competition in the wholesale or retail business in general or to the general competitive position of the grocery (not the salt) business of a particular wholesaler or retailer. Even Morton virtually conceded the difficulty (impossibility) of this assignment by pointing out that salt generally accounts for considerably less than one-half of 1 per cent of the gross business of the wholesaler or retailer.

If Morton's contention were correct, it was painfully clear to the Commission that it would have failed even though the evidence did show the required competitive effect (under its own theory of the case). The FTC hastened to point out that the same thing could be said of almost any single item carried. Thus, if this thinking were to prevail, it would completely nullify the Robinson-Patman Act with regard to the very grocery-store situation that Congress intended it to correct. Once more, the Commission's historical approach seems highly pertinent.

The Commission added another argument on this general issue of competitive injury. That it presented a hopeful if not extreme point of view should be obvious.

> We submit that it is not necessary in cases under the Robinson-Patman Act for the Commission in the first instance to do more than prove a difference in price to competitors. In order to furnish support for the inference as to effect on competition . . . the Commission should not be compelled to adduce hundreds and even thousands of pages of testimony in order to elicit examples and details and expert opinions to the effect that the person who pays the lower price obtains a competitive advantage.

Later, it went on to make the unusual suggestion that the "respondent should have to submit very convincing proof in order to warrant a court in holding that a Commission inference of injury to competitors was not a reasonable one."[17]

Morton's response to this suggestion was immediate: "It should rather quickly become apparent that the Commission may have wistfully ad-

---

[16] Brief of Respondent, *op. cit.*, p. 25.

[17] Brief of Petitioner, *op. cit.*, p. 39.

vanced the foregoing argument because of the complete inadequacy of its evidence on the question of injury."

With the terms defined, the petitioner and the respondent outlined their cases, intending to show the presence or absence of the required competitive injury. That rationale of the Commission's argument might be summarized as follows: (1) salt is a very competitive item; thus, it is highly desirable that the wholesaler "stay in line" with his competitors' prices; (2) discounts are important in determining the resale price; and (3) it follows that harmful effects would result from a "substantial" discount. Either the competitor would resell at a lower price and thus gain business or, if he did not lower his price, he would obtain higher profits and thus have a general competitive advantage which could be used to lower prices on other products.

Morton could hardly agree that profit was a significant criterion of the competitive effect prescribed by the act.[18] In the words of Morton, the Commission apparently felt that the "Robinson-Patman Act somehow guarantees equal profits as between all wholesalers and as between all retailers."[19] The FTC probably meant no such thing.

And, yet, this very disagreement is enlightening in the sense that it portrays one of the basic problems in the administration of the Robinson-Patman Act—that of the kind and degree of competitive effect required to show violation. The "rule of reason," if it exists, is highly generalized. One only knows, on the one hand, that any price discrimination would satisfy the requirement if it forced someone out of business. At the other end of the scale it is apparent that the mere presence of a price differential is not sufficient. Yet between these extremes lies a great "no-man's-land" inhabited by the competitive effects usually encountered in actual practice.

In any event, the volume of the "evidence" presented in this case was overwhelming. To the extent that witnesses represented extreme points of view, they were queried at some length about the "effects" of the discount structure. For example, wholesalers were asked what effect these discounts would have on their business. This might be a typical situation: "If you were paying $1.50 per case for Morton's Blue Label Salt while a competitor was paying $1.40, would your business be affected?" As might be expected, the witnesses usually answered in the affirmative. Other questions, similarly hypothetical, were asked of impressive numbers of witnesses.

However hypothetical or irrelevant the answers, it was quite clear that the role of the discount in determining the resale price was a crucial issue.

---

[18] It would have been interesting to know what standards Morton would apply in determining the legality of the competitive effect. One by one, it virtually eliminated almost every conceivable criterion that could have been applied. But, of course, this was the FTC's problem.

[19] Brief of Respondent, *op. cit.*, p. 35.

If the competitor took advantage of the discount to sell at a lower price (as some did), his margin was reduced. If he did not meet the price, his sales volume on salt (a close item) would fall. Also, being out of line on salt, in the opinion of some of the witnesses, would have an adverse effect on the wholesaler's other business as well. Perhaps this is a typical response:

Well, I might say that the generally accepted rule in the wholesale grocery business is this: If you are out of line on one particular item, why, it hurts all of your business, because it puts this doubt in the merchant's mind. "Well, if he is out of line on this, maybe he is out of line on something else," and all of your business is affected.[20]

Unfortunately, the Commission and the Morton Salt Company simply could not agree on the relationship (and the importance) of the discount in the resale price. At only one point was there even implied agreement on the resale price issue; there could be little question about chain stores. The A & P, for example, sold Morton's Blue Label Salt at 7 cents a package, or $1.68 a case. The most prevalent wholesale price was probably $1.65 a case; the wholesaler was virtually forced to charge the retailer more for the salt than A & P was charging at retail.

In the words of Morton, discounts "were not reflected in resale prices; the resale prices, not the purchase prices of a competitor, are all that interests most merchandisers, and some are even indifferent to resale prices; resale prices have some relation to cost, but the many variations in resale prices are attributable to a host of merchandising factors utterly apart from cost."[21]

This final argument is somewhat difficult to follow. At several points Morton suggested that there was little to be gained by examining either costs or resale prices, since these alone could furnish little hint as to competitive advantage. To determine this, said Morton, requires detailed knowledge of volume, turnover, overhead, warehousing and transportation costs, credit risks, and a virtually unlimited number of other merchandising factors.

This argument seemed to represent another attempt on the part of Morton to make the problem of proving competitive injury even more difficult than it is. Actually the real issue would seem to be the effect of one factor, the discount; all other factors must be assumed constant. It is as though one were trying to assess the competitive situation of a given wholesaler with and without the discounts. While this may not be feasible in any empirical sense, it seems wise to keep the objective in mind.

Morton argued further that one might have expected some "traces of this insidious injury" in the many years the discounts had been in ex-

---

[20] Brief of Petitioner, *op. cit.*, p. 50.
[21] Brief of Respondent, *op. cit.*, p. 42.

istence. To check the existence of any such "trace," Morton Salt tabulated its sales from 1937 through 1941 to discount and nondiscount wholesalers and retailers who testified before the Commission. The findings obviously had very little to do with the effect of the discounts and a great deal to do with some extraneous factors. Sales to nondiscount customers were relatively better in the areas studied—sales to nondiscount customers either decreased less or increased more than the sales of discount customers. Perhaps the most surprising thing of all is that these findings were even presented.[22] The Commission summarized its reaction to these sales tabulations with the withering observation that Morton had mistaken the unreliability of the figures as proof of the lack of effect of the discount system.

Perhaps enough of this argument has now been presented to suggest distressing complexities arising in any attempt to show the required competitive effect under the act.[23] Competition is by its very nature "injurious." The evidence of this injury, perhaps of necessity, is largely hypothetical. The interpretation of this evidence is largely subjective. This "reasonable" man, the one who is to draw all these inferences as to the effect on competition, is apparently an elusive individual.

THE SUPREME COURT'S DECISION

In a seven-to-two decision the Supreme Court reversed the circuit court and, in so doing, upheld the Commission's viewpoint. In summarizing the Supreme Court's opinion, one might think in terms of the answers given to the three basic questions upon which the argument centered.

1. *Was the General Quantity Discount System Discriminatory within the Meaning of the Robinson-Patman Act?* The Supreme Court said it was. In saying this, the Court rejected Morton's basic contention that its standard quantity discounts were not discriminatory because they were available to all on equal terms. "Theoretically, these discounts are equally available to all, but functionally they are not."

The Court made reference to the record. No single independent retailer and probably no single wholesaler bought as many as 50,000 cases or as much as $50,000 worth of table salt in any given year. A review of the legislative history of the Robinson-Patman Act made it "abundantly clear" to the Court that the act was passed to protect the small buyer and to deprive a large buyer of a competitive advantage solely because of

---

[22] For another reason as well. It seems inconsistent to argue in one vein that a host of factors affect competitive performance and then in another to present sales differences as a measure of only one factor, namely, the discount.

[23] For a thorough discussion of required competitive effects see H. Thomas Austern, "Required Competitive Injury and Permitted Meeting of Competition," in *Robinson-Patman Act Symposium* (New York: Commerce Clearing House, 1947), pp. 63–84.

his ability to buy large quantities, except to the extent that a lower price could be justified by the seller's diminished costs or by the seller's good-faith effort to meet a competitor's equally low price.[24]

2. *Did the Burden of Proving that Any Discriminatory Prices Were Justified by Cost Savings Rest upon the Commission or Morton Salt?* Here the Court agreed with the Commission and, for that matter, with Morton Salt too. First, there is the general rule that the person claiming the benefit of an exception must prove that he is entitled to it. And (as brought out in Question 1), a price differential is a price discrimination. Second, Section 2b of the act specifically imposes the burden of showing cost justification upon that party who has been shown to have discriminated.

3. *Was the Evidence Sufficient in Quantity and Quality to Support the Conclusion that the Quantity Discounts Had an Injurious Effect on Competition?* On this question the Supreme Court issued what may well be one of its more important proclamations in the antitrust area. It was not necessary that the Commission show that the discounts did *in fact* cause injury to competition but only that there is a *reasonably possibility* that they *may* have such an effect.[25]

With this frame of reference, the Court concluded that the Commission adequately supported its finding of competitive injury by showing that Morton had sold its goods to some customers "substantially" cheaper than it had sold like goods to competitors of these customers. Also, the Commission's finding that the discounts were sufficient to influence resale price was "in itself" sufficient to show injury (under the Court's newly proclaimed definition of the requisite effect).

Furthermore, the Commission "went much further in receiving evidence than the statute requires." Experts were offered to prove the tendency of injury from such prices. The evidence covers two thousand pages, largely devoted to this single issue—injury to competition.[26] The effective enforcement of the act would be greatly handicapped if the Commission were required to obtain testimony to show what is "self-evident"; namely, that there is a "reasonable possibility" that competition "may" be adversely affected when a "substantial" price differential exists. It is probably not an understatement to say that these utterances surpassed the Commission's wildest expectations. And it is certainly no understatement to suggest that the businessman is confused about the practical meaning of such terms as "substantial."

The Court took special effort to single out some of Morton's conten-

---

[24] It is indeed curious that in the face of such clarity the Court has only recently rendered a final decision on the "good-faith" issue in the Standard Oil of Indiana case.

[25] *Federal Trade Commission* v. *Morton Salt Co.*, 334 U.S. 37 (1948), Supreme Court of the United States on Writ of Certiorari to the U.S. Circuit Court of Appeals for the Seventh Circuit. Justice Black delivered the opinion.

[26] *Ibid.*, pp. 11–12.

tions. For example, it could not agree that the carload discounts should be ignored (1) because there are "obvious" cost savings associated with carload deliveries or (2) because less than one-tenth of 1 per cent moved in less-than-carload lots. Congress had not given carload discounts any "favored classification." These discounts, like all others, must be justified by actual cost savings (especially since the smallest merchants are most vitally affected).

The Court also attacked Morton's suggestion that the Robinson-Patman Act could not be applied to the case at hand, since salt was a very small item in most wholesale and retail businesses and thus could not exert the requisite effect on this "line of commerce." Congress intended to protect a merchant from discriminatory prices on any or all goods sold, whether they constituted a major or a minor portion of his stock. "There is no possible way effectively to protect a grocer from discriminatory prices except by applying the prohibitions of the Act to each individual article in the store."[27]

The Court had made its general position clear on this crucial issue of the quantity and quality of the competitive effect required under the Robinson-Patman Act.

Dissents are almost always interesting. In this case the dissent, by Justices Jackson and Frankfurter, was also significant in the sense that it made some incisive exploration as to the wisdom of two of the decision's more significant features. These two gentlemen thought that "the law as written by Congress and as always interpreted by this Court requires that the record show a reasonable probability of the effect. The difference between a *reasonable probability* and a *reasonable possibility* that the discount *may* have the effect"[28] in many cases would be decisive.

These honorable gentlemen knew of no other instance where the Supreme Court had ever held that such important administrative orders could hang on "so slender a thread of inference." They resented the "overtones of hostility to all quantity discounts." In their words, "The law of this case, in a nutshell, is that no quantity discount is valid if the Commission chooses to say it is not."[29]

This, their first indictment, certainly struck at the very heart of the majority opinion. But they had another complaint, also of the same order of magnitude. In their eyes the Robinson-Patman Act, as it relates to quantity discounts, strove for two effects. On the one hand, the act recognized that quantity discounts, unjustified by cost savings, could be used to give large buyers a discriminatory advantage over small buyers. On the other hand, the act also recognized that whatever economies result from quantity transactions should be passed on to the consumer. The Court, in their

---

[27] *Ibid.*, p. 10.
[28] Dissent, *ibid.*, p. 3.
[29] *Ibid.*

opinion, had failed to recognize this meaningful difference and had lumped both discounts together. Actually, these two types of discounts require "quite different inferences as to their effect on competition."

One was the "quota discount"—the $5,000 and $50,000 cumulative discount—which was not related to any apparent difference in handling costs but to volume only. Furthermore, only 54 of Morton's 4,000 customers qualified for this discount. Justices Jackson and Frankfurter agreed with the majority that this discount justified an inference of injurious effect (by their stricter test of "reasonable probability"). In fact, it was "almost inevitable" in their opinion that a 10- or 15-cent differential would have the requisite effect.

However, in the word of the dissenters, a very different problem was presented by the 10-cent carload discount. A consideration of the factors surrounding this discount made it very difficult to draw the inference that competition is "probably" affected by this discount. Also, and very important, this discount is not arbitrarily determined but is instead related to an obvious difference in handling and delivery costs.[30]

In any event, these two gentlemen pointed out that the practical effect of forbidding the carload discount is a 10-cent increase in the price of Morton's salt to 99.9 per cent of the customers, simply because the remaining one-tenth of 1 per cent were not in a position to accept carload shipments. This, they said, runs contrary to one of the prescribed objectives of the act. The majority has simply erred in not recognizing the essential difference between the "quota" discount and the carload discount. The latter should be permitted.

With this discussion of the background of the case, the arguments presented, and the Supreme Court's decision, it is now appropriate to consider the question of the effects of the case.

THE EFFECTS

If the consideration of the "effects" of this significant case is to be relevant, it is necessary that one distinguish, first, between the effects on various groups[31]—business, the legislative body, and the FTC—and, second, between observed or actual effects and those effects that one thinks should or may be taking place.

It is certainly not inconceivable that the gap between theoretical effects and actual effects is a substantial one. A systematic inquiry would probably reveal a time lag between the judicial edict and related business behavior due either to a fundamental inertia to unpleasant change or to a

---

[30] It should be mentioned that the majority did not imply that this discount could not be justified. It simply said that Morton did not justify the carload discount, and this, the majority pointed out, is required by the law.

[31] By a discussion of effects on each of several groups it is certainly not suggested that these effects are naturally independent. Quite obviously, what affects the FTC also affects business. And, one should hope, vice versa.

pervasive ignorance of such an "important" judicial decision. For example, the Supreme Court opinion in the Morton case could lead one to the conclusion that it will have a dramatic effect on quantity discounts. Yet, for a number of reasons, no such effects may actually be taking place. Perhaps the businessman is unaware of the Morton Salt decision and its implications. In this vein, it has been the writer's personal but limited experience that a number of executives are quite unaware even of the existence of the Morton Salt case. Thus, it is not at all inconceivable that one might currently find quantity discounts virtually ubiquitous, even though many are probably illegal.

In view of this, the present study is bound to be inadequate (inaccurate), since it contains only a fragment of what would have been a very useful but energetic sequel, a thorough empirical study of post—Morton Salt pricing behavior.

Effect on Business

At the outset, what can be said of the effect of this case on salt manufacturers? One would expect the most immediate response here. A personal inquiry has revealed a substantial if not heterogeneous reaction.[32]

Generally speaking, the Morton Salt Company and other salt firms no longer grant any quantity discounts, including carload discounts.[33] This complete about-face in pricing policy is remarkable when one recalls the dominant role of the quantity discount in the period before the FTC indictment.

The large buyers in particular have cause to be unhappy. Accustomed to a substantial price differential under the 5,000- and 50,000-case discount, they must now console themselves with whatever differential results from freight savings inherent in large shipments. Ironically enough, when one considers the remedial motives of those framing the Robinson-Patman Act, it is pressures such as these that lead large chains to further integrate their operations.

But not everyone is unhappy. This same personal inquiry indicated that the small salt manufacturer is quite content with the current state of things. His reasoning runs as follows: "I do not have production facilities in very many areas of the country. Freight rates are very important in delineating the marketing area to which I or any salt manufacturer can ship profitably (and competitively). However, the customers of 5,000 or 50,000 cases of salt are large grocery chains or large jobbers operating

---

[32] The writer communicated with several salt producers on the marketing implications of this case. Their response was most gratifying.

[33] There seems to be little question but that the carload discount could be justified in terms of selling, invoicing, and shipping costs. Why it was not (or has not been) is an interesting question. Perhaps the salt industry is simply in a state of severe but temporary reaction. Perhaps the salt people were attempting to dramatize the "consequences" of the decision. Or, probably more likely, perhaps the salt industry is in a state of strong demand and could not resist raising the price 10 cents a case.

a national chain of jobbing houses and warehouses which are spread over a region including several normal marketing areas. Thus, I am not able to sell these large customers (except by making a substantial competitive offer), since very few if any in my particular marketing area buy in such large quantities."

In the words of one small salt manufacturer: "Frankly, we were pleased when the case was decided as it was. Upon the removal of the quantity discounts, we were able to withdraw our competitive offers. We were also able to bid on business of former receivers of quantity discounts with a much better chance of receiving a share of the business. I believe that any other producer who has production facilities in only one, or perhaps two, producing areas had the same reaction."[34] It is quite interesting that the Commission did not include the effect of the quantity discounts on so-called first-line competition (other salt manufacturers) as part of its case.

One can only speculate as to the effect of the Morton Salt case on other segments of the business world. Certainly one can draw the obvious inference that almost any quantity discount is suspect, regardless of its standard availability or of its nature. For example, in the past, businessmen have operated under the time-honored theory that a carload discount is *ipso facto* an acceptable one. Those same businessmen seem to have arrived at the size of such discounts on a purely subjective basis, custom, expediency, or perhaps historical "competition" being the major criterion.

All this, however, has been changed inasmuch as the Court minced no words in singling out the carload discount; it, too, must be justified by actual cost earnings. Since 99.9 per cent of Morton's sales moved in carload lots, this dictum forces one to revise the prevalent assumption that the Court is only concerned with those discounts that are available to the very large buyers.

If, then, the businessman is to offer quantity discounts, he should have an "objective" basis for their determination. This can only mean an analysis of distribution costs, and yet can one honestly refer to distribution cost accounting as being "objective"? For example, consider for a moment the problem of joint costs and their allocation. While these may be annoying in the accounting of production costs, they are overwhelming in distribution. Warehouses store many products. Salesmen represent an entire line of products. Shipping departments and trucks do not limit themselves to one product.

The cumulative discount and the attendant problem of allocating costs through time are other intriguing accounting questions. It seems highly doubtful that the questions will be satisfactorily answered, but, even if they are, one still has the further question of how such a discount can be

---

[34] Letter to the writer, September 20, 1949.

justified, since it gives each manfacturer who takes advantage of it substantial discretion.

Perhaps the current situation with respect to the accounting of distribution costs is summed up well in these words: "For the most part, the efforts are experimental, sporadic, and perhaps somewhat speculative."[35] If nothing else, the Morton Salt case should serve as a real incentive to the growth of distribution cost accounting.

But one can be highly charitable and assume that the accountants become so ingenious that they solve the problem of measuring the costs of distribution alternatives. There is still the overwhelming problem of communication between the manufacturer and the courts. Is it possible to imagine the task of presenting the results of complex cost-accounting methods to judges? These gentlemen are hardly expert in the techniques of distribution cost analysis. Nor can they be expected to be. The result is that they either make incredible demands or take a more passive role and allow themselves to be hopelessly confused by cost-accounting experts and their conflicting statements.

Two recent cases help illustrate the point.[36] The American Can Company, involved in both, justified its quantity discount system on the basis of a painstakingly detailed cost analysis. The judges demonstrated their apparent lack of accounting acumen by suggesting that selling costs should have been shown to each individual customer (instead of classes of customers) and for each individual location. If the Supreme Court were to accept these requirements, it would virtually nullify the practical implementation of the cost justification proviso and cause the manufacturer (especially the large one) to become exceedingly wary of any quantity discount.

One may assume, then, that it is a difficult matter to implement the cost justification proviso of the Robinson-Patman Act. In view of the FTC's recent position that a "good-faith" effort to meet competition is not an adequate defense, it appeared as though the only safe pricing policy was the single price (thereby, of course, nullifying the Robinson-Patman Act). Very recently, however, the Supreme Court in the Standard Oil case[37] confirmed what seemed fairly clear even on the surface; namely, that a "good-faith" price cut was a valid justification. For the moment, at least, it appears as though the businessman, under certain perhaps unusual conditions, can charge price differentials and still avoid the FTC's wrath.

---

[35] Albert E. Sawyer, "The Commission's Administration of Paragraph 2(a) of the Robinson-Patman Act; An Appraisal," *George Washington Law Review*, VIII (January–February, 1948), 477.

[36] *Bruce's Juices, Inc.* v. *American Can Co.*, 87 F. Supp. 985 (D.C., Fla., 1949), and *Russellville Canning Co.* v. *American Can Co.*, 87 F. Supp. 484 (D.C., Ark., 1949). Both cases were at the district court level. See Herbert F. Taggart, "New Life for the Robinson-Patman Act," *Michigan Business Review*, II (March, 1950), 10–13.

[37] *Standard Oil Co. of Indiana* v. *Federal Trade Commission*, 340 U.S. 231 (1951).

Effects on the Legislative Segment

Congress, as a part of its first major overhaul in years of the Clayton Act and the Federal Trade Commission Act,[38] also became concerned over the Morton Salt decision and the majority opinion that it was only necessary to show that there be "reasonable possibility" that the discrimination "may" have the required effect. Apparently Congress was impressed by the testimony of some legal experts and businessmen who called the case, among other things, an "unfortunate dictum."

Thus, one of Congress' proposed amendments to the Clayton Act contained a provision to the effect that it was necessary to show a "reasonable probability" of the required effect. To the layman that distinction may seem an insignificant one. To the legal technician it was a major improvement.

It is hardly necessary that one become overly concerned with this unexpected surge of legislative activity, since the President vetoed the proposed legislation. It is possible, however, that the FTC will keep these legislative desires in mind in any future litigation.

Effect on the Federal Trade Commission

One can only speculate as to the effect of this decision on the Commission's future courses of action. The Court, with its dictum of the "reasonable possibility" and its suggestion that "substantial" price differential is in itself sufficient evidence of the required competitive effect, has presented the FTC with a liberal criterion. The vital question, of course, is one of whether the Commission will avail itself of this standard. Bogged down with a volume of work that is disproportionately large for its present staff, the Commission now must make the choice between alternatives—the prosecution of many more "violators" or the unpleasant and time-consuming search for evidence of competitive injury under the old standard. The temptation seems almost too great.

Members of the Commission disagree. For example, in statements on the Johnson Bill before a Senate subcommittee, Commission members were unusually consistent in their insistence that the requirement in the proposed legislation that there be a "reasonable probability" of the required competitive effect would "not alter the law as it has actually been applied."[39]

That the Robinson-Patman Act has adopted a new look can hardly be questioned. In the eyes of the anxious businessman, this can be interpreted to mean that he should employ quantity discounts only with the full realization that it is likely that he will be legally and financially embarrassed

---

[38] S. 236 (81st Cong., 1st sess.), bill on the competitive absorption of transportation costs.

[39] Statement by Joseph E. Sheehy before Senate Subcommittee on Trade Policies, January 25, 1949.

if the FTC or some "injured" competitor should decide this is desirable.[40] However, one should not forget that the large manufacturer is faced with an unalterable fact—he must sell a large volume of his product. The quantity discount is only one of the "incentives" that is available to him, and, if the legal or competitive situation requires it, there is every reason to believe that he will always conceive of appropriate alternatives.

---

[40] The probabilities of such embarrassment were considerably enhanced by a recent FTC order limiting quantity discounts on tires to a single carload. The Commission acted under the rarely used clause in the Robinson-Patman Act that permits the Commission to put a ceiling on quantity discounts if it finds existing discounts either "unjustly discriminatory" or "promotive of monopoly."